THE NUCLEAR THEME AS A DETERMINANT OF PAṬET IN JAVANESE MUSIC

Da Capo Press Music Reprint Series

Music Editor

BEA FRIEDLAND

Ph.D., City University of New York

This title was recommended for Da Capo reprint b
Frank D'Accone, *University of California at Los A*

THE NUCLEAR THEME AS A DETERMINANT OF PATET IN JAVANESE MUSIC

By

MANTLE HOOD

DA CAPO PRESS · NEW YORK · 1977

Library of Congress Cataloging in Publication Data

Hood, Mantle.
The nuclear theme as a determinant of patet in Javanese music.

(Da Capo Press music reprint series)
Reprint of the 1954 ed. published by J. B. Wolters, Groningen.
Bibliography: p.
1. Music–Java–History and criticism. 2. Music, Primitive. I. Title.
[ML345.J3H7 1977] 781.7'598'2 77-5680
ISBN 0-306-77419-4

This Da Capo Press edition of *The Nuclear Theme as a Determinant of Patet in Javanese Music* is an unabridged republication of the first edition published in Groningen and Djakarta in 1954. It is reprinted by arrangement with the author.

Published by Da Capo Press, Inc.
A Subsidiary of Plenum Publishing Corporation
227 West 17th Street, New York, N.Y. 10011

Manufactured in the United States of America

THE NUCLEAR THEME AS A DETERMINANT

OF

PAṬET IN JAVANESE MUSIC

ACADEMISCH PROEFSCHRIFT

TER VERKRIJGING VAN DE GRAAD VAN DOCTOR IN DE LETTEREN EN WIJSBEGEERTE AAN DE UNIVERSITEIT VAN AMSTERDAM, OP GEZAG VAN DE RECTOR MAGNIFICUS DR M. W. WOERDEMAN, HOOGLERAAR IN DE FACULTEIT DER GENEESKUNDE, IN HET OPENBAAR TE VERDEDIGEN IN DE AULA DER UNIVERSITEIT OP DINSDAG 1 JUNI 1954 DES NAMIDDAGS TE 4 UUR PRECIES

DOOR

MANTLE HOOD
GEBOREN TE SPRINGFIELD, ILLINOIS

PUBLISHED WITH THE SUPPORT OF THE PRINCE BERNHARD FUND AND THE UNITED STATES EDUCATIONAL FOUNDATION IN THE NETHERLANDS

J. B. WOLTERS — GRONINGEN, DJAKARTA — 1954

The following transliteration of Javanese words is used in the text: the (Dutch) oe is replaced by u, the consonant j by y, the double consonants dj and tj by j and ch respectively; the d and t are indicated by ḍ and ṭ if dental and by d and t if lingual, the mute e without an accent, the short e by è, and the long e (pronounced ā) as é; the initial mute h is omitted. The Dutch spelling has been retained in all quoted passages and also for the names of Javanese persons except for a few instances in which Javanese writers themselves have used the English transliteration.

SUATU PENDAHULUAN

untuk peladjaran ini mulai beberapa tahun lalu ketika seorang diantara kenal-kenalan saja memperkenalkan saja dengan beberapa piringan hitam jang membunjikan gamelan Djawa dan Bali. Bekas pengalaman itu masih hidup bergiap dalam ingatan saja. Warna bunji jang sekian istimewa dari orkes itu terus menangkap minat saja. Akan tetapi ada hal jang lain. Pola[2] jang sulit itu, teranjam dalam pantjaragambunjian menjatakan suatu deradjat susunan jang sangat tinggi, jang menantang pendengaran orang baru. Ketika itu pada rasa saja bunji itu sebagai tantangan jang menjukakan hati dan jang mungkin madjemuk rupanja.

Akan tetapi baharu beberapa tahun lalu, dalam mana saja diuntungi akan mempergunakan tempo jang dibutuhi untuk menjambut sebahagian dari tantangan itu, saja memahami betapa besar sifat menjenangkan hati dari tantangan itu dan betapa sungguh madjemuknja. Menurut pendapat saja, agar mulai mengerti musik itu, perlulah saja djuga mentjoba akan memahami bangsa, kadar-kadarnja menurut ilmu bangsa, 'adat isti'adatnja, kesusasteraannja, sandiwaranja, seni- dan agamanja. Agak ditengah-tengah angan[2] itu saja menginsafi bahwa saja, terpandang dari pihak tertentu, seorang penjelinap dalam keradjaan peradaban orang lain. Atas alasan jang sederhana jaitu bahwa saja menjukai bunji-bunjian musik Djawa itu, saja harap bahwa saja akan diterima baik.

Penjelidik tentang musik kebangsaan dan tentang ilmu-bangsa-musik mewakili beberapa anggapan, kejakinan dan alasan jang bermatjam-matjam. Oleh karena itu saja hendak mengatakan sepatah kata tentang maksud peladjaran ini dan tentang rasa hati dengan mana peladjaran ini disuguh. Meskipun peringatan[2] ini diutjapkan sengadja kepada *niyaga* Djawa, sipembatja jang biasa pun boleh berminat kepadanja.

Engkau, jaitu *niyaga* Djawa dan bangsa[2] Indonesia hidup dalam zaman dengan peralihan[2] besar. Pendjadian keekonomian dan politik menjebabkan bahwa engkau bersentuh dengan negeri[2] lain. Makin lama makin lebih deradjat penghidupan akan dinilai betalian dengan deradjat penghidupan jang berlaku pada bangsa[2] lain. Zaman itu ialah sezaman jang mengadjar banjak kepada manusia, pendidikan bertambah dan suatu bahasa kebangsaan ditjiptakan. Untuk masing[2] diantara engkau zaman itu ialah sezaman untuk pendapatan — jaitu pendapatan tentang keseorangan, tentang kemerdekaan seseorang dan tjara melahirkan diri untuk seseorang, tentang pikiran2 jang baru. Terpandang dari segala pihak zaman itu zaman jang membawa pembaruan jang besar.

Agaknja engkau menginsafi bahwa setiap kemerdekaan baru membawa pertanggungan djawab jang sesuai. Jang saja maksudkan ialah suatu pertanggungan djawab jang terchusus matjamnja. Pada waktu engkau sibuk untuk membangunkan bangsa baru engkau barangkali tidak lama bimbang hati akan menggantikan jang dulu dengan jang baru. Hal itu mudah dapat difahami. Akan tetapi musik engkau, wajang engkau, kesusasteraan engkau dan tjara melahirkan diri jang beradat tidak pernah akan digantikan oleh karena segala itu ialah sebagian dari engkau sendiri. Hal itu boleh berubah sebagaimana engkau sendiri boleh berubah, akan tetapi itu tjuma suatu keadaan menurut tab'i'at pada bangsa jang masih dalam tumbuhannja. Saja tidak mupakat dengan beberapa diantara sedjawat2 saja jang bersangka bahwa perubahan dalam musik engkau tidak akan mendjadi. Kami orang-asing barat, tidak berhak dan djuga tidak pandai akan "melindungi" musik engkau, akan mentjoba supaja musik itu tinggal takterubah. *Engkaulah* akan menerima segala jang kausuka dan menolak barang apa jang tidak kausuka. Segala hal dalam peradaban engkau jang tinggal bermakna kepada engkau, engkau akan mempertahankan dan semua jang tidak bermakna untuk engkau, engkau tidak akan mempergunakan lebih lama. Itu pun mudah dapat difahami. Akan tetapi pada waktu engkau masih sibuk selama masa perubahan barangkali ada hal hal jang kehilangan jang kemudian hari engkau hendak mengembalikan lagi. Djadi engkau mempunjai pertanggungan djawab kepada engkau sendiri untuk menjimpan *pengetahuan* tentang hal itu. Telah ada suatu hal sedemikian jang terdjadi lebih dahulu. Sudah lama lagu2 jang utama untuk *genḍing* ditulis dalam perkumpulan kraton. Biarpun beberapa diantara lagu2 itu tidak akan dimainkan beberapa tahun lamanja dan akan lepas dari ingatan sipemain, akan tetapi lagu2 itu tidak pernah akan hilang.

Kami, ahli-musik barat, boleh beladjar banjak dari engkau, *niyaga* Djawa. Kami dapat beladjar beberapa hal dari tjara latihan musik engkau, dari bangun irama pada *genḍing* engkau, dari tugas dan hal mempertahankan dari suatu pengertian sebagai *paṭet*, dari hal mengatur suara (intonasi) engkau waktu bernjanji, dari pemimpin gamelan engkau jang dapat didengar tetapi jang tidak kelihatan, dari perasa engkau untuk bermain bersama-sama, dari sifat karangan engkau jang tidak mengenai seorang diri.

Sebahagian dari maksud saja dalam peladjaran ini ialah akan mentjoba membantu ahli-musik barat supaja mereka itu mengerti musik engkau. Djikalau pendapat2 saja djuga dapat menambah suatu apa kepada pengetahuan engkau tentang teori musik Djawa, maka kebanjakan dari maksud saja dipenuhi.

Amsterdam
March 24, 1954.

MANTLE HOOD

A PREFACE

to this study began a number of years ago when an acquaintance introduced me to some recordings of Javanese and Balinese gamelan. The impression is still strong in my memory. The unique orchestral color caught my immediate interest. But there was something more. The intricate patterns interlacing this mosaic-in-sound suggested a high degree of organization that defied the ears of the newcomer. It struck me at the time as a pleasant and possibly complex challenge.

Not until the past few years, during which I have been privileged to devote the time necessary to meeting that challenge in part, have I realized just how pleasant and indeed how complex the challenge would be. I found that to begin to understand the music I must also seek to understand the people, their ethnic standards, their customs, literature, theatre, art and religion. Somewhere in the midst of these speculations it dawned on me that in a certain sense I was an intruder in the realm of another people's culture. On the simple grounds that I like the sound of Javanese music I hope I am a welcome intruder.

The investigators of folk music and ethno-musicology represent a number of diversified attitudes, convictions and motivations. For this reason I want to say something about the intention of this study and the spirit with which it is offered. Although these remarks will be directed expressly to the Javanese *niyaga*, they may also be of interest to the general reader.

You, the Javanese *niyaga* and the peoples of Indonesia, are living in a time of great transition. Economic and political development is bringing you in contact with other countries. Standards of living will more and more be appraised in relation to the standards maintained by other peoples. It is a time of great learning, of increased education and the creation of a national language. For each of you it is a time of discovery — the discovery of individuality, of personal liberty and personal expression, of new ideas. In every way it is a time of great newness.

You are probably realizing that each new freedom brings with it a corresponding responsibility. I am thinking of a particular kind of responsibility. In the busy times of building a new nation you may not hesitate long in replacing the old with the new. That is understandable. But your music, your wayang, your literature and traditional forms of expression will never be replaced because they are part of you. They may change, just as you yourself will change, but that is only natural to a growing nation. I do not agree with some of my colleagues who think that changes in your music should not occur. We Westerners do not have the right nor are we able to "protect" your music, to try to preserve it unaltered. *You* are the ones who will take what suits you and reject what does not. The things in your own culture which continue to have meaning for you, you will retain, and the things which are no longer meaningful, you will no longer use. That is also understandable. But during the activities of your changing times some things may be lost which you will later want to recover. So you have a responsibility to yourselves to preserve a *knowledge* of these things. A precedent is already established. Long ago the principal melodies of the *gendìng* were written down in the kraton collections. Even if some of them are not played for many years and fade from the musican's memory, they will never be lost.

We Western musicians can learn much from you, the Javanese *niyaga.* We can learn something from your methods of musical training, from the rhythmic structure of your *genḍing*, from the function and preservation of a concept like *paṭet*, from your voice control (intonation) in singing, from your gamelan conductor who is heard but not seen, from your feeling for playing in ensemble, from the impersonal quality of your compositions.

Part of my intention in this study is to try to help the Western musician understand your music. If my conclusions can also contribute something to your knowledge of Javanese music theory, then the greater part of my intention will be fulfilled.

ACKNOWLEDGMENTS.

Grateful acknowledgment is made: to my Promoter Prof. Dr. K. Ph. Bernet Kempers who has offered encouragement in this study since the beginning of my residence in the Netherlands; to Mr. Bernard IJzerdraat for his patient instruction in the techniques of the gamelan instruments and the intricacies of Javanese rhythm and his explanations of the dance; to Drs. R. L. Mellema for his assistance in the translation of the Javanese language, Bahasa Indonesia and Malay, for his detailed accounts of *wayang kulit*, and for the usage of his photographic studio and facilities; to Prof. Dr. R. A. M. Bergman of the Afdeling Culturele en Physische Anthropologie van het Koninklijk Instituut voor de Tropen for his personal interest in my research, for granting permission to photograph objects in the Museum which illustrate the text, and for his recommendation that the Instituut support the publication by subscription; to the entire staff of the Koninklijk Instituut v. d. Tropen for their endless cooperation and especially to Mrs. Aart Hazewinkel-Tio Siang Lian of the Centrale Boekerij and to Miss M. S. Reyers of the Handboekerij der Afdeling Culturele en Physische Anthropologie for their considerations in making reference materials available; to the

Stichting voor Culturele Samenwerking for their support of the publication by subscription; to the members of the Board of the Prins Bernhard Fonds for their generous financial support of the publication.

An especial gratitude is acknowledged for the whole-hearted support accorded me as a Fulbright grantee by the members of the Board of the United States Educational Foundation in the Netherlands; for their response to the exigencies which arose in connection with my research; for their recommendation to the U.S. Board of Foreign Scholarships that an extra year be granted for the consummation of this work; and finally for their timely financial support of the publication. I mention in particular Dr. Marshall Swan, Dr. D. M. E. Habbema, Dr. Arthur J. Mekeel, Mr. Fred Gammon and Mrs. Mae Van Doorne.

An acknowledgment of my manifold indebtness to Dr. Jaap Kunst can, at best, be only an adumbration of my gratitude. As a *guru* and friend he has given generously and untiringly of his time, his knowledge and experience, his interest and counsel. He has made available his private library, personal correspondence, field recordings, photographs, Javanese music manuscripts and countless other facilities, each of which has accelerated what might otherwise have been an interminable study. His suggestions and criticisms in connection with the manuscript have been invaluable, and the publication itself has been possible largely through his efforts to promote an interest in financing a costly undertaking. I am not a little indebted to him for his infectious love of Javanese music and all that is Java. No less important has been the encouragement and morale supplied by both Mr. and Mrs. Kunst during the past two years.

I am grateful to my wife for her vigilant and critical reading of the manuscript, for double checking the galley proof, for helping with the Index, for the thousand and one favors that allowed the work-in-progress an unfettered course.

Lastly, I appreciate the ceaseless cooperation and goodwill of J. B. Wolters, Publishers.

Amsterdam
March 24, 1954.

MANTLE HOOD.

CONTENTS

I.

GENERAL INTRODUCTION.

THE MUSIC OF CENTRAL JAVA has evolved through the centuries to its present form of expression under the tutelage of tradition. Tradition in artistic expression is sometimes regarded as a negative force which substitutes inertia for spontaneity and, by its sanction of imitation, precludes conscious creativity [1]). Its positive elements are too often overlooked.

In a broad application tradition supercedes the artifical boundaries of region and state to relate a greater or lesser number of peoples. It is through the persistence of tradition that a cultural area may be identified by language, dress, temperament, artistic expression and countless other manifestations of social unity. It is necessary to speak of the *persistence* of tradition because the history of all peoples is written in terms of migration and invasion, of commerce and trade, of cultural exchange and adaptation. These catalysts transform the "inertia" of tradition into a dynamic discipline which encourages order and prohibits anarchy in the evolution of cultural expression.

In the earliest imaginable stages of society perhaps inertia is the larger part of tradition. Perhaps at this level it can be said that imitation produces stagnation.

But the Indian Archipelago or, more specifically, the island of Java has had contact and trade with the advanced cultures of China, India and Further India since the beginning of the Christian Era. Migration and invasion have produced one powerful dynasty after another and introduced lasting infusions in language, in religion, in government, in artistic expression. Tradition as a dominant force in the evolution of the music of Central Java has not been lacking the necessary catalysts to transform inertia and imitation into a dynamic art form.

A historical survey of the Javanese-Hindu period and the post-Hindu times in Java [2]), interesting though it is, need not be of especial concern in the present study. It is sufficient to note that from temple reliefs, excavations, and Hindu-

---

1) Curt Sachs, *The Rise of Music in the Ancient World East and West* (New York: W. W. Norton, 1943), pp. 52—3.

2) See further Jaap Kunst, *Music in Java* (2nd ed., revised and enl.; The Hague: Martinus Nijhoff, 1949), I, 105—18; hereinafter cited as *MJ*.

Javanese and ancient Chinese literature we know that music held a high position in court life and also flourished among the people [1]). It is generally believed that today, however, the music of Java bears no essential likeness to that of India proper [2]).

The investigation of Javanese music might be said to have begun with a few superficial descriptions, dating from the early days of the Netherlands East India Company, found in *D'Eerste Boeck*, published in 1597 [3]). Scattered references appear after this until the remarkable descriptions offered by the Englishman Raffles, early in the 19th century [4]). The next really significant work, appearing in 1890, was Groneman's *De Gamelan te Jogjakarta* [5]), a publication which contains an introduction by Land (a summary of the pertinent facts already known up to that time) and numerous transcriptions of music.

From the beginning of the 20th century until the present time the investigations rapidly increased. Their number and worth prohibits individual comment [6]) beyond the mention of a few particularly outstanding sources.

The second edition of Jaap Kunst's two volume work *Music in Java* [7]) is one of the monumental contributions in the general field of ethno-musicology. The great quantity of detail on every aspect of Javanese music, a synthesis of the principal facts and an intensive treatment of Javanese music theory has made this publication a primary reference for all future investigations in this area of study [8]). Articles written by J. S. Brandts Buys, appearing primarily in the periodical *Djawa* [9]), are especially valuable for their perceptive comments about detailed musical practice. Besides these principal sources there are numerous lesser studies, each of which, in spite of a collective tendency toward repetition, affords bits of information that together assume some importance.

Javanese musicians themselves have contributed information and articles, and those of especial interest will be cited from time to time in the followings pages. The general nature of these sources deserves some comment.

Oral or written communications from the contemporary musicians of a culture under study are often not of direct help to the investigator. They sometimes provide an insight which leads to the eventual solution of a particular problem, or they may even supply the basis of a working hypothesis. Communications

---

1) *Ibid.*, 111—12.

2) *Ibid.*, 121.

3) Willem Lodewijckz, *D'Eerste Boeck*, De Eerste Schipvaart der Nederlanders naar Oost-Indie onder Cornelis de Houtman, 1595—1597, published in 1915 by the Linschoten-Vereeniging (The Hague: Martinus Nijhoff, 1915), p. 238, pl. 23 and 25 (pp. 128—9).

4) Thomas Stamford Raffles, *The History of Java* (London: Black, Parbury, and Allen, 1817), I, 469—72; also see Drama, Wayang, Dance.

5) (Amsterdam: Johannes Müller, 1890), 125 pp.

6) See further *MJ*, I, 7—8.

7) See footnote 2, p. 1.

8) See bibliography for other works by Kunst.

9) See bibliography for these and other articles by Brandts Buys.

of this type, however, are invariably expressed in subjective terms and cannot be taken at face value. Definitions, descriptions and explanations may contain mythological references; language difficulties and, of course, an Eastern orientation to music as a subject of rational investigation further complicates and often obscures the meaning of the informant. Music education in Java is conducted by demonstration and imitation, oral theorizing being almost unknown. These factors, therefore, restrict the usage of contemporary Javanese sources to the limited but important role of serving as referents for the confirmation of results reached by some other means.

There has been one noticeable lacuna among the copious publications of Western and Eastern writers — a systematic study of the music itself. The omission, actually, has probably persisted because of a number of contributing circumstances.

On first hearing gamelan music the Western musician is immediately impressed by the distinctive color of the orchestral complex. After his ear has become accustomed to the total sound of the gamelan, he begins to differentiate the various instrumental families according to their respective functions. A typical listener will notice first the two extremes of the Javanese orchestra: the large gongs, which are sounded periodically but not too frequently, and the *panerusan* instruments, which characteristically play rapid and elaborate melodic passages. The drummer may attract his attention next and subsequently the widely-spaced melodies sounded by the *saron* family and the beats of the "horizontal" gongs, which intersperse those of the larger vertical gongs.

The sequence of these observations may be significant. In a Western orchestra the same two extremes — the rapid figures of the strings and woodwinds and the underlying strength of the bases — are also prominent. In homophonic music, in fact, the two principals could be reduced to *the* melodic line (usually the "top" line) and the bass figures. The moving voices and orchestral colors of the harmonic texture and the instruments of the percussion section are not really secondary aspects of the symphony orchestra, but neither are they the most prominent elements.

Even after repeated exposures to gamelan music the Western listener is inclined to follow the rapid figurations and to hear everything else as "background". It is possible that, to a certain extent, this *method* of listening is also shared by the Javanese, but the *meaning* and result of the experience has quite another significance [1]).

In time, the Western listener will learn the functions of these several groups of instruments in relation to the whole. The widely-spaced melody of the saron group, he discovers, is actually the nuclear theme or melodic core of the composition, which is elaborated by the panerusan instruments and subdivided into regular phrases by the gong family. The drummer (or the two-string *rebab*, if

1) This matter can be more conveniently elaborated in Chapter VII.

it is present) is the audible, though not conspicuously-visible, conductor.

The members of the gamelan do not play from written music but only from memory [1]). The lack of written music and the difficulties involved in making full orchestral scores at the time of performance or rehearsal have resulted in a few scattered attempts at reproducing the music of the gamelan in Western notation. This factor has discouraged a systematic and comparative analysis of the music itself.

One element of the musical complex, however, has been preserved in several forms of Javanese music notation: the nuclear theme or principal melody [2]). It should be noted that although this melody predominates all others as it is sounded by the normally large number of saron(s), it strikes the listener as a "background" element in the composition, probably because the motion of the line is less active than the elaborations sounded by the panerusan instruments. This may easily be an added reason for ignoring the available music sources for comparative purposes — notwithstanding the fact that this nuclear theme is recognized as the *principal* melody.

It is precisely these long-neglected Javanese manuscripts which form the basis of the present study; and the publications indicated above provide a foundation on which the investigation has been constructed.

---

1) Recently there are a few — but very few — exceptions found in the modern schools where instruction in gamelan is given.

2) And sometimes includes certain other indications which will be discussed in Chapter III.

II.

FUNDAMENTALS OF JAVANESE MUSIC.

FOR THE READER WHO is thoroughly familiar with the general characteristics of Javanese music, the remarks immediately following are designed to clarify our particular selection of terms from among the synonymous or sometimes conflicting possibilities found in the nomenclature of Javanese studies. In a few instances terms have been chosen on the basis of convenience for the analysis rather than on the popularity of their common usage.

For the reader who is less familiar with gamelan music, the following particulars will provide a background which is adequate for the purposes of this study.

The fullest comprehension of Javanese music is possible only through a liberal acquaintance not only with performances or, second-best, recordings but also with the various other cultural expressions of the Javanese people. The dance, *wayang* (theatre), literature, religion, mythology are interwoven in a cultural pattern from which music is inseparable. Even such concrete forms as the famous batik [1]) and equally famous kris [2]) are associated with music. It is hoped that the reader will make generous use of the bibliography found in the appendix.

One sometimes hears a passing reference to the "music of Java and Bali". The basic contrasts between these two musics are explained by Ernst Schlager: „Obwohl Java besonders im 14. und 15. Jh. starken Einfluss auf die Musik Balis ausübte, ist die heutige Musik beider Inseln so verschieden, dass die Balinesen die javanische langweilig und die Javaner die balinesische Musik barbarisch finden. Während in Java die Sultanate Hüter der musikalischen Tradition sind, sind in Bali die Dörfer die Träger der Musikkultur. Darum ist in Bali die Musik weniger fixiert, die jedoch immer den Anschluss an die Tradition beibehält und in einer ständigen Entwicklung begriffen ist." [3])

1) J. S. Brandts Buys, „Een en Ander over Javaansche Muziek", *Programma van het Congres* (Gehouden van 27 tot en met 29 December 1929 ... ter gelegenheid van het Tienjarig Bestaan van het Java Instituut), pp. 53—4.

2) W. H. Rassers, „On the Javanese Kris," *Bijdragen Koninklijk Instituut*, 99 (1940), 503.

3) „Bali," *Die Musik in Geschichte und Gegenwart*, I (Basel: Bärenreiter, 1949—1951), 1110.

The Javanese know two tonal systems, the five-tone *sléndro* and the seven-tone *pélog* [1]). The former is said to be rather bright and invigorating and the latter is considered somewhat melancholy and sad [2]). Although mythology indicates that sléndro is older than pélog, ethnological evidence establishes the reverse order of their appearance, at least on the island of Java [3]).

The intervals formed by the five tones of the sléndro system are thought to be tending toward a functional equidistance in modern practice. This view of the matter may or may not be correct since an instrument with a truly equidistant scale is yet to be found. For the time being, however, it will be convenient to show an approximation of this scale in accordance with the generally accepted view, further comment on the subject being reserved for Chapter VII. The sequence of the scale given below represents the Javanese tones as they are found on the keys of the saron; the numbers placed between the tone names indicate the approximate size of the intervals expressed in cents [4]).

SLÉNDRO

barang		gulu		ḍaḍa		lima		nem		barang alit
	240		240		240		240		240	

The seven tones of pélog comprise a basic scale of unequal intervals, shown below as an average tuning would appear on the keys of the saron. (The higher *bem* is not found on the saron but is included parenthetically to complete the octave.)

PÉLOG

bem		gulu		ḍaḍa		pélog		lima		nem		barang		(bem)
	120		150		270		130		115		165		(250)	

Various scales are formed in either of the two systems by starting on different tones. The scale possibilities are further increased through the vocal practice (also possible on instruments with variable pitches) of deviating from these

1) There has recently been established the existence of a vocal scale which is neither sléndro nor pélog but a true anhemitonic pentatonic scale, found among the children's songs of East Java (according to an oral communication from Jaap Kunst).

2) Cf. *MJ*, I, 22—3.

3) See *ibid.*, 15—24.

4) 100 cents equal one half-tone of the European tempered scale; see A. J. Ellis, „Tonometrical Observations on some existing Non-Harmonic Musical Scales," *Proceedings* of the Royal Society (London: 1884).

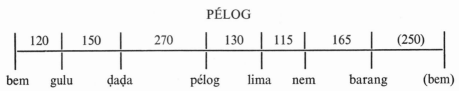

fundamental pitches or intercalating other tones between those of the basic scale [1]). The intricacies of the many theoretical scales require no elaboration here because we shall be concerned with only the nuclear theme and the idiophones on which it is played.

The principal scales of the pélog system do not consist of all seven tones. In each instance two of the seven tones have only an auxiliary function and are used as *sorogan* or temporary exchange tones for one of their adjacent neighbours in the basic scale [2]). A primary distinction among the principal scales is the choice of the two tones which serve as sorogan.

The three principal scales of sléndro can be classified according to *pațet* — *pațet nem*, *pațet sanga*, *pațet manyura*. Various definitions of *pațet* will be mentioned at the end of the chapter; but since the requirements of a *genuine* definition of pațet make up the larger part of this entire study, let us say, for the moment, that pațet is something like *mode*.

In each sléndro pațet *three* of the five tones have a particular importance in their occurrence as final notes of the long phrases (*gongan*) making up a com-

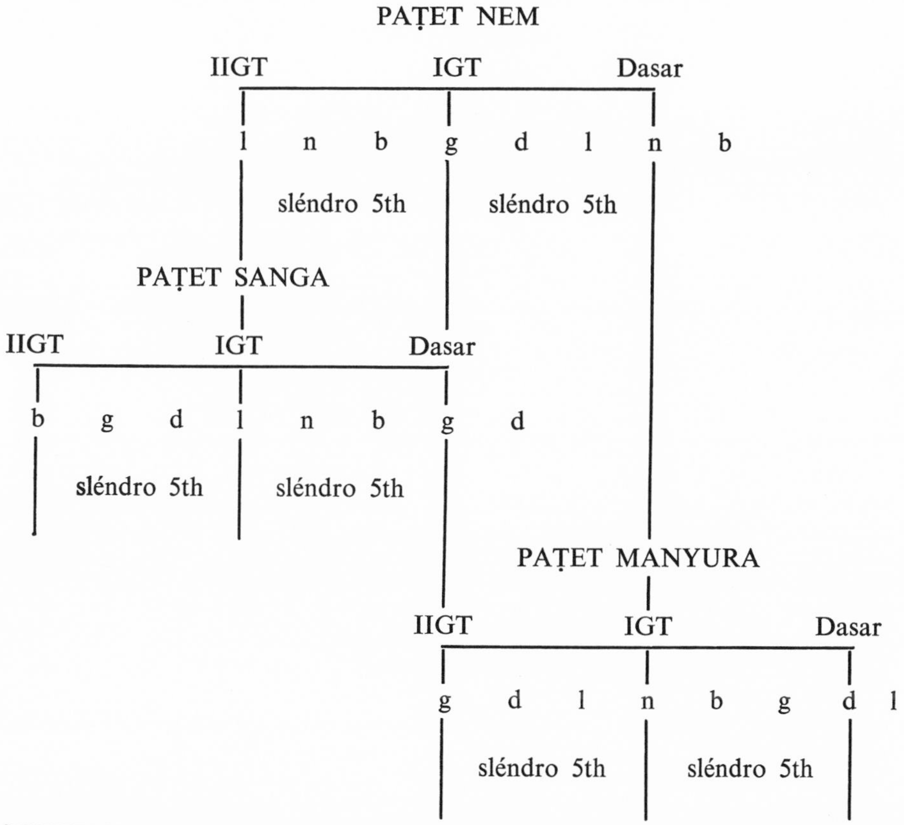

1) See *MJ*, I, 24—70.
2) See *ibid.*, 49—51.

position [1]). These *gong tones* or principal tones — conveniently designated as *dasar* [2]), *first gong tone* and *second gong tone* — lie a sléndro-"fifth" apart, *i.e.* the distance of *three* sléndro intervals. The principal scales of the three paṭet [3]) are also separated by a sléndro-fifth. The intervals between the principal scales of the three paṭet and their respective gong tones can be more clearly explained with the help of the following diagrams. The tone names are abbreviated with the first letter, *e.g.* b = *b*arang, g = *g*ulu, etc.; and IGT = first gong tone and IIGT = second gong tone.

The representation given above shows that the dasar of paṭet manyura lies a sléndro fifth *above* that of paṭet nem, and the dasar of paṭet sanga lies a fifth *below* that of paṭet nem. These details can also be represented in the five-tone principal scale of each paṭet by bringing the second gong tone within the octave of the other two gong tones:

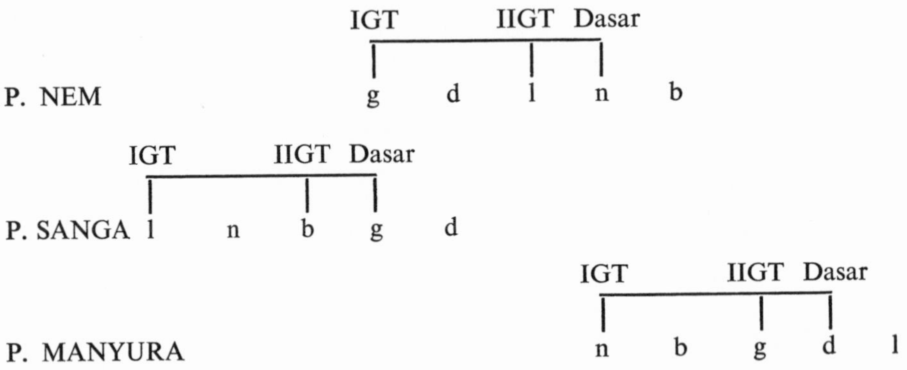

The gong tones of the three paṭet are shown below as they occur in the one-octave range of the saron keys:

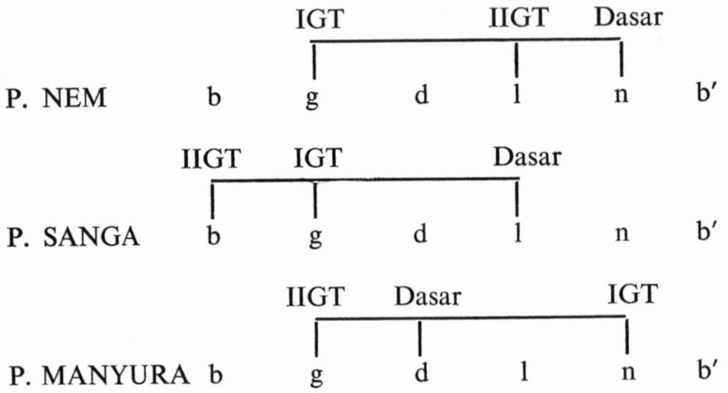

1) *Ibid.*, 70—83.

2) This term will be fully explained in Chapter VII.

3) Throughout this study the Javanese forms of singular and plural will be used, *e.g. one* patet or *three* patet, *one* saron or *several* saron.

This last arrangement shows the position occupied by the principal scale of each paṭet as represented by the notation of the nuclear theme and realized on the instruments of the saron group.

The pélog paṭet have a similar relationship; but a discussion of their scales can be postponed until the beginning of Chapter VIII. It will be sufficient for now to point out that the usage of sorogan or exchange tones, together with the gapped scale structure, creates two additional scale forms for each paṭet: *i.e.*, the principal scale, a high auxiliary scale and a low auxiliary scale.

The Principal Instruments

The nature and idiomatic function of the principal instruments is indicative of their respective importances in the gamelan. The usual instrumental classification (idiophones, chordophones, aerophones, membranophones) will be set aside in favor of an arrangement based on *function.*

Balungan Instruments

Although all the instruments of the gamelan are, to a greater or lesser extent, bound to the nuclear theme, certain of them play only this principal melody or *balunganing genḍing.*

The principal bearers of the nuclear theme are four types of single-octave *saron.* The saron has rather heavy, bronze (or, in the poorer village gamelan, iron) keys which rest on a wooden, trough-shaped case. The keys are held in place by pins, fixed in the edges of the case, which pass through small holes drilled near the two ends of each key. The bronze slabs are not in direct contact with the wooden frame but are cushioned by plaited ratan squares (cork or a woolen material is sometimes used) called *sumpilan* or *tawonan.* In the pélog tuning the saron has seven keys, one for each tone of the basic scale, comprising an unfinished octave; in sléndro there are six keys [1]), *barang alit* being added to complete the octave [2]).

The saron is played with a hard wooden mallet or *tabuh* held in the right hand, while the keys are damped with the left hand. If the tones of the principal melody lie far apart, the key is not damped but allowed to continue sounding.

The *saron panerus* has the highest pitch of the one-octave saron family. This instrument characteristically sounds each note of the nuclear theme *twice, e.g.* two quarter notes for every half note, and thus has a syncopating or duplicating function with regard to the balunganing genḍing. The *saron barung* is an octave lower in pitch, and the *saron demung* is tuned to the next octave below the saron barung. These two instruments play the nuclear theme without deviation. The lowest octave is represented by the somewhat antiquated *saron slenṭem,* an in-

---

1) Sometimes a saron is seen with a seventh key added as the highest tone in the series; *MJ*, I, 166.

2) See p. 6 and illus. p. 311 and p. 314.

strument which is struck on a boss located in the center of each key. The saron slenṭem also plays the notes of the nuclear theme but in some pieces omits the fourth beat of each measure [1]).

It is interesting to note that the *gendèr panembung* or (gendèr) *slenṭem gantung* (the construction of the gendèr family will be discussed presently, see illus. p. 312) sometimes plays *only* the *fourth beat* of every measure and therefore complements the role of the saron slenṭem. On the other hand, both the saron slenṭem and the slenṭem gantung may sound the nuclear theme in its entirety.

When they are present, in smaller orchestral combinations, the three older forms of *bonang* (described below), having only a one-octave range, also play the nuclear theme [2]). The modern two-octave *bonang panembung* (lowest in pitch of the bonang group) is found only in Jogyakarta; it is used, among other functions, to play the "essence", *i.e.* a simplification, of the principal melody [3]). Occasionally, even the *bonang barung* (the middle-size bonang) does little more than sound the balungan tones [4]).

An idea of the volume of sound issuing from the balungan instruments is indicated by the following description of the number of these cantus-firmus instruments used in the gamelan. "In the large orchestras of the nobility in the Principalities [Central Java] and of the Chinese music-lovers the sarons, especially the sarons *barung* and *demung*, are often present in remarkably large — and always even — number: *e.g.* four demungs and eight S. barung, which enables a truly imposing unison melody-effect to be obtained ... The following combination may be considered as normal: 2 demung, 2 or 4 saron barung, and in addition one, or sometimes two saron panerus. When the saron *slenṭem* is present, it is usually in duplicate. In the event of a greater number of sarons barung and demung being used, the number of S. panerus and S. slenṭem is not increased." [5])

Interpunctuating Instruments

The flow of the nuclear theme is divided into phrases by the members of the gong family. The longest of these divisions is provided by the regular punctuations of the great *gong ageng* or *gong geḍé*, and one or more of these phrases (*e.g.* 8, 16, or 32 measures in length) are called *gongan*. The large gong may be up to one metre in diameter and weigh as much as 150 pounds. It is hung vertically from a stand or *gayor* and struck on its central boss or beating knob with a large round tabuh or, preferably, with the clenched fist. The deep, dark sonorous tone of the Javanese gong ageng is unrivaled by gongs from

---

1) Beat four of the Javanese notation but actually beat one in the transcription; this will be fully explained in the following chapter.

2) See *MJ*, I, 155—157.

3) *Ibid.*, 158; see illus. p. 313.

4) *Ibid.*, 167; see illus. p. 313.

5) *Ibid.*, 166—7.

any other part of the world; the pitch is about 30 to 40 vibrations per second. Sometimes the gong ageng is replaced by the smaller *gong suwukan* which has a tone about one octave higher.

The gongan, in turn, is subdivided into shorter phrases by a medium-size vertical gong, the *kempul* (usually only in the smaller forms of composition) and *always* by the *kenong*, a "horizontal" gong form. In a sixteen-measure gongan, for example, the kempul is sounded on the first beat of the sixth, tenth and fourteenth measures; the kenong on the fourth, eighth, twelfth and (coinciding with the gong ageng) on the sixteenth measures. A small horizontal gong, flatter in shape than the kenong, called the *keṭuk*, is sounded at the beginning of all the odd-numbered measures. Thus, every measure except the second begins with a stroke on one of these interpunctuating instruments.

The horizontal gong, shaped like a deep inverted bowl, has a central boss which is struck with a cylindrical, wooden tabuh wrapped along the striking surface with heavy cord. The gong is placed on crossed cords strung from the four sides of a supporting frame.

The Javanese have an infallible sense for onomotopoetic names: the *gong ageng* (pronounced AH-gung) has the deepest, fullest sound; the *kenong* (accent on -nóng) has a high, clear sound; the *kempul* (accent on -pul) a penetrating but modulated tone; the *keṭuk* (accent on -ṭuk) a short "cluck" produced by damping as the instrument is struck. (See the illus. pp. 314—15.)

Panerusan Instruments

The *panerusan* instruments exist in several multi-octave forms and characteristically play elaborations of the nuclear theme. The style of these paraphrasing melodies is, to a certain extent, determined by the nature of the various instruments. Since the particular parts for these instruments are not preserved in the Javanese notation of the nuclear theme, however, we shall consider them only in brief [1]).

The gendèr has thin bronze keys suspended in a frame over bamboo resonators. A disc-headed tabuh with a padded edge is held by the player in each hand; and the keys are damped by the fingers, thumb or heel of the thumb of the same hand which strikes them. The melodies are often elaborate, especially in the smallest gendèr, *gendèr panerus*, and require extremely supple wrists for their execution. The gendèr panerus and the next larger size, the *gendèr barung*, have two complete octaves or sometimes a few tones more. The one-octave slenṭem gantung and the single-octave demung have been discussed above.

The *bonang* consists of a series of bronze sounding kettles (or small horizontal gongs) supported by crossed cords strung in a wooden frame. The older one-octave forms were mentioned above. The modern two-octave forms are found in three sizes: the *bonang panerus* (the highest), the bonang barung and the

---

1) See *ibid.*, 122—240.

bonang panembung (see above). These instruments are played with two cylindrical, wooden tabuh, similar to those used for the kenong or keṭuk, the tones being damped, in this case, with the tabuh itself. The bonang panerus and barung have rather variable functions. In fast pieces they may do little more than reinforce or syncopate the nuclear theme; in slower pieces the same style is followed with only a little more melodic and rhythmic variation.

The *gambang kayu* is a kind of wooden xylophone, three to four octaves in range, played with two tabuh which have long resilient handles and a padded, disc-shaped head. Producing a much more mellow sound than its Western counterpart, the gambang kayu plays rapid elaborations of the nuclear theme in a variety of styles [1]).

The *rebab* is a two-stringed bowing lute, probably of Persian-Arabic origin [2]), which, in the softer orchestral pieces, has a rather elaborate melodic function. It does not depart too much, however, from the cantus firmus. The *suling* or end-blown flute and the human voice are used in soft (*alus* = refined) gamelan pieces and may deviate considerably from the nuclear theme in their independent melodies.

Rhythm Instruments

Rhythm is one of the most important elements in gamelan music and yet, for the Westerner, one of the most difficult to comprehend fully. I am indebted to Mr. Bernard IJzerdraat [3]) for his explanation of an approach to understanding rhythm as a subtle but primary force in Javanese music.

One might assume that the player of the gong ageng, who, for example, strikes one tone every sixteen measures, performs a very simple task; or the keṭuk player, who sounds one note in every other measure; or the kenong and kempul in their four-measure phrases. The task is not so simple. To consider the shortest phrase first, the keṭuk player must not merely "count" to eight in order to play "in time" but must *feel* the rhythm of his individual line in relation to the whole.

I suggest that two components are necessary to rhythm: 1. recurrence or repetition; 2. a pattern in which one unit is stressed: *e.g.*

The first four beats do not establish a *rhythm* until they are repeated, and it is the accent on "four" which causes the eigth beats to be recognized as two groups of four. The repetition also creates *two lines* of rhythm:

---

1) See *ibid.*, 185—90; see illus. p. 316.

2) *Ibid.*, 220; see illus. p. 317.

3) The conductor of the Dutch study-group, gamelan *Babar layar* at the Royal Tropical Institute in Amsterdam. Mr. IJzerdraat's facility on all the instruments of the gamelan and the excellent performances of Babar layar are testimony to the fact that a comprehension of and feeling for gamelan music are not inaccessible to the Western world. Performances by this group are sometimes broadcast to Java, where they are very favorably received.

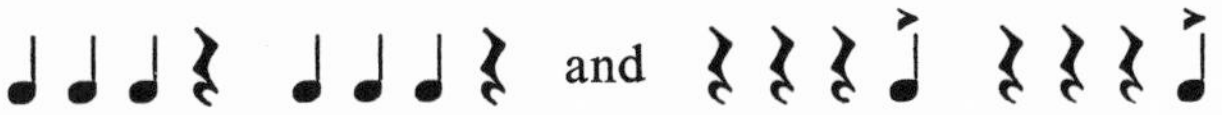

Together, these might be represented in the following way:

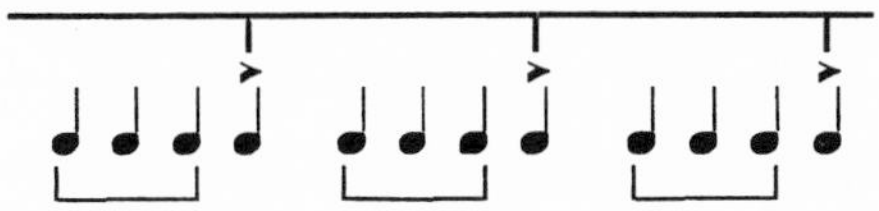

If each of the four beats is sounded by a different instrumental timbre, we might imagine *four* lines of rhythm. If the second beat in each group were replaced by a rest, still *another* line of rhythm would be established.

We can apply this example to the role of the principal interpunctuating instruments. In the diagram given below, each symbol represents one measure (actually the fourth beat of the measure); the diagram contains the last beat of one gongan, a full gongan and the first two measures of another. G = gong; N = kenong; T = keṭuk; P = kempul; W = wela (the second measure of the gongan from which the kempul is omitted, therefore a rest).

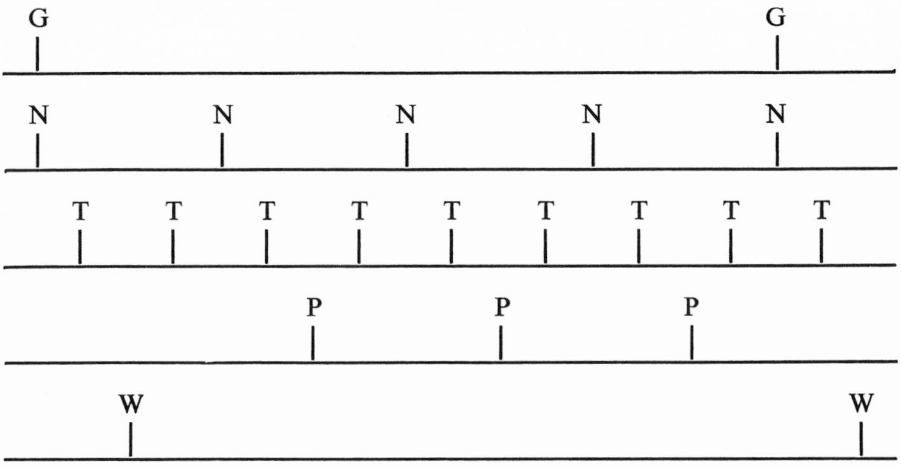

The Javanese "measure" consists of four beats or time units called *keteg*. The fourth keteg of every measure (like the first beat in Western music) is *felt* as having slightly more weight than the other three. This quadratic division can be extended to the rhythmic lines indicated for the interpunctuating instruments above. For example, the *fourth* kenong beat (N) of a gongan, coinciding with the gong ageng (G), will be *felt* as having slightly more weight than the preceding three beats. The *second* beat will have a little more weight than beats one and three. In other words, the stress is on *two-FOUR;* in Western music it is on *ONE-three*.

Each instrument, therefore, not only is part of the whole rhythmic complex but also contains within its own rhythmic line the two necessary components:

repetition and a pattern with one unit which is (felt as) stressed. Unless the individual player manages to capture this large sense of his rhythmic contribution, the true spirit of gamelan music is lacking [1]).

To these multi-rhythms created by the interpunctuating instruments must be added the variable *melodic* rhythms contained in the nuclear theme. Sometimes these coincide with the principal points of the gongan subdivisions, and sometimes not. The syncopations, paraphrasing and elaborations of the panerusan instruments add still other cross-rhythms. It is little wonder that I heard someone remark once, at his first gamelan concert, "How do they all manage to finish at the same time?"

This question leads us to a short discussion of the "invisible" conductor of the gamelan: the *kenḍang* player or drummer. The first responsibility of the kenḍang is to maintain a steady tempo and to signal clearly an accelerando or ritardando indicative of a change in tempo. To this fundamental function the drummer adds various lines of rhythm (see above) which may be a reflection of the nuclear theme or the interpunctuating instruments or the panerusan instruments or may be a combination of any of these. Needless to say, a feeling for the *total* rhythmic structure is essential to this very complicated and important task. On the other hand, the Javanese drummer is not a *prima donna* of the gamelan; virtuostic exhibition is not practiced in Central Java.

The principal types of kenḍang will be mentioned later in connection with the Javanese notation of the nuclear theme.

The Genḍing

The kinds and number of Javanese *genḍing* or orchestral compositions are extensive [2]), but for present purposes we shall be concerned with three principal types and the mention of a fourth.

The large genḍing consist of a *short introduction* (the *bubuka* or *buka*), an *introductory movement* (the *mérong*) and the *principal movement* (the *munggah*). This larger form will be discussed at the beginning of Chapter VIII and need not occupy further attention until then.

The *ladrang* (plural *ladrang*) and the *ketawang* (plural *ketawang*) consist of a bubuka, an introductory *gongan* and a principal movement. In the ladrang each gongan is sixteen measures long and has the following colotomic structure, arranged by four-measure phrases or *kenongan, i.e.* divisions marked by the regular occurrence of a kenong beat; (W = wela = "rest"):

---

[1]) This comes as second nature for the Javanese but is something of a problem for the Western musician. As a beginner on these instruments I have, when playing in the gamelan, deliberately neglected the larger aspect of the rhythmic line and fallen back on the simple: 1-2-3-*4*, 1-2-3-*4*. Mr. IJzerdraat *invariably* noticed the difference in the result!

[2]) See *MJ*, I, 295—346.

T W T N
T P T N
T P T N
T P T N
G

The ketawang has eight-measure gongan:

T P T N
T P T N
G

The nuclear themes of these two forms of genḍing have the same characteristics as those of the larger genḍing (see Chapter VIII) and, for the purpose of an extensive comparative analysis, have the advantage of being shorter. The larger of the two manuscripts used for this study contains a few ketawang and a few *gangsaran*; the rest are ladrang.

The *gangsaran* will be omitted from the analysis because they are a kind of medley which begins and ends on an extended monotone and lack a bubuka [1]).

As a convenience, a slightly different terminology will be used for designating the parts of the ladrang and the ketawang. The short introduction will be indicated by the term *bubuka opaq-opaq*; the one introductory gongan, which immediately follows, will be called the *bubuka genḍing* in order to distinguish this section from the gongan of the genḍing proper [2]). The bubuka genḍing is *not* repeated but proceeds directly to the genḍing proper; the gongan of the principal movement, on the other hand, *are* repeated a variable number of times.

Some Definitions of Paṭet

To return briefly to the larger aspects of the paṭet concept, various "definitions" are given below [3]). Appropriate comment will be withheld until the beginning of Chapter III.

R. M. Jayadipura: "paṭet is the couch or bed of a melody." [4]) Jakub and Wignyarumeksa: "the paṭet serves to allow the genḍing to sit down (nglungguhake)" [5]). Suryaputra: "paṭet is the harmonic relation between the pitch of a piece of music and the vibrations of the atmosphere at certain moments of the day or night [6]). R. M. Sarwaka: "the distinction between a given paṭet and

---

1) See *ibid.*, 302—3.

2) Cf. J. S. Brandts Buys, „Omtrent Notaties en Transscripties en over de Constructie van Gamelanstukken," *Djawa*, XIV (1934), 137—8.

3) See *MJ*, I, 72—3.

4) *Ibid.*, 72.

5) Djakoeb and Wignjaroemeksa, „Lajang anjoeroepaké pratikelé bab sinaoe naboeh sarto panggawéné gamelan," *Volkslectuur*, no. 94 (1913).

6) Soerjapoetra, „Javaansche Muziekontwikkeling en Westersche Muziek," *Djawa*, I, Prae-Adviezen II (June, 1921), 118.

another one is based upon a difference in *chengkok* (melody or melodic line) [1]. Sulardi: "what is called paṭet is really preluding (grambyanganing) on an instrument according to certain rules, from which the nature of the compositions to be performed shall become evident" [2]. Sastrasuwignya: "by paṭet is meant the singing of the ḍalang to the accompaniment of the rebab, gender, gambang, suling, kenḍang and the gong" [3].

---

1) *MJ*, I, 72.

2) R. Bagoes Soelardi, ,,Serat pradongga," *Widya poestaka*, no. 2 (1918).

3) Soehardha Sastrasoewignja, in collaboration with R. Wiradat and K. Kodrat, ,,Ringkesaning kawroeh padalangan ringgit poerwa ing Soerakarta" (,,Kadjawen"), Volkslectuur nos. 70 to 54 (September 2, 1931 to July 6, 1932).

III.

CONSIDERATIONS IN THE ANALYSIS.

> "All these definitions [of paṭet] ... are either incomplete or too superficial. A genuine definition, *i.e.* one which would convey to us all essential characteristics of the conception, and, thereby, indirectly, the differences existing between the different kind of paṭets, has not yet, as far as I am aware, been formulated" [1].
>
> . . . . . .
>
> "We have here, as in so many other cases, an *intuitive* not an intellectual knowledge: a good niyaga from the Principalities immediately distinguishes one paṭet from another, without ever making a mistake: he is, however, incapable of explaining how or why he does so" [2].

THE INITIAL AIM of this study was not prompted by any romantic notions concerning the conquest of the reputedly illusive paṭet concept, but rather by the conviction that the nuclear theme and the instruments entrusted with this principal melody were the most important elements of the gamelan — elements which could provide a clue to the order and logic of Javanese musical expression, if my long-held presumptions were correct [3]. From indications early in the analysis it appeared that certain practices might be associated with each paṭet. While this discovery in itself required no alteration of my original objective, I must confess that it provided a focal point which considerably augmented my interest in the investigation. The actual working of the paṭet concept, then, will be of primary concern in the following pages.

The Javanese Manuscripts

The nuclear theme or principal melody of the genḍing distinguishes that piece from all others. The members of the gamelan do not read music as they play

---

1) *MJ*, I, 72.

2) *Ibid.*, 73.

3) If in his haste to get at the crux of the matter the reader has by-passed the *preface*, he would oblige me by turning back a few pages now.

but perform from memory, having learned, in the first place, through a process of imitation. If a particular genḍing should not be played for some time and consequently should be forgotten, that composition would completely disappear from the repertoire. To prevent such a loss many of the nuclear themes have been collected and set down in one of several forms of Javanese notation.

In addition to the nuclear theme the notation may also give indications for the interpunctuating instruments (gong, kenong, kempul, keṭuk), occasionally the beats of the bonang panembung, the essential drum patterns and sometimes a general indication of tempo and the register (high or low) in which the panerusan instruments are to play. Certain kinds of cipher notation contain only the nuclear theme and the symbols of the interpunctuating instruments.

Either type of „short score" is sufficient because the panerusan parts are guided by the nuclear theme, and the kenḍang patterns exist in several standard types which are elaborated by the individual player. J. S. Brandts Buys makes the following comment regarding the parts represented in the various forms of Javanese notation: „Practisch hoort men den cantus firmus dus, enorm sterk, door de saron's hameren, binnen hun één-octaafs-bestek. De aanduiding, hoe dat thema zou (hebben) kunnen worden ontvouwd door een rebab b.v., is dus werkelijk niet van zoo veel belang" [1]). (Practically, therefore, the cantus firmus is heard enormously strong, hammered out by the sarons within their one-octave range. Consequently, an indication of how that theme might have been realized by a rebab, for example, is actually not of so much importance.)

The two collections used for this study represent different types of notation. The larger manuscript is from Jogyakarta and contains one hundred genḍing noted in the *kraton* (royal court) "checkered" script. This copy, part of a larger collection originally made *ca.* 1895, was presented to Jaap Kunst by R. T. Wiraguna, a muscially-gifted official of the Kraton in Jogya.

An illustration of the checkered-script notation for a sléndro ladrang and a pélog ketawang will be found on p. 318 and p. 319, respectively. The lines of the vertical "staff" represent the saron tones of each scale system: six in the sléndro script (reading from left to right): barang, gulu, ḍaḍa, lima, nem, barang alit; seven in the pélog script: bem, gulu, ḍaḍa, pélog, lima, nem, barang. One of the lines in sléndro (lima) and two of the lines in pélog (lima and pélog) are sometimes made heavier than the others as an aid in reading the notation [2]). The horizontal lines crossing these tonal indications represent the *keteg* (heartbeat) or rhythmic unit. Every fourth keteg is also printed a little heavier than the other three, thus representing both the fourth beat and the "bar line" simultaneously. The dots placed on the intersections of the vertical and horizontal lines indicate the notes of the nuclear theme. The signs to the right of the vertical staff indicate the basic drum pattern; the symbols on the left represent the

---

1) „Het Gewone Javaansche Tooncijferschrift (Het Salasche Kepatihan-Schrift)," *Djawa*, XX (1940), 90 (footnote).

2) *MJ*, I, 351.

occurrence of the principal colotomic instruments. In the transcriptions of these pieces the drum indications are omitted and the colotomic symbols are replaced by the letters "T", "N", "P", and "NG" for "keṭuk", "kenong", "kempul", and "kenong-gong". A clue to the written indications appearing at the top of the script can be seen by turning to the transcription of the sléndro ladrang on pp. 273—4 and the pélog ketawang on pp. 297—8.

The second manuscript, copied *ca.* 1925, is Solonese and was presented to Jaap Kunst by H. H. Mangku Nagara VII, ruling Prince of the Mangku Nagaran State. This collection is in cipher notation. Seventeen compositions in pélog paṭet lima are used from the manuscript, and an illustration of one of them will be found on p. 319. The numbers 1—7 indicate the sequence of pélog tones: bem, gulu, ḍaḍa, pélog, lima, nem, barang. The small circle above a cipher is the symbol for the keṭuk, a "g" indicates the large gong, "N" represents the kenong and "k" the kempul. No drum signs are included. The other letters and symbols, *e.g.* "C" and "$" and the information to the right of the notation gives directions for playing which can be compared with the transcription given on p. 291.

The principal objective in the analysis is to discover those elements of compositional practice which occur with a regularity sufficient to establish a fundamental norm for the individual paṭet, for the paṭet of sléndro, for the paṭet of pélog, and finally for the paṭet of both tonal systems. Accordingly, a separate chapter is devoted to each of the three sléndro paṭet and another to a summary of the sléndro system with resulting conclusions; the pélog system is treated in a similar manner; and the final chapter consists of a comparison of both tonal systems with conclusions.

In order to be able to see both the forest and the trees minor practices will be given less attention. Certain artistic devices will occasionally be called to the reader's attention, but stylistic treatment and, more especially, the nuance of thematic development and form are minor considerations. Although most of the genḍing are interesting from this standpoint alone, an evaluation of style and the minutia of form tend to be somewhat subjective and perhaps are better served by the individual reader's interpretation.

In this comparatively large number of genḍing (a total of 117 titles) [1]) it would be surprising if some of the compositions, by whatever standards we are finally able to establish, were not particularly *good* pieces of music. It would be equally surprising if we were to find no "unrepresentative" genḍing. On the other hand, such irregularities, in themselves, may provide the very exceptions which prove the rule. It should also be noted that "copyists' errors" are not

---

1) According to Jaap Kunst the entire repertoire of all of Central Java consists of no more than approximately 800 genḍing. No one collection contains all of them; the largest collection, the kraton MS of Jogya, has about 500-odd genḍing, and these are almost entirely the larger forms of compositions. See further *MJ*, I, 347—8.

unknown in manuscripts of this type [1]), and further that it is common practice or, better stated, it is *mandatory* that in the copying of certain genḍing used for religious purposes at least *one* mistake *must* occur in the copy, a perfect copy, in this instance, being considered sarcriligious! [2]) Notwithstanding the probable existence of such imperfections, I promise not to take refuge in these pecadillos when discussing problematical genḍing — at least not more than once or twice.

An adequate number of representative genḍing from each paṭet are given in detailed analysis, and complete transcriptions of these pieces appear in the appendix. A structural chart representing the four-measure melodic sections (*kenongan*) of the genḍing is presented at the beginning of each analysis, and pertinent music examples illustrate the text. The genḍing from each paṭet which are not shown in detailed analyses are included in the individual paṭet summaries of important structural elements.

The scale used for transcribing the sléndro genḍing from the kraton notation is given below with its approximate sléndro equivalents:

The intervals and the actual pitch of the saron keys do not, of course, coincide with the notes given. The absolute pitch of barang, for example, may vary from one gamelan to another by as much as a whole tone or more [3]). This transcription-scale was selected primarily to maintain an approximation of the fifth relationship among the three principal tones of each paṭet [4]).

I hesitated a long while before deciding to use a Western-scale transcription for the genḍing. After becoming accustomed to the kraton script, I found that for comparative purposes it was much more quickly read than a transcription. On the other hand (so went the debate), perhaps it was asking too much to expect the reader to become acquainted with two or three kinds of script. So, actually, I have settled for a compromise. It will take the reader only a few minutes to learn that "c" is really not "c" but barang and that "d" is actually gulu, etc. Throughout the analysis I shall refer to the tones of the melodic line only by their Javanese names, so that any tendency to associate Western pitches with tonal designations may be at a minimum.

The scale used for the transcription of pélog genḍing will be discussed at the beginning of Chapter VIII.

---

1) Cf. J. S. and A. Brandts Buys-Van Zijp, „Javaansche Gending's bij Land en bij Seeling," *Djawa*, XVIII (1938), 142, 196—7.

2) *MJ*, I, 280.

3) Cf. *ibid.*, II, 574—5.

4) See pp. 7—9; see further *MJ*, I, 71, 84, 94, 97—8.

In practice the time value given the keteg or smallest rhythmic unit of the kraton script is, of course, relative to the tempo or tempos at which a genḍing is played. If, in the four keteg of one measure, there are notes on the second and fourth horizontal lines, this indicates that the saron player allows each tone to sound for the duration of two keteg, damping the first note only as the second is sounded. Depending on the tempo, these two notes could be written as half notes, as whole notes or even as double whole notes. For analytical purposes, however, *each keteg* of the transcription will receive the constant value of one quarter note, and general directions for tempo will be stated above the appropriate parts of the genḍing. In some compositions the nuclear theme consists of only one tone every four keteg. This will be indicated in whole notes. The duration of sound issuing from a struck bronze key — again depending on the tempo — may, in practice, not sustain itself effectively for so long as four keteg (although the sustaining power of the saron key is surprising). The notation of a whole note, however, is justified if for no other reason than the fact that an indication for damping is given only by the appearance of the next tone in the script — in this instance, another whole note.

It has been mentioned earlier that in Javanese music a slight stress is felt (though not necessarily executed) on *two-FOUR*, and consistent with this rhythmic pulse the final gong (and kenong) occur on the *fourth* beat of the measure. In transcription this beat becomes the first beat of the following bar. To Western ears the gong beat is actually heard as sounding on *one* rather than on *four*. This shift of one beat is maintained in all complete and excerpted transcriptions, the entire genḍing, as it were, being moved one beat forward.

In order to afford the inclusion of a maximum number of analyses the exposition of various compositional devices is given in detail only once. As similar practices occur in subsequent genḍing, they are pointed out and the pagination of the first example cited for comparison, at least until such devices are reasonably familiar to the reader.

Terminology

The Western musician who writes about non-European music occupies an anomalous position. If, for example, his subject of inquiry is Javanese music, he discovers that the Javanese writings in themselves are not expressed in terms which are understandable nor, consequently, acceptable to himself nor to his colleagues. His task, then, is to employ scientific method in his research and to express his results in terms which will be understood and are acceptable to the Western musician. But there are inherent difficulties in this simple objective. If he uses the terminology of Western music in an analogous application, he may be criticized as being "Western-influenced". If he does not use the abstract symbols familiar to the Western musician, he may not be able to communicate his findings. There are few investigators who, at one time or another, have not been, justly or unjustly, accused of being Western in their thinking [1]). Usually such accusations are founded on a misinterpretation of the author's intention.

In order to minimize similar misinterpretations I should like to say a few words about the music terms used in this study.

In the following pages it will frequently be necessary to make a specific reference to either of two tones separated by the interval of a fifth. There are several phrases which could be used to designate one of these tones in such a way that the reader is reminded of the fifth relationship. For example: "I am referring to the tone *x*, the lower of the two tones delimiting the interval of a fifth", or "we are speaking here of the tone *y* which, we must bear in mind, lies a fifth above the tone *x*". Frequent designations of this kind would be something of a nuisance. For this reason I have chosen to use the term "tonic" to indicate the lower note of the fifth interval and the term "dominant" to indicate the upper note. These terms are reserved for only that fifth interval which appears to be the most important in each paṭet. At the risk of seeming tedious I point out further that these two terms and any similar words which are familiar to the Western reader are not intended in the literal sense in which they are understood in Western musical practice but are offered only as convenient symbols. The term "cadence" will also be used and is meant to indicate a melodic formula which occurs with some regularity at the ends of a musical sentence or other points of repose. The *function* of these tones and melodic formulas, we shall assume, may or may not have features in common with Western musical practice. The reader will oblige me by holding such judgements in abeyance until the proper time, namely, Chapters VII, XI and XII. In those places I shall try to present the pertinent facts as objectively as possible.

(If, at this point, the reader is reminded of a certain Hollywood trademark which goes, "Any correspondence between actual persons, living or dead ...". I can only say: any correspondence between Javanese tones of resolution, real or imaginary, and tonic-dominant is purely coincidental.)

Indonesian terms not already presented and defined in the foregoing pages will be explained as they occur in the course of the analysis.

---

1) Manfred F. Bukofzer, „The Evolution of Javanese Tone-Systems," *Papers* read at the International Congress of Musicology, held at New York Sept. 11 to 16, 1939 (New York: 1944), p. 242; but cf. Jaap Kunst, *Around von Hornbostel's Theory of the Cycle of Blown Fifths*, Mededeling LXXVI of the Indisch Instituut (Amsterdam: 1948), p. 31; and see pp. 115—20.

IV.

SLÉNDRO PAṬET NEM.

THE THREE GONG TONES of paṭet nem are the tones nem, gulu and lima, referred to as dasar, first gong tone and second gong tone respectively. The word "dasar" and its Sundanese musico-technical application will be considered in Chapter VII. The terms "first gong tone" and "second gong tone" were previously discussed [1]) and will serve — together with "dasar" — as convenient labels in the analysis. In the general sense they will be called "gong tones" or "principal tones" and in the specific sense by their particular names. The reader should avoid any prejudice toward the inference that the melodic or structural importance of a given tone is necessarily related to the classification "first" or "second" or "dasar".

The first few examples in the analysis will be treated in considerable detail so that both the minor and the major features of the genḍing are brought to the reader's attention. These early analyses should be read along with constant reference to the corresponding transcriptions appearing in the appendix. When the characteristics of the genḍing become more familiar, the reader, at his own discretion, may not wish to follow the transcriptions in such great detail.

Analysis of the Genḍing

The Jogyanese collection contains seventeen genḍing listed by the scribe in sléndro paṭet nem. Two of these, nr 13 and nr 14, are gangsaran and have therefore been omitted [2]); two others, nr 4 and nr 12, were incorrectly labeled and will be included in their proper paṭet group. Of the remaining thirteen examples seven have been selected for detailed analysis, and the other six are included in the statistical summaries in the latter part of this chapter. In both categories of these examples particular attention should be given to three structural sections of the genḍing: the bubuka opaq-opaq, the bubuka genḍing and the last gongan of the piece. The structural position of each of these three sections gives them a greater importance than the other parts of the genḍing. The bubuka opaq-

1) See pp. 7—9.
2) Cf. p. 15.

opaq is the short introduction. The bubuka genḍing immediately follows the bubuka opaq-opaq and unlike the subsequent gongan is almost never repeated but leads directly to the genḍing proper. Its name as well as its position suggest that it may be a formal extension of the short introduction. The position of the final gongan of the piece, of course, is important in terms of resolution.

The structural table appearing on p. 25 is typical of the analyses of all ladrang and should be read in the following manner:

"B.Op." indicates the bubuka opaq-opaq, the short introduction which concludes with the first stroke on the large gong.

"B. Gd." indicates the bubuka genḍing, which is normally sixteen measures long and ends with the second stroke on the large gong.

"GN I, GN II" etc. indicate the individual gongan of the genḍing proper. Each of these structural divisions is also sixteen measures long and terminates with a gong beat.

"A B C" etc. indicate the four-measure divisions of the gongan into *kenongan*, so-called because a stroke on the kenong falls on the last beat of the four-measure phrase. If the melodic pattern of one kenongan is also used for other kenongan (with perhaps a change in the initial or the ultimate note), these four-measure phrases are indicated by the same letter, e.g. "A". A small deviation other than that of the first or last note is distinguished by "A*" and is explained below the table. Kenongan which have different melodic patterns are indicated by different capital letters, e.g. "A B C D".

"g l n" etc. indicate the names of the sléndro tones *n*em, *l*ima, *ḍ*aḍa, *g*ulu, *b*arang (from high to low) and represent the tone sounded simultaneously with the kenong on the last beat of the four-measure phrase.

"*A B A*" indicate the architectonic form.

"Kenḍang 2" indicates the type of kenḍangan employing two drums, the *kenḍang genḍing* and the *penunṭung* or *ketipung* [1]. Some genḍing use "kenḍang 1", i.e. only one drum, the kenḍang genḍing or the *chiblon* [2]. The art of kenḍang playing is a separate study in itself [3] and need only concern us here in the general indication: *kenḍang 1* or *kenḍang 2.*

The bubuka opaq-opaq is given both in the original kraton script and in transcription. These together with the structural table and pertinent music examples in the text will, in the later analyses, serve for a general perusal of the material without requiring detailed reference to the complete transcription. The symbols appearing to the left and right of the checkered script were explained

1) *MJ*, I, 213—14; see illus. p. 317.

2) *Ibid.*, 212—13.

3) See *ibid.*, 209—19.

in the previous chapter [1]). The reader is again reminded that the kenong-gong symbol  falls on the fourth keteg of the kraton script, which in transcription becomes the first beat of the following measure and is indicated by NG.

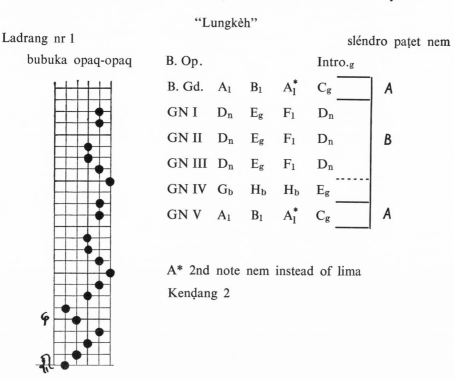

"Lungkèh"

Ladrang nr 1 — sléndro paṭet nem

bubuka opaq-opaq

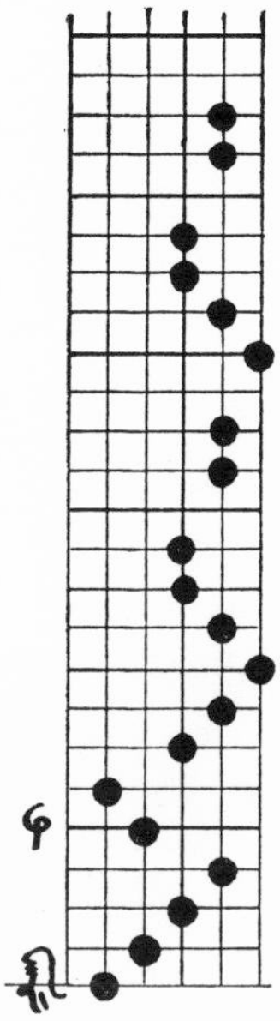

B. Op.				Intro.$_g$	
B. Gd.	A_l	B_l	A^*_l	C_g	A
GN I	D_n	E_g	F_l	D_n	
GN II	D_n	E_g	F_l	D_n	B
GN III	D_n	E_g	F_l	D_n	
GN IV	G_b	H_b	H_b	E_g	
GN V	A_l	B_l	A^*_l	C_g	A

A* 2nd note nem instead of lima

Kenḍang 2

transcribed (see appendix pp. 265—6).

The structural table of "Lungkèh" indicates that the ladrang has a ternary form. The four kenongan of the bubuka genḍing are repeated as gongan V, comprising the two *A* sections; the *B* section is a binary structure, gongan I, II and III forming the first part and gongan IV the second part. The preponderance of the three gong tones nem, gulu and lima (destignated by the lower-case letters)

1) See p. 21.

appearing as the ultimate constituents of the kenongan and gongan indicates their general melodic and structural importance. On p. 266 of the appendix the complete transcription shows that the occurrence of the colotomic instruments — the keṭuk (T), the kenong (N), the kempul (P) and the gong (G) — is typical of the ladrang form. The kenḍang-two pattern is regular.

Bubuka opaq-opaq

The three gong tones carry the principal melodic emphasis in the bubuka opaq-opaq. In the beginning measures nem (dasar) is the strongest tone with its rhythmic figure of bars 1—2 and 3—4. The tones lima (second gong tone) and barang are used as important neighbor notes, and gulu (first gong tone) appears as the last note of measure five and as the final tone of the bubuka opaq-opaq in bar seven. The descending scale passage from nem to gulu (bar 6—7) can be described as a cadence from dasar to first gong tone or from "dominant" to "tonic". The reader should again be cautioned not to infer that the term "tonic" necessarily indicates a melodic goal or a tone of resolution. The four notes (or, including the neighbor tone barang, six notes) preceding this cadence appear to be a slight variation of the same cadence.

In brief summary: the tone nem, using lima and barang as neighbor notes, serves as the melodic core of the first four measures. In measure five there is an incomplete cadence to gulu, which is fully stated in the final measure as a simple scale passage descending from nem to gulu. The tone ḍaḍa is omitted from the first cadence and leads to the full cadence in bar six, where it occurs again as a passing note.

Bubuka genḍing

The sixteen measures of the bubuka genḍing are constructed from a figure appearing in the bubuka opaq-opaq in bars 5—6—7:

In the bubuka genḍing this figure is altered in the following way: the time value of every note has been doubled, and the tone ḍaḍa appears between each note of the figure as a kind of pedal or pivot tone. It will be expedient at this point to acquaint the reader with an element of musical practice characteristic of Jogyakarta.

> "... it happens sometimes — in the real genḍings always, after they have 'fallen' (*tiba*, H. J. [High Javanese] *nḍawah*), i.e. in the second part of these compositions — that the *saron barung* does not only sound the cantus firmus, but, in addition, each time between the tones of this nuclear theme, another tone, always the same one for quite a long time, whereby the impression is created that this nuclear theme is, as it were, curled like a festoon around a fixed pivot, or, to put it another way, hanging upon a straight

line. This continually recurring tone is called *pancher*, meaning literally: a pole used to mark out part of a field ... A pancher is beaten only when the nuclear theme-tones lie far apart, as is the case in *wirama rangkep*; it saves the playing from losing some of its equilibrium and firmness owing to the time-intervals between the tones of the cantus firmus being too long" [1]).

To return to the bubuka genḍing under discussion, it should be pointed out that since the pivot tones on ḍaḍa appear *as notes of the nuclear theme itself*, this is *not* an example of the pancher practice explained by Kunst, in which an *additional* tone is sounded each time between the notes of the nuclear theme. In this instance, however, ḍaḍa functions as what might be termed a "quasi-pancher", comprising at the same time part of the cantus firmus.

In the fragment of the bubuka genḍing given below, the underscored notes are those appearing in the figure taken from the bubuka opaq-opaq.

N.B. To avoid sounding ḍaḍa three times in succession the tone nem has been substituted in measure twelve. This type of substitution is also common practice in the usage of a regular pancher [2]). In measures nine and thirteen, on the other hand, ḍaḍa appears in the double capacity of pancher and melodic tone.

The gong tone lima in measure eight is used, perhaps, as a bridge tone from the final gulu of the bubuka opaq-opaq to the reiterated phrase (bars 9—12) which continues through the third kenongan. At this point the sequence is interrupted (after a pancher tone) by a repetition of lima again serving as a bridge- or transition-tone to the basic cadential formula nem-lima-ḍaḍa-gulu (plus a short extension: ḍaḍa-gulu) which closes the gongan.

Summarized quickly: the melodic material of the bubuka genḍing is taken from the bubuka opaq-opaq and used in augmentation and with a quasi-pancher or pedal note on ḍaḍa. The three gong tones and the gulu cadence are important throughout.

---

[1]) *MJ*, I, 168.

[2]) According to Mr. IJzerdraat.

Gongan I, II, III

The first three gongan of the genḍing proper are identical. The final tone of the gongan is nem, and the second kenongan (the midpoint) ends with the same cadential formula that closes the bubuka opaq-opaq.

The first kenongan (four-measure phrase) begins with the neighbor note barang and continues in a descending scale passage from tonic (gulu) to dominant (nem). The "descending" motion is established by the initial step downward from gulu to barang. The one-octave limit of the demung or saron, however, requires that the next "descending" step be substituted by a leap up to nem, because the lower octave of nem is not available. As we shall see later, this one-octave limit rather frequently forces a disjunct movement in what might otherwise be a simple ascending or descending scale passage, and this circumstance assumes a considerable importance.

The principal melodic tones of the first part of the kenongan, then, are the tones gulu (which, after the neighbor note barang, is a continuation of the preceding gong tone gulu that ends the bubuka genḍing) and its fifth, nem. The last part of the kenongan is another descending scale, this time between ḍaḍa and nem (see example on p. 30 under discussion of the tone nem). The relation of these two tones will be more fully treated farther on in this chapter.

The two important intervals of the first kenongan are also prominent in the bubuka opaq-opaq. The interval gulu-nem is established in the final cadence. The omission of the tone ḍaḍa from the cadence of measure five and its delay until the beginning of measure six results in the interval ḍaḍa-nem — the second important interval of the kenongan under discussion.

The important elements of the second kenongan are not new to us. The tone lima acts as a bridge- or transition-tone between the last nem of kenongan one and the concluding element of kenongan two, i.e. a repetition of the cadential formula from the bubuka opaq-opaq. The "bridge" is further strengthened by the ḍaḍa-nem interval. After the initial neighbor note ḍaḍa, the whole of kenongan two is an exact augmentation of the bubuka opaq-opaq beginning with lima of measure five.

The principal melodic elements of kenongan three are the cadence from nem to gulu and the final transition tone lima. This material is derived from the last three measures of the bubuka opaq-opaq. The transition tone lima leads to kenongan four which, except for the initial note, is a repetition of kenongan one and ends with the descending scale passage from ḍaḍa to nem.

The chief melodic features of the gongan as a whole can most easily be seen from the structural table. The tones ending each of the four kenongan (the lower-case letters) are nem, gulu, lima and nem — the three gong tones. Nem begins and ends the gongan. The melodic material of gongan I, II and III is based on the bubuka opaq-opaq.

Gongan IV

The importance of the tone nem is continued and emphasized in the beginning of gongan IV first by its prolongation and then by the quarter-note rhythmic figure. The first kenongan features the tone nem, the second and third kenongan (which are identical) use the transition tone lima in descending motion leading to gulu and on to the initial tone nem of the fourth kenongan. The first three kenongan are based on an elaboration of the figure beginning in the third (and first) measure of the bubuka opaq-opaq, and kenongan four continues as an exact augmentation of the last two measures of the bubuka opaq-opaq.

Gongan I-II-III and gongan IV have the appearance of an antecedent-consequent structure. The two parts are related by the importance in each section of nem and the ḍaḍa-nem interval. The question-response construction is also strengthened by the appearance of the gulu cadence at the midpoint of each of the first three gongan and its reappearance at the end of gongan IV. Finally, the importance of nem in the first three gongan and the resolution to gulu in the fourth gongan can be reduced to the interval of the fifth or dominant-tonic.

Gongan V

The final gongan is a literal repetition of the bubuka genḍing and closes, therefore, with the gulu cadential formula.

General Summary

The bubuka opaq-opaq features the three gong tones and ends with a cadence in the form of a descending scale passage from nem to gulu. This short introduction provides the basis of thematic development for the whole of the genḍing.

The bubuka genḍing is constructed on an augmentation of the gulu cadential formula derived from the bubuka opaq-opaq.

In gongan I, II and III the three principal tones form the melodic framework, and the tone nem is the melodic goal.

Gongan IV continues the melodic importance of nem and, passing through the transition tone lima, closes on the gulu cadential formula.

Gongan V is an identical repetition of the bubuka genḍing.

The three critical sections — the bubuka opaq-opaq, the bubuka genḍing and the final gongan — use the same melodic material and each end with a descending cadence from nem to gulu.

The melodic importance of each tone can be summarized as follows:

> *Gulu,* by its position in both the detailed and the architectonic structure, has the chief melodic importance. It appears as the final gong tone in the bubuka opaq-opaq, the bubuka genḍing, gongan IV and V. It is used consistently — both at the conclusion of gongan and kenongan — in the cadential formula:

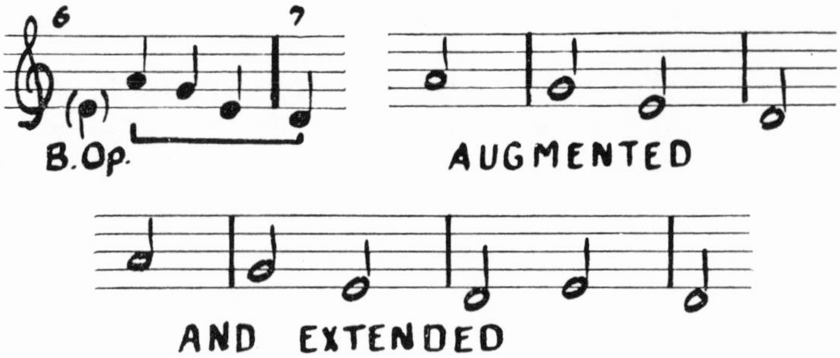

Nem is the second tone in melodic importance. It appears as the fifth or dominant of gulu both in the cadential formula and in the relation of gongan I, II and III to the other gongan. It is used at the end of gongan and kenongan in a cadential formula built on the interval ḍaḍa-nem, which, for the present, we may refer to as a dominant cadential formula:

Lima is used in cadential support of both gulu and nem at the kenongan divisions and other places within the gongan.

Barang first appears as a neighbor note in the bubuka opaq-opaq and continues in that function or as a passing tone throughout the genḍing.

Ḍaḍa achieves a secondary importance in its relation to nem and is also used in passing and as a quasi-pancher.

N.B. In the following pages the terms „cadence", „cadential formula" and „formula" will be used interchangeably to denote certain regular or standard sequences of tones, wherever they might occur within the course of the genḍing. The actual cadence or primary cadence, i.e. denoting partial or full repose in the musical sentence, will be made evident in the text.

"Dirodo Meto"

Ladrang nr 2 — sléndro paṭet nem

bubuka opaq-opaq

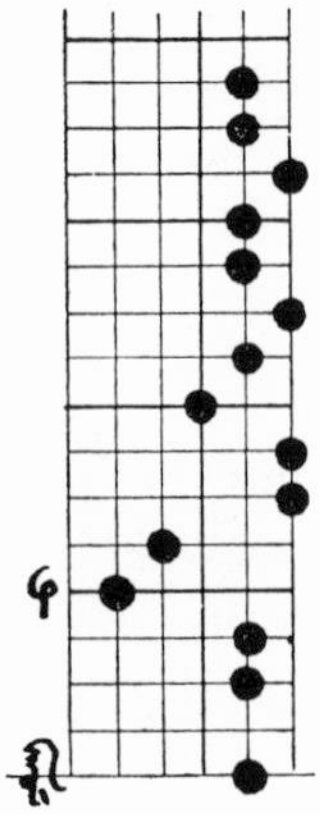

B.Op.				intro$_n$	
B.Gd.	A_n	B_g	C_g	C_g	A
GN I	D_g	D_g	E_l	B^*_n	A
GN II	F_n	F_n	F_n	F^*_g	B
GN III	G_n	G_n	H_b	I_n	B
GN IV	J_n	B_g	C_g	C_g	A′

B* cadence to nem instead of gulu
F* „ „ gulu „ „ nem
Kenḍang 2

transcribed (see appendix p 267)

„Dirodo meto" has a ternary structure with *A* consisting of two gongan, *B* of two gongan and *A′* of the final gongan. The bubuka genḍing and the final gongan have three identical kenongan. The structural table shows the prominence of the three gong tones at kenongan and gongan divisions. The complete transcription indicates that the pattern for the colotomic instruments and for the kenḍang 2 are regular.

Bubuka opaq-opaq

In essence the bubuka opaq-opaq consists of an extension on the tone nem (with its neighbor barang) leading to a gulu cadence, extended by a reiteration of nem. The gulu cadence is interrupted in bar three by the repeated tone barang, introducing the interval lima-barang before the passage finishes with ḍaḍa and gulu. The melodic goal of the introduction is nem, preceded by a gulu cadence.

Bubuka genḍing

The bubuka genḍing prolongs the tone nem (from the bubuka opaq-opaq), which is further increased in importance by the whole note and half note immediately following. The first and second kenongan follow quite closely (in augmentation) the melodic material of the bubuka opaq-opaq. The material is simplified in kenongan one by the omission of barang and the sounding of nem only twice instead of five times, and in kenongan two by not interrupting the descending scale with the tone barang. Kenongan two closes on the gulu cadence extended to ḍaḍa-barang-gulu. Kenongan three and four are identical and are a repetition of the gulu cadence with a quasi-pancher on ḍaḍa.

The melodic material is based on the bubuka opaq-opaq.

Gongan I

The quasi-pancher technique of the preceding two kenongan is continued in the first two kenongan of gongan I. The tone *nem* now serves as quasi-pancher instead of ḍaḍa. The example given below has underscores marking the notes of the cadential formula with the initial nem replaced by ḍaḍa (see N.B.); the same practice was observed in „Lungkèh", but here the role of the two notes is reversed.

The first three notes of kenongan three continue the quasi-pancher idea, and then a gulu cadence and the transition tone lima lead to the fourth kenongan. The material of the fourth kenongan is an augmentation of the material beginning in bar two of the bubuka opaq-opaq (on the tone barang), which omits the two barang of bar three, resulting in the uninterrupted scale from barang *alit* to gulu. This is extended by the tones barang-gulu and the dominant.

The material of gongan I is based on the bubuka opaq-opaq.

Gongan II

The first three kenongan are identical and are built on a ḍaḍa-nem formula plus a variation of the gulu cadence (given below) in which the omission of ḍaḍa (x) is perhaps justified by the conspicuous position of this tone two bars earlier, *i.e.* as the beginning of the dominant (nem) cadence. An extension, barang-gulu to dominant, closes the kenongan.

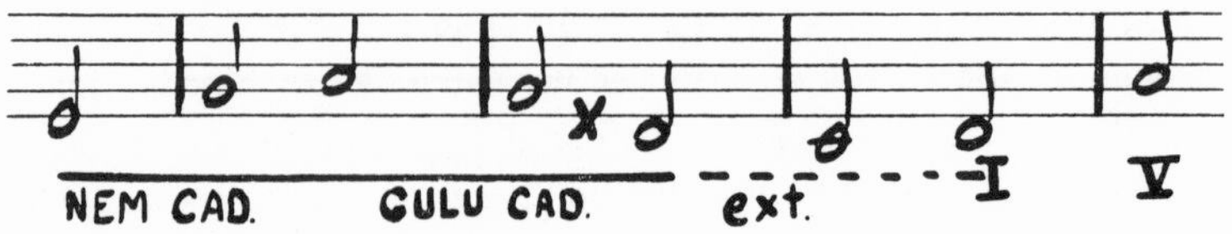

The fourth kenongan begins in the same way (ḍaḍa-lima-nem) but finishes with a *complete* gulu cadence and an extension to ḍaḍa-gulu.

The material is rather freely based on two elements of the bubuka opaq-opaq: the gulu cadential formula and the final gulu-nem interval of bar four.

Gongan III

The first kenongan begins with an incomplete gulu cadence starting on lima. The transition tone lima is repeated, and a complete ascending gulu cadence, *i.e.* gulu-ḍaḍa-lima-nem, follows. The second kenongan consists of a descending and ascending form of the gulu cadence connected by the transition tone lima. Kenongan three consists of gulu with its neighbors ḍaḍa and barang. In kenongan four the transition tone lima leads to the I—V interval plus the ḍaḍa-nem cadence.

The material is rather freely derived from the bubuka opaq-opaq.

Gongan IV

The first kenongan begins with the lima-barang interval (prepared in the bubuka opaq-opaq) and closes with the tone nem. The last three kenongan are identical to those of the bubuka genḍing.

The material is based on the bubuka opaq-opaq.

General Summary

The bubuka opaq-opaq establishes a gulu cadence extended to a reiteration of the dominant. The introduction also provides the basis of thematic deveopment for the rest of the genḍing.

As indicated by the structural table the melodic goal of each successive gongan after the bubuka opaq-opaq alternates from nem to gulu. These two tones are also in evidence at the kenongan devisions.

The three critical structural sections are constructed from the same melodic material: each concludes with a variation of the gulu cadential formula; the introduction includes an extension to the dominant.

The melodic importance of each tone can be summarized as follows:

Gulu is the tone of primary importance, occurring as the final note of the bubuka genḍing, gongan II and the final gongan IV. It appears in the descending cadential formula, sometimes with an extension. An ascending formula is also used in gongan III:

Nem is second in melodic importance, appearing as the fifth or dominant of gulu in the cadential formula and serving in alternation with gulu as the final note, either in a simple I—V or in the ascending gulu cadence shown above. The ḍaḍa-nem formula appears in gongan II and III in the ascending form:

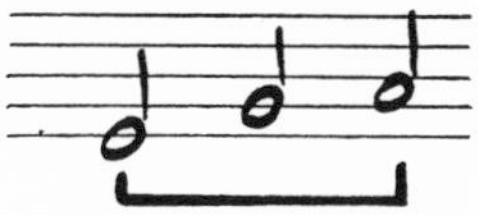

Lima is used in cadential support of gulu and nem as a tone of transition.
Ḍaḍa is used as a passing note, and quasi-pancher and achieves a secondary importance in its relation to nem.
Barang is used chiefly as a passing or neighbor note.

"Babat Kencheng"

Ladrang nr 8 — sléndro paṭet nem

bubuka opaq-opaq

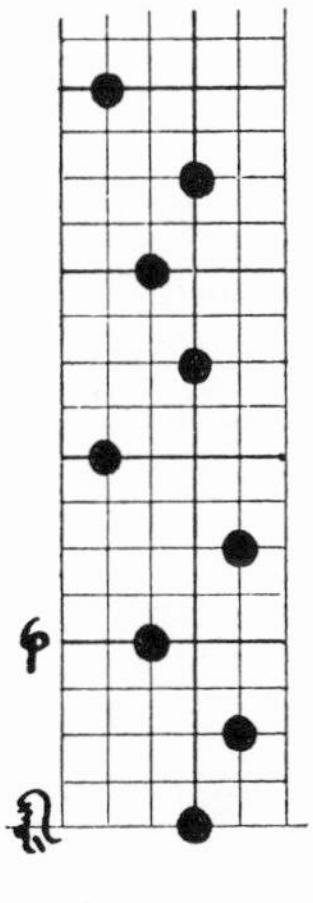

B.Op.				intro$_1$	
B.Gd.	A_l	A_l	B_d	C_g	A
GN I	B_d	C_g	D_d	E_l	B
GN II	A_l	A_l	B_d	C_g	A

Kenḍang 2

transcribed (see appendix p. 268)

„Babat Kencheng" is a „whole-note" piece which uses a true pancher [1]) on the tone barang. The ladrang has a ternary form: the bubuka genḍing and the last gongan are identical and represent the *A* sections; gongan I comprises the *B* section. The colotomic pattern and the kenḍang two pattern are regular.

N.B. Unless stated to the contrary all subsequent genḍing have a regular colotomic structure and kenḍang pattern.

Bubuka opaq-opaq

The principal outline of the bubuka opaq-opaq is an ascending gulu cadence (underscored tones) with an extension to lima on the final gong. The melodic weight of the three principal tones is about even.

Bubuka genḍing

The first two kenongan are identical; they begin on the neighbor note (of nem) barang and then use three of the last four notes from the bubuka opaq opaq:

Kenongan three is based on the first two measures of the bubuka opaq-opaq; and kenongan four is a descending gulu cadence.

The melodic high points of the first two kenongan are nem and the transition tone lima; in the third kenongan ḍaḍa is prominent and leads to nem and the gulu cadence of kenongan four.

Gongan I

The first two kenongan of gongan I are the same as the last two of the bubuka genḍing. Kenongan three is a rearrangement of the last four notes of the bubuka opaq-opaq; kenongan four, after the neighbor note barang, outlines the three gong tones of the last two measures of the bubuka opaq-opaq. Kenongan three and four combined are a variation of the gulu cadence with an extension to the dominant (nem) and lima.

Gongan II

Gongan II is the same as the bubuka genḍing, ending on a gulu cadence.

---

1) See pp. 26-7.

General Summary

The three critical sections are related melodically and cadentially. The bubuka opaq-opaq is a variation of an ascending gulu cadence with an extension to lima; the other two sections end with a gulu descending cadence. The widely-spaced notes of the genḍing show a general derivation from the bubuka opaq-opaq.

The melodic importance of each tone:

Gulu is the final note of the bubuka genḍing and gongan II and is important in the bubuka opaq-opaq in the ascending cadence.
Nem as the dominant of gulu has a melodic importance in the cadences.
Lima is used as the final note of the bubuka opaq-opaq and gongan I and in each case is preceded by a variation of the gulu cadence.
Daḍa is used as a passing note and has a secondary importance in relation to nem.
Barang is a tone of melodic variety in its function as a true pancher.

"Kandang Walang"

Ladrang nr 10 — sléndro paṭet nem

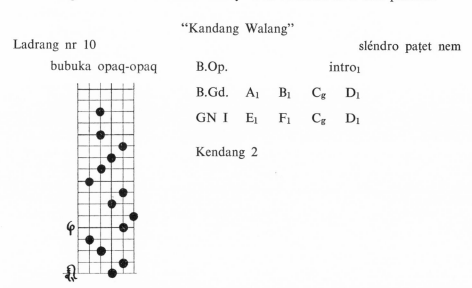

bubuka opaq-opaq

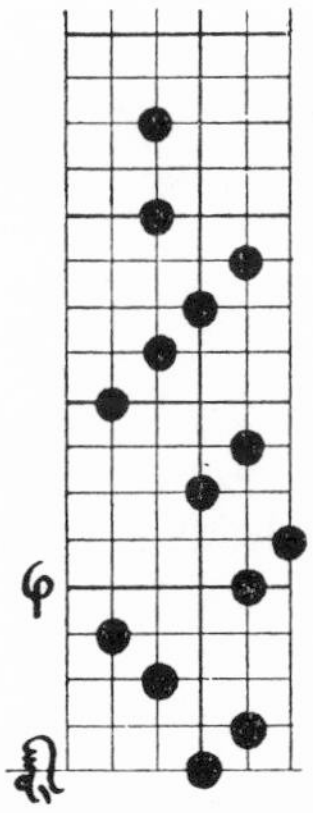

B.Op.			intro$_l$	
B.Gd.	A_l	B_l	C_g	D_l
GN I	E_l	F_l	C_g	D_l

Kendang 2

transcribed (see appendix p. 268)

"Kandang Walang" is a very short ladrang but holds some interest for our survey in that it is one of the two ladrang which end on a tone other than tonic or dominant. In this example the final note is lima, the second gong tone. The ladrang is also interesting in its rhythmic variety: it begins in whole notes, proceeds to half notes and for one kenongan continues in quarter notes.

The form of the two gongan might, by analogy, be called a double period, the last half (gongan I) being repeated eight times. The last two kenongan of the final gongan are identical to those of the bubuka genḍing.

N.B. The letter "T" (keṭuk) at the beginning of the penultimate measure and the letters "NG" (kenong-gong) at the end of the transcribed bubuka opaq-opaq will be understood in all following genḍing but will not be shown.

Bubuka opaq-opaq

The opening interval ḍaḍa-nem leads directly to a gulu cadence followed by a leap up to the dominant (plus the neighbours on either side) and a close on a variation of the ascending gulu cadence. In the last cadence the tone lima is omitted and then added as a short extension. The important elements of the bubuka opaq-opaq are: the primary descending gulu cadence; a leap up to the dominant, a leap back to an ascending gulu cadence as an extension of the primary cadence.

Bubuka genḍing

The first kenongan is in whole-note values and is taken from the last part of the bubuka opaq-opaq beginning with barang in measure three — gulu and nem of bar four are omitted. The second kenongan imitates the beginning of the bubuka opaq-opaq except for the first tone lima of bar two which is saved for the last note of the kenongan. The last two kenongan, except for the addition of the two neighbor notes between the two initial ḍaḍa, are an exact augmentation of the bubuka opaq-opaq.

As in the bubuka opaq-opaq, the principal features of the bubuka genḍing are a descending and an ascending gulu cadence connected by the dominant.

Gongan I

The first kenongan is built on the gulu-nem interval of the bubuka opaq-opaq (in this case gulu "descends" to nem) plus the final ascending gulu cadential variation. The second kenongan is in quarter notes; it begins with an elaboration of the ḍaḍa-nem interval from the bubuka opaq-opaq. After the bridge tone lima the kenongan closes on the gulu cadential variation. The third and fourth kenongan return to half-note values and are identical to those of the bubuka genḍing.

General Summary

The material of the bubuka opaq-opaq provides the basis of thematic development for the rest of the genḍing and consists principally of a descending and ascending gulu cadence separated by the dominant.

The three critical sections use the same melodic material and have the same final cadences. It should be noted that lima, as the final note of each of these three sections, is directly preceded by a regular gulu cadence.

The melodic importance of each tone:

Gulu, although it is not used as a final note and appears only twice at kenongan divisions, preserves its melodic importance in the cadential formulas of the bubuka opaq-opaq and subsequent gongan.

The *descending* scale from gulu to nem (kenongan one, gongan I) was also seen in the ladrang (nr 1) "Lungkèh" (kenongan one, gongan I-II-III) and is given below:

Nem is important as the dominant or fifth of gulu in the cadential formulas.

Lima is used as the final note of each section but is always preceded by a gulu cadence.

Ḍaḍa achieves a secondary importance in relation to nem.

Ḃarang appears as a neighbor note and once as a passing note.

"Rojo Hanggolo"

Ladrang nr 11 — sléndro paṭet nem

bubuka opaq-opaq

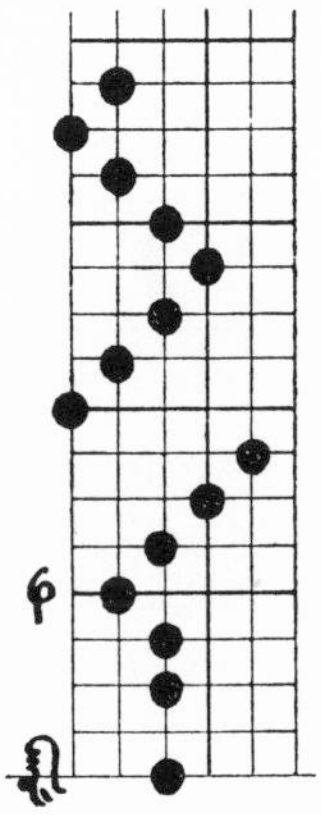

B.Op.				intro$_d$	
B.Gd.	A_b	B_b	B_b	C_d	A
GN I	A_b	B_b	B_b	D_l	
GN II	E_l	E_l	E_l	F_b	B
GN III	G_n	G_n	H_n	I_n	
GN IV	J_b	B_b	B_b	C_d	A′
GN V	A_b	B_b	B_b	C_d	

Kenḍang 2

transcribed (see appendix p. 269)

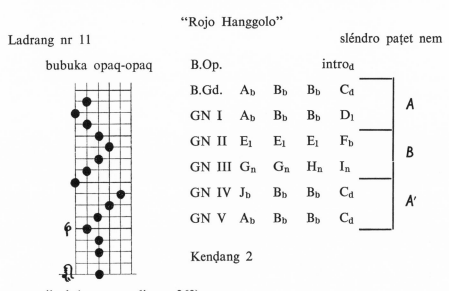

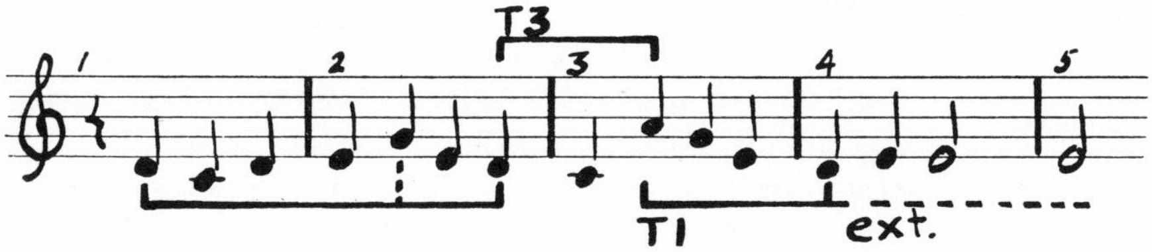

As indicated by the structural table "Rojo Hanggolo" is the second example which ends with a note other than tonic or dominant — in this instance the tone is ḍaḍa. The piece is so constructed that the tones of the kenongan divisions (lower-case letters) are not truly indicative of the principal notes of the gongan, the chief tones, as it were, occuring before or after these structural points. In

Western music something analogous is effected in the practice of "writing across the bar-line" of "breaking the tyranny of the bar-line".

The gongan comprise a ternary form: **A** represents the bubuka genḍing and gongan I, **B** indicates gongan II and III, and **A′** designates gongan IV and V. The bubuka genḍing and the final gongan are identical.

Bubuka opaq-opaq

The chief melodic goals of the bubuka opaq-opaq have been indicated by brackets above and below the transcription. The first shows the ascending-descending line gulu-lima-gulu, the second (placed above the staff) is the descending scale from tonic to dominant (also shown in the summary of nr 10), and the last bracket (below) indicates the gulu cadential formula with an extension on the tone ḍaḍa.

Bubuka genḍing

Kenongan one is an elaboration of the first three notes of the gulu cadence (measure three of the bubuka opaq-opaq) and ends on barang. The melodic drive, however, is toward the tone gulu which is the first note of kenongan two. At this juncture of the two kenongan appears the figure indicated by the upper bracket in the bubuka opaq-opaq, but in retrograde:

The meaning of "T3" and "T4" will be discussed farther on.

The second and third kenongan are identical, and these two plus the fourth kenongan are an exact augmentation of the entire bubuka opaq-opaq, except that the final extension to ḍaḍa is altered. The melodic outline of the whole gongan might be summarized as: nem, gulu-lima, gulu cadence extended.

Gongan I

The first three kenongan of gongan I are identical to those of the bubuka genḍing. The last kenongan is based on bars 2—3 of the bubuka opaq-opaq, the principal melodic points being the three gong tones in the order: gulu, nem, lima. In contrast to the bubuka genḍing, then, the melodic goal of this gongan is not the gulu cadence but the transition tone lima; this transitional role of lima is foreshadowed in the first two measures of the bubuka opaq-opaq.

Gongan II

Kenongan one, two and three of gongan II are identical. They are based on the first three measures (beginning with the second gulu) of the bubuka opaq-opaq. In these kenongan all three gong tones are important, and lima marks the structural divisions. In the fourth kenongan the material consists of fragments of the bubuka opaq-opaq: the first interval barang-nem from the beginning of bar three (bubuka opaq-opaq); the interval nem-barang from the beginning of bar one; the interval barang-lima from the limits of the scale passage in bars 1—2. Barang provides a tone of melodic variety and is the final note of the gongan. In reality, however, the bar line is "shifted"; barang is actually the neighbor note of the opening gulu in gongan III.

Gongan III

The first two kenongan of gongan III are based on the figure indicated by the upper bracket in the bubuka opaq-opaq, nem being extended to include its neighbor tones. Kenongan three begins with the transition tone lima followed by an ascending gulu cadence and ends on lima. The fourth kenongan, after the neighbor note barang, consists of a descending and ascending gulu cadence.

The melodic outline of the gongan is gulu-nem, lima, and an ascending gulu cadence to nem. The material is based on the bubuka opaq-opaq.

Gongan IV

The first kenongan continues the importance of nem. Nem and its neighbours proceed to a slight variation of the gulu cadence which is extended by barang as a neighbor to the first note of the second kenongan, gulu. The last three kenongan are identical to those of the bubuka genḍing.

Gongan V

The entire gongan is the same as the bubuka genḍing.

General Summary

The bubuka opaq-opaq features the three gong tones, gulu, lima, nem, and closes with a descending gulu cadence and an extension to ḍaḍa. The introduction provides the melodic material for the whole genḍing.

The melodic goal of the bubuka genḍing is a gulu cadence with an extension including lima, nem and ḍaḍa.

The first three kenongan of gongan I are the same as those of the bubuka genḍing (featuring the three gong tones). The fourth kenongan ends on the transition tone lima.

The three gong tones are about equally important in gongan II. Lima marks the kenongan divisions and barang introduces melodic variety and ends the gongan.

Gongan III uses all three gong tones and ends with an ascending gulu cadence to nem.

Gongan IV and V (except for the first kenongan of gongan IV) are the same as the bubuka genḍing.

The three critical sections — the bubuka opaq-opaq, the bubuka genḍing and the final gongan — use the same melodic material and all end with a gulu cadence extended to ḍaḍa.

The melodic importance of each tone:

Gulu never appears at the gongan or kenongan divisions and yet, because of the prominence of the gulu cadence throughout the genḍing, must be considered the most important tone melodically. The ending of the three critical sections are gulu cadences extended to ḍaḍa.

Nem is the second tone of melodic importance because of its cadential function as the dominant of gulu. It is the final note of gongan III, appearing in an ascending gulu cadence.

Lima is the tone of transition and serves in cadential support of gulu and nem. It is also the final note of gongan I.

Ḍaḍa appears as the final note of the bubuka opaq-opaq, the bubuka genḍing gongan IV and V and is always preceded by a gulu cadence. Ḍaḍa also appears as a passing note.

Barang introduces some melodic variety, is the final note of gongan II, and is used as a passing tone.

Cadences

We have now seen four types of gulu cadences. Only one of these has appeared at the ends of the three critical sections, and that is type one (T1) shown below. Its retrograde form (T2), appearing at the close of gongan III, will also be found in later examples at critical points. Type three (T3) was pointed out within the melodic line of the bubuka opaq-opaq, and type four (T4) occurred within the body of the bubuka genḍing. The tone barang alit (*i.e.* barang 8va) may be optional as shown by the small note.

It should be noted that if a T3 cadence immediately follows a T1 cadence or a T4 immediately follows a T2, the effect is nothing more than a gulu cadence extended to nem in the first instance or extended to gulu in the second. This can be shown by the following examples:

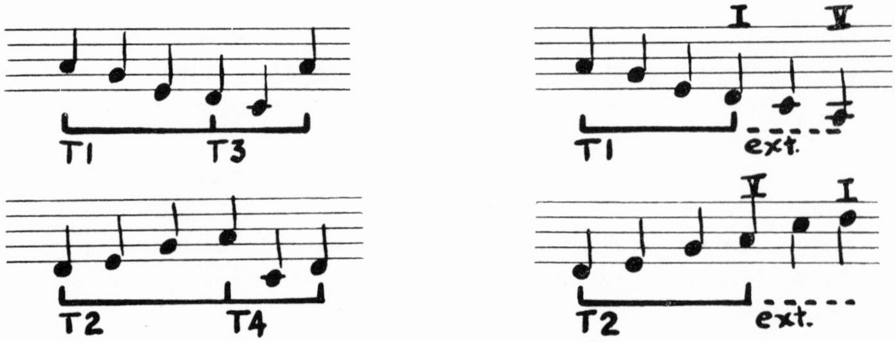

When the T3 cadence continues to the tone lima, *i.e.* gulu-barang-nem-lima, other considerations arise. These will be taken up presently.

“Gupuh”

Ladrang nr 15 slèndro paṭet nem

bubuka opaq-opaq

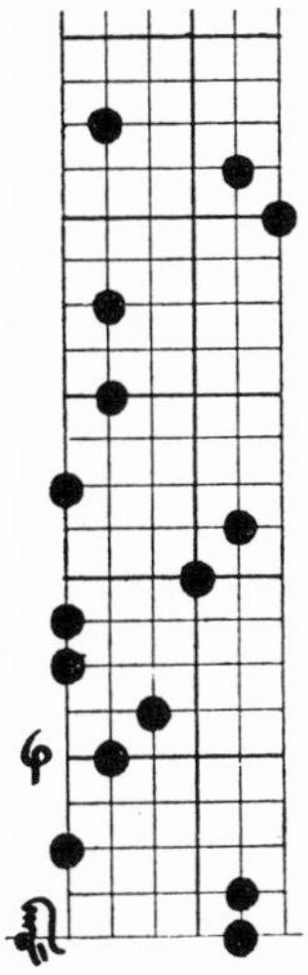

B.Op.				$intro_n$	
B.Gd.	A_n	B_g	C_g	D_n	A
GN I	E_n	B^*_g	C_g	D_n	A
GN II	E_n	B^*_g	C_g	D_n	A
GN III	E^*_g	F_l	F_l	D_n	B
GN IV	E^*_g	F_l	F_l	D_n	B

B* rhythmic subdivision of the initial nem

E* neighbor quarter notes added before final gulu

Kenḍang 1

transcribed (see appendix p. 270)

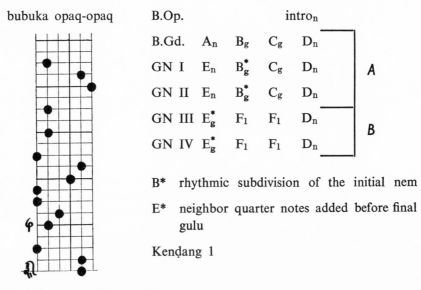

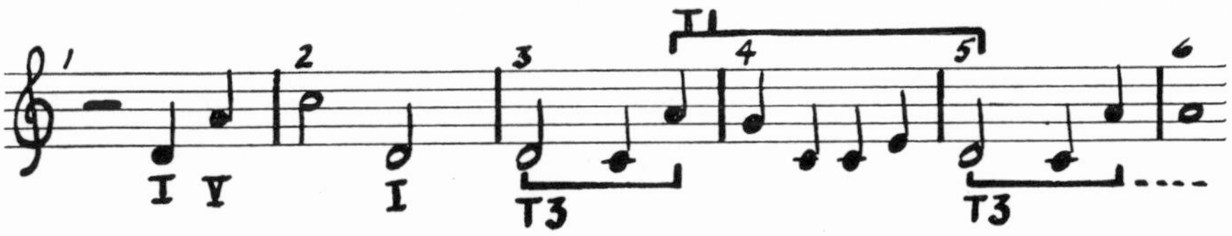

This genḍing has a rather ambiguous introduction which, together with other factors, suggests a partial transposition. The matter will be discussed in some detail under the heading Bubuka opaq-opaq below.

The general form of the ladrang “Gupuh” is binary: *A* consists of the bubuka genḍing and gongan I and II, and *B* consists of gongan III and IV. The identical kenongan ending every gongan result in a sort of verse-refrain construction within the larger two-part form. The gongan and kenongan divisions indicate the importance of the three gong tones.

Bubuka opaq-opaq

The bubuka opaq-opaq is built on several forms of the tonic-dominant interval: the simple I–V and the T3 and the T1 cadences indicated by the brackets. The descending T1 cadence is interrupted midway by a reiteration of barang. These two barang, together with those appearing in each of the T3 cadences, produce a kind of pedal-note effect. The first (half-note) gulu of bar three begins, theoretically, a descending scale passage which ends on the nem of bar five. The half-note value of gulu in bar five, however, establishes the T1 formula as the primary cadence, and the following two quarter notes and half note appear to form an extension to the dominant. The intended extension to nem is perhaps more clearly stated at the end of the bubuka genḍing (and all the following gongan) as a simple I—V following the ascending (T2) gulu cadence.

It is also possible to look at the bubuka opaq-opaq in a slightly different way. If we ignore the half note value of gulu in bar five and look at the sequence beginning in bar four: ḍaḍa-gulu-barang-nem, we recognize the ḍaḍa-nem cadence given in the analysis of "Lungkèh" (p. 30). The example cited in "Lungkèh" is *within* the gongan, while in this present example the ḍaḍa-nem formula *closes* the bubuka opaq-opaq. Its importance, however, is considerably lessened by the half-note gulu which concludes the T1 formula. In this case, the weight of gulu confirms the paṭet nem gulu cadence as primary. It is possible that the exposure of ḍaḍa — caused by the barang interruption of the descending gulu cadence — is designed to throw into relief the secondarily important ḍaḍa-nem interval as a "dominant" cadence. As stated in the foregoing paragraph, however, the T3 cadence is not repeated at the ends of the following gongan, but a I—V extension to nem is used following a T2 cadence. So it is difficult to marshal support for the dominant cadence as a planned artistic device. But there is still another possible explanation.

The somewhat "sensitized" ḍaḍa and the gong tone nem outline a descending scale passage which will be commonly found in Chapter VI in connection with sléndro paṭet manyura. In paṭet manyura (to anticipate slightly) the tone nem is "tonic" and ḍaḍa is its fifth or dominant. Even though the *rhythmic* values of the bubuka opaq-opaq outline the T1 paṭet nem cadence as primary, the mere presence of the ḍaḍa-nem cadence in this conspicuous position suggests paṭet manyura. The table of paṭet transposition given in the appendix (p. 259) shows that this ladrang is known in both paṭet nem and paṭet manyura. The basic metric unit of "Gupuh" is the quarter note. This relatively lively movement (there are also a few sixteenth notes) is much more characteristic of paṭet manyura than of paṭet nem,[1] and a general comparison of the "Gupuh" transcription with those of the other paṭet nem genḍing confirms the manyura "character" of the piece in question. It seems reasonable to assume that the original "Gupuh" is in paṭet manyura, and that the paṭet nem version is its transposition. It also appears likely that when the genḍing was transposed, all or, more probably, *part* of the bubuka opaq-opaq was retained in the original paṭet. The body of the genḍing seems to be in paṭet nem. On the assumption that part of the original paṭet manyura introduction was retained, the bubuka opaq-opaq has been transposed a fifth lower for comparison with the thematic material of the rest of the genḍing. The

---

1) *MJ*, I, 338.

reader may be interested in comparing both the original and the transposed bubuka opaq-opaq with the melodic material of the genḍing. It is likely that a few rhythmic changes were made and perhaps a few notes altered in the original bubuka opaq-opaq in order to give it an acceptable paṭet nem cadence (see the first paragraph under the heading Bubuka opaq-opaq above).

transposed

bubuka opaq-opaq

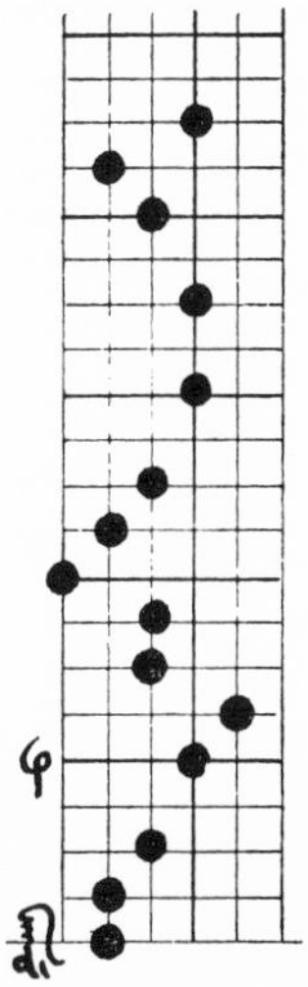

transcribed and transposed

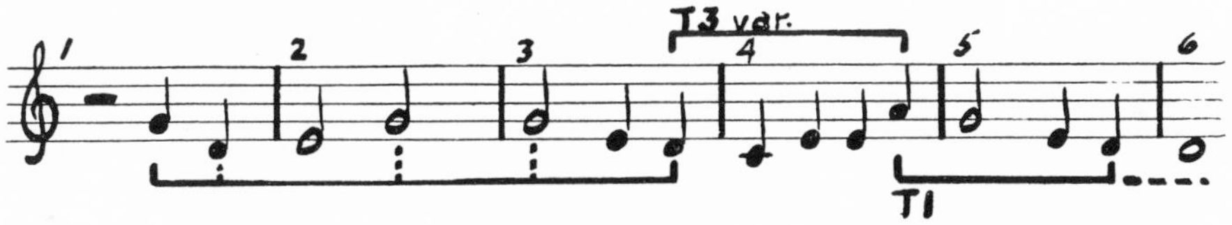

The eligibility of this transposed version as a "real" paṭet-nem introduction gains some strength when the general structure of this bubuka opaq-opaq is compared with that of nr 11 "Rojo Hanggolo". The first lower bracket indicates several gulu-lima intervals in the first three measures, the upper bracket shows a T3 variation, and the second lower bracket outlines a regular T1 cadence. The important intervals, then, are gulu-lima and gulu-nem with the interval ḍaḍa-nem of bar four perhaps having a secondary importance.

Bubuka genḍing

The first kenongan fixes the importance of nem, and the second kenongan creates a kind of fantasy on the T1 cadence which is fully stated at the end of the kenongan. The first half of the third kenongan contains the first three notes of the bubuka opaq-opaq followed by the concluding T1 cadence. This complete figure is repeated in the latter half of the kenongan. Kenongan four opens with the gulu-lima interval and proceeds to an ascending gulu cadence (T2) which is extended by the gulu-nem interval.

The material is based on the transposed bubuka opaq-opaq and is used rather freely in development, a characteristic practice of genḍing which have a relatively lively movement.

Gongan I, II

The first two gongan of the genḍing proper are identical. Kenongan one is a continuation of the gulu- (barang-gulu-) nem interval that closes the bubuka genḍing. Kenongan two is the same as kenongan two of the bubuka genḍing except that the initial quarter note nem is anticipated by two sixteenth notes on nem. The last two kenongan are identical to those of the bubuka genḍing. The material is rather freely based on the transposed bubuka opaq-opaq.

Gongan III, IV

Gongan III and IV are identical. The first kenongan is the same as that of gongan I and II except that the last measure is in quarter notes instead of half notes, the added notes being the neighbors of the final gulu. Kenongan two and three are identical and appear to begin with the last two measures of the bubuka opaq-opaq in retrograde and slightly extended. The final bar and a half seems to be taken from the following (underscored) part of the bubuka opaq-opaq:

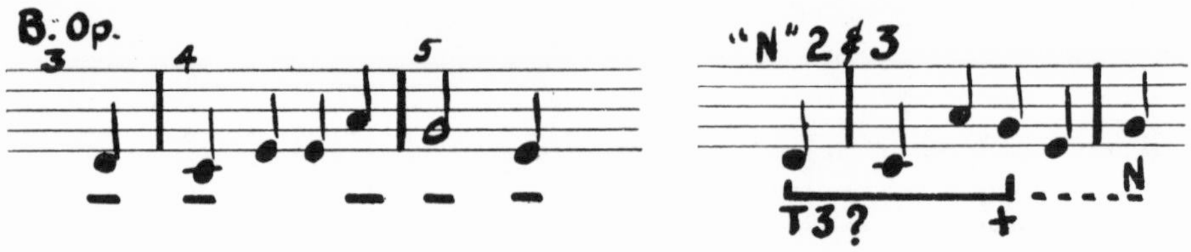

At first glance this appears to be a T3 cadence extended to lima (+). The principal melodic points of these two kenongan, however, indicate that although gulu and nem are important, the tone lima has a principal role as a tone of transition leading to the strong cadential statement of the last kenongan. Lima is the melodic goal of the first part of the kenongan as well as the last part, and in both instances there is an extension on the tone lima. To return to the cadence under discussion, the important function of lima in these two kenongan suggests that the *primary* interval is from gulu to lima (not gulu to nem) — a descending scale passage which goes one step beyond the T3 formula (normally ending on nem, the dasar) and concludes with the second gong tone lima. We shall consider this formula more fully in the analysis of the next genḍing.

The fourth kenongan is identical to those of the preceding gongan.

The thematic material appears to be based on the transposed bubuka opaq-opaq and developed rather freely.

General Summary

In the transposition from paṭet manyura the genḍing has retained all or part of the original bubuka opaq-opaq. When this introduction is transposed a sléndro fifth lower, the resulting bubuka opaq-opaq has a typical paṭet-nem construction and provides the basis for a somewhat free thematic development. The T1 cadence closing the transposed bubuka opaq-opaq and the gulu-nem interval it includes is the basis of every kenongan.

The three critical sections are related melodically. The final cadence of the transposed introduction and those of the bubuka genḍing and the final gongan are variations of the same thing: a descending scale passage from nem to gulu on the one hand and an ascending scale passage from gulu to nem (extended by I—V) on the other.

The melodic importance of each tone:

Gulu appears as the final note of the transposed bubuka opaq-opaq and is used at kenongan divisions but not at the close of the gongan. Its role as "tonic" in the principal cadence (the T1 or T2) used throughout the genḍing makes gulu one of the two most important tones.

Nem is the final note of all gongan (and ends the nontransposed introduction). This prominent position and its dominant relation to gulu give the tone nem an equal or superior importance to gulu in this piece. It is the melodic goal. Whether this genḍing ends on a kind of Javanese "dominant", however, had better be decided in Chapter VII.

Lima appears as a tone of transition and in cadential support of gulu and nem.

Ḍaḍa is used as a passing note and sometimes has a minor importance in relation to nem.

Barang produces some melodic varity by its frequent occurrence as a neighbor note and passing note.

"Gègèr Sakuto"

Ladrang nr 7 — sléndro paṭet nem

bubuka opaq-opaq

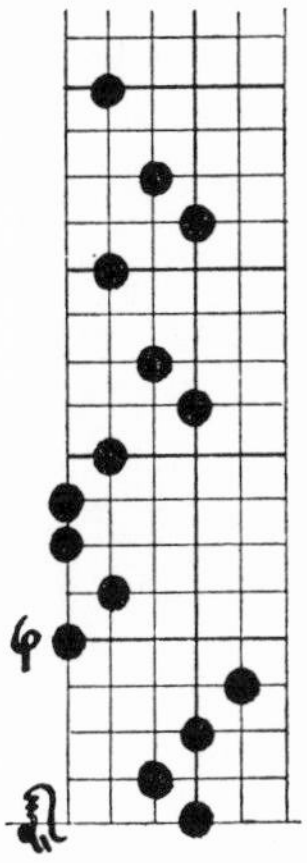

B.Op.				intro$_l$	
B.Gd.	A_l	A_l	A_l	B_n	
GN I	B^*_n	B^*_n	B^*_n	C_g	A
GN II	D_g	D_g	E_g	F_l	B
GN III	G_l	G_l	G_l	B_n	A′

B* first two notes changed

Kenḍang 2

transcribed (see appendix p. 271)

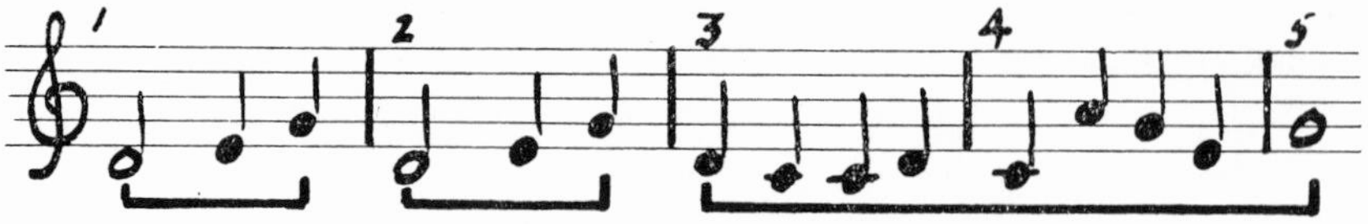

The structural table of "Gègèr Sakuto" shows that only the last kenongan of the bubuka genḍing and the final gongan are identical. In a restricted sense, therefore, the general structure might be indicated as a binary or rounded binary form. As will be shown, however, the melodic emphasis of the first three kenongan is quite similar in both the bubuka genḍing and gongan III and seems actually to indicate a ternary form.

This genḍing offers an example (the only one found) of a piece which is apparently transposed from paṭet sanga with the retention of the original bubuka opaq-opaq. The cadence indicated by the long bracket under the transcription of the introduction was mentioned in the analysis of nr 15 "Gupuh" where the tone lima functions as a tone of transition in two *inner* kenongan, leading to a gulu cadence in the final kenongan. The interval outlined by this cadence is gulu (descending) to lima. Although there is some justification for its usage at transitional sections within the gongan, the present example prominently displays this cadence at the close of the bubuka opaq-opaq. This ladrang, it should be noted, is the only paṭet nem genḍing which uses such a cadence at the close of one of the three critical sections. It is possible to imagine that a good paṭet nem introduction ending with a lima transitional cadence could be constructed; but this does not appear to be such an example.

In the transcription each of the three brackets delimits the interval gulu-lima. Among the earlier analyses we found that sometimes the gulu-lima interval had some importance. Between those examples and the present one, however, there is one striking difference: this bubuka opaq-opaq does not contain the gulu-*nem* interval, whereas in the earlier analyses it was precisely this interval which occupied the most prominent role.

It is again necessary to anticipate the results of a later chapter. In the chapter devoted to sléndro paṭet sanga we shall learn that the tone lima bears the designation "tonic" and that gulu is its fifth or "dominant". If the bubuka opaq-opaq is examined from the paṭet-sanga viewpoint, the three brackets indicate the dominant-tonic interval, and, incidentally, the final cadence *includes* the (paṭet-sanga) second gong tone barang — just as in paṭet nem the T1 (or T2) cadence *includes* the second gong tone lima. But the matter of comparison will be appropriate a few chapters later.

The paṭet transposition table indicates that "Gègèr Sakuto" also appears in another collection in paṭet sanga. This listing together with the strong paṭet-sanga introduction provide a reasonable substantiation for our tentative assumption that the original bubuka opaq-opaq was retained in the transposition to paṭet nem. The transcription given below has been transposed one fifth higher than the original. If our assumption is correct, this should scan as a characteristic paṭet-nem introduction.

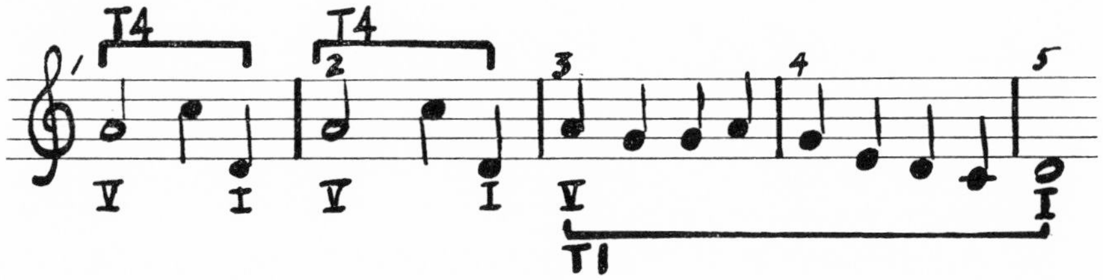

The concluding gulu cadence and the number of dominant-tonic intervals (indicated by the T4 brackets) are strong evidence that our position is justified.

Although we shall not dwell too long on the detailed analysis of the individual gongan, a brief comparison on the basis of derived thematic material is in order — not only because it supports our contention but also because it hands us something of a surprise too.

Bubuka genḍing

The first three kenongan of the bubuka genḍing seem to be based on bars 2—3 of the transposed bubuka opaq-opaq with the omission of gulu. The fourth kenongan continues with nem and its neighbors and then an ascending T2 cadence, the retrograde form of the T1 which closes the bubuka opaq-opaq.

Gongan I

The first three kenongan are like the fourth kenongan of the bubuka genḍing except for the first two notes. In this version the opening bars of the bubuka opaq-opaq again provide the basic material, but this time the tone gulu *is* included (cf. the beginning of the first three kenongan of the bubuka genḍing). The fourth kenongan is based on bars 3—4—5 of the transposed bubuka opaq-opaq — ḍaḍa is added at the beginning of the passage and substituted for barang as a neighbor note before the final gulu.

Gongan II

Kenongan one and two are identical. They begin with the neighbor note ḍaḍa (continued from the preceding gongan) leading to a T2 and a T1 cadence. Kenongan three and four offers a real surprise. If we include the final gulu of kenongan two, the melody comprising these last two kenongan is an exact augmentation of the original *paṭet-sanga bubuka opaq-opaq*.

Gongan III

The first three kenongan are identical and bear a resemblance to those of the bubuka genḍing. The material is based on the first three measures of the

the transposed bubuka opaq-opaq, the tone barang being taken in the lower octave once. The final kenongan is the same as that of the bubuka genḍing.

General Summary and Conclusions

The transposed bubuka opaq-opaq provides the basis of thematic development for all of the genḍing except the last two kenongan of gongan II. The three critical sections use the same melodic material; the transposed introduction ends with a T1 cadence and the other two sections end with a T1.

The melodic importance of each tone:

Gulu appears as the final note of the transposed bubuka opaq-opaq and the first gongan. It achieves its usual prominence by the frequent usage of the gulu cadence (T1 or T2).

Nem appears as the final note of the bubuka genḍing and the last gongan in a T2 cadence.

Lima is used in a transitional cadence at the end of gongan II, leading to the final gongan. It also appears in the same cadence in the original bubuka opaq-opaq.

Daḍa is used as a neighbor or passing note.

Barang, by the frequency of its occurrence, introduces a certain melodic variety as a neighbor or passing note.

There remains one slight mystery — the last half of gongan II. If, as the evidence indicates, the original bubuka opaq-opaq was retained in the transposition of the genḍing, and, consequently, must be transposed in order to examine the thematic relationship between the introduction and the rest of the genḍing, how can we explain the exact (augmented) quotation of the original paṭet-sanga bubuka opaq-opaq in this paṭet-nem version of the genḍing?

It might be profitable to examine this question in a general sense in as much as nr 15 "Gupuh" and nr 16 and nr 17 (listed farther on in the statistical summaries) are equally concerned in this practice of retaining an original bubuka opaq-opaq in transposition. Perhaps the practice has arisen out of respect for the original genḍing, or perhaps it is intended merely as an artistic device in which a familiar genḍing is announced by its bubuka opaq-opaq in the original paṭet, the disclosure of the actual paṭet being thus deliberately withheld until the genḍing proper is established. On the strength of either of these possibilities the quotation of the original bubuka opaq-opaq in nr 7 "Gègèr Sakuto" seems justified. It is also significant that this quotation was used at the close of the penultimate gongan in the *characteristic transitional function of lima.*

We must conclude that the last two kenongan of gongan II have been retained (like the bubuka opaq-opaq) in the original paṭet, or the whole of gongan II has been added to the original genḍing in order to provide the paṭet-sanga quotation. It is interesting to note that the two kenongan preceding this quotation consist of nothing but T1 and T2 cadences, as though paṭet nem were being strongly confirmed before the paṭet-sanga quotation is introduced.

Whether tradition or artistic license has established this practice and how consistently it is practiced we have not been able to determine from the available material. The ladrang nr 3 (entered in the statistical summaries), for example, is listed in Kunst's *Music in Java* [1]) as existing in both paṭet nem and paṭet manyura. The Jogyanese collection used for this study contains only the paṭet-nem version, which has a normal paṭet-nem bubuka opaq-opaq and subsequent gongan. There are two possible conditions: 1) nr 3 in paṭet nem is the original genḍing, and the one in paṭet manyura must be its transposition; 2) nr 3 has been transposed *including the bubuka opaq-opaq*, and the paṭet-manyura genḍing is the original. If the first condition obtains, it tells us nothing regarding the choice between fixed tradition and artistic license as an explanation of the transposed bubuka opaq-opaq. If number two is correct, then we should be inclined to favor artistic license or individual choice or whimsy as an explanation. There is additional evidence, however, which inclines toward the first condition and its open question. Nr 3 also appears in Groneman's *Gamelan te Jogjakarta* in two different places, [2]) first as a nuclear theme and second in score form. The two Groneman versions are listed as being in paṭet nem, their bubuka opaq-opaq are in paṭet nem and the three critical structural points end with a T1 cadence. In view of the fact that nr 3 appears three times in important collections in paṭet nem and is listed elsewhere only once in pateṭ manyura, it seems relatively safe to assume that the genḍing in paṭet nem is the original.

Summary and Conclusions

It was mentioned in the beginning of this chapter that the seven genḍing chosen from paṭet nem were *representative* pieces. This merits repetition in order to emphasize the fact that they are not necessarily *typical* genḍing. Every type of exception or irregularity which appears in the paṭet nem group is illustrated by one of the foregoing examples. On the other hand, certain devices occur with a regularity sufficient to suggest that there exists some kind of standard or norm or, perhaps most accurately stated, discipline which serves as the foundation of compositional practice. It is this discipline, as we shall see, which regulates and preserves the identity and individuality of the paṭet.

The principal features of this practice can best be determined by summarizing the chief elements of each of the thirteen genḍing. The summary is arranged in four tables.

The first two tables are designed to indicate something of the general form of the genḍing. In Table I the first colum gives the number and corresponding title of each gending, and only the number will be repeated in the other three tables.

---

1) *Ibid.*, II, 596.
2) (Amsterdam: Johannes Müller, 1890), p. 95 nr 2, pp. 105—17.

Column two indicates the architectonic form of each piece. The term "rounded binary" indicates a "*B*" section in which the closing kenongan is the only recurrence of "*A*" material. As was stated earlier, this is at best a broad representation of form and is admittedly limited in value. The third column represents a comparison between the bubuka genḍing and the final gongan on the basis of identical kenongan. If three kenongan appearing in the bubuka genḍing are repeated in the last gongan of the piece, this is indicated by the number 3. If one kenongan of the bubuka genḍing is also used in the last gongan, this is indicated by the number 1. In the rare instance in which *one* kenongan of the bubuka genḍing appears *twice* in the last gongan, it is shown by the number 2. The value of this comparison is its direct indication of the melodic relationship between these two critical sections of the genḍing. The actual melodic relationship will be somewhat greater than the results indicate because only *identical* and not similar kenongan have been included.

Table I

Title	Form	Same kenongan B.Gd./final GN
nr 1 — Lungkèh	Intro — ternary	4
,, 2 — Dirodo Meto	,, — ,,	3
,, 3 — Girang-Girang	,, — rounded binary	1
,, 5 — Peksi Bajah	,, — ternary	3
,, 6 — Herang-herang Kudus	,, — ,,	1
,, 7 — Gègèr Sakuto	,, — ,,	1
,, 8 — Babat Kencheng	,, — ,,	4
,, 9 — Pisang Bali	,, — ,,	1
,, 10 — Kandang Walang	,, — double period (2 gongan)	2
,, 11 — Rojo Hanggolo	,, — ternary	4
,, 15 — Gupuh	,, — rounded binary	1
,, 16 — Sekar Gadung Puletan	,, — ternary	4
,, 17 — Rangsang	,, — ,,	3

Summary: 10 ladrang are ternary
2 ,, ,, binary
1 ,, is a double period

On the basis of identical kenongan appearing in the bubuka genḍing and the final gongan: all 13 ladrang have at least 1 kenongan identical in both sections, and of these 13:

4 ladrang have 4 kenongan identical in both sections
3 ,, ,, 3 ,, ,, ,, ,, ,,
1 ,, has 2 ,, ,, ,, ,, ,,
5 ,, have 1 ,, ,, ,, ,, ,,

In all ladrang the last kenongan of the bubuka gending and the closing kenongan of the piece are the same.

Table II indicates the detailed structure of each gongan on the basis of repeated kenongan. Although these statistics probably have no correlation with paṭet practice, they show the relative importance of the compositional device *repetition* in Javanese music. The first column (after the title numbers) indicates the number of gongan in each genḍing which repeat no kenongan within the sixteen measures, *e.g.* ABCD or BDGH; the second column shows the number of gongan in each genḍing which repeat one kenongan, *e.g.* AABC or ABBC or ABCC; the third column indicates that two kenongan are repeated, *e.g.* ABAB or ABBA or AABB; the fourth column indicates that one kenongan is used three times in a gongan, *e.g.* AAAB or FCFF; the last column indicates that all four kenongan are identical, *e.g.* AAAA.

Table II

Genḍing	ABCD	AABC	AABB	AAAB	AAAA
nr 1		6			
„ 2		4			1
„ 3	2			3	
„ 5	3	1	3		
„ 6	2	1	1	1	
„ 7		1		3	
„ 8	1	2			
„ 9				3	
„ 10	2				
„ 11		5		1	
„ 15	3	2			
„ 16	2	3			
„ 17	6				
Total:	21	25	4	11	1

Summarized on the basis of a total of 65 gongan:

33.9%	repeat no kenongan				—	ABCD
40.3%	„	1	„		—	AABC
6.5%	„	2	„		—	AABB
17.7%	„	1	„	3 times	—	AAAB
1.6%	„	1	„	4 „	—	AAAA

Table III represents a summary of the cadence closing the three critical sections of the genḍing — the bubuka opaq-opaq, the bubuka genḍing and the final gongan, shown in columns one, two and three, respectively. The symbol "T1" indicates a gulu cadence and "T2" its retrograde form. The figure "T2 + I/V" indicates a T2 cadence extended by the gulu-nem interval. "T1 + ḍaḍa" indicates a T1 cadence with an extension to the tone ḍaḍa. "T1 (trsp)" indicates a bubuka opaq-opaq which in the transposition of the genḍing was retained in the original paṭet and here has been transposed in order to show the cadential structure of the original genḍing. If I/V appears without any "T" number, it means that the gulu-nem interval was used without other cadential preparation.

Table III

Genḍing	B.Op.	B.Gd.	Final GN
nr 1	T1	T1	T1
„ 2	T1 + V	T1	T1
„ 3	T1	T1	T1
„ 5	T1	T1	T1
„ 6	T2	I/V	I/V
„ 7	T1 (trsp)	T2	T2
„ 8	T2	T1	T1
„ 9	T2	T1	T1
„ 10	T1 + lima	T1 + lima	T1 + lima
„ 11	T1 + ḍaḍa	T1 + ḍaḍa	T1 + ḍaḍa
„ 15	T1 (trsp)	T2 + I/V	T2 + I/V
„ 16	T1 (trsp)	T1 + V	T1 + V
„ 17	T1 (trsp)	T2	T2

In summary:	T1	T2	T3	T4	I/V		
B.Op.	10	3	0	0	0	=	100 % T1 or T2
B.Gd.	9	3	0	0	1	=	92.3% T1 or T2
Final GN	9	3	0	0	1	=	92.3% T1 or T2

The melodic importance of each tone can be seen in Table IV. Column one indicates the final note of the genḍing. Column two indicates the principal fifth interval, its importance being determined by its melodic prominence and frequency of occurrence. Column three indicates the tone of transition or bridge tone used in support of tonic and dominant. In the following chapters a distinction will be made between these two functions; in paṭet nem, however, one tone seems to fulfill both functions and will be shown in the column headed "Trans". Column four indicates a true pancher as specified in the musical directions (which, of course, does not appear in the notes of the nuclear theme recorded in the kraton script). Column five indicates a "quasi-pancher" or pedal note which is used for at least two consecutive kenongan.

Table IV

Genḍing	Final	Pr.5th	Trans.	Pancher	Q-pancher
nr 1	gulu	gulu-nem	lima		ḍaḍa
,, 2	,,	,, ,,	,,		ḍaḍa/nem
,, 3	,,	,, ,,	,,		
,, 5	,,	,, ,,	,,	barang	
,, 6	,,	,, ,,	,,		
,, 7	nem	,, ,,	,,		
,, 8	gulu	,, ,,	,,	barang	
,, 9	,,	,, ,,	,,		
,, 10	lima	,, ,,	,,		
,, 11	ḍaḍa	,, ,,	,,		
,, 15	nem	,, ,,	,,		
,, 16	,,	,, ,,	,,	barang	
,, 17	,,	,, ,,	,,	,,	
Summary:	gulu 7 nem 4 lima 1 ḍaḍa 1	gulu-nem	lima	barang	variable

Of the 11 genḍing using either gulu or nem as the final note 63.6% end on gulu and 36.4% on nem.

From these four tables it is possible to determine the principal elements of compositional practice. Those regular features which pertain to the paṭet concept in general and those which are peculiar only to paṭet nem cannot be clearly distinguished until we have had the opportunity to examine and compare paṭet sanga and manyura.

The figures in Table I indicate that most of the ladrang have a ternary form and show that consistent with this three-part construction the sixteen measures of the bubuka genḍing and those of the final gongan of the piece are related melodically. The detailed analyses of the seven exemplary genḍing revealed that the material of the bubuka opaq-opaq was used, to a greater or lesser extent, as the basis of thematic development throughout the genḍing. Together these two practices establish the fact that a *melodic* relationship exists among the bubuka opaq-opaq, the bubuka genḍing and the final gongan. These three critical sections also have a marked *cadential* relationship as shown by the figures in Table III.

The percentages summarized below Table III establish the T1 or gulu cadence and (less often) its retrograde form, the T2 cadence, as typical of paṭet nem genḍing. Table IV shows that the tones gulu and nem are used as the final note in eleven of the thirteen genḍing. The two exceptions — one ending on lima and one on ḍaḍa — are both "prepared" by gulu cadences (see Table III). The general rule can be formulated: gulu is the preferred final note; sometimes its fifth nem is used; and on the rare occasion when another tone appears as the final note, it is preceded by a T1 (or T2) cadence in confirmation of the principal fifth-interval gulu-nem.

The three gong tones have the primary importance: gulu (first gong tone) as tonic, nem (dasar) as dominant, and lima (second gong tone) as a cadential support. Lima is the tone of transition (see Table IV) or, as indicated by the individual analyses, the tone which serves in cadential support of the principal tonic-dominant interval. A few comments regarding the "peculiar nature" of the tone lima (to Western ears) may not be amiss at this time.

The usage of the words "tonic" and "dominant" were justified on the grounds of convenience in indicating two principal tones separated by the interval of a fifth. It has also been made clear that "tonic" is not necessarily indicative of a melodic goal or tone of resolution. The results of paṭet nem, however, rather strongly suggest that gulu may actually be *some* kind of "tonic" and that nem, its fifth, may also be eligible as a dominant. Although an evaluation of this question must wait until Chapter VII, the suggestion that such a tonic idea is admissable might in turn produce unwarrented speculations on the position and function of the tone lima. The reader might too quickly conclude that the behavior of lima is reminiscent of the Western subdominant, and that one practice in Javanese music can be reduced to the authentic cadence of European music — IV-V-I!

The analyses have established the cadential function of these three gong tones. It has also been pointed out that the dominant lies a sléndro fifth above tonic and the second gong tone a fifth below tonic. But even these suggestive conditions do not necessarily justify the conclusion that lima can be considered a "sub-dominant". The interval between gulu and lima may be described variably as a too-small fourth or a too-large third. If the bubuka opaq-opaq of a number of different genḍing are played on one and the same saron demung, the Western ear may in one instance "correct" the gulu-lima interval to the fourth and in another to the third. Colin McPhee has commented on the apparent instability of the tone lima (Balinese "dung" or "doeng"), [1]) and Jaap Kunst cites other instances in which fixed intervals give the impression of being unstable [2]).

We shall manage a more precise comprehension of the function of the Javanese tones if the matter of analogy is limited to only those applications which really serve as a convenience in the analysis. The term "secondary dominant" or "dominant of the dominant" might be introduced to point out the fifth relationship between ḍaḍa and (the dominant) nem (cf. p. 30).

---

1) „The Balinese Wajang Koelit and its Music," *Djawa*, XVI (1936), 9—10 and p. 10 footnote 2.

2) *MJ*, I, 100 footnote 1; and „Music in Nias," *Internationales Archiv für Ethnographie*, XXXVIII (Leiden: E. J. Brill, 1939), 45 footnote 8 ff.

The extent to which this has an analogous application to the function of the secondary dominant in Western music is not of particular concern in the present study. The „dominant", "secondary dominant", "tertiary dominant", the "subdominant", "secondary subdominant" *ad infinitum* has elsewhere been applied to Javanese music. [1]) In the course of the analysis it may be noted that the centers of melodic movement persistently maintain a fifth relationship [2]). At the reader's choice he may apply these terms as he sees fit if it will aid his understanding of the melodic movement. In order not to obscure the primary concepts in paṭet practice, however, Western terminology will be restricted to "tonic", "dominant" and occasionally "secondary dominant".

To return to the original point of departure, lima, therefore, may best be described as a bridge tone or transition tone which is used in cadential support of gulu and nem. The detailed analyses show that lima may appear as the final note of an inner gongan as a tone added to the T3 cadential formula. Two types of T3 and T4 cadences can be distinguished: one type used in connection with tonic and dominant (shown below as T3 and T4), and one used in a transitional function which includes the second gong tone lima (shown as T3+ and T4+). The T1 and T2 cadences are also given for comparison.

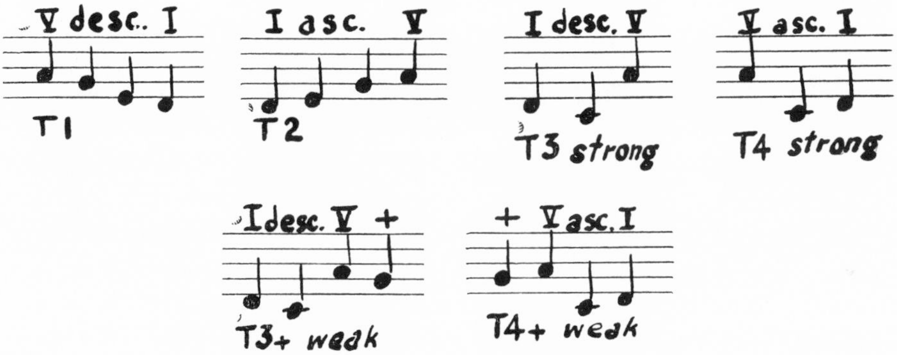

The T4+ cadence is not actually a transitional cadence because it ends on the tonic gulu. It has been included, however, since it is the retrograde form of the T3 formula and may occasionally be found within a gongan.

The above examples show that the typical (T1) cadence is a descending scale passage from dominant to tonic or (less often) the retrograde (T2) form of that figure. Both formulas, it should be noted, contain all three gong tones. The T3 formula appears within the gongan but is not used as a final cadence unless it is preceded (one example, nr 16) by a gulu cadence. In this case the T3 formula actually becomes nothing more than an extension of the T1 cadence (see p. 40). The T3+ and T4+ formulas are *not* used at critical points in paṭet nem because

---

1) J. S. and A. Brandts Buys-Van Zijp, „Javaansche Gĕṇdings bij Land en bij Seelig," *Djawa*, XVIII (1938), 212—13, 220.

2) Cf. *MJ*, I, 71—2.

they are typical of paṭet sanga. We might say, then, that the T3 and T4 cadences are *stong* cadences in as much as they identify paṭet nem and the T3+ and T4+ forms are *weak* in paṭet nem because of their importance in paṭet sanga.

Barang and ḍaḍa have less important roles than those of the three gong tones. Both of these tones occur chiefly as passing notes or as neighbor notes, but each of them occasionally assumes a minor importance. Barang, by the frequency of its occurrence and its conspicuous position as the lowest and highest tone of the one-octave saron scale, sometimes functions as a tone of melodic variety. Generally, however, barang appears to be the least important of the five tones. Ḍaḍa is somewhat stronger in its occasional minor importance as a secondary dominant. The ḍaḍa-nem interval is sometimes used within the gongan in a cadential formula beginning on ḍaḍa and descending in a scale passage to nem, a sléndro fifth "below". (see p. 30).

In connection with the practice of transposing a genḍing and retaining the original bubuka opaq-opaq, the T3+ cadence mentioned above and the ḍaḍa-nem cadence merit some further consideration. The T3+ cadence from gulu to lima suggests paṭet sanga; the familiar appearance of this cadence at transitional points, on the other hand, may justify its limited usage in a more important position as the result of this transposition device. The same circumstance applies in a lesser degree to the "dominant" cadence on nem. Although the cadence ḍaḍa-gulu-barang-nem immediately suggests paṭet manyura, this interval can also be identified with the "dominant" of paṭet nem and on these grounds may be justified in occasionally being admitted to a conspicuous position in the bubuka opaq-opaq at the dictates of artistic license.

Both ḍaḍa and nem are used as quasi-pancher or pedal notes. Only two genḍing, however, employ such a device for as long as two kenongan (eight measures), and this number of examples is insufficient to be indicative of a consistent practice. Since other tones are also used for the duration of one kenongan in this capacity it is probable that the quasi-pancher can be considered variable.

A brief summary of the principal points:

1. The bubuka opaq-opaq is a particular elaboration, combination or variation of cadential formulas, the principal cadence being the T1 formula. The bubuka opaq-opaq provides the basis of thematic development for the entire genḍing.
2. Through the thematic development of the bubuka opaq-opaq the T1 cadential formula becomes the melodic framework of the genḍing. The particular variation of that formula in the bubuka opaq-opaq accounts for the distinctiveness of the introduction and consequently the genḍing itself.
3. The three critical sections of the genḍing — the bubuka opaq-opaq, the bubuka genḍing and the final gongan — are closely related melodically and cadentially.

4. The "inner gongan" may be related to the bubuka genḍing, may be a distinct development of the melodic material, may be a combination of these two conditions or may be chiefly of a transitional nature. Any of the theoretical cadences, T1, T2, T3, T4, or the "dominant" cadence on nem may be found at these inner gongan.
5. The T1 cadence is typical of paṭet nem genḍing, but all the theoretical possibilities of a cadence descending or ascending between tonic and dominant may be found within the course of the genḍing.
6. The three gong tones occupy the principal melodic and structural roles: gulu (first gong tone) as "tonic", nem (dasar) as "dominant", and lima (second gong tone) as a cadential support for tonic and dominant and as a tone of transition. Barang and ḍaḍa are used as passing or neighbor notes and may also have slightly more important functions: the former as a tone of melodic variety and the latter as a kind of "secondary dominant" to nem.

V.

SLÉNDRO PAṬET SANGA

THE THREE GONG TONES of paṭet sanga are gulu as dasar, lima as first gong tone, and barang as second gong tone. The same general procedure followed in the paṭet nem analyses will also be used for the genḍing of paṭet sanga. The terms "tonic" and "dominant" are again used to designate the two tones delimiting the most important fifth-interval.

Analysis of the Genḍing

The large Jogyanese manuscript contains twenty-three genḍing listed by the scribe in sléndro paṭet sanga. The ladrang nr 35 and the ketawang nr 38, however, were incorrectly labeled and will be included in their proper place in paṭet manyura. The ladrang nr 12, on the contrary, which was listed by the scribe as belonging to paṭet nem is actually in paṭet sanga and is accordingly included with these genḍing. This makes a total of twenty-two pieces: nineteen ladrang and three ketawang.

Nine of the twenty-two genḍing will be presented in detailed analysis, and the remaining thirteen are included in the statistical summaries.

„Uluk-Uluk"

Ladrang nr 19 — sléndro paṭet sanga

bubuka opaq-opaq

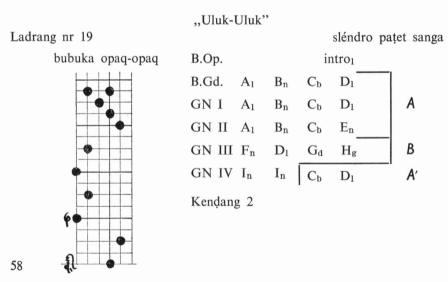

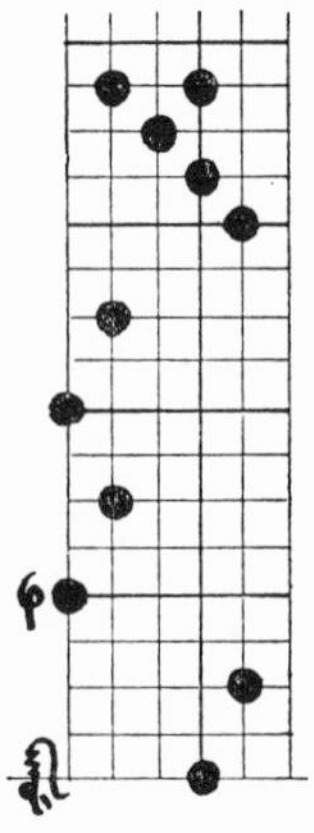

B.Op.				intro$_l$	
B.Gd.	A_l	B_n	C_b	D_l	
GN I	A_l	B_n	C_b	D_l	A
GN II	A_l	B_n	C_b	E_n	
GN III	F_n	D_l	G_d	H_g	B
GN IV	I_n	I_n	C_b	D_l	A′

Kenḍang 2

transcribed (see appendix p. 272)

"Uluk-Uluk" is an unusual "whole-note" piece in its usage of both ḍaḍa (rare) and barang as true pancher[1]) beginning (after the bubuka genḍing) in the genḍing proper. The form of the ladrang is designated as ternary; the brief return (two kenongan) of *A* material in the last gongan, however, might as easily justify the term "rounded binary".

The melodic highpoints are indicated by the structural chart: lima is important in the bubuka opaq-opaq and the *A* section; nem (as we shall see) serves as a tone of transition at the close of gongan II, leading to the *B* section which terminates on the dominant gulu; the return to *A'* is again via the tone nem, and the final gongan ends on lima, the tonic.

Bubuka opaq-opaq

The optional tones given at the beginning of the introduction form (the inversion of) the principal fifth-interval in paṭet sanga, namely lima-gulu. If lima is taken as the first note of the bubuka opaq-opaq, the first three notes are the tonic-neighbor-tonic, *i.e.* lima-ḍaḍa-lima; if gulu is used, the first three notes are a short ascending scale from dominant to tonic, *i.e.* gulu to lima. The second measure consists of the interval nem-gulu and raises the possibility that in paṭet sanga the dominant (nem) of the dominant (gulu) may have a function which is similar to that of the "secondary dominant" in paṭet nem (cf. p. 56). From the tone gulu in measure two to the end of the bubuka opaq-opaq is an extended T3 cadence. The bold bracket begins with the gulu of measure three in order to show the simple form of the cadence. It should be noted that in paṭet nem this cadence appears at *inner* points in which lima has a transitional function. In paṭet sanga this formula appears at important structural points as a descending cadence from dominant to tonic.

Bubuka genḍing

The sixteen measures (and therefore the sixteen notes) of the bubuka genḍing are built on the basic T3 cadence of the bubuka opaq-opaq. The first two notes are a continuation of the descending scale begun in the introduction (the total passage being a retrograde version of bar one). The next two notes plus kenongan two are a continuous descending scale from nem to nem. This could be considered a filling-in of the nem-gulu interval of bar two (bubuka opaq-opaq) continued to bar four or thought of as a retrograde version of the first four notes of the

1) Cf. *MJ*, I, 168—9.

bubuka opaq-opaq with a barang continuation. Kenongan three is a reiteration of the gulu-barang figure from bar three, and kenongan four finishes the quotation of the bubuka opaq-opaq, with a complete T3 cadence. The material is derived from the introduction.

Gongan I, II

All of gongan I and the first three kenongan of gongan II are the same as the bubuka genḍing. The fourth kenongan of gongan II differs from that of the preceding gongan only in the exchange of the last two notes. This juxtaposition places nem in a transitional position, as the final note of the gongan, leading to the *B* section.

Gongan III

The first kenongan consists of an alternation of barang *alit* and nem, the first two notes (barang *geḍé* and nem) of bar four in the bubuka opaq-opaq. The second kenongan is the same as the fourth kenongan of the bubuka genḍing, *i.e.* the T3 cadence. The third kenongan is made up of the first three notes of the bubuka opaq-opaq, which are extended by ḍaḍa leading to kenongan four. In kenongan four the tone nem descends to gulu as a retrograde form of the four-note scale beginning the bubuka opaq-opaq.

Gongan IV

The first kenongan uses a slight variation in retrograde of the scale from the beginning of the introduction. The second kenongan is a variation of that scale in the normal order. The last two kenongan are the same as those of the bubuka genḍing.

General Summary

The three gong tones lima, gulu and barang are featured in the bubuka opaq-opaq and end the introduction with a T3 cadential formula. The bubuka opaq-opaq provides the basis of thematic development for the rest of the genḍing. The last two kenongan of the bubuka genḍing and the final gongan are identical. The three critical sections end with the same T3 cadence.

The melodic importance of each tone:

Lima is the tone of principal melodic importance, being used as the final note in the bubuka opaq-opaq, the bubuka genḍing, gongan I and the final gongan IV in the T3 cadence. A less important cadential formula appears at the beginning of the bubuka opaq-opaq, the T1 shown below with the T3:

Gulu as the dominant of lima is second in melodic importance and is used as the gong tone of the *B* section in gongan III.
Nem appears in a transitional function at the end of gongan II (leading to the *B* section) and frequently at the midpoints of other gongan (cf. second kenongan endings in the structural table).
Barang is used as a tone of melodic variety and true pancher.
Ḍaḍa is used as a passing note and true pancher.

"Gondo Yonni"

Ladrang nr 24 — sléndro paṭet sanga

bubuka opaq-opaq

B.Op.			$intro_l$		
B.Gd.	A_l	B_b	C_g	D_l	A
GN I	A_l	B_b	C^*_g	D_l	A
GN II	A_l	B_b	C^*_g	D_l	A
GN III	E_l	F_b	C^*_g	D_l	B
GN IV	E_l	F_b	C^*_g	D_l	B

C* barang added as second note
Kenḍang 2 (symbols apparently forgotten by the scribe after the B.Gd.; see illus. p. 318)

transcribed (see appendix p. 273)

The structural table of "Gondo Yonni" shows an interesting consistency in the position and usage of the three gong tones. The lower-case letters indicate that the same order is used for *each* gongan — lima, barang, gulu, lima — and it is worthy of note that the *tonic* lima begins the gongan, barang (*second gong tone*) is at the midpoint of the gongan, and the *dominant* gulu directly precedes the final *tonic* lima which closes the gongan. The position of barang at the midpoint suggests that it may function in cadential support of tonic and dominant. The genḍing has a binary form: the bubuka genḍing, gongan I and II comprise the *A* section; and gongan III and IV constitute the *B* section.

Bubuka opaq-opaq

The bubuka opaq-opaq offers an excellent example of a dominant-tonic "conscious" introduction. Its total composition consists of five cadential formulas, indicated by the appropriate brackets. The first is a variation of the T3 cadence found in nr 19 "Uluk-Uluk" and in essence is a descending scale from dominant to tonic. The T4 cadence is a retrograde version of the T3, barang alit being used in this instance instead of the lower octave, and is therefore an ascending scale from tonic to dominant. The next two cadences, T2 and T1, are three-note scales, the first ascending from dominant to tonic, the second descending from tonic to dominant. The final cadence is a regular T3 formula. The last four brackets represent "model" cadences and will be referred to later in analyses which may use variations of these.

Bubuka genḍing

The whole of the bubuka genḍing is a slight elaboration of the bubuka opaq-opaq in augmentation. The first two notes of kenongan one are a continuation of nem including the neighbor barang alit, and the following tones comprise the T2 cadence, which is repeated. After this somewhat fragmentary beginning the second kenongan starts with the second note of bar two (gulu, in the bubuka opaq-opaq) and continues through kenongan four in an augmented quotation of the entire bubuka opaq-opaq. The final T3 cadence of kenongan four is slightly extended by the addition of the tone ḍaḍa before the final lima.

Gongan I, II

Gongan I and II are the same as the bubuka genḍing except that an extra barang has been added as the second note of the third kenongan. All the material is derived from the bubuka opaq-opaq.

Gongan III, IV

Gongan III and IV are identical. The first kenongan is an extension of the figure from bar two of the bubuka opaq-opaq. Kenongan two uses the exact figure found in the introduction (except for the prolongation of gulu) and then repeats it in retrograde. Kenongan three and four are the same as those of gongan I and II. All the material is from the bubuka opaq-opaq.

General Summary

The bubuka opaq-opaq consists of five cadential formulas or scale passages between dominant and tonic which provide the basis of thematic development for the entire genḍing. The third and fourth kenongan of the bubuka genḍing and the final gongan are identical. The three critical sections, therefore, are closely related both melodically and cadentially.

The melodic importance of each tone:
Lima is the tone of primary importance and occurs as the final note of the bubuka opaq-opaq and all gongan; it is used in any one of the four cadences indicated by the brackets under the transcribed bubuka opaq-opaq.
Gulu is second in melodic importance; it appears in the four types of cadences as the fifth of lima and closes the penultimate kenongan of each gongan.
Barang is prominent in the T3 and T4 cadences and is used in a transitional function and in cadential support of dominant and tonic at the midpoint of each gongan.
Nem achieves a secondary importance in relation to gulu (as the dominant of the dominant) and is conspicuous in the T3 and T4 formulas because of the leap from or to barang, necessitated by the one-octave range of the demung.
Ḍaḍa is used as a passing note.

"Konchang"

Ladrang nr 23 slédro paṭet sanga

bubuka opaq-opaq

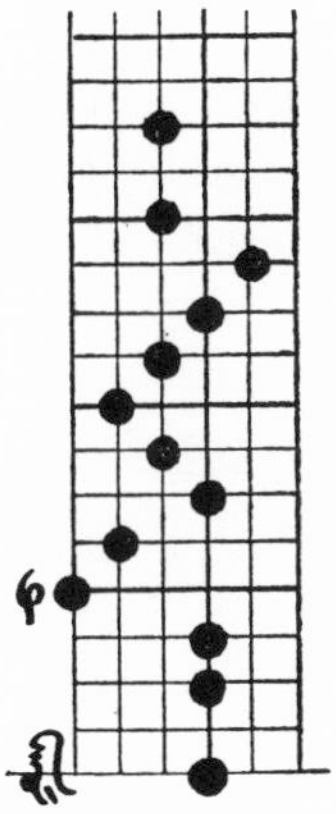

B.Op.			intro$_l$		
B.Gd.	A_l	B_n	C_n	D_l	A
GN I	D'_l	D''_n	E_n	D'_l	A
GN II	D'_l	D''_n	E_n	D'''_l	A
GN III	F_l	F_l	G_n	D'''_l	B
GN IV	F_l	F_l	G_n	D'_l	B

D′ begins with 2 quarter notes instead of a half note and ḍaḍa is added as a neighbor note
D″ variation in ending
D‴ variation in ending
Kenḍang 2

transcribed (see appendix p. 274)

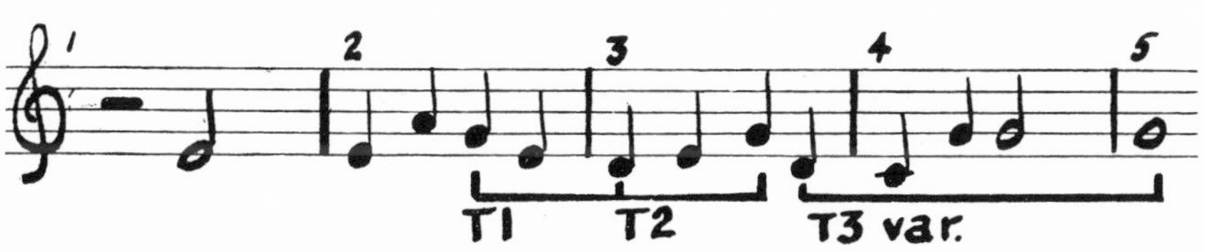

The general form of "Konchang" has been indicated as rounded binary. The development of the fourth kenongan of the bubuka genḍing in gongan I and II seem to bind these first three parts together to form the *A* section;

gongan III and IV make up the *B* section. The repetition of the same fourth kenongan (with minor changes) in each gongan creates a kind of verse-refrain structure within the larger binary design.

Bubuka opaq-opaq

The bubuka opaq-opaq begins with the two neighbors of lima — ḍaḍa and nem — and three cadences follow, as indicated by the brackets. There is nothing unusual about the first two, a simple T1 and T2 formula. The final cadence, however, is a T3 in which the tone nem has been omitted. An examination of the final kenongan of the bubuka genḍing, gongan I and gongan IV, as well as other kenongan, indicated in the structural chart as "D" or some variety of "D", leaves little doubt that the final cadence of the bubuka opaq-opaq is a T3 formula in which nem is withheld only to be revealed in subsequent quotations of the bubuka opaq-opaq.

Bubuka genḍing

Kenongan one and two of the bubuka genḍing are in whole notes. The first two notes (taking the final tone lima of the introduction as a beginning) complete a T1 formula. A scale passage beginning with nem (from bars 2—3 of the bubuka opaq-opaq) then continues through barang to nem again. In the first kenongan nem is actually used as a neighbor note preceding the T1 formula (note that lima, the first note of the cadence, falls on the kenong beat) which continues to gulu in kenongan two. Gulu begins a T3 cadence that is completed by the first lima of kenongan three. Kenongan three is a retrograde version (underscored) of the following figure from the bubuka opaq-opaq with the addition of a quasi-pancher on lima sometimes merging with the regular lima of the melodic pattern:

becomes

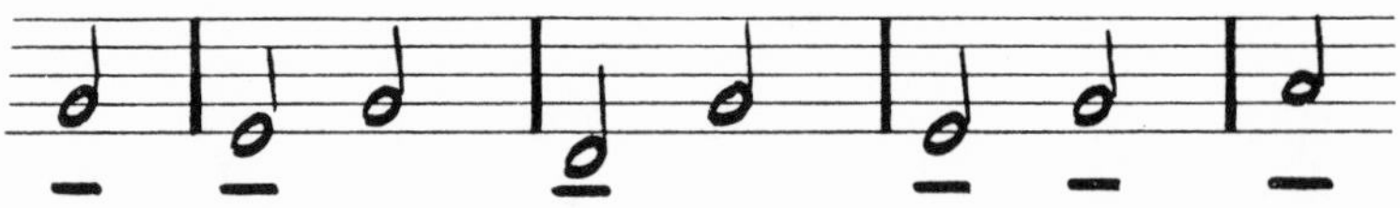

The fourth kenongan is a repetition of the entire bubuka opaq-opaq except that the final T3 cadence is now completed by the addition of nem and is slightly extended.

Gongan I

The first and fourth kenongan of gongan I are identical. These kenongan are the same as the last kenongan of the bubuka genḍing except that they begin with a rhythmic subdivision of the first note and add ḍaḍa as a neighbor note. Kenongan two is the same as the first and last kenongan except for the final measure, where the sequence of the last three notes is altered to end on nem. Kenongan three begins with the neighbor note barang followed by a scale passage from nem to a reiteration of gulu, a leap to lima and back again to a retrograde form of the same scale. This is taken from bars 2—3 of the bubuka opaq-opaq.

In kenongan one, two and four ḍaḍa achieves a minor importance through reiteration and in its fifth relationship to nem. The entire gongan is derived from the introduction.

Gongan II

The first three kenongan are the same as those of gongan I. The fourth kenongan is the same as that of the bubuka genḍing except that the final T3 cadence (last measure and a half) is replaced by an extended T2 formula. The material is based on the bubuka opaq-opaq.

Gongan III

Kenongan one and two are identical and consist of two T4 formulas (the first one is begun with the neighbor note nem) followed by a scale from lima to nem and back to lima with an extension. Kenongan three introduces melodic variety by a reiteration of the tone barang (after the initial nem); and a retrograde variation of the figure in bars 2—3 (T2 and T1) of the bubuka opaq-opaq ends the kenongan. The fourth kenongan is the same as that of gongan II. The material is freely derived from the introduction.

Gongan IV

The first three kenongan are the same as those of gongan III. The last kenongan is the same as that of gongan I.

General Summary

The bubuka opaq-opaq is built on three of the four possible cadential formulas. The tone nem is omitted from the final T3 cadence, perhaps as an artistic device. The entire bubuka opaq-opaq is quoted several times in the genḍing itself, and in these instances the tone nem appears in the T3 cadence, suggesting the deliberate design of the T3 variation of the introduction.

The bubuka opaq-opaq provides the thematic material for the genḍing; and the three critical sections are related melodically and cadentially.

The melodic importance of each tone:

Lima is the most important tone as tonic in the cadential formulas and as the final note of the bubuka opaq-opaq, the bubuka genḍing and all gongan.

Gulu is second in melodic importance as the dominant of nem.
Nem is the tone of transition (cf. the kenongan endings in the structural chart).
Barang is used in cadential support of lima and gulu and as a tone of melodic variety.
Daḍa appears as a neighbor and passing note but achieves a minor importance through reiteration and its fifth relationship to nem.

"Udan Sejati"

Ladrang nr 18 slé ndro paṭet sanga

bubuka opaq-opaq

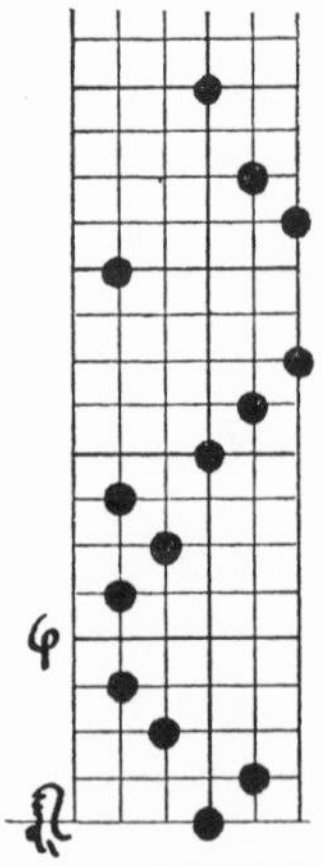

B.Op.				intro$_l$	
B.Gd.	A_l	A_l	B_b	C_l	A
GN I	D_l	D_l	E_g	E_l	A
GN II	A_l	A_l	B_b	C_l	A
GN III	D_l	D_l	E_g	E_l	A
GN IV	A_l	A_l	B_b	F_b	A
GN V	G_b	H_b	H_b	I_b	B
GN VI	G_b	H_b	H_b	$I_{(l)}$	B

Kenḍang 2

transcribed (see appendix p. 275)

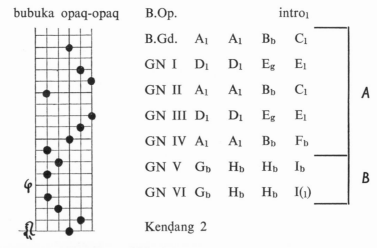

"Udan Sejati" has a binary form, **A** consisting of the bubuka genḍing and the first four gongan and **B** consisting of gongan V and VI. The rather long **A** section has a rondo construction; this will merit some comment presently. The lower-case letters of the **A** part indicate the prominence of lima and the cadential support of gulu and barang. The **B** section features barang and has a questionable final note.

Bubuka opaq-opaq

The T4 and the T3 cadences both employ barang alit and quite naturally so if we imagine the half-note gulu one octave higher (which, of course, is not possible on the balungan instruments). If gulu alit were available, the ascending scale from the half-note tonic to the half-note dominant and the descending form from the imaginary gulu alit back again to lima would be perfectly conjunct movements. The extended T2 formula may be an extension of the preceding T3 cadence. This will be more apparent in an examination of the final gongan of the genḍing.

Bubuka genḍing, gongan II

The bubuka genḍing and gongan II are identical. The first two kenongan of these gongan are alike and consist of an augmentation of the figure beginning with gulu in bar four of the bubuka opaq-opaq and continuing to the gong. Two extra gulu have been added in measure three, actually as a rhythmic subdivision of the original version. The derivation of kenongan three and four can most easily be seen by considering them together. The total eight measures (kenongan three and four) consist of a very long extension of the T3 cadence taken from bar two of the bubuka opaq-opaq, using barang geḍé instead of (the octave higher) barang alit. Gulu serves in the double capacity of quasi-pancher and melodic tone.

Gongan I, III

Gongan I and III of the *A* section are identical. The four kenongan may be examined in pairs: the first two are alike, and kenongan three and four are alike except for the final note. The first pair is built on the same figure from the bubuka opaq-opaq that is used in the last two kenongan of the bubuka genḍing, *i.e.* bar two starting with the note gulu to the end of the T3 cadence (first note of bar three). This time, however, the note serving in the double capacity of quasi-pancher and melodic tone is barang, and, as in the bubuka opaq-opaq, barang alit is used instead of the lower octave. The last two kenongan consist of a long extension of the last four-note figure of the bubuka opaq-opaq with nem serving as quasi-pancher.

Gongan IV

The first three kenongan of gongan IV are the same as those of the bubuka genḍing. The fourth kenongan differs from that of the bubuka genḍing only in the final measure. The T3 cadence is not complete (and extended), but instead the tone nem is repeated as a tone af transition to the *B* section, and in anticipation of the *B* section the final note of the kenongan is barang.

Gongan V

Gongan V features the tone barang as a tone of melodic variety. The first three kenongan are constructed on the T1 and T2 cadences. The first kenongan is from bar three of the bubuka opaq-opaq with the addition and frequent reiteration of the tone barang. The second and third kenongan are identical and consist of a T2—T1 formula (bars 3—4 of the introduction) extended to barang. This extension introduces a T1 formula which includes the second gong tone barang, just as in pațet nem the T3 cadence was extended to include the second gong tone lima. The extended T1 cadence and its retrograde version are given below; the second gong tone barang is indicated by +:

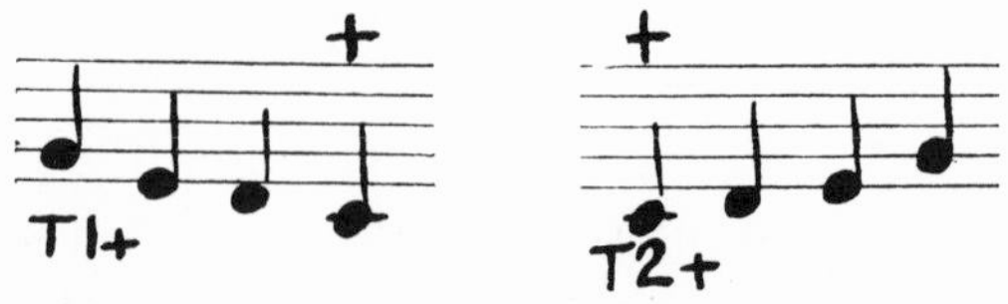

The end of kenongan three forms the first half of a T3 formula which is completed and extended in kenongan four. The fourth kenongan completes the T3 cadence and makes an extension on a combined T1—T2 plus nem-barang. The whole passage is a variation of bars 2—3 from the bubuka opaq-opaq in retrograde. The example shown under gongan VI below is also applicable to this kenongan except for the last two notes which in the example are omitted entirely. In this kenongan (of gongan V) these two notes nem-barang form a transition to gongan VI. The material is derived from the bubuka opaq-opaq.

Gongan VI

The first three kenongan are the same as those of gongan V. The fourth kenongan is also identical to that of gongan V except that the last two notes are omitted. This is the only example in the entire collection which does not show a final note of the nuclear theme sounding with the final gong. The obvious guess would be that the scribe simply forgot the last two notes. But I wonder if that explanation is not a little too easy? We have noticed in an earlier example that the kenḍang symbols were forgotten (nr 24, p. 61) after the bubuka genḍing; this is understandable, since at that point the genḍing proper continues on the following page. It is reasonable to imagine the omission of two whole kenongan when copying two identical gongan; but the accidental omission of precisely the last two notes of the piece . . . it hardly seems accidental. So far as I have been able to find out "Udan Sejati" is not used in connection with sacred occasions, otherwise we might assume that religious motivation had prompted a deliberate error or omission.[1]) I suggest that resolution is achieved without the addition of the two "omitted" notes and that artistic whimsy has chosen not to repeat lima or gulu with the final gong. But perhaps the reader can decide for himself.

The last two notes of kenongan three and all of kenongan four are given below. The brackets should be compared with the similar indications given in the transcribed introduction. The two passages accomplish the same purpose

1) See p. 20.

cadentially; and the one from gongan VI seems to indicate that the T2 cadence of the bubuka opaq-opaq is intended as an extension of the T3 cadence. Whether in the final gongan this extension is meant to include nem and barang (as in gongan V) seems to me a minor point.

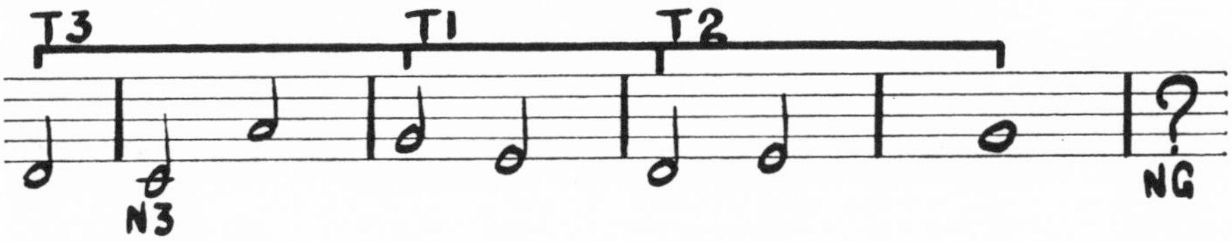

The Rondo

In the Jogyanese manuscript of 100 titles there are only two genḍing which have a rondo construction: "Udan Sejati" with a rondo **A** section in sléndro paṭet sanga, and "Udan Mas" a ladrang in pélog paṭet nem which uses the rondo form throughout. It is interesting that the two pieces are similar in both their titles and rondo character. "Udan Mas" is very popular in Central Java (we shall examine this piece at some length later on); its title means "*Golden* Rain". "Udan *Sejati*" means "*Real* Rain", and as we might surmise, it seems to be some kind of parody on "Udan Mas". The elements of contrast between the alternating gongan of the **A** section in "Udan Sejati" are not so obviously nor strongly stated as in the alternating sections of "Udan Mas". It will be better, therefore, if the reader returns to this interesting aspect of "Real Rain" after an exposure to (the analysis of) "Golden Rain", at which time a footnote will provide the clue to the composer's probable intention in this paṭet sanga ladrang.

General Summary

The bubuka opaq-opaq is constructed on a series of lima-gulu cadential formulas, the most important probably being a T3 cadence with an extension. The melodic material for the genḍing is derived from the introduction. The three critical sections are related melodically and cadentially, but the bubuka genḍing and the final gongan are not identical in any of their kenongan. The melodic relationship is achieved through the circumstance that the material for both of these sections is taken from the *same* figures in the bubuka opaq-opaq although their developments are different. The cadences of the bubuka opaq-opaq and the final gongan are both T3 formulas with an extension; the final cadence of the bubuka genḍing is also a T3 formula but without an extension.

The melodic importance of each tone:

Lima has the primary importance as tonic of the basic cadential formulas and as the final note of the bubuka opaq-opaq, the bubuka genḍing, gongan I, II, III and (?) VI.

Gulu is second in importance as the fifth of lima.
Barang is used in cadential support of dominant and tonic and as a tone of melodic variety in the *B* section.
Nem is used as a tone of transition and a secondary dominant.
Ḍaḍa is used as a neighbor note and passing tone.

"Madu Bronto"

Ladrang nr 28 — sléndro paṭet sanga

bubuka opaq-opaq

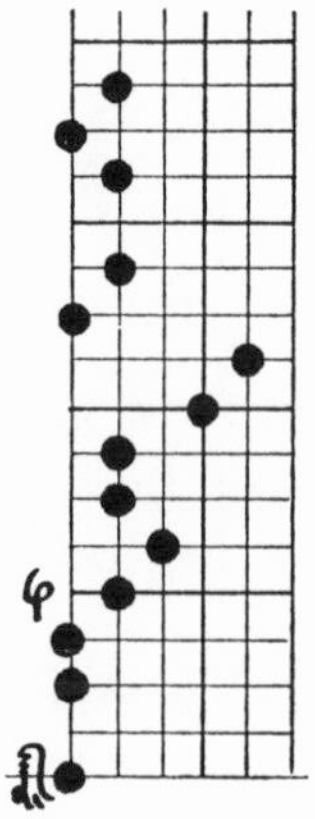

B.Op.			intro$_b$		
B.Gd.	A_b	B_l	C_l	D_l	*A*
GN I	E_l	D_l	F_g	G_b	*B*
GN II	H_b	E_l	C_l	D_l	*A′*

Kenḍang 1

transcribed (see appendix p. 276)

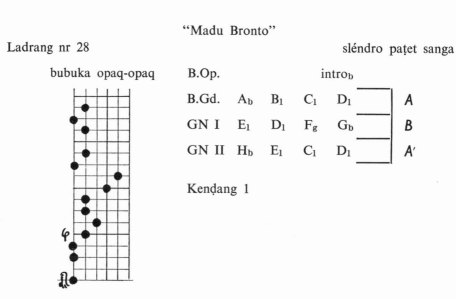

"Madu Bronto" has a simple ternary form: the bubuka genḍing represents the first part; gongan I the second part; and gongan II the *A′* section. The final note of the bubuka opaq-opaq and the following gongan alternates between barang and lima; the kenongan divisions are made up entirely of the three gong tones.

One of the principal points of interest in "Madu Bronto" is the fact that two other genḍing in the collection have exactly the same bubuka opaq-opaq. Nr 32 "Bronto Asmoro" and nr 27 "Chlunṭang" each will be examined briefly and compared with "Madu Bronto" primarily with respect to the development of thematic material. The melodic importance of each tone will be seen to be consistent with the standard practices found in the foregoing paṭet sanga analyses and will not be given particular attention.

Bubuka opaq-opaq

The first cadence of the bubuka opaq-opaq is a T3 formula and appears to be the principal cadence. The second cadence is a variation of a T1 formula extended to include the second gong tone barang (see example on p. 85). This has not been indicated by a bracket but only by a dotted line because it is actually an extension of the T3 cadence. The beginning of measure three could also be interpreted in terms of the tonic-dominant interval, lima-gulu, extended by the neighbors of gulu to the second gong tone barang.

Bubuka genḍing

The first two kenongan follow very closely the beginning figure of the bubuka opaq-opaq which ends with the lima of bar three, the end of the T3 cadence. The bubuka genḍing begins with whole notes and in the last half of the second kenongan changes to half notes. The third kenongan immediately introduces quarter notes in a rather free elaboration of the figure starting in bar two on barang and ending on gulu of bar four. This figure is used forward and backward and forward again, continuing in kenongan four to a slightly elaborated T3 cadence (from bars 2—3 bubuka opaq-opaq).

Gongan I

Kenongan one is an elaboration of the beginning of the bubuka opaq-opaq including the T3 cadence. Kenongan two is the same as that of the bubuka genḍing. Kenongan three is a rather free fantasy on the figure barang-nem-lima of bars 2—3 and ends with the gulu-ḍaḍa figure of bars 3—4. Kenongan four is a slight elaboration of the entire bubuka opaq-opaq; and the last two bars provide a good example of the T1 formula extended to include barang. At this midpoint of the genḍing barang is again reminiscent of lima's transitional function in paṭet nem.

Gongan II

Kenongan one uses the three-note figure from bars 3—4 of the introduction, *i.e.* ḍaḍa-gulu-barang, with a quasi-pancher on ḍaḍa. The second kenongan is the same as the first kenongan of gongan I. The general outline of this first half of gongan II is similar to that of the bubuka genḍing. The last two kenongan are identical to those of the bubuka genḍing.

In conclusion: although its development is rather elaborate, the melodic material of the genḍing is very closely related to the bubuka opaq-opaq.

"Bronto Asmoro"

Ladrang nr 32 — sléndro paṭet sanga

bubuka opaq-opaq	B.Op.				$intro_b$	
(see nr 28)	B.Gd.	A_b	B_l	C_l	B_l	A
	GN I	A_b	B_l	C_l	B_l	A
	GN II	A_b	B_l	C_l	B_l	A
	GN III	B_l	B_l	D_n	E_b	B
	GN IV	B_l	B_l	D_n	E_b	B

Kenḍang 1

"Bronto Asmoro" presents a considerable contrast to the foregoing "Madu Bronto". Nr 28 has the basic note value of a quarter note; nr 32 contains only whole notes and uses a pancher on barang. Nr 28 is a short ternary form; nr 32 is twice as long and in binary form. (See appendix p. 277).

Bubuka genḍing, gongan I, II

The four kenongan consist of an extended T3 cadence (taken from bars 2—3 of the bubuka opaq-opaq): a repetition of gulu-barang in the first kenongan, a complete T3 in kenongan two, a repetition of nem-lima in kenongan three, and a complete T3 cadence in kenongan four. This bubuka genḍing (and gongan I and II) have a general outline which is similar to that of the bubuka genḍing of nr 28.

Gongan III, IV

The first two kenongan are the same as the second (and fourth) kenongan of the bubuka genḍing, *i.e.* a T3 formula. The third kenongan repeats the first three notes of the T3 formula. Kenongan four is an augmentation of bars 3—4, *i.e.* gulu-ḍaḍa-gulu-barang, and (like the introduction) provides an extension to the preceding T3 cadences.

Gongan III and IV resemble gongan I of nr 28. Kenongan one, two and four have the same general outline; in kenongan three the sequence of gulu-nem as melodic highpoints is reversed.

In conclusion: the whole-note design of nr 32 affords little opportunity for melodic development. The genḍing therefore consists of very direct quotations from the bubuka opaq-opaq; nr 32 and nr 28 have the same general outline.

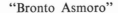

“Chlunṭang”

Ladrang nr 27 — sléndro paṭet sanga

bubuka opaq-opaq	B.Op.				$intro_b$
(see nr 28)	B.Gd.	A_b	B_n	C_l	D_l
	GN I	E_l	E_l	E_l	F_b
	GN II	G_g	G^*_n	H_l	I_l

G* last measure altered to end on nem
Kenḍang 1

In contrast to the ternary and binary forms of the two preceding genḍing “Chlunṭang“ is through-composed. Although the basic note value is again the quarter note, this ladrang is less active than nr 28, *i.e.* it has more half- and whole-notes. The three gong tones are prominent in the structural table, the final notes alternating between barang and lima. (See appendix p. 278).

Bubuka genḍing

The first three kenongan are in whole notes and seem to be a fragmentary version of the T3 formula in retrograde (almost completed in kenongan two). The fourth kenongan is in half notes; the first three measures are based on bars 3—4 of the bubuka opaq-opaq and the final two notes complete a T3 cadence. This bubuka genḍing is related to those of nr 28 and nr 32 by the basic outline of the T3 cadence. Although its fragmentary development tends to set it somewhat apart from the other two genḍing, the reiteration in kenongan three of the last two notes of kenongan two is the same device used in nr 32.

Gongan I

The first three kenongan are identical. They are based on the first two bars of the bubuka opaq-opaq (including beat one of bar three). The figure barang-gulu-barang is used as a kind of pedal in the extended T3 cadence. Kenongan four begins with a variation of bars 2—3 in retrograde and closes with a passage based on the figure of bars 3—4.

Kenongan one and two show a general correspondence to those of nr 28 (gongan I) and nr 32 (gongan III). Kenongan three is like the first two and is therefore not related to the corresponding kenongan of nr 28 and nr 32. The fourth kenongan is similar in melodic outline to that of nr 28 (gongan I) and nr 32 (gongan III).

Gongan II

Kenongan one and two (alike except for the last measure) are elaborations of the T3 formula extended by a T1 cadence (*i.e.* an elaboration of the entire bubuka opaq-opaq). The last measure of kenongan two adds a T2 formula plus nem to the extension. In the first half of kenongan three the importance of nem (and its neighbors) is continued. The last half uses the figure from the bubuka opaq-opaq beginning with the second gulu of bar three and ending with barang of bar four. This passage continues to complete a slightly-extended T3 formula. Kenongan four consists of a series of T2—T1 formulas leading to a final T3 cadence, the whole kenongan being a reversal of the cadential sequence stated in the bubuka opaq-opaq.

The embellishments of this gongan are numerous; consequently it might be convenient to describe the melodic highlights of the entire gongan. The melodic emphasis of the first kenongan is on lima and gulu; kenongan two is the same except for the ending leading to nem; in kenongan three nem continues as a transition tone and the melodic highpoints: nem, gulu, lima; kenongan four stresses gulu and lima and ends with a T3 cadence. The material of the first two kenongan do not seem to be generally related to any of the kenongan of nr 28 and nr 32. The third and fourth kenongan, however, correspond to those of nr 28 (gongan II).

General Summary 28, 32, 27

One bubuka opaq-opaq provides the basis of thematic development for each of the three genḍing — "Madu Bronto", "Bronto Asmoro", and "Chlunṭang". Each genḍing is highly individual in its melodic structure and form, and yet each shows a thematic relationship — sometimes fragmentary, sometimes direct — to the bubuka opaq-opaq. The three different developments of the *single* theme are also seen to have a general relationship. Melodic variations on a given theme in Western music show a similar kind of relationship. The analogy is valid only as it applies to one bubuka opaq-opaq used for several different genḍing; the relationship of the individual gongan of *one* genḍing to their bubuka opaq-opaq is not an example of a variations technique any more than the melodic development of a theme or motif in Western music is an example of this technique.

In all three genḍing the melodic importance of each tone is consistent with the pertinent characteristics found in the summaries of the preceding paṭet sanga genḍing.

"Barang Ganjur"

Ketawang nr 39 slèndro paṭet sanga

bubuka opaq-opaq

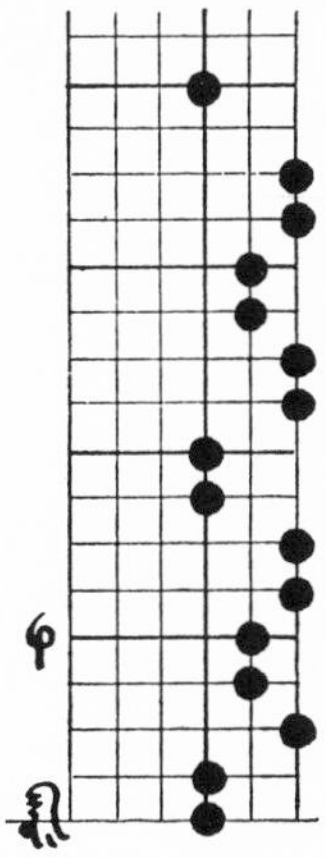

B.Op.			$intro_l$
B.Gd.	A_l	A_l	A
B.Gd.	A_l	A_l	A
B.Gd.	A_l	B_b	A
GN I	C_b	D_b	A
GN II	E_l	F_n	B
GN III	G_l	H_l	B
GN IV	I_b	J_l	B
GN V	I_b	J_l	B
GN VI	A_l^*	A_l^*	A′
GN VII	A_l^*	B_b^*	A′

A* is an elaboration of *A*
B* is an elaboration of *B*
Ketawang kenḍang 2
transcribed (see appendix p. 279)

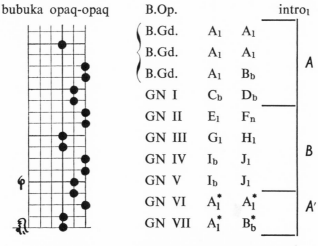

There are three ketawang in the paṭet sanga group. The eight-measure construction of the individual gongan produces a structural table typified by that of "Barang Ganjur" given above. This ketawang makes two departures from the norm: the bubuka genḍing consists of *three* eight-measure gongan, and this is normally two eight-measure phrases (*i.e.* the equivalent of one sixteen-measure gongan of a ladrang). The extra gongan can best be explained, perhaps, as a product of artistic license. The second curious aspect is the omission of the dominant gulu in the bubuka opaq-opaq. The brackets have been left open at one end to indicate that the T3 cadence is missing its initial note gulu; otherwise the cadence is complete: barang (alit), nem and lima. This same bubuka opaq-opaq (also used for nr 40 "Gajah Endro") and the one cited in the foregoing analyses in connection with nr 28, nr 32 and nr 27 are the only two bubuka opaq-opaq in paṭet sanga which are used for more than one genḍing.

"Barang Ganjur" has a ternary form: *A* including the bubuka genḍing and gongan I, *B* composed of gongan II, III, IV and V, and *A′* a return of the last two gongan of the bubuka genḍing in elaboration. The gongan in each of the three large parts are more closely related than the structural table can accurately indicate. The last half of "D" in gongan I is an elaboration of the last half of "B"; the first half of "H" in gongan III is like the first half of "F" in gongan II; the last half of "J" in gongan IV and V is like the last half of "H" of gongan III.

The colotomic pattern is regular for the ketawang form, and the kenḍang-two pattern typical of the ketawang is also regular.

Bubuka opaq-opaq

The introduction begins on lima and then, as pointed out above, features two incomplete T3 cadences. These cadences are further varied slightly by the repetition of barang alit before the final lima in each instance.

Bubuka genḍing

The first two (eight-measure) gongan of the bubuka genḍing are a simplification and augmentation in whole notes of the first three measures of the bubuka opaq-opaq beginning with barang alit. This melodic outline is continued in the first half of the third gongan (*i.e.* in the first kenongan), and the final kenongan uses the same pattern but in the last two bars employs half notes, so that lima is reached more quickly, and a short extension follows. The material is derived directly from the bubuka opaq-opaq and in essence amounts to an incomplete T3 cadence.

Gongan I

The first kenongan features the tone barang alit and the lima-barang interval (most clearly seen in the beginning of kenongan two). The second kenongan stresses lima and adds a short fantasy on the three tones of the bubuka opaq-opaq.

Gongan II

Kenongan begins with a T4—T3 formula (using barang alit) and offers the first suggestion that gulu may have been intentionally withheld from the bubuka opaq-opaq because here it is very conspicuous. Lima is reiterated and followed by a T2 formula. This is extended in kenongan two, where nem assumes some prominence.

Gongan III, IV, V

Gongan III through gongan V are rather free fantasies in which the three notes of the bubuka opaq-opaq appear with some regularity and are interspersed with melismatic passages covering the whole scale.

Gongan VI, VII

The last two gongan can be considered together. They are an elaboration of the last two gongan of the bubuka genḍing in which the original whole-note values now become half notes. There is also one other important difference. The bubuka genḍing was seen to be a rather direct augmentation (and simplification) of the bubuka opaq-opaq — including the omission of gulu. In the last two gongan the missing gulu is supplied in the elaborated T3 cadences for three successive kenongan; the final kenongan returns to a pattern (in diminution) similar to that which closes the bubuka genḍing (and bubuka opaq-opaq), *i.e.* gulu is omitted from the cadence.

General Summary

The bubuka opaq-opaq is composed of two T3 cadences from which the dominant gulu has been omitted. The appearance of gulu in the last two gongan suggests that its omission from the bubuka opaq-opaq was prompted by artistic choice. The thematic material of the genḍing is derived directly from the introduction in some gongan and is a very free fantasy in others. The three critical sections are related melodically and cadentially.

The melodic importance of lima and gulu is typical of paṭet sanga genḍing. Nem is used as a tone of transition, barang is important as a tone of melodic variety and a cadential support, and ḍaḍa is used chiefly as a passing and neighbor note.

"Wani-Wani"

Ladrang nr 12 — sléndro paṭet sanga

bubuka opaq-opaq

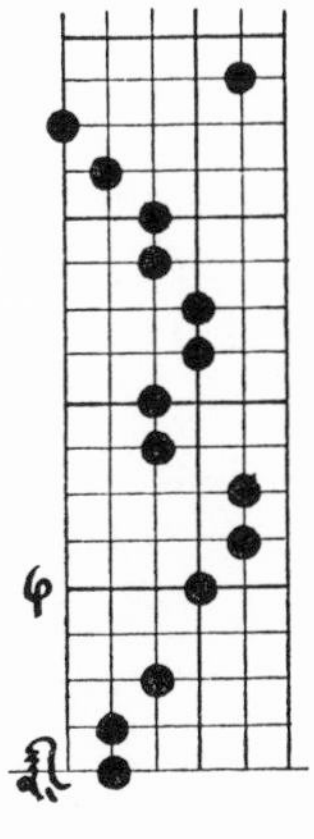

B.Op.				$intro_g$	
B.Gd.	A_g	A_g	B_n	C_l	A
GN I	D_l	D_l	E_d	F_g	B
GN II	G_g	G_g	H_n	C_l	A′

Kenḍang 2

transcribed (see appendix p. 280)

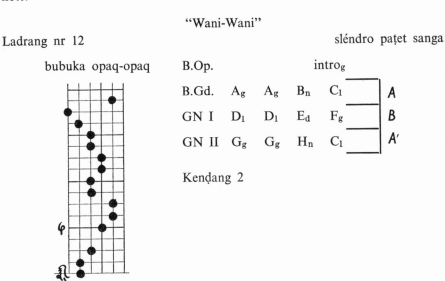

The most interesting aspect of "Wani-Wani" is the difficulty it seems to cause collectors and scribes in assigning it to the correct paṭet. Although I shall leave the regular procedure followed in the analyses and pursue principally the question of paṭet indications, one factor should be noted: the return of the *A′* section in the final gongan is an elaboration of the first three kenongan of the bubuka genḍing and an almost exact repetition of the fourth kenongan.

Bubuka opaq-opaq

The introduction begins with a dominant of the dominant, *i.e.* nem to gulu. This is followed by an extended T2 formula which finally concludes with the half note lima in bar four. From lima a short scale passage descends to gulu in a T1 cadence. This is the *first* T1 cadence we have found at the close of one of the three critical sections and therefore becomes a little suspect.

There is yet another way in which this introduction might be regarded. Since the piece was originally assigned to paṭet nem, one might consider the scale passage beginning with nem in bar three (ignoring the half-note value of lima) and descending to gulu as a typical T1 cadence from dominant to tonic in *paṭet nem*. The short passage from gulu of bar one to lima of bar two — in paṭet nem the tonic to the second gong tone — was established in Chapter IV as not an unusual feature of a paṭet nem introduction. The first three notes — nem, barang, gulu — could also be said to be a T3 cadence in paṭet nem, *i.e.* dominant ascending to tonic.

As will be shown farther on, I believe that such an interpretation is only partly justified, in fact, is too much simplified.

Bubuka genḍing

The melodic essence of kenongan one and two is the interval lima-gulu — the tonic-dominant of paṭet sanga. Including the final note of kenongan two, kenongan three begins with a T2 formula going to the dominant gulu and ending on nem, the dominant of the dominant. The fourth kenongan continues the tone nem which leads to the dominant gulu, a leap up to lima and then a T4 formula ascending from lima to gulu. This is followed by a T3 cadence descending from gulu to lima, which closes the bubuka genḍing. The entire gongan is *lima-gulu* centered and closes with a *regular T3 paṭet sanga cadence.*

Gongan I

The first two kenongan are identical and begin with an elaboration of a paṭet sanga T3 formula and end with a T2 formula on lima. The third kenongan is a kind of fantasy on the three tones of the paṭet sanga T1 (or T2) formula, namely, gulu, ḍaḍa, lima. Kenongan four features lima at the midpoint and gulu at the end and consists of three interrupted scale passages built on the T1—T2 cadence. The entire gongan is constructed principally of *paṭet sanga formulas.*

Gongan II

This gongan is an elaboration of the bubuka genḍing and therefore shows the same melodic characteristics, ending with a paṭet sanga T3 cadence.

In conclusion we can say that the melodic course of "Wani-Wani" shows the gulu-lima interval to be the principal fifth-interval of the piece. In addition to this the final notes of each gongan are alternately gulu and lima. The kenongan subdivisions suggest further the importance of the gulu-lima interval, and the tone nem in the bubuka genḍing and gongan II and the tone ḍaḍa in gongan I occupy a lesser importance. Finally, the T3 cadences closing the bubuka genḍing and the final gongan are the most conclusive evidence that "Wani-Wani" is indeed in paṭet sanga.

But there is yet another twist to the story of "Wani-Wani". An almost identical version appears in Groneman's *De Gamelan te Jogyakarta.* [1] If the reader is interested in making a comparison, a few hints may save him time. Although J. P. N. Land (who made the transcriptions) shows a bubuka opaq-opaq, his version of the piece actually begins (according to our version) with the last note of the second kenongan of the bubuka genḍing and continues with minor deviations (especially in note values) to the second gong (the first gong in Land's transcription). Land's gongan II is a simplified version of our gongan I, and his gongan IV is almost identical with our gongan I; his gongan III and V are very close to our gongan II. In short, Land has written out two of the specified eight repetitions of gongan I and II, the first containing a simplification of (our) gongan I.

J. S. Brandts Buys devotes considerable time and space to the correction of the transcriptions found in Groneman's publication, [2] but he misses two rather conspicuous points in connection with "Wani-Wani". In the first place he says that the bubuka opaq-opaq of the kraton script (the original manuscript from which our collection was copied) is much shorter than the one given by Land and is therefore not suitable for comparison. [3] As indicated above, the version in the Groneman collection does *not* have a bubuka opaq-opaq (by comparison to the kraton script) but begins in the middle of the bubuka genḍing. In the second place Brandts Buys indicates that the kraton-script version is in sléndro paṭet nem and attempts to show that Land has incorrectly labeled his version by assigning it to sléndro *paṭet manyura!* [4]

In regard to Brandts Buys' general criticism I can agree that Land's transcription is erroneously labeled. But I add further that the kraton version is also incorrectly labeled as sléndro paṭet nem. Finally I submit that all three of these versions are practically identical and clearly indicate that the proper paṭet classification is *sléndro paṭet sanga.*

---

1) (Amsterdam: Johannes Müller, 1890), p. 72.
2) See bibliography: *Djawa*, XIV, XV, XVI, XVIII.
3) *Djawa*, XVIII (1938), 182.
4) *Ibid.*, 207—8.

There is one more point to consider. The paṭet transposition table appearing in the appendix (p. 260) shows that "Wani-Wani" appears in major collections twice in paṭet sanga (one being my correction of the Jogyanese manuscript), once in paṭet manyura (*i.e.* in the Groneman collection, shown above to be incorrectly labeled) and finally once in *pélog paṭet nem.* Although it is too early to discuss fully the implications of paṭet transposition, it is significant that the general rule for transposition from one tonal system to another (*e.g.* pélog to sléndro) indicates that a *pélog paṭet nem* genḍing is preferred, if transposed to sléndro, in *sléndro paṭet sanga* and *vice versa.* [1])

Now to return to a discussion of the bubuka opaq-opaq: it was pointed out that the T1 formula in paṭet sanga is not likely as a *closing* cadence; a paṭet nem interpretation was weakened by the half-note value of lima beginning bar four. I should like to venture the following opinion regarding the possible history of "Wani-Wani".

Perhaps the *original* genḍing was in *pélog paṭet nem;* it was then transposed not to its parallel sléndro paṭet (sanga) but to sléndro *paṭet nem* (a lesser transposition practice sometimes used). The original *sléndro* version was therefore in paṭet nem. Subsequently it was in turn transposed to sléndro paṭet sanga (where it should have been in the first place) *with the retention of the original sléndro bubuka opaq-opaq,* i.e. in paṭet nem, and the time value of one or more notes of the introduction was altered to make it more acceptable in paṭet sanga. Perhaps because the original *sléndro* version and the original *pélog* version were both in *paṭet nem* the piece has erroneously born this label, even though the three versions mentioned above indicate a preference for "Wani-Wani" in sléndro *paṭet sanga,* the *parallel* paṭet of pélog paṭet nem.

In support of this supposition I give below the bubuka opaq-opaq transposed a fifth lower. This not only shows an acceptable paṭet sanga T3 cadence (note the misplaced weight of the half note in bar four caused by the "adjustment" of the former paṭet nem version to paṭet sanga) but also provides a suitable basis of comparison for the melodic material of the genḍing itself.

Summary and Conclusions

The fundamental compositional practices of paṭet sanga genḍing can be determined by summarizing the chief elements of each of the twenty-two pieces. Four tables similar to those used in the summary of paṭet nem will be suitable.

---

1) See further pp. 127—8.

Although a brief indication of the purpose of each table is given below, a full explanation can be had by referring to the corresponding tables in Chapter IV.

Table I indicates the architectonic form of the genḍing and the correspondence between the bubuka genḍing and the final gongan on the basis of identical kenongan (the three ketawang are not included).

Table I

Title	Form	B.Gd./final GN
nr 12 — Wani-Wani	Intro — ternary	1
„ 18 — Udan Sejati	„ — binary	0
„ 19 — Uluk-Uluk	„ — ternary	2
„ 20 — Wirangrong	„ — „	4
„ 21 — Jangkrik Ginggong	„ — binary	0
„ 22 — Dempel	„ — ternary	4
„ 23 — Konchang	„ — rounded binary	1
„ 24 — Gondo Yonni	„ — „ „	2
„ 25 — Sobrang Barang	„ — ternary	4
„ 26 — Sulung Ḍayung	„ — rounded binary	1
„ 27 — Chlunṭang	„ — through-composed	0
„ 28 — Madu Bronto	„ — ternary	2
„ 29 — Gondo Suli	„ — through-composed	1
„ 30 — Bujang Daleman	„ — period repeated	4
„ 31 — Bronto Moro	„ — ternary	2
„ 32 — Bronto Asmoro	„ — binary	1
„ 33 — Bronto Kingkin	„ — ternary	2
„ 34 — Gaḍung Mlaṭi	„ — binary	0
„ 36 — Kumandang	„ — „	0
„ 37 — Laras Dijo	„ — ternary	ketawang
„ 39 — Barang Ganjur	„ — „	„
„ 40 — Gajah Endro	„ — through-composed	„

Summary: 10 genḍing are ternary
8 „ „ binary
3 „ „ through-composed
1 ladrang is a period repeated

On the basis of identical kenongan appearing in the bubuka genḍing and the final gongan: of the 19 ladrang 14 have at least 1 kenongan identical in both sections, and of these 14:

4 ladrang have 4 kenongan identical in both sections
5 „ „ 2 „ „ „ „ „
5 „ „ 1 „ „ „ „ „

In these ladrang the last kenongan of the bubuka genḍing and the closing kenongan of the piece are the same except in nr 32 (in which the repetition occurs in the second kenongan).

Table II indicates the patterns of kenongan repetition in a gongan and is arranged according to type. It shows the number of each type used in every ladrang (the ketawang are omitted).

Table II

Genḍing	ABCD	AABC	AABB	AAAB	AAAA
nr 12		3			
„ 18		5	2		
„ 19	4	1			
„ 20		1		2	
„ 21	4				
„ 22	1	5			
„ 23	1	2		2	
„ 24	5				
„ 25	4	2			
„ 26	5	1			
„ 27	1	1		1	
„ 28	3				
„ 29	2				
„ 30				2	
„ 31	3	2			
„ 32		5			
„ 33	5				
„ 34	3	2			
„ 36	4				
Total:	45	30	2	7	0

Summarized on the basis of a total of 84 gongan:

53.6%	repeat no kenongan				— ABCD
35.8	„	1	„		— AABC
2.3	„	2	„		— AABB
8.3	„	1	„	3 times	— AAAB

Table III presents a summary of the cadences closing the three critical sections of the genḍing. The indication "T3 + barang" or "T3 + T2" signifies a T3 cadence extented to the tone barang or by a T2 formula. "T3 — gulu" indicates a T3 cadence from which the tone gulu is apparently withheld deliberately and added at a later critical point (*e.g.* see the analysis of nr 39 and nr 23).

Table III

Gendịng	B.Op.	B.Gd.	Final GN
nr 12	T3 (trsp)	T3	T3
„ 18	T3 + T2	T3	T3 + T2
„ 19	T3	T3	T3
„ 20	T3	T3 + T1	T3 + T1
„ 21	T3 – nem	T3	T3
„ 22	T3	T3	T3
„ 23	T3 – nem	T3	T3
„ 24	T3	T3	T3
„ 25	T3 + barang (trsp)	T3	T3
„ 26	T3	T3	T3
„ 27	T3 + barang	T3	T3
„ 28	T3 + barang	T3	T3
„ 29	T3	T3	T3
„ 30	T2	T2	T2
„ 31	T3	T3	T3
„ 32	T3 + barang	T3	T3+barang
„ 33	T3	T3	T3
„ 34	T3	T3	T3
„ 36	T3	T3	T3
„ 37	T3	T3	T3
„ 39	T3 – gulu	T3 – gulu	T3+barang
„ 40	T3 – gulu	T3 – gulu	T3

In summary:	T3	T4	T1	T2	I/V	
B.Op.	21	0	0	1	0	= 95.5% T3
B.Gd.	21	0	0	1	0	= 95.5% T3
Final GN	21	0	0	1	0	= 95.5% T3

Table IV indicates the melodic importance of each tone. It was shown in the foregoing chapter that in pațet nem the tone lima functions as the tone of transition and is also used in cadential support of dominant and tonic. Although these two functions cannot always be distinguished categorically, the following applications are intended: the "tone of transition" generally refers to the tone used as a bridge between gongan, between the two halves of one gongan, between kenongan or even smaller units in the lively pieces; the "tone of cadential support" is generally a bridge tone appearing between tonic and dominant, which receives some emphasis in the variations and elaborations of the primary cadential formulas. The tone of transition in pațet sanga is sometimes shared by both nem and barang and is indicated in the column headed "Trans". In the individual analyses barang was seen in the function of cadential support, although sometimes there appeared to be no especial tone serving in this capacity. The emphasis of barang in cadential passages may be created by repetition, by its frequent appearance as a neighbor of gulu or occasionally by its usage as the ultimate note of a cadential extension. This cadential emphasis also gives barang a secondary melodic importance; the two functions, cadential support and melodic variety, will be indicated under the heading "Mel. Var."

The other column headings are the same as those used for Table IV of patet nem.

Table IV

Genḍing	Final	Pr.5th	Trans.	Mel.Var.	Pancher	Q-pancher
nr 12	lima	lima-gulu	nem	barang		lima
,, 18	,,	,, ,,	nem/barang	,,		gulu/nem/ barang
,, 19	,,	,, ,,	nem	,,	ḍaḍa/barang	
,, 20	gulu	,, ,,	,,			nem
,, 21	lima	,, ,,	nem/barang	barang		
,, 22	,,	,, ,,	,, ,,	,,		
,, 23	,,	,, ,,	nem	,,		
,, 24	,,	,, ,,	barang	,,		
,, 25	,,	,, ,,	nem/barang	,,		
,, 26	,,	,, ,,	,, ,,	nem		
,, 27	,,	,, ,,	nem	barang		barang
,, 28	,,	,, ,,	,,	,,		
,, 29	,,	,, ,,	nem/barang	nem		
,, 30	,,	,, ,,	nem		barang	
,, 31	,,	,, ,,	nem/barang	barang		
,, 32	barang	,, ,,	,, ,,	,,	barang	
,, 33	lima	,, ,,	,, ,,	,,		barang
,, 34	,,	,, ,,	,, ,,	,,		
,, 36	,,	,, ,,	,, ,,	,,		barang
,, 37	,,	,, ,,	,, ,,	,,		gulu
,, 39	barang	,, ,,	nem	,,		barang
,, 40	lima	,, ,,	,,	,,		
Summary:	lima 19 gulu 1 barang 2	lima-gulu	nem/barang	barang	barang	variable

Of the 20 genḍing using either lima or gulu as the final note 95.0% end on lima and 5.0% on gulu.

The above summaries together with the details emphasized in the individual analyses establish certain consistent practices. Some of these, *e.g.* the separate functions of the three gong tones, are similar to those of paṭet nem. A detailed comparison, however, will be reserved for Chapter VII.

Table I indicates that the paṭet sanga genḍing are about evenly divided between ternary and binary forms. The melodic relationship between the bubuka genḍing and the final gongan is rather strong on the basis of identical kenongan, and the individual analyses show that melodic similarity often exists when the kenongan of the two sections are not identical. The detailed analyses also reveal that the bubuka opaq-opaq provides the basis of thematic material for melodic development in the body of the genḍing. These two considerations together establish a strong melodic relationship among the three critical sections. The equally strong cadential relationship of these three parts can be seen from the figures in Table III.

The percentages summarizing Table III establish the T3 cadence, a descending scale passage from dominant to tonic, as typical of paṭet sanga genḍing. Rarely one of the tones of this formula is omitted from the cadence of the bubuka opaq-opaq (once also in the bubuka genḍing, *viz.* nr 39) but appears at the following critical point in a full cadence. Occasionally the T3 cadence is extended by a T1 or T2 formula. The T4 cadence does not appear at any of the three critical points but may be found within the genḍing, *e.g.* as shown in the bubuka opaq-opaq of nr 24 and nr 18. The four cadences are given below, and the tone barang has been included in the T1 and T2 formulas (+) on the assumption that the second gong tone may be an essential part of the cadential formula.

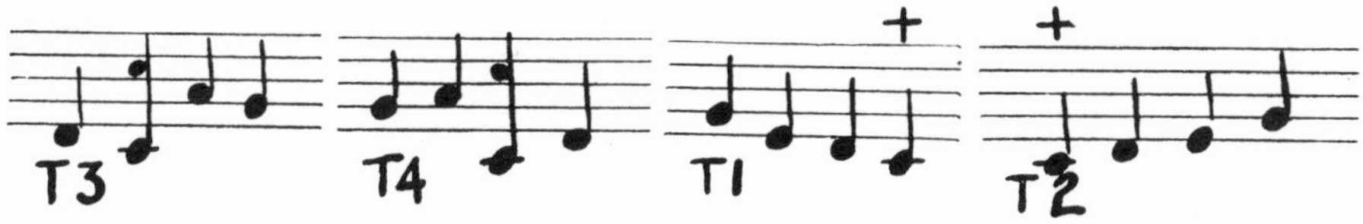

The summary of Table IV establishes lima as the preferred final note, and its fifth, gulu, appears once in that capacity. The second gong tone barang is used twice as a final note preceded, in both instances, by a T3 cadence and therefore resulting in a regular resolution with an extension to barang. Only the three gong tones appear as final notes. The important fifth-interval is lima-gulu. The second gong tone barang has some importance in its cadential support of lima and gulu created through the emphasis of barang in elaborations of the formula. Barang also functions as a tone of melodic variety, shares the honors with nem as a tone of transition, and serves as a true pancher. In conclusion, the three gong tones have the primary importance: first gong tone lima as "tonic", dasar gulu as its „dominant", and second gong tone barang as a cadential support for tonic and dominant and as a tone of melodic variety.

Nem is used as a tone of transition and sometimes appears as a dominant of the dominant gulu in the formula:

or

To avoid confusion with the T1 and T2 cadences of paṭet nem this formula is not used at important structural points. Perhaps the secondary-dominant role of nem is also intended by the following variation of the T3 formula (*e.g.* see the bubuka opaq-opaq of nr 18):

Ḍaḍa is the one tone of the five which is rather slighted, appearing as a passing or neighbor note with an occasional secondary importance in relation to nem. Although in one genḍing ḍaḍa is named along with barang as a true pancher, this is a very rare occurrence. [1]

The pedal note or quasi-pancher is variable.

A brief summary of the principal points:

1. The bubuka opaq-opaq is a particular elaboration, combination or variation of cadential formulas, the principal cadence being the T3 formula. The bubuka opaq-opaq provides the basis of thematic development for the entire genḍing.
2. Through the thematic development of the bubuka opaq-opaq the T3 cadential formula becomes the melodic framework of the genḍing. The particular variation of that formula in the bubuka opaq-opaq accounts for the distinctiveness of the introduction and consequently the genḍing itself.
3. The three critical sections of the genḍing — the bubuka opaq-opaq, the bubuka genḍing and the final gongan — are closely related melodically and cadentially.
4. The "inner gongan" may be related to the bubuka genḍing, may be a distinct development of the melodic material, may be a combination of these two conditions or may be chiefly of a transitional nature. Any of the paṭet sanga cadences may be found at these inner gongan.
5. The T3 cadence is typical of paṭet sanga genḍing, but any of the theoretical formulas between tonic and dominant may be found within the body of the piece.
6. The three gong tones occupy the principal melodic and structural positions: the "tonic" lima; its "dominant" gulu; and the tone of cadential support and melodic variety, barang. Nem is used as a tone of transition, sometimes sharing this function with barang. Ḍaḍa is used as a passing or neighbor note.

---

1) *MJ*, I, 168.

VI.

SLÉNDRO PAṬET MANYURA.

THE THREE PRINCIPAL TONES of paṭet manyura are the dasar ḍaḍa, the first gong tone nem and the second gong tone gulu. The terms "tonic" and "dominant" will again be used to designate the two tones of the principal fifth-interval. The general procedure followed in the analyses will be similar to that used in paṭet nem and sanga.

Analysis of the Genḍing

Nr 41 through nr 60 of the Jogyanese manuscript are ladrang listed in paṭet manyura. Although this number includes twenty different titles, it represents only seventeen different compositions. The ladrang nr 47 "Gaja Bengok" and nr 48 "Machan Géro" are identical; nr 49 "Machan Angop" and nr 50 "Simo Nebak" are identical; and nr 53 "Panyutro" and nr 54 "Prawiro Tomo" are also identical. In the summaries and elsewhere, therefore, each of these three different ladrang will be referred to by a double number, *e.g.* nr 47—48, or by the double number and the two appropriate titles.

To these seventeen paṭet manyura genḍing will be added the ladrang nr 4 and nr 35 and the ketawang nr 38 which also seem to belong to this paṭet rather than to that one to which they were assigned by the scribe. Of the total number of twenty genḍing eight are presented in detailed analysis as representative examples, and the complete group is included in the statistical summaries.

"Gonjang"

Ladrang nr 57 — sléndro paṭet manyura

bubuka opaq-opaq

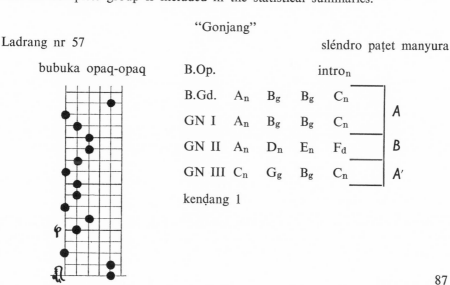

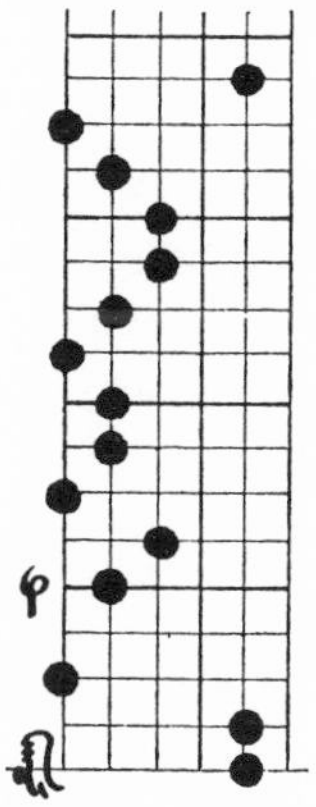

B.Op. intro$_n$

B.Gd.	A_n	B_g	B_g	C_n	A
GN I	A_n	B_g	B_g	C_n	
GN II	A_n	D_n	E_n	F_d	B
GN III	C_n	G_g	B_g	C_n	A′

kenḍang 1

transcribed (see appendix p. 280)

"Gonjang" has a ternary form with **A** consisting of the bubuka genḍing and gongan I, **B** of gongan II and **A′** of gongan III. Only the three gong tones appear at the kenongan divisions, and nem occupies the principal position at the close of the gongan.

Bubuka opaq-opaq

The bubuka opaq-opaq is built on two cadences. The T4 cadence of bars 1—2 is an ascending formula from tonic to dominant, and the T3 cadence is a descending scale from dominant to tonic, in this instance considerably extended. The repetition of gulu in bar three and its half-note value in bar four give this tone some importance in the T3 cadence. In bar three gulu is used in cadential support of ḍaḍa and in measure four in cadential support of both ḍaḍa and nem. The two tones beginning and ending the cadence, namely ḍaḍa and nem, are, of course, the two most important tones.

Nr 60 uses this same bubuka opaq-opaq and has a general melodic relationship to "Gonjang".

Bubuka genḍing, gongan I

The bubuka genḍing (and gongan I) is constructed from elements of the T3 cadence: the first kenongan states the complete formula; kenongan two and three are identical and reiterate the first two tones of the cadence, ḍaḍa and gulu; kenongan four begins with lima as a kind of bridge tone (this function will be more apparent in subsequent examples) and ends with ḍaḍa-barang(alit)-nem, the tone gulu not being repeated in the fourth kenongan.

The whole gongan might be considered an extension of the T3 formula of kenongan one or, in the restricted sense, the "cadence" may be described in terms of the fourth kenongan only, *i.e.* dominant-tonic.

Gongan II

The first kenongan is the same as that of the bubuka genḍing, namely, a T3 cadence. The second kenongan stresses the interval gulu-nem, an interval which seems to have a minor importance in the bubuka opaq-opaq due to the half-note value of gulu in bar four. Kenongan three continues the importance of the tone nem, and kenongan four consists of ḍaḍa with its neighbors.

Gongan III

The first kenongan is the same as the fourth kenongan of the bubuka genḍing, *i.e.* dominant-tonic. The second kenongan is based on bars 3—4 of the bubuka opaq-opaq and is extended in kenongan three. The third and fourth kenongan are identical to those same kenongan in the bubuka genḍing. The chief melodic points of the last three kenongan are: gulu, gulu, and ḍaḍa-nem.

General Summary

Typical of the usual "whole-note" piece the melodic material of this genḍing shows a general derivation from the bubuka opaq-opaq. The bubuka genḍing and the final kenongan have three identical kenongan, one of which is the final kenongan, and are therefore related melodically and cadentially. The cadences of these two sections could be considered in the broad sense as extended T3 formulas or in the restricted sense (last kenongan only) as a simple dominant-tonic (expressed in the statistical summary by (T3) V/I).

The melodic importance of each tone:

> *Nem* as the final tone of the bubuka opaq-opaq, the bubuka genḍing, gongan I and III and as the "tonic" of the primary fifth-interval is the most important tone.
> *Ḍaḍa* as the final tone of gongan II and the "dominant" of nem is second in importance.
> *Gulu* appears at kenongan divisions, is used in cadential support of nem and gulu and has some importance in the bubuka opaq-opaq.
> *Lima* is used as a neighbor note, perhaps as a bridge tone.
> *Barang* appears as a passing and neighbor note.

"Gonjang Sèrèt"

Ladrang nr 58 slèndro paṭet manyura

bubuka opaq-opaq

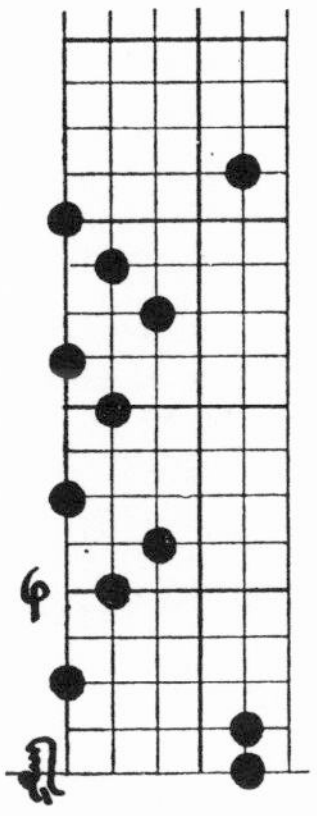

B.Op.			intro$_n$		
B.Gd.	A_n	B_g	C_g	D_n	A
GN I	E_n	F_g	C_g	D_n	
GN II	E_n	G_n	H_n	I_d	B
GN III	J_n	K_g	C_g	D_n	A′

kenḍang 1

transcribed (see appendix p. 281)

The ternary form of "Gonjang Seret" is less regular in the length of its three parts than most genḍing: **A** consists of two and a half gongan, *i.e.* the bubuka genḍing, gongan I and the first half of gongan II. The last half of gongan II and the first half of gongan III comprise the **B** section. The **A′** section is the last half of gongan III. The kenongan of the **A** section are related in the following way: "F" is an elaboration of "B", and the first half of "G" is similar to "F". The kenongan "H" which begins the **B** section is precisely the same pattern as "C" except that it appears a fifth higher, as though the melody had modulated.

Bubuka opaq-opaq

The bubuka opaq-opaq of "Gonjang Sèrèt" is very much like that of nr 57 "Gonjang". It is perhaps no accident that their titles are also similar. (*Gonjang* means "to swing or to rock", and *gonjang sèrèt* "to swing in a circle") [1]. The cadential statements of nr 58 are more simply achieved than in nr 57, and beyond that the two introductions are the same. The development of the two genḍing, however, is quite different from the standpoint of elaboration. Nr 57 is a whole-note piece; nr 58 has the quarter note as a basic rhythmic unit and includes some sixteenth-note passages. It is worthy of note, on the other hand, that the tones appearing at the kenongan divisions of both genḍing are identical.

The bubuka opaq-opaq consists of an extended T4 cadence and a simple T3 formula. The tone gulu appears as a half note in measure two and again at the beginning of bar four.

Bubuka genḍing

The first kenongan consists of a T3 formula in whole notes. The basic unit becomes the half note in kenongan two which begins with a reiteration of the dominant ḍaḍa, followed by tonic and a T4 cadence. This formula and the extension following are an augmentation of the beginning of the bubuka opaq-opaq. In kenongan three and four the basic unit is the quarter note, and the eight measures are an elaboration and extension of a T3 cadence. The figure used forward and in retrograde is from bar two (or bars 3—4) of the bubuka opaq-opaq. The cadence is extended in the last half of kenongan four by a T1 and T2 cadence. As can be seen from the example below, the T2 formula causes a delay or interruption in the final statement of the T3 cadence which is finally completed in the last measure of the kenongan.

[1] *Javaans-Nederlands Handwoordenboek*, (Groningen: J. B. Wolters, 1938).

(The two sixteenth notes on ḍaḍa are an example of *ngenchot*. In the checkered script a dot appears on the line of beat one, the line of beat two, and the space in between these two lines. The first two tones are muted immediately after the keys are struck (indicated by a connecting tie), and the third, i.e. beat two, is allowed to sound. It would be correct theoretically to represent this by two eighth notes followed by a quarter; but the sound has the effect given above [1]). The melodic weight of gulu foreshadowed in the bubuka opaq-opaq might account for the slight variation in this final T3 cadence which returns to gulu before the leap up to nem, an example of second gong tone in cadential support of tonic.

The material of the bubuka genḍing is derived from the bubuka opaq-opaq.

Gongan I

The first kenongan may be considered either as a continuation of the final four-note figure of the bubuka genḍing (now in half notes) or as a variation and elaboration of the T3 cadence. In view of the fact that the second kenongan is quite clearly an elaboration of kenongan two of the bubuka genḍing and that kenongan three and four are identical to those of the bubuka genḍing, it seems probable that kenongan one can be considered in that same relationship.

Gongan II

The first kenongan is the same as that of gongan I. The first half of kenongan two is the same as that corresponding section of gongan I (a reiteration of ḍaḍa). The second half of kenongan two begins with the tone lima (perhaps as a tone of transition), followed by the tonic-dominant closing with a T1 formula. In the third kenongan this same three-note scale, lima-nem-barang, begins the *B* section. The pattern of this kenongan is exactly the same as that of kenongan three of gongan I except that it lies a fifth higher. The tone barang alit is used in reiteration as a tone of melodic variety. Lima serves as a tone of transition to kenongan four and runs like a tonal thread through this kenongan, always on the unimportant beats of the measure. Kenongan four consists of a chain of T1 and T2 cadences which were first introduced as an extension of the T3 cadence closing the bubuka genḍing.

Gongan III

Kenongan one is an elaboration of a T1 and T2 formula. Kenongan two continues to stress nem and ḍaḍa in the first two bars with a T1 and T2 formula;

[1] Cf. *MJ*, I, 353.

this is followed by a figure in the third measure which, through the interval gulu-nem, leads to a closing T1 formula extended to gulu-barang-gulu, *i.e.* the beginning of a T3 formula. This figure is reiterated in the last two kenongan which finish with a T3 cadence. The last two kenongan are identical to those of the bubuka genḍing.

General Summary

The melodic material of the *A* and *A′* sections is closely derived from the bubuka opaq-opaq. The material of the *B* section is quite free. The three critical sections are related melodically and cadentially.

The importance of each tone:

> *Nem* as the final note of the bubuka opaq-opaq, bubuka genḍing, gongan I and III and as the tonic of the primary cadential formulas is the most important tone.
>
> *Ḍaḍa* as the fifth of nem and as the final note of gongan II is second in importance.
>
> *Gulu* appears in cadential support of nem and ḍaḍa.
>
> *Lima* functions in the *B* section as a tone of transition.
>
> *Barang* appears as a tone of melodic variety in the *B* section and otherwise is used as a passing or neighbor note.

"Lèngkèr"

Ladrang nr 44 slėndro paṭet manyura

bubuka opaq-opaq

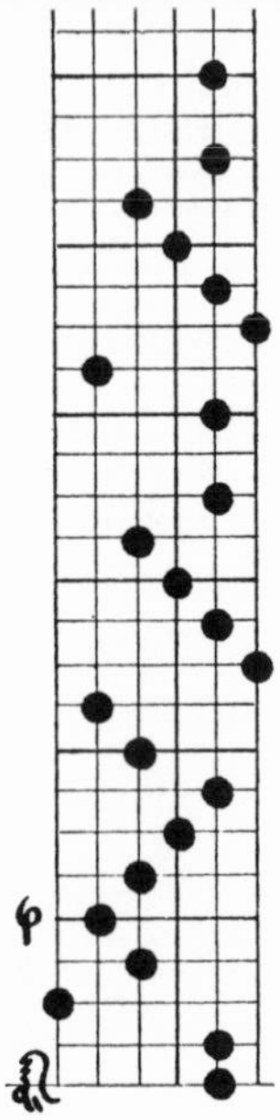

B.Op.				intro$_n$	
B.Gd.	A_n	A_n	A_d	B_n	
GN I	A_n	A_n	A_d	B_n	*A*
GN II	A_n	A_n	A_d	B_n	
GN III	C_b	D_n	E_n	F_d	*B*
GN IV	G_n	H_n	I_d	B_n	
GN V	J_n	H_n	I_d	K_b	*A′*
GN VI	L_n	M_n	N_d	O_n	

kenḍang 2

transcribed (see appendix p. 282)

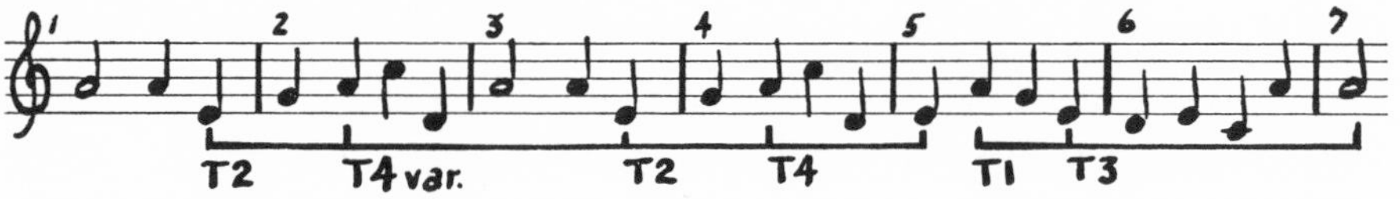

"Lèngkèr" has a ternary form. *A* consists of the bubuka genḍing, gongan I and II; *B* consists of gongan III, IV and V; and *A′* consists of gongan VI – actually a simplification of the bubuka genḍing. The structural table shows a prominence of nem and ḍaḍa at kenongan divisions and the complete absence of gulu.

Bubuka opaq-opaq

The rather long bubuka opaq-opaq features the three gong tones in a series of cadential formulas. As indicated by the brackets each of the four theoretical possibilities is represented. The T4 variation of bars 2–3 could also be interpreted as an incomplete T4 rather than a variation in which nem is repeated before sounding ḍaḍa. I am personally inclined to the latter interpretation because of the parallel structure of bars 1–2 and bars 3–4, the immediate goal of which is revealed at the beginning of bar five in the termination of a T4 cadence. Perhaps the repetition of ḍaḍa in the final T3 cadence is intended as a "dominant" answer or echo or equivalent of the "tonic" interruption of the T4 cadence of bar three.

Bubuka genḍing, gongan I, II

The bubuka genḍing and the first two gongan are identical. Kenongan one and two are identical and begin with the dominant ḍaḍa, followed by an almost exact augmentation of the measures 1–2 and the tone nem of bar three of the bubuka opaq-opaq (barang ageng, *i.e.* barang geḍé, being used instead of the octave higher). Kenongan three continues in exactly the same way except that it is quoting the second version of this figure from the bubuka opaq-opaq, which begins in bar three and ends with the first note (ḍaḍa) of bar five. The first two kenongan and the third kemongan, therefore, are identical except for the final note which is nem in the former and ḍaḍa in the latter. Kenongan four continues the augmentation of the bubuka opaq-opaq with the addition of an extra gulu in the last measure of the T3 cadence. The bubuka genḍing, gongan I and II are almost a literal quotation (in augmentation) of the bubuka opaq-opaq. The three gong tones are featured; and gulu, as the penultimate note of each kenongan, is used in cadential support of nem and ḍaḍa.

Gongan III

Kenongan one is based on the figure beginning with barang (alit) of bars 4–5 of the bubuka opaq-opaq and features barang, as a tone of melodic variety, and ḍaḍa. The first half of kenongan two is constructed on the figure beginning with ḍaḍa of bars 5–6, and the last half is taken from bars 3–4 and ends with a T1 formula. Kenongan three begins with a reiteration of lima, perhaps as a bridge tone, and continues with the gulu-nem scale of bars 5—6 (bubuka opaq-opaq) in retrograde. Although lima receives the major emphasis in the first half of kenongan three, it is revealed in its neighbor relation to ḍaḍa as the last half of the kenongan begins with the other neighbor note gulu and again sounds ḍaḍa in the start of a T2 formula. Kenongan four ends with a T1 cadence which is approached by ḍaḍa and its neighbors. The material is a free fragmentation of bars 5—6, the nem-gulu scale. The melodic material of the gongan is rather freely based on the bubuka opaq-opaq.

Gongan IV

All of kenongan one and the first half of kenongan two is based on bars 1—2 of the bubuka opaq-opaq, beginning with the tone ḍaḍa. The last half of kenongan two is a simple T3 cadence and corresponds to the end of the bubuka opaq-opaq. Kenongan three and four are an elaboration of bars 5—6 of the bubuka opaq-opaq, kenongan four being identical to that of the bubuka genḍing. All the material is derived from the bubuka opaq-opaq.

Gongan V

The whole of kenongan one is a variation of a T3 cadence (the position of ḍaḍa and lima in the first half of the kenongan is exactly reversed as compared with kenongan three of gongan III). The second kenongan is the same as that of gongan IV. Kenongan three is identical to that of gongan IV except for the last note which begins a further extension of the T3 cadence in kenongan four. Kenongan four is an elaboration and extension of a T3 cadence. The material of the gongan is based on the bubuka opaq-opaq.

Gongan VI

The final gongan is a simplification of the bubuka genḍing, the essential notes of the first two kenongan being a T1 formula and those of the third and fourth kenongan being a T3 cadence.

General Summary

The melodic material of the genḍing is based on the bubuka opaq-opaq. The three critical sections are related melodically and cadentially.

The melodic importance of each tone:

Nem as the final note of the bubuka opaq-opaq, the bubuka genḍing, gongan I, II, IV and VI and as the tonic of the principal fifth-interval is the most important tone.

Ḍaḍa as the final note of gongan III and the penultimate kenongan of all other gongan and as the dominant of nem is second in importance.

Gulu functions in cadential support of nem and ḍaḍa.

Lima has a minor importance as a tone of transition.

Barang is used as a passing or neighbour note and achieves some importance as a tone of melodic variety.

"Chèlèng Mogok"

Ladrang nr 51 sléndro paṭet manyura

bubuka opaq-opaq

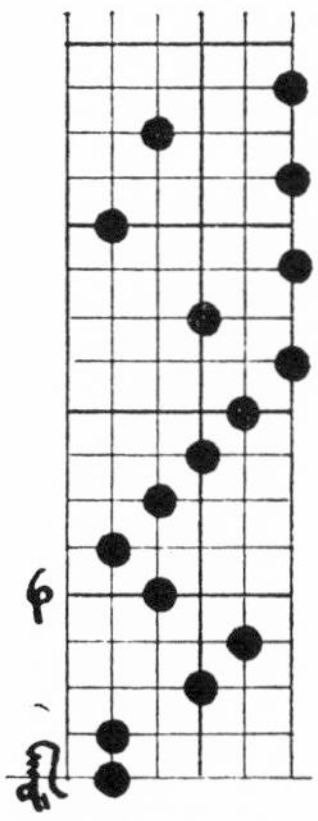

B.Op.				intro$_g$		
B.Gd.	A_g	A_g	A_g	B_n		*A*
GN I	C_n	C_n	C_n	D_g		*B*
GN II	A_g	A_g	A_g	B_n		*A*

kenḍang 2

transcribed (see appendix p. 283)

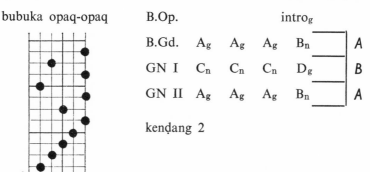

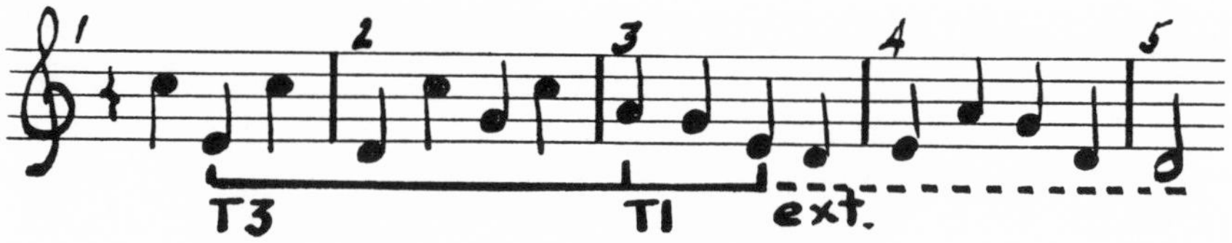

The ternary form of "Chèlèng Mogok" is quite regular: the bubuka genḍing forms the *A* section, gongan I the *B* section and gongan II the return of the *A* section. The kenongan divisions feature only nem and gulu, but a close inspection of the melodic material shows that gulu is appearing in its regular function as a cadential support for both nem and ḍaḍa.

Bubuka opaq-opaq

The introduction begins with a T3 cadence elaborated by a quasi-pancher on barang alit which in measure two also serves as part of the cadence itself. The cadence is further varied by the appearance of ḍaḍa in bar two as the lower neighhor of the final nem. The T1 formula beginning in measure three is an extension of the T3 cadence, which in turn is extended first by the neighbor note gulu in bar three and then by leap up to nem-lima-gulu.

Bubuka genḍing, gongan II

The first three kenongan of the bubuka genḍing and gongan II are taken from bar three of the bubuka opaq-opaq and consist of a T1 formula and its retrograde form T2 with lima functioning as a bridge tone between the ḍaḍa and gulu of each kenongan. The fourth kenongan begins with lima as a neighbor note leading to ḍaḍa, followed by the lower neighbor gulu and a T2 cadence beginning on nem and slightly extended in the last measure. This material is based on a retrograde version of bars 2—3—4 of the bubuka opaq-opaq.

Gongan I

The first three kenongan are identical and are an exact augmentation of the elaborated T3 cadence beginning the bubuka opaq-opaq (bars 1—2—3), barang serving as a quasi-pancher in all three kenongan. Kenongan four continues the bubuka opaq-opaq quotation in augmentation beginning with the second note of bar three and adds the tone ḍaḍa in the last measure.

General Summary

The melodic material of the genḍing is derived from the bubuka opaq-opaq. The three critical sections are related melodically and cadentially.

The melodic importance of each tone:

Nem as the final note of the bubuka genḍing and gongan II and as the tonic of the primary fifth-interval is the most important tone.
Ḍaḍa, although it does not appear as the final note of kenongan nor gongan, is prominent as the dominant of nem in the cadential formulas throughout the genḍing and therefore must be considered the second tone in importance.
Gulu as the final note of the bubuka opaq-opaq and gongan I as well as the kenongan divisions of the bubuka genḍing and gongan II has a considerable importance; it functions in cadential support of tonic and dominant.
Lima appears as a neighbor and passing note and has a minor importance as a bridge or transition tone.
Barang introduces some melodic variety as a passing note, neighbor note and quasi-pancher.

"Gaja Bengok" and "Machan Géro"

Ladrang nr 47—48 slèndro paṭet manyura

bubuka opaq-opaq

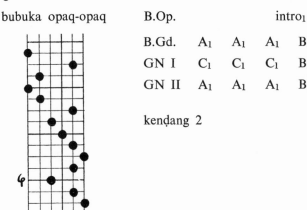

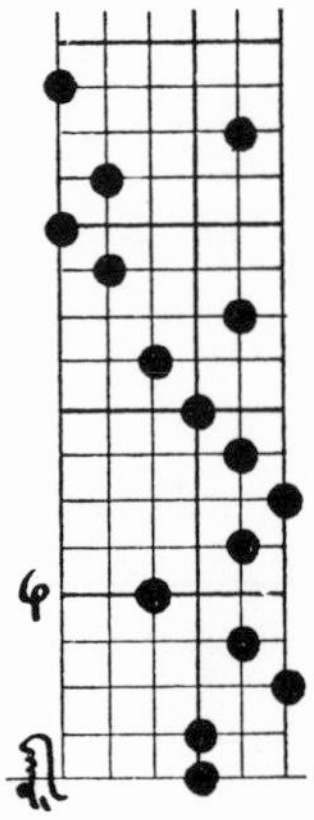

B.Op.			intro$_1$		
B.Gd.	A_1	A_1	A_1	B_1	A
GN I	C_1	C_1	C_1	B_1	B
GN II	A_1	A_1	A_1	B_1	A

kenḍang 2

transcribed (see appendix p. 284)

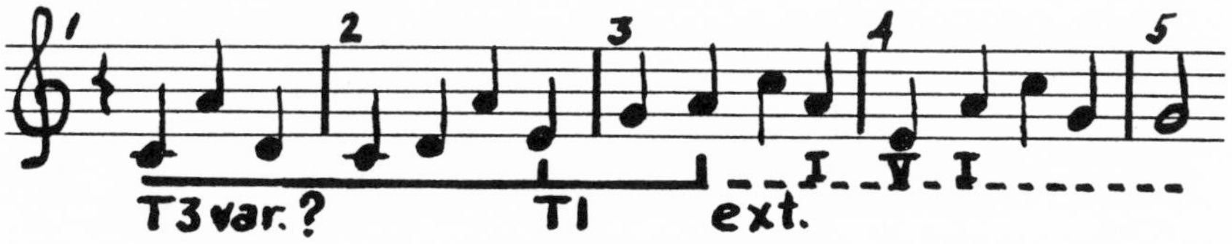

"Gaja Bengok" (or by its other title "Machan Géro") is interesting for two reasons: lima is the only tone used at kenongan and gongan divisions; the bubuka opaq-opaq presents a problem in its cadential intention.

The ternary form of the ladrang is symmetrical: the bubuka genḍing comprises the *A* section, gongan I the *B* section and gongan II the return of the *A* section.

Bubuka opaq-opaq

The first two measures of the introduction might be interpreted as a fragmentation and elaboration of a T3 cadence, even though the tone ḍaḍa is withheld until the last note of measure two. At that point ḍaḍa also begins a T1 formula which is extended by the repeated interval nem-ḍaḍa-nem, this in turn being extended by the two neighbors of nem: barang alit and lima.

There are several choices in the selection of the primary cadence. Beginning with measure four we might be satisfied that the simple dominant-tonic interval, with an extension to lima, is the principal cadence. Or, enlarging on this position slightly, we might include the last nem of bar three, yielding a I—V—I cadence extended. Another view of the matter might suggest that the T1 formula beginning in measure two is the principal cadence and that the V—I and continuation is merely an extension. Still another interpretation might indicate that the essential cadence is a variation of the T3 formula and that the rest of the introduction is an extension of this cadence. This last interpretation is somewhat strengthened by the manner in which the genḍing itself is developed melodically.

Bubuka genḍing

The first three kenongan of the bubuka genḍing are identical and consist of an elaboration of a T3 cadence to which is added the tone lima as a bridge or transition note. This figure is similar to the first two measures (including the first beat of bar three) of the bubuka opaq-opaq, described above as a variation of the T3 formula. The argument that these three kenongan and the beginning measures of the bubuka opaq-opaq are similar variations of the same thing (a T3 formula) is somewhat reinforced by the fact that the melodic material of kenongan four is an almost exact augmentation of the bubuka opaq-opaq beginning with the second note of bar three (an extra nem is added in the last measure). In other words, the first three kenongan are clearly based on the bubuka opaq-opaq from bar one to the first note of bar three, and the fourth kenongan continues the quotation of the introduction to the final lima. The whole gongan, therefore, is closely related to the bubuka opaq-opaq with the essential difference that the elaboration in the first three kenongan of the bubuka genḍing is more clearly identified as a variation of a T3 formula than the similar material of the introduction.

Gongan I

The first three kenongan of gongan I are a strict augmentation of the bubuka opaq-opaq (the initial barang is taken an octave higher) from the first note of bar one to the first note of bar three. The fourth kenongan (like that of the bubuka genḍing) completes the augmentation of the material from the bubuka opaq-opaq. In short, the whole gongan is an almost-perfect augmentation of the introduction.

Gongan II

Gongan II is the same as the bubuka genḍing.

General Summary

In essence the two **A** sections of this ladrang consist of an elaborate variation of a T3 cadence with a long extension. The **B** section has a very similar construction except that it quotes the opening T3 pattern of the bubuka opaq-opaq quite literally.

The introduction provides the melodic material for the whole of the genḍing. The three critical sections are related melodically and cadentially.

The importance of each tone:

Nem, although it never appears as the ultimate constituent of any of the kenongan or gongan, must still be indicated as the most important tone melodically because of its tonic position in the principal fifth-interval. The extension to lima no more nullifies its position in relation to the melodic movement than would an ending in Western music on the supertonic [1]) or dominant [2]) nullify an implied tonic.

Ḍaḍa in its fifth-relation to nem is second in importance.

Gulu is used in cadential support of nem and ḍaḍa throughout the genḍing.

Lima achieves a real importance as the final note of each subdivision, both kenongan and gongan. Its chief function, however, seems to be that of a bridge or transition tone, *e.g.* between the repeated kenongan of each gongan. This transitional role might also apply to lima as the final note of all gongan except the last, where it appears as an extension of nem (or actually the T3 cadences of the preceding kenongan).

Barang is used as a passing and neighbor note.

---

1) *e.g.* Yugoslavian folk songs; cf. Vinko Žganec and Nada Sremec, *Croatian Folk Songs and Dances*, (Zagreb: Seljačka Sloga, 1951), p. 229.

2) *e.g.* Spanish folk songs.

"Richik-Richik"

Ladrang nr 43 sléndro paṭet manyura

bubuka opaq-opaq

B.Op intro$_n$

B.Gd. A_n B_g C_g D_n } period

GN I E_n F_g G_g D^*_n } repeated

D* barang added as first note

kenḍang 2

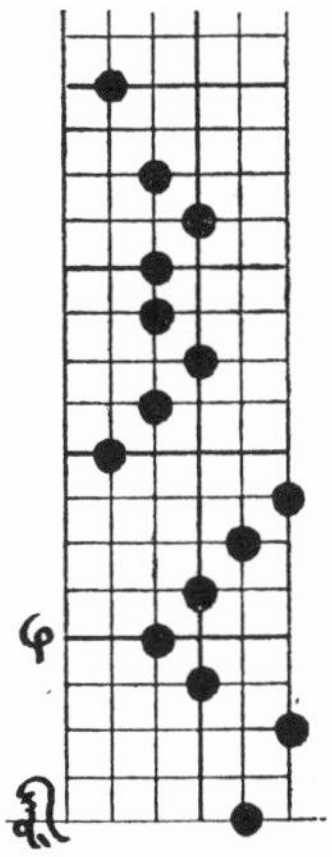

transcribed (see appendix p. 285)

"Richik-Richik" is a simple period or gongan which is repeated in elaboration. This genḍing has been selected primarily because of the cadential extensions used in the bubuka opaq-opaq and the following gongan. In the last example, nr 47—48, there were several interpretations possible in trying to determine where exactly a primary cadence ended and an extension began. In "Richik-Richik" the indications are more definite.

Bubuka opaq-opaq

The brackets below the transcription of the bubuka opaq-opaq indicate the T3 cadence followed by a long extension on nem. The two upper brackets label the two parts of this extension as a combination of a T1 and T2 formula. The reiteration of the tone ḍaḍa in bars one and two provides a rhythmic weight which firmly establishes this tone as the beginning of the T3 cadence; gulu begins the introduction as a cadential support for ḍaḍa. The theoretical cadence is satisfied when nem is reached in measure three, *i.e.* a descending scale passage from ḍaḍa (dominant) to nem (tonic). The continued descending scale to ḍaḍa and return to nem — or, expressed in the symbols of the above example, the T1—T2 formulas — are merely an extension on the tone nem.

Bubuka genḍing

The first three kenongan are in whole notes. The first repeats the ḍaḍa-nem interval, the second is based on the lima-ḍaḍa-gulu figure of bars 2—3 in the bubuka opaq-opaq, and the third kenongan is a scale passage from nem to gulu. The fourth kenongan is in half notes and consists of a T1 and T2 formula slightly extended. This, of course, comes from bars 3—4—5 of the bubuka opaq-opaq.

Gongan I

The first kenongan is based on bars 2—3—4 of the bubuka opaq-opaq. The second kenongan consists of ḍaḍa with its neighbors plus a T1 formula extended to gulu. Kenongan three begins with the T2—T1 formula (from the last two bars of the introduction) followed by the transition tone lima, leading to ḍaḍa and the beginning of a T3 cadence (bar two of the bubuka opaq-opaq). This cadence is completed in kenongan four and extended by a T1—T2 formula (bars 3—4—5 of the introduction). It was pointed out above that the first three kenongan are an elaboration of those of the bubuka genḍing. Through this elaboration it is possible to see the melodic intention of the bubuka genḍing.

General Summary

The bubuka opaq-opaq consists of an extended T3 cadence which provides the basis for melodic development in the rest of the genḍing. The three critical sections are related melodically and cadentially.

The melodic importance of each tone:

Nem as the final tone of the bubuka opaq-opaq and both gongan and as the tonic of the principal fifth-interval is the most important tone.
Ḍaḍa is second in importance as the dominant of nem.
Gulu serves in cadential support of nem and ḍaḍa.
Lima functions as a tone of transition.
Barang is used as a neighbor and passing note.

Ladrang nr 45 "Tlosor" sléndro paṭet manyura

bubuka opaq-opaq

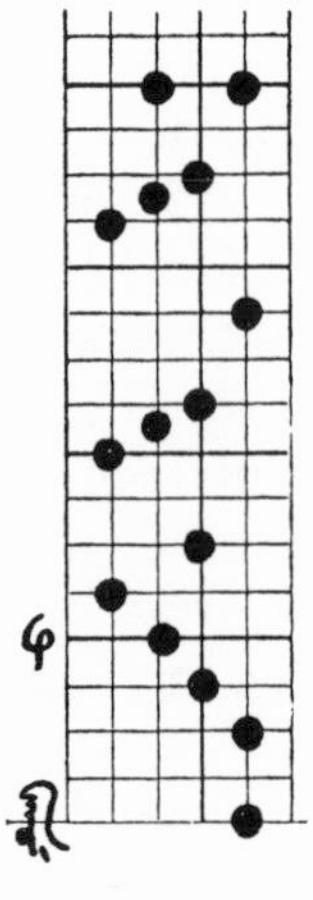

B.Op.			intro$_n$		
B.Gd.	A_b	A_n	A_b	B_n	A
GN I	A^*_n	A^*_n	A^*_n	B_n	A
GN II	A^*_n	A^*_n	A^*_n	B_n	A
GN III	A^*_n	A^*_n	C_n	D_g	A
GN IV	E_b	F_g	E_b	F_g	B
GN V	E_b	F_g	G_n	H_n	B
GN VI	A_n	A_n	A_n	B_n	A′

A* adds a rhythmic subdivision of lima in the third measure
kenḍang 2

transcribed (see appendix p. 285)

"Tlosor" has been included in the detailed analyses as an example of what appears to be a Javanese scherzo [1]). The "joking" aspect of the ladrang will best be understood by a brief analysis of each gongan. The usual summary will be omitted.

The ternary form has three sections of rather unequal lengths: *A* consists of the bubuka genḍing and the first three gongan ("C" and "D" are actually transitional kenongan); *B* consists of gongan IV and V; *A'* is a return of the bubuka genḍing in the form of gongan VI.

Bubuka opaq-opaq

The optional half notes appearing in the first measure are dominant and tonic, *i.e.* ḍaḍa and nem, the principal fifth-interval in paṭet manyura. The rhythmic patterns which follow the opening half notes, however, tend to emphasize nem and gulu. Certainly the tone ḍaḍa is slighted rhythmically until the first beat of measure four in which it appears at the beginning of the closing T2 cadence.

Bubuka genḍing

The three principal tones of paṭet manyura are studiously avoided in the first half of the bubuka genḍing until the last note, nem, of kenongan two (the midpoint of the gongan). The melody consists of a simple alternation of lima and barang alit, the two neighbor notes of nem, with a prolongation of lima (a whole note) occurring in the middle of each kenongan. The third kenongan continues the same pattern, ending on barang alit. In the fourth kenongan the tone lima leads to the first appearance of ḍaḍa which is then followed by gulu (in cadential support), another lima, another gulu and finally a T2 cadence from ḍaḍa to nem. Kenongan four is based on bars 2—3—4 of the bubuka opaq-opaq.

The melodic intention of the bubuka genḍing seems to be an avoidance of the principal tones until nem at the midpoint and the cadential material of the last kenongan. The first three kenongan suggest that something is being concealed from the listener — perhaps, if the T3 cadence is important in paṭet manyura, it is the identification of the paṭet itself. On the other hand, the deliberate repetitions of lima and barang alit manage, by this delay, to increase the importance of nem as the midpoint and final note of the gongan. Since we are analyzing

1) According to the *Javaans-Nederlands Handwoordenboek* „tlosor-tlosor" means to creep or crawl (as a snake or tree root over the ground).

paṭet manyura genḍing and because kenongan four ends with a T2 cadence (the important melodic points can be summarized as ḍaḍa-lima-ḍaḍa-nem), we might conclude that the importance of nem and the final cadence create no mystery regarding the identity of the paṭet.

But there also exists the possibility that this gongan suggests paṭet nem rather than paṭet manyura. With only nem and its two neighbors appearing in the first three kenongan there is actually no clear indication of paṭet. The tone nem, it must be remembered, is also important in paṭet nem as the dasar or dominant. To lead us further astray the tone gulu in the fourth kenongan could be interpreted as part of a regular T2 cadence ending on the paṭet-nem dominant, *i.e.* on the tone nem. If we re-examine the bubuka opaq-opaq from this paṭet nem orientation, a similar re-adjustment of cadences might take place. Beginning with nem of the first measure we could describe two successive gulu T1 cadences (to do this successfully, of course, we must ignore the alternate tone ḍaḍa given below the initial nem) followed by the paṭet-nem bridge-tone lima and a final gulu T2 cadence. The unusual rhythmic patterns of the bubuka opaq-opaq further point to this interpretation — in fact, in my opinion, so obviously that the idea becomes a little suspect.

But we shall come nearer the solution of our musical puzzle in the subsequent gongan.

Gongan I, II

Gongan I and II are identical and differ only slightly from the bubuka genḍing. The first three kenongan of gongan I and II are like those of the bubuka genḍing except for the following small changes: in each kenongan the whole note lima is replaced by a half note and two eighth notes, giving this tone an increased emphasis; the first and third kenongan of gongan I and II end on nem instead of barang alit, thereby strengthening the position of nem. Kenongan four is the same as that of the bubuka genḍing.

These two gongan, therefore, bring us no closer to the paṭet riddle.

Gongan III

The first two kenongan are the same as those of the preceding gongan I and II. The third kenongan consists of two T2 formulas (from the last measures of the bubuka opaq-opaq), each ending with a whole note on nem. Kenongan four consists of a T2 and T1 cadence extended to gulu. These last two kenongan, as a transition to the *B* section, begin to suggest (for the first time) paṭet manyura.

Gongan IV

Kenongan one and three and kenongan two and four respectively are identical. Half of the gongan (therefore one kenongan of each of the two pairs indicated above) is presented in the following example, with appropriate brackets designating the paṭet manyura cadences.

The example indicates that each half of gongan IV contains all four of the theoretical paṭet-manyura cadential formulas; and even with the addition of the final gulu (which, as seen in earlier paṭet manyura genḍing, is always an allowable extension) this melodic material could be nothing other than paṭet manyura.

Gongan V

The first two kenongan are the same as those of gongan IV (given in the example above). Kenongan three consists of a T2 formula followed by a reiteration of nem and its neighbors. The fourth kenongan begins with the transition tone lima leading to the dominant ḍaḍa and the second gong tone gulu, and the gongan closes with a T2 cadence. This gongan also confirms paṭet manyura.

Gongan VI

Except for two small changes the final gongan is the same as the bubuka genḍing, re-stating, as it were, the initial proposition of the musical riddle. The two changes are perhaps worthy of note. The final tone of kenongan one and kenongan three is now *nem* instead of the neutral or questioning barang alit which appears in the bubuka genḍing.

Observations

The following devices contribute to the mystery of paṭet in "Tlosor": 1) an ambiguous bubuka opaq-opaq which avoids both the T3 and T4 formulas; 2) an *A* section that continues the ambiguity and the avoidance of the T3 and T4 cadences; 3) a transition of two kenongan features the paṭet manyura T1 and T2 cadences quite clearly but still avoids the T3 and T4 formulas; 4) finally the T3 and T4 cadences establish paṭet manyura in the *B* section; 5) a return to ambiguity in the final gongan.

The three critical sections (usually models of paṭet construction) are ambiguous; and the middle section of the ternary form (normally the freest part of the genḍing) is a direct statement of the primary paṭet manyura cadential formulas.

"Liwung"

Ladrang nr 42 slendro paṭet manyura

bubuka opaq-opaq

original transposed

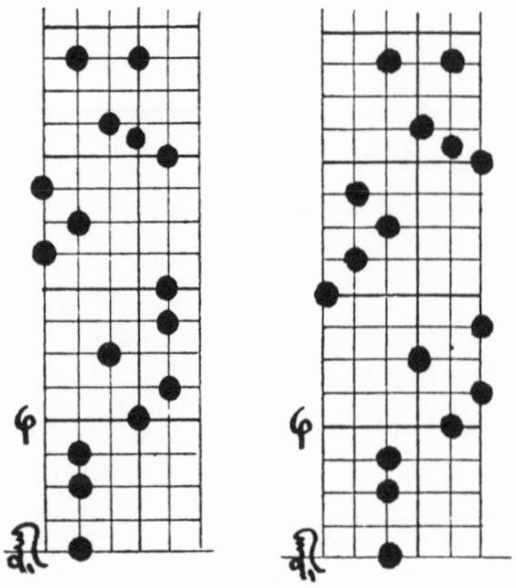

B.Op.				intro$_{g\ (d)}$	
B.Gd.	A_g	A_g	B_n	C_n	double period
B.Gd.	D_n	D_n	D_n	A^*_g	
GN I	A_g	A_g	B_n	C_n	repeated
GN II	D_n	D_n	D_n	A^*_g	

A* first note ḍaḍa instead of nem

kenḍang 2

transposed and transcribed (see appendix p. 286)

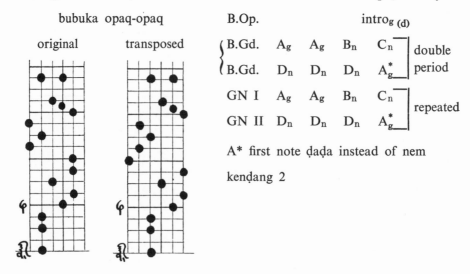

"Liwung" is another example which seems to have a bubuka opaq-opaq in the wrong paṭet, but it adds a complication to the question of paṭet transposition encountered earlier.

The form of the ladrang is a double period repeated, the first statement composed of a double bubuka genḍing (two gongan in length) and the second composed of gongan I and II. Gongan I and II are repeated eight times with a pancher on barang.

Bubuka opaq-opaq

The bracketed cadential formulas of the transposed and transcribed bubuka opaq-opaq given above indicate that a transposition of the original version (which is in paṭet sanga) one step higher produces a true paṭet manyura introduction. The conspicuous tonic-dominant construction needs no elucidation. It is worthy of note that this transposed version is almost identical to the bubuka opaq-opaq of the paṭet manyura ladrang nr 41 "Kondo" given below for the sake of comparison.

It is interesting, too, that nr 41 also has a double bubuka genḍing and that it is a whole-note genḍing.

Although the transposition of the "Liwung" introduction is justified for the reasons given above, there remains something of a problem as to how or why the original paṭet-sanga introduction came to be recorded in the checkered script. It was shown earlier that when a genḍing is transposed from its *original* paṭet to another paṭet, the *original* bubuka opaq-opaq may be retained, perhaps as a token of respect. The paṭet transposition table on p. 260, however, shows that "Liwung" is found in two collections in paṭet nem and in two others in paṭet manyura, but it is not listed in any of these sources in paṭet sanga [1]. Paṭet nem is not likely to be the original paṭet because a transposition of the paṭet sanga introduction to paṭet nem results in a weak bubuka opaq-opaq.

We can only surmise that the original genḍing was in pateṭ sanga and that for some reason — perhaps over a long period of time — it came to be preferred in paṭet nem or manyura, the original being lost through disuse.

The gongan

The first gongan of the bubuka genḍing and gongan I are idential; and they further complicate the paṭet gender of "Liwung". The first two kenongan are identical and consist of a *paṭet nem* T1 formula. The third kenongan features nem and the fourth kenongan features gulu (the dominant and tonic, respectively, of paṭet nem).

The second gongan of the bubuka genḍing and gongan II are identical; they are in paṭet manyura. The first three kenongan are the same and consist of a T3 cadence, the last of which is extended in kenongan four to ḍaḍa (the dominant) and gulu (the second gong tone).

Conclusion

As it is recorded in the kraton script, "Liwung" appears to be a mixture of all three sléndro paṭet. "Liwung" is also known in paṭet manyura played with a pancher on *ḍaḍa* instead of barang [2]; this change would certainly strengthen the paṭet manyura character.

---

1) N.B. This genḍing should not be confused with „Lawung" or „Lawoeng" which does appear in paṭet sanga but is a different piece; cf. Paul J. Seelig, *Genḍing Djawi* (Bandung: J. H. Seelig & Son, 1922), p. 88.

2) *MJ*, I, 168.

The preceding analyses show that the genḍing of paṭet manyura are more individual in their variations from the "norm" than the compositions of paṭet nem and sanga. The representative examples include cadential sections in which the principal cadence is often followed by an extension. In some instances the extension itself is a secondary cadential formula. The rhythmic patterns and different note values appearing in a single genḍing exhibit a greater variety in

Table I

Title	Form	Bd./Final GN
nr 4 — Sekar Pépé	Intro — rounded binary	4
„ 35 — Ladrang Kuwung	„ — ternary	4
„ 38 — Panji Ketawang	„ — „	ketawang
„ 41 — Kondo	„ — binary	1
„ 42 — Liwung	„ — double period (2 GN) repeated	4
„ 43 — Richik-Richik	„ — period repeated in elaboration	1
„ 44 — Lengker	„ — ternary	4 (simplified)
„ 45 — Tlosor	„ — „	4
„ 46 — Jagung-Jagung	„ — „	4
„ 47—48 — Gajah Bengok-Machan Géro	„ — „	4
„ 49—50 — MachanAngop-Simo Nebak	„ — „	4
„ 51 — Chèlèng Mogok	„ — „	4
„ 52 — Chèlèng Minggok	„ — „	4
„ 53—54 — Panyutro-Prawiro Tomo	„ — period repeated	4
„ 55 — Semar Mantu	„ — ternary	4
„ 56 — Chino Nagi	„ — „	4
„ 57 — Gonjang	„ — „	4
„ 58 — Gonjang Sèrèt	„ — „	2
„ 59 — Téjo	„ — through-composed	1
„ 60 — Sekar Tanjun	„ — ternary	3

Summary: 14 genḍing are ternary
2 „ „ binary
3 „ „ a period repeated
1 „ is through-composed

paṭet manyura than in the other two paṭet. More freedom in the selection of the final note, the use of non-typical melodic sections (*e.g.* nr 45), and the greater melodic elaboration characteristic of the livelier nature of paṭet manyura pieces tend further to set this paṭet apart from the other two.

The basis of compositional practice, however, can be isolated by a summary of the principal features of each of the twenty paṭet manyura genḍing. The four tables employed in the two preceding paṭet summaries will again suffice. A brief indication of the function of each table is repeated below, and a full explanation can be found in Chapter IV.

Table I indicates the architectonic form of the genḍing and the correspondence

Table II

Genḍing	ABCD	AABC	AABB	AAAB	AAAA
nr 4		3		2	
„ 35	2		3		
„ 41	5	1			
„ 42		2		2	
„ 43	2				
„ 44	4			3	
„ 45	1	1	1	4	
„ 46		4			2
47—48				3	
49—50				3	
nr 51				3	
„ 52				3	
53—54		2			
nr 55				3	4
„ 56				6	
„ 57	1	3			
„ 58	4				
„ 59	3	1			
„ 60	3				
Totaal:	25	17	4	32	6

Summarized on the basis of a total of 84 gongan:

29.8%	repeat no kenongan				— ABCD
20.2%	„	1	„		— AABC
4.8%	„	2	„		— AABB
38.1%	„	1	„	3 times	— AAAB
7.1%	„	1	„	4 times	— AAAA

of the bubuka genḍing and final gongan on the basis of identical kenongan (the one ketawang is not included).

On the basis of identical kenongan appearing in the bubuka genḍing and the final gongan: of the 19 ladrang 19 have at least one kenongan identical in both sections, and of these 19:

14 ladrang have 4 kenongan identical in both sections
1 „ has 3 „ „ „ „ „
1 „ „ 2 „ „ „ „ „
3 „ have 1 „ „ „ „ „

The last kenongan of the bubuka genḍing and the final kenongan of the piece are the same except in nr 41 and 42.

Table II indicates the patterns of kenongan repetition in the gongan and is

Table III

Genḍing	B.Op.	B.Gd.	Final GN
nr 4	T3	T3	T3
„ 35	T3 + barang	T3 + barang	T3 + barang
„ 38	T1	T1	T3 + T1
„ 41	T3 + V	(T3) T1	T1
„ 42	T3 + V (trsp)	T3 + V/gulu	T3 + V/gulu
„ 43	T3 + T1/T2	T3 + T2	T3 + T1/T2
„ 44	T3	T3	T3
„ 45*	T2	T2	T2
„ 46*	(T3) I/V + gulu	T3	(T3) I/V + gulu
47—48*	V/I + lima	(T3) V/I + lima	(T3) V/I + lima
49—50*	(T3) V/I + gulu	T2	T2
„ 51*	(T3) V/I + gulu	T2	T2
„ 52*	T3 (trsp)	T2	T2
53—54*	T1 + gulu	I/V + gulu	I/V + gulu
nr 55	T3	T3	T3
„ 56*	T1 + gulu	T1 + gulu	(T3) T1 + gulu
„ 57	T3	(T3) V/I	(T3) V/I
„ 58	T3	T3 + nem	T3 + nem
„ 59*	(T3) V/I	(T3) T2	(T3) T2
„ 60	T3	T1	T1

In summary:	T3	T4	T1	T2	I/V	
B.Op.	11	0	3	1	5	= 55.5% T3; 20.0% T1 or T2
B.Gd.	7	0	5	5	3	= 35.0% T3; 50.0% T1 or T2
Final GN	8	0	3	5	4	= 40.0% T3; 40.0% T1 or T2

arranged according to type. It shows the number of each type used in every ladrang (the ketawang is omitted).

Table III gives a summary of the cadences closing the three critical sections of the genḍing. The symbols used in this table are similar to those found in Chapters IV and V, the principal difference being that a cadence enclosed in parenthesis and preceding another cadence, *e.g.* (T3) T1 + gulu, indicates that the parenthetical cadence may or may not be considered the primary cadence and everything

Table IV

Gd.	Final	Pr. 5th	Trans.	Cad.Sup.	Mel. Var.	Pancher	Q-pancher
nr 4	nem	nem-ḍaḍa	lima	gulu			
,, 35	barang	,, ,,		,,			
,, 38	ḍaḍa	,, ,,	lima	,,			
,, 41	,,	,, ,,	,,	(,,)			
,, 42	gulu	,, ,,		(,,)		barang	
,, 43	nem	,, ,,	lima	,,			
,, 44	,,	,, ,,	,,	,,	barang		
,, 45	,,	,, ,,	,,	,,	lima/barang		lima
,, 46	gulu	,, ,,	,,	(,,)	barang		nem
47—48	lima	,, ,,	,,	,,			
49—50	nem	,, ,,	,,	,,	barang		ḍaḍa/barang
nr 51	,,	,, ,,	,,	,,	,,		lima/barang
,, 52	,,	,, ,,	,,	(,,)	,,		nem/barang
53—54	gulu	,, ,,		,,			
nr 55	nem	,, ,,	lima	,,	barang		barang
,, 56	gulu	,, ,,	,,	(,,)	lima		ḍaḍa/barang
,, 57	nem	,, ,,		,,			
,, 58	,,	,, ,,	lima	,,	barang		
,, 59	,,	,, ,,	,,	,,			
,, 60	ḍaḍa	,, ,,	,,	,,			
Summary:	nem 11 ḍaḍa 3 gulu 4 lima 1 barang 1	nem-ḍaḍa	lima	gulu	barang	barang	variable

Of the 14 genḍing using either nem or ḍaḍa as the final note 78.5% end on nem and 21.5% on ḍaḍa.

following it, consequently, interpreted as an extension. In the example cited above, therefore, the T3 cadence might be considered the principal cadence and the T1 and gulu merely an extension; the parenthesis, on the other hand, indicates that the connection between the T3 and the T1 formulas is not an uninterrupted scale passage, and so the latter formula, *i.e.* the T1 ,will be considered as the primary cadence in the summaries. The symbols "T3 + T1/T2", given for the bubuka opaq-opaq of nr 43 (cf. the detailed analysis p. 99), do indicate the T3 cadence as primary and the T1 and T2 as an extension.

Table IV indicates the melodic importance of each tone. In Chapter IV the tone of transition and the tone of cadential support were combined in the functions of the tone lima. One column headed "Trans." was therefore sufficient for paṭet nem. In Chapter V nem and sometimes both nem and barang served as the tones of transition in paṭet sanga. An additional column headed "Mel. Var" was needed to indicate those times in which the cadential support provided by the tone barang became melodically prominent. In the Table IV of paṭet manyura another column must be added, namely, the "Cad. Sup.", *i.e.* the tone of cadential support. To repeat briefly: in paṭet nem the tone of transition and the tone of cadential support could be shown in one column, and because barang appeared only a few times as a tone of melodic variety a separate indication was not shown in summary; in paṭet sanga the tone of transition and the tone of melodic variety (and cadential support) were indicated in two different columns; in paṭet manyura three columns are needed to show these separate functions. The parenthesis in the "Cad. Sup." column indicate that the cadential function of gulu is not particularly obvious.

A comparison of the basic practices of paṭet manyura with those of the other two paṭet will be reserved for Chapter VII. The following conclusions can be formulated from the above tables.

Table I indicates that the paṭet manyura genḍing are predominantly ternary in form. The identical kenongan of the bubuka genḍing and the final gongan show a strong melodic relationship between these two sections. The detailed analyses indicate that the bubuka opaq-opaq provides the basis of thematic material for melodic development in the body of the genḍing. These two considerations together establish a close melodic relationship among the three critical sections; the corresponding cadential relationship of these three parts can be seen from the figures in Table III.

The percentages summarizing Table III indicate that the T3 cadential formula and the T1 or T2 cadences occur with about the same frequency. The rather large percentage of T3 cadences in the bubuka opaq-opaq total is somewhat offset by the predominance of T1 or T2 cadences in the figures for the bubuka genḍing. The final gongan shows a frequency of forty percent for both the T3 and the T1 or T2 formulas. The theoretical cadences are given below. The tone gulu (+) has been added to the T1 and T2 formulas on the assumption that the second gong tone may be an essential part of the cadential formulas.

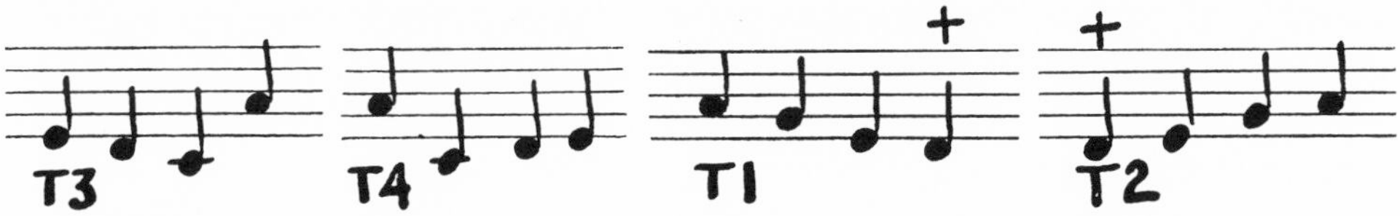

In paṭet nem and in paṭet sanga *one* type of formula was found to be typical, *i.e.* if T1 and its retrograde form T2 are considered as one type and T3 and T4 are regarded as one type. The fairly even usage of T3 and T1 (or T2) cadences appearing in the summary of Table III for paṭet manyura, however, would suggest that there is *not* a typical formula in this highest of the three paṭet. Actually this may not be the case. There are several factors which might render a different interpretation of these results:

1) The bubuka opaq-opaq employs the T3 cadential formula in 55.5% of the genḍing and the T1 or T2 in only 20.0% of the pieces — a peculiar lack of balance if the two basic formulas are really meant to be considered as equally representative of paṭet manyura.

2) It is possible (probable?) that the parenthetical T3 cadences shown in the Table are indeed the primary cadences and that the continuations are actually extensions.

3) In paṭet nem and in paṭet sanga the typical formula is one which *includes* the second gong tone *within* the scale delimited by dominant and tonic (marked "+" in the examples below):

Paṭet Nem

Paṭet Sanga

Although the T1 formula in paṭet manyura establishes a cadential bridge between tonic and dominant, it is lacking the second gong tone. If the second gong tone is *added*, a *weak* T1 formula (cf. pp. 55-6) results which is indistinguishable from the T1 cadence of paṭet nem. Such a weak cadence may appear as an exceptional practice or as a cadential extension but could hardly qualify as a representative or typical cadence of paṭet manyura. In this connection it is worthy of mention that the little Javanese scherzo "Tlosor" (nr 45) uses the T1 and T2 formulas (with and without the addition of the second gong tone) in the *ambiguous* sections while the T3 (and T4) formula are withheld as a means of announcing the paṭet identity in the B section (see p. 103).

4) There is also some question of how representative this group of twenty paṭet manyura genḍing may be. A check of these titles against the available lists of other collections [1]) shows that only eleven of the genḍing appear in those

[1]) See paṭet transposition table p. 260.

records. If the nine genḍing which appear only in this collection (marked in Table III by an asterisk after the title number) are eliminated, the following percentages can be shown:

	T3	T1/T2
B.Op.	90.9%	9.1%
B.Gd.	54.5%	36.4%
Final GN	72.7%	18.2%

5) The *shape* of the T3 formula caused by the disposition of its four notes within the one-octave compass of the saron demung is more readily distinguishable from the typical formulas of paṭet nem and paṭet sanga than is the T1 or T2. The T3 formula, beginning with the tone ḍaḍa, descends conjunctly two more steps (ḍaḍa-gulu-barang) and then makes a wide leap up to the tonic nem. The shape of this formula is easily contrasted with that of paṭet nem (four conjunct descending tones) and that of paṭet sanga (two conjunct tones descending, followed by a leap up to two more conjunct tones descending). The paṭet manyura T1 formula, on the other hand, might be confused with the typical formula of paṭet nem. It is perhaps worthy of note that if the paṭet manyura T3 cadence uses barang alit instead of the (lower octave) barang ageng (in that case having the same *shape* as the T3 formula of paṭet sanga but sounding one step higher), the T3 formula is then preceded (*e.g.* nr 41 and 42) or followed (*e.g.* nr 43 and 51) by a strong T1 formula (without the addition of the second gong tone).

6) Although no direct substantion for his opinion is offered, J. S. Brandts Buys recognizes the sequence ḍaḍa-gulu-barang-nem (*i.e.* the T3 cadence) as characteristic of paṭet manyura [1]).

The weight of all these factors leads to the following conclusion: although either the T3 or *strong* T1 (or T2) cadence readily identifies paṭet manyura, the T3 formula — a descending scale passage from dominant to tonic — is the typical cadence.

The summary of Table IV establishes nem (first gong tone) as the preferred final note with a second choice about evenly shared by its fifth, ḍaḍa (dasar), and gulu (second gong tone). Gulu as well as lima (once) and barang (once) are used as the final notes of extensions following a characteristic cadential formula (usually T3 but sometimes T1). The important fifth-interval is nem-ḍaḍa. The statistics from Table IV together with the summaries of the individual analyses yield the conclusion that nem as tonic, its fifth, ḍaḍa, as dominant, and the second gong tone gulu, used in cadential support of tonic and dominant, are the tones of primary importance in paṭet manyura. Although lima is used quite consistently as a tone of transition, it is not numerically prominent; rarely it may be featured as a tone of melodic variety (nr 45 and 56).

1) J. S. and A. Brandts Buys-Van Zijp, „Javaansche Gending̣s bij Land en bij Seelig," *Djawa*, XVI (1936), 242.

Barang occurs once as the only example of a true pancher. Barang is sometimes very prominent as a tone of melodic variety and otherwise appears as a passing or neighbor note. The pedal note or quasi-pancher is variable.

A brief summary of the principal points:

1. The bubuka opaq-opaq is a particular elaboration, combination or variation of cadential formulas, the principal cadence being the T3 formula. The bubuka opaq-opaq provides the basis of thematic development for the entire gendhing.
2. Through the thematic development of the bubuka opaq-opaq the T3 cadential formula becomes the melodic framework of the gendhing. The particular variation of that formula in the bubuka opaq-opaq accounts for the distinctiveness of the introduction and the gendhing itself.
3. The three critical sections of the gendhing — the bubuka opaq-opaq, the bubuka gendhing and the final gongan — are closely related melodically and cadentially.
4. The "inner gongan" may be related to the bubuka gendhing, may be a distinct development of the melodic material, may be a combination of these two conditions or may be chiefly of a transitional nature. Any of the theoretical cadences may be found at these inner gongan.
5. The T3 cadence is typical of pathet manyura gendhing, although the T1 or T2 formula is rather frequently used. Any of the theoretical types may be found within the body of the piece.
6. The three gong tones occupy the principal melodic and structural importance and their functions are: first gong tone nem as "tonic", dasar dhadha as "dominant", and second gong tone gulu as the tone of cadential support. Lima functions as a tone of transition but is not numerically prominent in the melodic line. Barang is either slighted as a passing or neighbor note or is featured as a tone of melodic variety.

VII.

SLÉNDRO: SUMMARY AND CONCLUSIONS.

IN CHAPTER II WE CONSIDERED several Javanese definitions of paṭet, but in every instance the language was either too figurative or too general to be of much value in formulating a method for paṭet identification or in determining the structural and compositional techniques which maintain the concept itself. In the following comparison we shall try to discover what structural characteristics the three sléndro paṭet have in common and try to isolate those details which determine and preserve the individual paṭet.

The Five Sléndro Tones

The melodic importance of each of the five sléndro tones varies from one paṭet to another. The principal functions are summarized below:

NEM — as dasar in paṭet nem is the *dominant*
— in paṭet sanga is the *tone of transition*
— as first gong tone in paṭet manyura is the *tonic*

LIMA — as second gong tone in paṭet nem is the *tone of transition* and serves in cadential support of the dominant and the tonic
— as first gong tone in paṭet sanga is the *tonic*
— in paṭet manyura is the *tone of transition*

ḌAḌA — in paṭet nem is a „secondary dominant"
— in paṭet sanga is a *passing tone*
— as dasar in paṭet manyura is the *dominant*

GULU — as first gong tone in paṭet nem is the *tonic*
— as dasar in paṭet sanga is the *dominant*
— as second gong tone in paṭet manyura serves in cadential support of the dominant and the tonic

BARANG — in paṭet nem is the *tone of melodic variety* and occasionally *pancher;* when not melodically prominent is used as a passing note
— as second gong tone in paṭet sanga is the *tone of melodic*

variety, occasionally *pancher*, and serves in support of the dominant and the tonic
— in paṭet manyura is the *tone of melodic variety*, occasionally *pancher*, and when not melodically important, occurs as a passing tone.

These particulars can also be arranged according to the characteristic function of the three principal tones:

In all paṭet the *first gong tone* functions as *tonic*
„ „ „ „ *dasar* „ „ *dominant*
„ „ „ „ *second gong tone* „ in support of dominant and tonic
and also has a secondary function which differs slightly in each paṭet:
in paṭet nem it is the *tone of transition*
„ „ sanga „ „ „ *tone of melodic variety*
„ „ manyura „ „ used primarily in support of dominant and tonic.

It was stated earlier that the terms "tonic" and "dominant" are used as a matter of convenience for the Western reader in that they provide a familiar nomenclature which quickly identifies either of the two tones separated by the interval of the fifth (or its inversion, the fourth). The reader was cautioned not to infer that the usage of "tonic" and "dominant" supposed an Indonesian equivalent to our concept of tonality.

The above summary, however, indicates a striking consistency among the three paṭet in the function of the first gong tone as tonic and the function of dasar as dominant, a fact which suggests that the relation of *first gong tone* and *dasar* to *paṭet* may be somewhat akin to the relation of our *tonic* and *dominant* to tonality. I do not mean to imply that *tonality* and *paṭet* are similar concepts (much less that they are by any means equivalent), but simply that the *function* of tonic and dominant and the *function* of first gong tone and dasar in relation to their own tonal concepts are much alike. This idea also seems to be acceptable to the Indonesians themselves. The well-known Javanese musician and educator Ki Hadjar Déwantara in his small book *Leidraad behoorende bij den Cursus over De Javaansche Muziek* [1]) (a booklet used in the schools for teaching singing) says that the first gong tone in sléndro may be compared with the tone "do" in the European song and further describes this principal tone as "babon ing laras" (the mother of the scale). Inferring from this description that Déwantara as much as re-christened the first gong tone with the name "dasar", Jaap Kunst makes the following comment: "In this representation of the scale structure, therefore, the real, ancient Javanese dasar is dethroned by the principal gong-tone, to which it has even ceded its name. No doubt this is to be attributed to

1) Groningen: J. B. Wolters, 1930.

the influence of European musical theory." [1]) As we shall see presently, however, it seems likely that the error is not Déwantara's but rather an erroneous inference on the part of Kunst. The faulty interpretation probably results from the loss of lingual finesse in the translation of Javanese terms into another language, in this instance into Dutch. Although the further pursuit of this question of terminology may at first strike the reader as a kind of etymological splitting of hairs, I believe that a fundamental concept is involved and that the details will prove to be pertinent. For this reason it will be expedient to look more closely at Kunst's usage of the word "dasar".

In attempting to throw some light on the paṭet question he says: "To my mind the nearest approach to the conception 'paṭet' may be achieved by the formula: '*all scales possessing the same tone of the basic scale as central tone* (*dasar*) *form together one paṭet*'." [2]) He adds in a footnote, "I am using here — and also occasionally further on — when discussing the Central Javanese tonal systems, some of the Sundanese terms (such as *dasar* . . .) BECAUSE THE EQUIVALENT JAVANESE TERMS ARE LACKING or at any rate, have not come to my knowledge." [2]) (The capital letters are mine.) From these comments two observations should be held in mind: first, the theoretical scales in each paṭet have a central tone *dasar* or, as we have labeled it, *dominant;* second, the Jogyanese have no musical equivalent for "dasar".

A little later Kunst continues:

"... we may point out once more that, although the dasar may be recognized as such in any composition, even by European ears — especially in vocal music and when played on the rebab — it definitely does not occupy the predominant position in the scale which, in Western music, has been acquired by the tonic. In this connexion it is significant that in the Principalities, there does not exist a special term to indicate this tone (the word *dasar*, in *this* musico-technical signification, is, it appears, exclusively Sundanese), and that, both in Solo and in Jogya, during the many years covering my attempts to investigate the paṭet problem, nobody has ever drawn my attention to the central position of any particular tone in each of the paṭets as far as regards the melody; nay, it was evident from the fact that when I asked questions about the possibility of such a thing that people were of opinion that all the principal tones of the scale had perfectly equal melodic rights.
"This, however, is quite definitely not the case. A representation of the mutual relation between the three sléndro paṭets, as given by Ki Hajar Déwantara, can, in the nature of things, be justified only when there exists, in each of those scales, a definite central point — since all three consist of the same five tones. A dasar, at any rate a central or principal tone is, one might say, *sous-entendu.* It seems to be such a *sine qua non* in a scale that, in Central Java, it is not generally accounted for (any longer)

1) *MJ*, I, 87.
2) *Ibid.*, 73.

consciously. A man like Ki Hajar Déwantara, however, must surely have felt the necessity for such a scale-centre quite *consciously;* for this reason he indicated the lowest in each of the three tone-sequences given by him, as [*N.B.*] *dasar*, or 'the tone which serves to support the laras'." [1])

From this passage there are two additional points to keep in mind: one, the dasar does not have the predominant position in the scale that the tonic does in Western music; two, there is a necessity for *some* principal tone.

Then, even though he implies that a Western influence must be responsible for Déwantara's misapplication of the term "dasar", Kunst makes the statement:

> "Notwithstanding this it should be recognized that this principal [first] gongtone, a fifth below the dasar, is hardly secondary in importance to the dasar itself. They both (as well as the other, the secondary [second] gongtone, which is another fifth lower again [or, brought within the same octave, a fourth higher]) function as melodic *foci*, as 'bases of tension'; one might describe them, therefore . . . as melodic 'pillar-tones'." [2])

One more point to remember: Kunst's indication of the importance of the first gong tone, which we have been calling *tonic* (and the importance of the second gong tone) is in agreement with the results of our analysis.

Now we shall look more closely at Déwantara's booklet. This work, published in Javanese script and consequently accessible to few Western readers, is found in very few libraries. In my opinion it is one of the most important Javanese treatises on music that has come to my attention. These conditions justify the quotation of pertinent passages at some length. The Dutch translation was made by Tjokro-Soehartjo.

To facilitate singing instruction in the schools Déwantara suggests the usage of a solmization with a movable tonic or "do". Although one might be inclined to think of the 11th-century Guido of Arezzo in connection with solmization, [3]) this method is by no means exclusive to the West. The Hindu syllables of solmization appear in the treatise *Natya Sastra*, attributed to Bharata of the 6th century; [4]) the Chinese employed a system of tone-syllables, and the ancient Greeks used *tah, ta, toh, teh* (τα, τη, τω, τε) as syllables representing the tones of the descending tetrachord; [5]) in Bali the syllables used are *ding, dong, dèng, dung, dang*, representing, in this case, constant pitches, *i.e.* a non-movable tonic. [6])

Déwantara uses the last syllable of the Javanese names for the numbers

---

1) *MJ*, I, 84—87.

2) *Ibid.*, 87.

3) *Baker's Biographical Dictionary of Musicians* (4th ed., rev. and en.; New York: G. Schirmer, 1940), p. 445.

4) Willi Apel, *Harvard Dictionary of Music* (Cambridge: Harvard University Press, 1944), p. 332.

5) *Ibid.*, p. 690.

6) Colin McPhee, „The Balinese Wajang Koelit and its Music," *Djawa*, XVI (1936), 8—11; and see Ernst Schlager, „Bali," *Die Musik in Geschichte und Gegenwart*, I (1949—1951), 1110—11.

1 through 5: thus, *dji* (*sidji*) = 1, *ro* (*loro*) = 2, *loe* (*teloe*) = 3, *pat* (*papat*) = 4, *mo* (*limo* or *lima*) = 5.

"De toonaanduiding of in het Hollandsche de noot is hier gebaseerd op de Javaansche toonladder, die verdeeld is in de sléndro- en pélogtoonladder, welke een heel verschil vormt met de Europeesche toonladder. Geheel onjuist zal het daarom zijn door: 1-2-3-4-5 te lezen als: do-re-mi-fa-sol, daar beide toonladders, Javaansche en Europeesche, in wezen anders klinken. De overeenkomst zit alleen in het principe van de aanduiding en in de uitdrukking der rhythmiek [duration of the tones]. De toonaanduiding: 1-2-3-4-5 moet aldus gelezen of gezongen worden: dji-ro-loe-pat-mo, en moet men hierbij steeds denken aan de Javaansche toonladder d.w.z. in navolging van de gamelan-tonen.

"De toon of noot 'dji' vormt de basis van de laras. Met 'basis van den laras' wordt hier bedoeld den toon, waarmee een lied [N.B.] eindigt. Hij kan ook genoemd worden 'de moeder van den laras' [*babon ing laras*] . . . . . Onze toon 'dji' is dus uiteraard te vergelijken met de 'do' in den Europeeschen zang, waar bij 'do' genoemd wordt de grondtoon [tonic].

"De andere noten ro-loe-pat-mo zijn dus de opeenvolgende hoe langer hoe hooger wordende tonen van 'dji', steeds echter de gamelantonen als maatstaf dienende, niet dus de Europeesche muziek." [1])

(The indication of pitch, or in Dutch the note, is here based on the Javanese scale which is subdivided into sléndro and pélog, a very different form from that of the European scale. It would be completely inaccurate, therefore, to read 1-2-3-4-5 as do-re-mi-fa-sol because the Javanese and the European scales do not sound alike. The conformity lies only in the principal of the indication and in the expression of the rhythm [duration of the tones]. The indication: 1-2-3-4-5 must be read or sung as follows: dji-ro-loe-pat-mo, and the Javanese scale must always be kept in mind, *i.e.* in imitation of the gamelan tones.

(The tone or note "dji" forms the basis [Tjokro-Soehartjo's translation of *dasar*] of the laras. By "basis of the laras" is meant the tone with which a song [N.B.] ends. It can also be called "the mother of the scale [*babon ing laras;* laras = sound, tone, pitch, key or mode [2])] . . . Our note "dji" is, therefore, naturally comparable to the "do" in the European song, in which "do" is called the tonic.

(The other notes ro-loe-pat-mo, consequently, are the tones lying successively higher [and lower] than "dji". The gamelan tones, however, always serve as the standard and not European music.)

In connection with paṭet he says:

"Wij hebben dus gezien dat de noot [solmization syllable] dienen moet als aanduiding van elken toon afzonderlijk in de toonladder.

---

1) Déwantara, *op. cit.*

2) *Javaans-Nederlands Handwoordenboek* (Groningen: J. B. Wolters, 1938).

"De paṭet nu duidt de hoogte aan van de tonen, die in een bepaald lied voorkomen." [1])

(Consequently we have seen that the note [solmization syllable] must serve as the indication of each separate tone in the scale.

(Now the paṭet indicates the pitch of the tones which appear in a particular song.)

He then arranges the three sléndro paṭet according to their solmization scales and actual scales, 1 or *dji* in each case representing tonic:

paṭet nem	*paṭet sanga*	*paṭet manyura*
1 — dji — gulu	1 — dji — lima	1 — dji — nem
2 — ro — ḍaḍa	2 — ro — nem	2 — ro — barang
3 — loe — lima	3 — loe — barang	3 — loe — gulu
4 — pat — nem	4 — pat — gulu	4 — pat — ḍaḍa
5 — mo — barang	5 — mo — ḍaḍa	5 — mo — lima

This arrangement confirms our conclusion that gulu, lima and nem are the tonics of the scales in paṭets nem, sanga and manyura respectively. But in order to discover the correct interpretation of the word "dasar" one more reference is necessary.

Returning for a moment to Kunst's inference that the dasar has been "dethroned by the principal gongtone" we find that he adds this interesting footnote: "There is an — at any rate *verbal* — analogy to this in Western musical theory: although the tonic should undoubtedly be regarded as the most important tone in the scale, it is the fifth step that is called the *dominant*. The conception dominant is rendered by R. M. A. Kusumadinata [a Sundanese] by the term *patokaning laras*." [2]) According to the *Javaans-Nederlands Handwoordenboek* "patokaning laras" means the tone which "fixes" or holds the paṭet firm or steady; and according to the same source "dasar" may mean: the foundation (of a textile or color), the bottom (of a lake or sea), the bed (of a river), the basis (of geometry).

The definitions of the two Javanese terms seem to me to be in perfect accord: the tone which holds the paṭet steady could as well be described as the foundation or the basis of the paṭet. These terms also suggest a larger or more fundamental concept than is indicated by the function of the first gong tone or tonic, namely, the delimitation of the scale.

A brief recapitulation of the main points: 1. Kunst has shown that there is a central tone known to the *Sundanese* as "dasar" common to the theoretical scales of each paṭet; [3]) 2. "dasar" as a *musical* term is not known to the *Jogyanese*; 3. dasar does not occupy the predominant position in the scale

1) Déwantara, *op. cit.*
2) *MJ*, I, 87.
3) *Ibid.*, 56—70.

which tonic does in Western music; 4. a central or principal tone is *sous-entendu;* 5. the principal gong tone is hardly secondary in importance to dasar.

Déwantara says that *dji* or 1 forms the *basis* of the laras, and then he goes on to explain that *basis* refers to the tone with which a song *ends*. Although Dewantara's usage of the Javanese term *dasar* is intended as a *non-musical* abstraction, *viz*. "basis," it is not surprising that Kunst might interpret this term in its *Sundanese* musical application, especially since he has shown that "a dasar" is the central tone common to the theoretical scales of a given paṭet. We also agree that *some* central or *principal* tone is *sous-entendu*. But in this case *the* principal tone referred to by Déwantara is the first gong tone, and this tone is further distinguished from others (*e.g.* dasar) when he explains that *basis* refers to the tone with which a song ends. Add to this the fact that the Jogyanese have no equivalent word for the musical concept "dasar" and we must reach the conclusion that Déwantara is speaking of the *function of the first gong tone* with respect to a system of solmization and that Kunst, because of his own convictions regarding the *function of dasar* as a central tone of theoretical scales, mistakenly infers that Déwantara, influenced by Western music, has indeed "dethroned the real, ancient dasar" and incorrectly (point 3 above) dubbed it the equivalent of the Western "do".

There remains an interesting residue from the solution of our etymological mixture, point 5 given above. Although (as indicated by point 3) Kunst never ventures the opinion at any time that dasar is to be compared in a real sense with the Western tonic, [1]) the following passage makes one wonder if there is not a slight, unconscious prejudice in that direction which perhaps was influential in the interpretation of Déwantara's book:

> "Sundanese music does not, anymore than European music, inevitably finish on one and the same tone of the scale, but, in common with Western music, there does exist a certain preference in this respect. As we know, the predominant majority of European folksongs finish on the fundamental tone (tonic) of the prevailing tonality; but it may also happen that the last note of the melody is the fifth (dominant) or the third (mediant). This also applies to the Gregorian chant, though to a lesser degree: there, in addition to the *finalis* we also have the *confinales*.
>
> "Something very similar characterizes Sundanese music. Preference is given, in each of the paṭets — at any rate in the Sumedang and Garut districts — to the tone lying either a pélog- or a sléndro-fifth under the *dasar*." [2])

Before concluding this discussion of the structural importance of dasar and first gong tone, I should like to call attention to a few more details concerning the function of each tone. The tones gulu, lima and nem are not only the tonics of paṭet nem, sanga and manyura, respectively, but also function as the three gong tones of paṭet nem: gulu as first gong tone, lima as second gong tone and

---

1) Also see *MJ*, I, 73 and footnote 3.

2) *MJ*, I, 70.

nem as dasar. Stated in another way, it could be said that these three tones not only fulfill their regular function in paṭet nem but also, as three tonics, become the piling which support the triple arch of the sléndro paṭet, each separated by the span of a fifth. Theoretically there could be two additional paṭet, one having ḍaḍa as tonic and one using barang. But from the analysis there is no such indication, and Déwantara makes the statement: "Naar het karakter onzer liederen mag de ḍoḍo evenals de barang niet als grondtoon worden gebruikt." [1] (According to the character of our songs ḍaḍa and also barang may not be used as tonic.) The analysis showed that in each paṭet there is a tendency to avoid one of the five tones, and it is precisely these two tones which are "slighted" melodically. [2] In paṭet sanga the tone ḍaḍa appears, for the most part, as a passing note. It functions once as a principal tone, *i.e.* in paṭet manyura as dasar or dominant. In paṭet nem and manyura the tone barang may achieve some importance as the tone of melodic variety or appear only as a passing note. It also serves only once as a principal tone, namely, the less-important second gong tone in paṭet sanga. Perhaps because barang never functions as a dominant or a tonic it is, for this reason, considered uniquely qualified as the tone of melodic variety and the normal true pancher — the dual position it occupies in all paṭet.

We have seen that the word "tonic" and our designation of the tones performing that function in each of the three sléndro paṭet are acceptable to the Javanese themselves, [3] and that our usage of the term "dominant" finds justification in the Sundanese definition of that word by virtue of its interchangeability with the meaning of dasar. Together these confirmations indicate that at least *two* principal tones lying a sléndro fifth apart — the first gong tone, which the analysis has shown to be the preferred finalis, and the dasar, the next choice for a final tone — are fundamental to the concept of paṭet. At first glance Kunst's statistics — showing the second gong tone to be second in frequency as the final tone and the dasar to be third in occurrence as finalis [4] — would appear to conflict with our results. Actually, quite the reverse is true. The two apparently different conclusions tend rather to support one another. In this study the designation "final note" is applied to the last note of the entire genḍing. Kunst's figures represent the final tone *of each gongan* in the genḍing. His results, therefore, support our conclusion that the second gong tone in all three paṭet functions in cadential support of tonic and dominant, in as much as it is frequently

---

1) Déwantara, *op. cit.*

2) The tone lima might also be included; although lima functions as a tone of transition in paṭet manyura, it is numerically inconspicuous.

3) There is yet another reference which by inference adds support to this conclusion. In a discussion of various forms of modulation (*MJ*, I, 99) Kunst says that according to the Jogyanese Raden Kodrat „all genḍings sléndro P. nem, whose gongan finish on *lima, might possibly* modulate to P. sanga, and those whose gongan finish on *nem*, to P. manyura." In each case the tone which makes a modulation possible is the *tonic* of the paṭet to which the modulation leads.

4) Cf. *MJ*, I, 78—82.

the final tone of the *inner* gongan. In a moment the second gong tone will merit further attention in the discussion of cadential formulas, but first a few concluding remarks about dominant and tonic.

From an aesthetic viewpoint, in my opinion, the relative importance of the first gong tone and the dasar cannot be compared by a Western musician. To suggest that the Javanese *hear* these two principal tones as we hear our tonic and dominant — or more especially as we hear *their* tonic and dominant — would indeed be ridiculous. A tendency to correct non-European intervals to those of his own scales disqualifies the Western musician. [1] Aesthetic judgements, in this case, must remain the special property of the Javanese themselves.

It is possible, however, to make a few observations concerning the structural importance of these two tones. The Sundanese definitions of *dasar* or *patokaning laras* (dominant) suggest that a major importance is attached to this tone. The position of dasar as a central tone in the construction of Javanese scales has been previously established by Kunst and offers a convincing explanation for the importance placed on dasar by the Javanese niyaga. It was shown above that the three paṭet also have an interdependence based on the first gong tone as tonic. A hasty conclusion might lead to the idea that the Sundanese are "dasar-conscious" and the Jogyanese "tonic-conscious", that the former emphasize (what amounts to) a theoretical importance and the latter a practical importance — two concepts separated by a sléndro fifth. It is true that the theoretical function of dasar is acceptable to the Sundanese; this is certainly *one* aspect of paṭet. Déwantara has very clearly stated the role of the first gong tone in explaining his system of solmization. This is another aspect of paṭet. Both elements will be necessary, later in this chapter, in summarizing the essential features of paṭet.

The Cadential Formula

Among his speculations on the paṭet problem Kunst says, "... there are certain indications that the essential being of the paṭet is not exclusively determined by the gong-tones and the pitch ... Thus it is not quite impossible that ... there is a difference in the turn of the melody, especially in the manner in which the kern-melody [nuclear theme] reaches the finish of the gongphrases ..." [2]

The function of tonic and dominant assume a more tangible importance by the characteristic manner in which they are used melodically. In all paṭet the basic melodic patterns that make up the bubuka opaq-opaq and those which close the bubuka genḍing and the last gongan of the genḍing were seen to be a simple scale passage between dominant and tonic. The particular disposition of the principal melody within the one-octave range of the saron causes these scale passages, in effect, to assume a slightly different shape for each paṭet. The four theoretical cadential formulas created by this melodic movement are given

1) Curt Sachs, *Rise of Music* ... (New York: W. W. Norton, 1943), pp. 25—6.
2) *MJ*, I, 90.

below for each paṭet. On the assumption that the second gong tone *may* be an important part of the cadence, it has been included (marked by a +), even though the scale passage between dominant (V) and tonic (I) is complete without it.

All of these theoretical possibilities may be found in a general examination of the genḍing (see appendix p. 266ff). It has been shown that these formulas may be used in their basic form as given above or, to a greater or lesser degree, may be elaborated and extended. At the three critical points — the end of the bubuka opaq-opaq, the end of the bubuka genḍing and the close of the final gongan — one type and (less often) its retrograde form can be distinguished as typical of each paṭet. The above examples have been arranged so that the typical formulas and their retrograde versions appear in the first and second vertical columns respectively.

The non-typical formulas are found in the third and fourth columns. In paṭet nem and in paṭet manyura the inclusion of the second gong tone results in what has been referred to as a "weak" cadence, *i.e.* one which could be confused at critical points with the typical cadence of another paṭet. T3 and T4 of paṭet nem would be indistinguishable from the typical cadences of paṭet sanga. In paṭet manyura T1 and T2 are the same as the typical formulas of paṭet nem. When these weak cadences are used within the body of the genḍing, however, and are supported at the critical points by the typical formulas, the maintenance of the true paṭet is not threatened. The analysis of paṭet manyura revealed that the T1 and T2 cadences were rather frequently used but *without* the second gong tone. This *three-tone* cadence ending on ḍaḍa or nem could not be mistaken for the T1 and T2 cadences of paṭet nem. The same holds true for the T3 and T4 cadences of paṭet nem, which, without the second gong tone, could not be confused with those of paṭet sanga. T1 and T2 of paṭet sanga are distinctive with or without the addition of the second gong tone. The following conclusions, therefore, can be formulated: in sléndro the non-typical cadences which include the second gong tone, and may be confused with the typical formulas of another paṭet, are "weak" cadences; the omission of the second gong tone in such non-typical formulas makes them "strong" cadences; some non-typical cadences are "strong" with or without the inclusion of the second gong tone.

The summary of each paṭet has indicated that when a non-typical cadence is used at critical points, it is preceded (with rare exception) by the typical formula. In the three instances (nr 11, nr 35, nr 47—48) in which a genḍing ends with a tone other than one of the three gong tones a similar practice obtains. In other words, the tonic is affirmed by a typical cadential formula. Even the second gong tone as a final tone is prepared by the typical cadence, although sometimes (*e.g.* in paṭet manyura) it is shortened to merely V—I or I—V. In conclusion, then, the *resolution* of a genḍing is achieved through a final statement of dominant and tonic (the principal fifth-interval), usually in the form of the typical cadence.

If the cadences given in the first vertical column above were to be arranged without the limitation of the saron octave, they could be represented as follows:

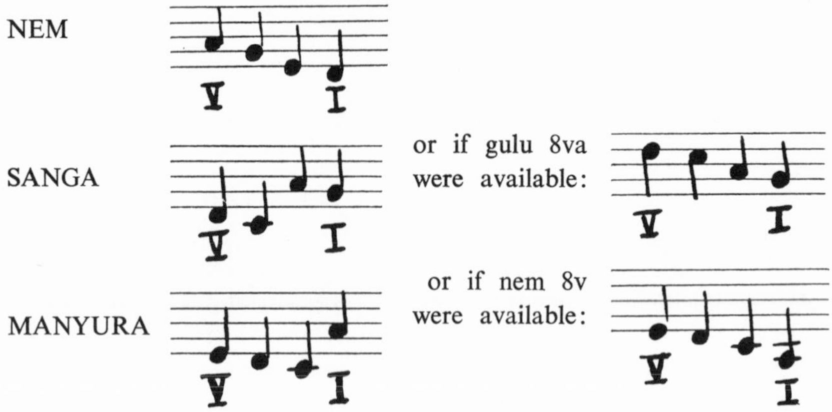

This representation is not intended to show the relative pitch of the paṭet but rather to indicate that the typical cadence in all three paṭet is actually a descending- (occasionally an ascending-) scale passage between dominant and tonic. With some justification one could speak of the *tonic* cadential formula. As was previously pointed out, however, the preponderance of sound issues from the balungan instruments bound to the single octave [1]) and does, in effect, produce the cadences as they are shown in the first column.

The tonic cadential formula of each paṭet has a melodic "shape" that is clearly distinguishable: the conjunct scale in paṭet nem; two steps descending, a leap up to two more descending steps in paṭet sanga; three steps descending and a wide leap up in paṭet manyura. Although these cadences may occur in elaboration, such devices as the usage of the quasi-pancher or neighbor tones or even the rather rare stylistic device of omitting one of the principal tones and waiting

[1]) See p. 10 and p. 18.

until the cadence of a subsequent critical point to add it, these variations only thinly veil the basic shape of the cadence. It is also probable that the ear of the Western listener is so occupied with the colorful lines of the panerusan parts that he would not recognize these cadences without making a very conscious effort in that direction. On the other hand, it appears probable that the Javanese is unconsciously aware of the endings of the critical points in the genḍing (as well as the "inner" cadences) — cadential points which to him are a clear indication of the paṭet being used. In Western music we also have an unconscious awareness of cadences. Tonic may be preceded by the dominant harmony in a variety of forms: with the addition of the seventh, the ninth, the omission of the fifth, even of the fifth and the third; it may be deceptively resolved; any of these harmonic elaborations may be expressed in a purely melodic form. Yet few listeners would have to listen consciously to determine whether a cadence had been reached. We do not have, it is true, a particular *pattern* peculiar to a particular key or mode. But the process of recognition is no more complicated in the one form than in the other. I should say that in Western music the ability to follow audibly a set of melodic variations on a given theme requires something of the same process but on a more complex level. It seems reasonable to assume that the paṭet-conscious Javanese are thoroughly familiar — consciously or unconsciously — with the tonic cadential formulas characteristic of the sléndro paṭet.

There is also the possibility that the Javanese perception of the cadential melodic patterns sounded on the demung may be a rather conscious awareness. Another reference to Déwantara provides a general indication: "Although the paṭet to which each song is suited can be lowered or raised, according to the capacity of the student's voice, I should still recommend that the given paṭet be used as much as possible because *in essence the determination of the paṭet is originally derived from the gamelan, which in a very real sense is bound to firm rules.*" [1]) (The italics are mine.) If the principal consideration in distinguishing paṭet were differences in pitch *only*, it is unlikely that the author would be so emphatic with students of singing classes in recommending the original paṭet because "in essence . . . etc." It is true that he does not specify just what those firm rules are, but at least the possibility that the cadential formula is one of them seems admissible. The following quotations, however, from a paper by Tjokrahadikoesoema are a little more pointed. In his discussion of gamelan sléndro he says, "I take the demung as the foundation because this sets the key or mode [paṭet]." [2]) And a little farther on, "The demung gives the correct wilet. For this reason it plays simply the ḍongḍing [nuclear theme] without any variation. If the demung plays variations on the theme, there exists the danger that the whole genḍing as a result will be lost." [3]) The two remarks together indicate

1) Déwantara, *op. cit.*

2) From a manuscript submitted in competition in 1924; see further J. S. Brandts Buys, „Uitslag van de Prijsvraag inzake een Javaansch Muziekschrift," *Djawa*, IV (1924), 1—17.

3) *Loc. cit.*

that the demung part, *i.e.* the nuclear theme, sets the paṭet. As well as being a general confirmation of our results, this pronouncement suggests (if a short deduction is allowable — from paṭet to nuclear theme to cadential formula) that the Javanese themselves may be aware of the cadential patterns and their importance. A little farther on, in a discussion of the bubuka opaq-opaq we shall examine more fully the usage of the cadence in relation to the melodic material of the nuclear theme.

I do not mean to imply that pitch, for the Javanese, is not a factor in paṭet identification nor that the cadential formula is *the* hallmark of paṭet. But perhaps it will be possible to understand more clearly their relative importance. Kunst raises another question in connection with the paṭet problem. "... why has P. 9 [paṭet sanga] not been permanently regarded as the lowest of the three paṭets, but has in practice become the middle one (as it were through raising it by an octave), whereas the pélog paṭet 5 [paṭet lima] which is in the same position [the lowest of the pélog paṭet] (also, *e.g.* in the wayang-night subdivision) has retained its original place?" [1])

This will need some explanation. Only the sléndro paṭet can be used in the musical accompaniment for the most important type of *wayang kulit*, *i.e. wayang purwa* (*wayang* = theatre; *kulit* = leather [puppet]; *purwa* = old), and these are appropriate for the following periods of the wayang night: paṭet nem is used from the early part of the evening until about midnight; from midnight until three o'clock in the morning is the period for paṭet sanga; from three o'clock until dawn paṭet manyura is used. The character of the pieces in paṭet nem is rather quiet; paṭet sanga genḍing are of a livelier nature and the paṭet manyura repertoire is the most lively of all. This sense of climax is also consistent with the stories of the wayang. [2])

It was explained in Chapter II that the relative pitch of the three paṭet places paṭet sanga as the lowest, paṭet nem in the center and paṭet manyura as the highest. [3]) On pp. 120-1 the same relative positions of the paṭet were explained on the basis of a tonic or first-gong-tone relationship. In the above quotation Kunst is implying that it would seem reasonable to expect paṭet sanga, the lowest in pitch, to be used in the first portion of the wayang night and paṭet nem during the second period — whereas in practice the reverse is true. The supposition gains some strength in an examination of the three *pélog* paṭet as they are used in the accompaniment for the lesser wayang kulit, *i.e. wayang geḍog* (wayang with flat wooden puppets) and the *wayang wong* (wayang with human actors) during performances of the autochthonous Panji stories. (Sléndro, exclusively, is used for the stories of the Hindu repertoire.) In the forms of wayang which use pélog the *time* divisions of the wayang night are quite the same as they are for sléndro, with this principal difference: paṭet lima, the lowest in pitch, is used

1) *MJ*, I, 89.
2) *MJ*, I, 338—45; and see J. S. Brandts Buys, *Djawa*, XVI (1936), 234.
3) pp. 7—8.

in the *first* period; paṭet nem, occupying the central position in pitch, occurs in the *second* period. [1]) This would appear to be the "normal" order and does justify Kunst's question. Why indeed is paṭet sanga used for the second instead of the first period of the wayang night?

A possible explanation arises again in terms of the one-octave range of the demung. When the three sléndro paṭet are brought together within the same octave and arranged according to their respective *tonics* or first gong tones (in Kunst's "ancient nuclear triplet" they are arranged according to *dasar* in a range of almost three octaves) [2]), the sequence is: the tone gulu of *paṭet nem,* lima of *paṭet sanga* and nem of *paṭet manyura.* This sequence does correspond to the sléndro periods of the wayang night and offers some support to the importance of pitch in this relationship. If the *tonic* sequence is accepted in explanation of the sléndro paṭet, however, must we then turn to the *dasar* sequence for an explanation of the pélog paṭet? This would seem to be as much a rationalization as a solution.

The Javanese musician Djajengoetara, in his definition of paṭet and his description of its function, says, "Only he who is well versed in Javanese music studies can say from which paṭet a particular genḍing comes. Because only such a man is able to make some connection between the proper gamelan type and the lakon [the wayang story]." [3]) If paṭet identification itself can be so closely tied to wayang, it is suggestive of two things: first, the sléndro paṭet in their respective periods of the wayang night and the pélog paṭet, used during the same periods must have something in common *if,* as our writer says, the wayang story (hence, any one of its three periods and the story elements characteristic of them) can furnish a clue to paṭet identification; second, since the actual pitch of the sléndro paṭet and the actual pitch of the pélog paṭet do not appear in the same sequence within the three wayang periods, the relationship between the paṭet of the two systems cannot be based on a general correspondence of their pitch sequence. This second point eliminates the tempting rationalization presented above, namely, that a tonic sequence might explain the order of sléndro paṭet in wayang and that a dasar sequence might serve the same purpose for pélog.

Before trying to isolate the features which are common to the paṭet of sléndro and pélog we might first attempt to substantiate the implication in Djajengoetara's statement, first, that there *is* some "wayang bond" common to the paṭet of both systems, and second, *which* of the sléndro paṭet correspond, in this sense, to those of pélog. In a discussion concerning paṭet transposition another Javanese musician, Tirtanata, presents the paṭet of the two systems by pairs, according to their suitability for transposition. "All genḍing pélog paṭet barang can be played in sléndro paṭet manyura [this arrangement is consistent with the third

1) *MJ*, I, 343—5.

2) *MJ*, I, 49—51, 84.

3) From a manuscript submitted in competition in 1924; see further J. S. Brandts Buys, *Djawa*, IV (1924), 1—17.

period of the wayang sequence]. Also, the genḍing pélog paṭet gangsal [lima] and paṭet nem can be played in sléndro but then in paṭet nem or paṭet sanga." [1]) The last two pairs are consistent with the sequence of the first and second periods — *if* the small word "or" is meant to indicate exclusive parallels between paṭet lima and sléndro paṭet nem and between pélog paṭet nem and paṭet sanga. But I have had access only to the Dutch translation and cannot be positive. On the same subject Tjakrahadikoesoema says: "Not every genḍing should be played on both pélog and sléndro. There are also those which should not be played on both pélog [paṭet lima and paṭet nem] and pélog [paṭet] barang. There are known, however, genḍing bonangan which can be played on both [genders of] pélog. Pélog has three paṭet: paṭet gangsal [lima], paṭet nem and paṭet barang which in sléndro correspond respectively with paṭet lasem [nem], paṭet sanga and paṭet manyura." [2]) Whether this correspondence between pélog and sléndro is meant to apply to transposition practice or is merely a restatement of the well-known correspondence based on the wayang sequence is difficult to say. A likely interpretation of these two ambiguous Javanese references, however, is suggested by the figures appearing in the paṭet transposition table on pp. 259—61 of the appendix. Although there are exceptions (to be discussed later), the preferred practice establishes a *general rule of transposition* which is consistent with the paṭet sequence of the wayang night.

We might now examine the two systems briefly to discover what similarities exist between the parallel paṭet of the wayang sequence. A detailed comparison of sléndro and pélog must wait until the analyses which make up the latter part of this study have been examined. At this time, however, for the sake of convenience, one element of the pélog results — the cadential formula — can be anticipated. As the analysis will show, the typical formula for sléndro paṭet nem has the same general pattern — a simple descending scale passage of four tones — as the cadential formula of pélog paṭet lima. The typical formula of sléndro paṭet sanga has the same general pattern — two steps descending and a wide leap up to two more descending steps — as that of pélog paṭet nem. If a standard-of-pitch comparison had been valid, we would have expected to find the shape of the typical formulas of the two pélog paṭet appropriate in a juxtaposition of the above representation. Since, however, the cadential patterns of the parallel pairs do correspond, the shape of the typical cadential formula offers a plausible explanation for the seeming inconsistency between the sequences of the first two paṭet of sléndro and pélog in the wayang night. A comparison of the sléndro paṭet manyura and the pélog paṭet barang necessitates a detailed examination of the pélog system and for this reason will be postponed until the final comparison of the two tonal systems.

I should like to venture an opinion on how, actually, these cadential formulas

---

1) From a manuscript submitted in competition in 1924; see further J. S. Brandts Buys, *Djawa*, IV (1924), 1—17.

2) Tjahrahadikoesoema, *op. cit.*

may in turn correspond to the climactic build-up, from calm to more excitement to the most excitement, which characterizes the sequence of the three periods of the wayang night. Let us consider for a moment the degree of melodic tension achieved by the three patterns. A simple descending scale passage of four tones is typical for the first wayang period. As melodic movement this creates a minimum tension, suitable to the relatively quiet mood of the opening period. In the second period the typical pattern suggests a classic rule of disjunct movement in a melodic line: two steps descending, a wide leap up and the melody turns back on itself again in a descending step. This pattern produces more melodic tension than a simple scale passage but also lessens the effect produced in the wide leap, by the final step-wise movement. This pattern of the second wayang period contains more excitement than the first pattern. The typical cadence of the third period in sléndro and at least one form of pélog paṭet barang generates the most tension: three descending steps and a wide leap up, which is not resolved at all. This psychological argument, based on such simple melodic lines, is somewhat reinforced by the reminder that the nuclear theme is sounded with great volume, that the elaborations of the formula and the heterophony of the panerusan instruments may increase its basic psychological effectiveness and that the general character of the genḍing increases in liveliness with each period of the wayang night.

The Bubuka Opaq-opaq

Thus far, three aspects of paṭet have been examined: tonic (first gong tone), dominant (dasar) and their melodic relation to one another as it is represented by the cadential formula. The fourth aspect of paṭet contains all of these elements in the highly concentrated form of the bubuka opaq-opaq.

Probably the most singular feature of the bubuka opaq-opaq is its individuality. It has been shown that the basic outline of this short melody can be reduced to the cadential formula and that the unique variation of that formula characteristic of each bubuka opaq-opaq is responsible for the distinctiveness of these introductions. They may consist of little more than a simple cadential statement or, at the other extreme, may be a rich elaboration involving all four of the theoretical cadences. The analysis showed that these few measures constitute a thematic nucleus which is used throughout the genḍing as a basis for melodic development. It was also indicated by the analysis that considerable freedom may be shown in the usage of this melodic material, and that in a few instances the correspondence between the genḍing proper and the bubuka opaq-opaq is of such a general nature that derivation would be difficult to establish. This fourth aspect of paṭet will be better understood if we can discover what requirements the "ideal" bubuka opaq-opaq should fulfill.

From Jaap Kunst comes the following comment regarding its function: "During this introduction the players have an opportunity of getting into the atmosphere of the piece to be played and ensure proper 'team-work'. Frequently this buka contains some anticipatory fragments of the genḍing which is to follow it." [1]) One requirement, then, it must set the mood of the piece.

Brandts Buys makes a little stronger statement regarding the relation of the bubuka opaq-opaq to the genḍing proper. He has been examining the literal meaning of *opaq-opaq*, "undulating or rippling in water." [2]) Although he finds this description fitting, especially if the introduction is played on the rebab (or, in my opinion, on the gendèr, gambang kayu or suling), he says, "Maar die term [for the bubuka opaq-opaq] schijnt een zoo-maar mijmeren-met-tonen te suggereren. Nu hadden we echter altijd gedacht, dat een góéde beboekå heelemáál verband hield met zijn genḍing; èn .... een slèchte heelemaal niét. Hetgeen bevestigd werd door een deskundig Javaan, die eens tegen ons zei: Zéker; een boekå móét iets hebben van de genḍing zèlf. Als ze het maar werkelijk dóén!" [3]) (But that term seems to suggest nothing more than a musing- [or daydreaming-] with-tones. Now we had always thought, however, that a *good* bubuka *always* had a connection with its genḍing; *and* .... that a *bad* one did *not*. This was born out by a Javanese expert who once said to us: *Certainly;* a boeka *must* have something of the *genḍing itself*. If only they *would!*).

He then refers to an old kraton collection of nineteen pélog-paṭet-lima genḍing in which one bubuka opaq-opaq was used once, one was used for four genḍing, one for another five and one for nine genḍing. After a comparison of these (which is not included in the article) he reaches the conclusion, "... dat de relatie tusschen aanhef en genḍing toch sterker is, dan men zou vermoeden. Het ziet er uit, als had de Javaan, — denkelijk [m]eer bij instinct dan met opzet! — die inzetten zóó geschapen, dat ze met hun geringe verbizondering wel haast in iédere genḍing momenten moeten vinden die er een weerkaatsing, een echo van schijnen; en als kiest hij daarenboven uit de beschikbare boeka oepaq-oepaq de met de onderhavige genḍing verwantste." [4]) (... that the relation between the introduction and the genḍing is yet stronger than one might suspect. From this it appears as if the Javanese — probably more by instinct than intention — had so fashioned the contents that in their slight peculiarities they must find moments in almost *every* genḍing in which a response, an echo appears; and as if he choses, moreover, from the available bubuka opaq-opaq the one most related to the genḍing under consideration.) After an analysis of the pélog genḍing "Pengrawit" he points out in conclusion that the melodic kernel of the bubuka opaq-opaq is none other than the pélog tone series: bem, gulu, ḍaḍa, lima — the typical cadential formula (see pp. 166—7) of pélog paṭet lima.

Brandts Buys indicates (as do a *few* examples in our analyses) that one bubuka

---

1) *MJ*, I, 311.

2) J. S and A. Brandts Buys-Van Zijp, „Omtrent Notaties en Transscripties en over de Constructie van Gamelanstukken," *Djawa*, XIV (1934), 137.

3) *Loc. cit.*

4) *Ibid.*, 138.

opaq-opaq may be used for more than one genḍing. It should be noted, however, that the present study includes 117 genḍing (from two different collections) representing all six paṭet, and that the collection mentioned by Brandts Buys included only nineteen genḍing, all in pélog paṭet lima. It seems reasonable to conclude that the wider sampling is more representative. On the strength of these circumstances, therefore, the general rule can be made: each genḍing has its own bubuka opaq-opaq; and as the exception: one bubuka opaq-opaq is sometimes used for more than one genḍing.

To summarize Brandts Buys' points: there are good and bad bubuka opaq-opaq; a good one must reflect something of the genḍing itself; the bubuka opaq-opaq is constructed in such a way that it will fit a number of genḍing, and the matter of appropriateness comes down to the proper selection of a bubuka opaq-opaq for a particular genḍing. I believe that Mr. Brandts Buys has the cart before the horse. It seems far more reasonable to assume that a genḍing is composed through a process of melodic development on a given theme or bubuka opaq-opaq, than to suppose that a genḍing is created quite apart from a thematic referent and is then "fitted" to the most suitable, already-existing introduction. I suggest, further, that the very question of what, exactly, a *good* and a *bad* bubuka opaq-opaq really is, has been the source of Brandts Buys' improbable conclusion. Let us try to determine the necessary requirements.

The basis of the bubuka opaq-opaq is the cadential formula. If it is nothing more than a simple cadence, such an introduction will establish "mood" or, better, "mode" or, still better, "paṭet" just because it *is* a scale passage between the correct dominant and tonic. But such a frugal statement would hardly be enough to ensure "team-work" on the part of the players nor would "fragments" of it be especially recognizable in the genḍing. This bare outline of the cadence, then, must be considered a *bad* bubuka opaq-opaq but, on the strength of its correct cadential formula, one which might generally "fit" an x number of genḍing. A *good* bubuka opaq-opaq, on the other hand, is one that not only establishes paṭet through its essential outline of the cadential formula but also creates a *particular* variation of that formula, providing, at the same time, suitable material for melodic development in the genḍing proper. Theoretically, then, an x number of genḍing can be composed on this original theme also.

If this little melody, this "daydreaming-with-tones", establishes paṭet and also provides the material for the whole piece, there would seem to be justification in saying that *the bubuka opaq-opaq is the most important single element of the Javanese genḍing.* We turn again to the Javanese themselves for confirmation. Brandts Buys supplies a lead when he mentions, in passing, the fact that in the old kraton collection the notation of the bubuka opaq-opaq was not written in a vertical column like the rest of the script but appeared in a horizontal form, one note following another, *as part of the title.* [1]) The Sulardi collec-

[1]) *Ibid.*, 137.

tion, although noted in cipher script, is a modern survival which gives the bubuka opaq-opaq as part of the superscription. Another indication of the importance of the bubuka opaq-opaq in the minds of the Javanese might be mentioned in connection with paṭet transposition. The paṭet summaries of sléndro show that in the transposition of a number of genḍing the bubuka opaq-opaq has been retained in the original paṭet. It is not improbable that this practice is indicative of a certain respect for and quite certainly the importance of the original (or, in a general sense, *any*) bubuka opaq-opaq.

At this time it might be appropriate to review some of the Javanese definitions of paṭet mentioned at the close of Chapter II. Sulardi's definition now may hold more meaning for us, "... what is called paṭet is really preluding [grambyangan] on an instrument according to certain rules from which the nature of the compositions to be performed shall become evident." In a general sense this certainly applies to the bubuka opaq-opaq; in the specific sense Sulardi is referring to the *paṭetan* or *lagon*, a short melody sung with accompaniment between the genḍing used for the wayang performances "... to imbue the listeners with the spirit of the prevailing paṭet and to saturate the atmosphere with it ..." [1] Transcriptions of the principal paṭetan are entered in the appendix of Kunst's *Music in Java;* and a comparison of these vocal melodies with the tonic formulas revealed in the foregoing analyses provides added confirmation of our results and clarifies, at the same time, Sulardi's definition. The "Lagon Sléndro Paṭet Nem Wetah", [2] for example, ends with the typical T1 formula of paṭet nem, a descending scale passage from nem to gulu. The "Lagon Sléndro Paṭet Manyura Wetah" [3] is the same as the "Lagon Paṭet Sanga Wetah" except that it is one step higher and is lengthened by a final phrase. The paṭet sanga version ends with a descending scale passage from gulu to lima (dominant to tonic), and the paṭet manyura paṭetan ends with a descending scale from the dominant ḍaḍa to the tonic nem, extended by an extra phrase descending to the dominant ḍaḍa. Not being restricted to a one-octave range as is the saron, these vocal melodies end with conjunct scale passages.

Another definition from Chapter II was earlier dismissed as being too general. The cadential formula, as the core of the bubuka opaq-opaq, in turn forms the skeleton of the melodic development which makes up the genḍing proper. In this sense, therefore, the simple structural framework — the cadential formula — might indeed be thought of as "... the couch or bed of the melody," a definition of paṭet by R. M. Jayadipura. And from R. M. Sarwaka — "the distinction between a given paṭet and another one is based upon a difference in *chengkok*" (melody or melodic line) — we have another definition that seems more admissible from what has been learned of the nuclear theme. Even the rather

1) *MJ*, I, 319.
2) *Ibid.*, II, 501.
3) *Ibid.*, 513.

restricted definition: "by paṭet is meant the singing of the ḍalang to the accompaniment of the rebab, gendèr, gambang, suling, kenḍang and the gong" from Sastrasuwignya contains implications that are more clearly understood in terms of the paṭet sequence of the wayang night.

Structure of the Ladrang

The three critical structural sections — the bubuka opaq-opaq, the bubuka genḍing and the final gongan of the piece — are related in two ways. The general practice of using the tonic cadential formula to close each of these sections was established in the summaries of the individual paṭet. In addition to this cadential "link" there is a rather consistent correspondence in the melodic material of the three sections.

It will be convenient to look first at the similarity between the bubuka genḍing and the final gongan. [1] A comparison can be most easily made on the basis of the number of kenongan which are identical in both sections. A comparative summary is given below.

Paṭet nem

All 13 ladrang have at least 1 kenongan identical in both sections, and of these 13:

4 ladrang have 4 kenongan identical in both sections
3 ,, ,, 3 ,, ,, ,, ,, ,,
1 ,, has 2 ,, ,, ,, ,, ,,
5 ,, have 1 ,, ,, ,, ,, ,,

In all ladrang the last kenongan of the bubuka genḍing and the closing kenongan of the piece are the same.

Paṭet sanga

Of the 19 ladrang [2] 14 have at least 1 kenongan identical in both sections, and of these 14:

4 ladrang have 4 kenongan identical in both sections
5 ,, ,, 2 ,, ,, ,, ,, ,,
5 ,, ,, 1 ,, ,, ,, ,, ,,

In 13 of these ladrang the last kenongan of the bubuka genḍing and the closing kenongan of the piece are the same.

Paṭet Manyura

All 19 ladrang [2] have at least 1 kenongan identical in both sections, and of these 19:

[1] Cf. J. S. Brandts Buys, *Djawa*, XIV (1934), 161.
[2] The ketawang are omitted.

14	ladrang	have	4	kenongan	identical	in	both	sections
1	,,	has	3	,,	,,	,,	,,	,,
1	,,	,,	2	,,	,,	,,	,,	,,
3	,,	have	1	,,	,,	,,	,,	,,

In 16 of these ladrang the last kenongan of the bubuka genḍing and the closing kenongan of the piece are the same.

The detailed analyses reveal that in the ladrang of all paṭet even those kenongan of the bubuka genḍing and the final gongan which are not identical usually have marked melodic similarities.

In conclusion, then, elements of the bubuka genḍing are repeated — identically or similarly — in the final gongan.

The analyses of the individual genḍing show that the bubuka genḍing is usually closely tied to the bubuka opaq-opaq. In some instances a small figure from the short introduction provides the material, and in others the entire bubuka opaq-opaq itself is used. Among the latter examples the quotation may be identical (*i.e.* the same note values), augmented, combined with a pedal note or quasi-pancher, etc. On the basis of the above summary this relationship between the bubuka opaq-opaq and the bubuka genḍing can be extended proportionately to the final gongan. This direct or slightly-modified quotation of the introduction in the other two critical structural sections offers further substantiation of our point of issue with Brandts Buys regarding the intrinsic function of the bubuka opaq-opaq.

It is not surprising that this relationship between the beginning and the end of the genḍing frequently results in a ternary form. Although the summary of architectonic forms given below may afford a rough indication, like all reductions of musical compositions to such cold structural terms as "sonata form" or "A B A", it conveys nothing of the artistic merit and variety of each genḍing. Some of those designated as "ternary" have binary "B" sections; some of those labeled "binary" might better be called "verse-refrain" or, because the last kenongan is taken from the "A" section, might be termed "rounded binary" or "ternary". The following summary is offered as a general indication of form.

Paṭet Nem

10	genḍing	—	intro.:	ternary
2	,,	—	,,	binary
1	,,	—	,,	double period (two gongan)

Paṭet Sanga

10	genḍing	—	intro.:	ternary
8	,,	—	,,	binary
1	,,	—	,,	period (one gongan) repeated
3	,,	—	,,	through-composed

Paṭet Manyura

14 genḍing	—	intro.:	ternary
2 ,,	—	,,	binary
3 ,,	—	,,	period (one gongan) repeated
1 ,,	—	,,	through-composed

The genḍing of paṭet nem and manyura are principally ternary in form, while those of paṭet sanga are about evenly divided between ternary and binary forms. A few genḍing are through-composed (it is interesting to note that even in these the last kenongan is usually a repetition of the last kenongan of the bubuka genḍing) or a period repeated. Although the results of paṭet sanga tend to set it apart from the other two paṭet, there is actually nothing to indicate that form in itself is connected with paṭet identification.

The detailed structure of the individual gongan on the basis of the number of kenongan repeated within the sixteen measures has been presented in detail in the summary of each paṭet. For the sake of comparison the principal figures are repeated here. 1)

Paṭet Nem

In the gongan of 13 ladrang (a total of 65 gongan) some combination of the pattern (e.g.) AABC occured 40.3% of the time, and the pattern (e.g.) ABCD (no kenongan repeated) was used 33.9% of the time.

Paṭet Sanga

In the gongan of 19 ladrang (a total of 84 gongan) some combination of the pattern AABC occured 35.8% of the time, and the pattern ABCD was used 53.6% of the time.

Paṭet Manyura

In the gongan of 19 ladrang (a total of 84 gongan) some combination of the pattern (e.g. AAAB occured 38.1% of the time, and the pattern ABCD was used 29.8% of the time.

The patterns for kenḍang one or two are generally uniform in all ladrang. The kenḍang two pattern typical for the ketawang is regular in the four examples found in this collection.

The colotomic pattern of four kenongan to a gongan and the appropriate keṭuk and kempul subdivisions are consistently used in all ladrang. The colotomic pattern of two kenongan to a gongan and the appropriate keṭuk and kempul subdivisions are consistently used in all ketawang.

---

1) The ketawang are omitted.

Paṭet Transposition

The basic rules governing the transposition of genḍing from one tonal system to another were previously pointed out. Further comment in this connection will be withheld until the final comparison of sléndro and pélog. An indication of the transposition practice within the sléndro system can best be seen by studying the chart given in the appendix, pp. 259—60. The original numbering of the collection of 100 genḍing has been retained so that those pieces (nrs 4, 12, 35, 38) which were incorrectly labeled may be seen in their proper paṭet group and at the same time can be related numerically to that paṭet to which they were mistakenly assigned by the scribe. It is possible that the sources listed at the head of the chart also contain errors in their paṭet designations. We assume, however, that such errors are at a minimum, and that the comparatively large number of sources consulted tend to cancel out possible errors and yield generally reliable statistics.

The chart shows the following transpositions:

> Of the 13 paṭet-nem genḍing a total of 6 are transposed: 4 appear in paṭet manyura and 2 in both paṭet sanga and paṭet manyura.
> Of the 22 paṭet-sanga genḍing a total of 5 are transposed: 3 appear in paṭet manyura and 2 in paṭet nem.
> Of the 23 paṭet-manyura genḍing [1] a total of 3 are transposed: 2 appear in paṭet sanga and 1 in both paṭet nem and paṭet sanga.

From these figures we can conclude that in sléndro a genḍing in one paṭet may be transposed to either of the other two paṭet. Genḍing appearing in only *one* paṭet in three or more collections might be taken as an indication that such genḍing (for some reason not readily apparent from our analyses) are considered unsuitable for transposition. Perhaps the character of the piece or its association with a specific wayang connotation is responsible for this restriction. [2] The percentage of transposed genḍing would appear to diminish from paṭet nem to paṭet sanga to paṭet manyura. This may be misleading, however, because the titles of genḍing in the last two paṭet (particularly paṭet manyura) often do not appear at all in the other collections.

Preservation of Paṭet

The exposition of the sléndro paṭet in Curt Sachs' *The Rise of Music in the Ancient World East and West* [3] is somewhat misleading. Mr. Sachs says, "The question of mode is not easily answered. Java had [sic] three *sléndro* modes, but they have no importance today, and even their distinghuishing features are nearly forgotten. They are played on the same instruments and in the same

---

1) Three genḍing are duplicated but carry different titles; see further Chapter VI.
2) Cf. *MJ*, I, 91, 338—45.
3) New York: W. W. Norton, 1943.

range and scale and only differ in their main notes, which in the orchestra are emphasized by single strokes of the large gong. But not even these chief notes are beyond doubt." [1]) In support of his last statement he cites Kunst's statistics, based on a survey of *all* gongan, representing the frequency with which the first gong tone of each paṭet occurs as finalis. From these percentages Sachs concludes, "This means disintegration." [2]) And a little farther on, "It seems that the modes or, better, the melodies ascribed to the modes, matter today only from the standpoint of choosing the adequate time for performance . . . ." [3])

To begin at the beginning, I believe the present study establishes the fact that the Javanese *have* three sléndro paṭet or modes. Even at the time of Mr. Sachs' publication there were no important sources which denied the effective existence of three sléndro paṭet. Knowing that Jaap Kunst's *Music in Java* (or more especially the first edition [4]) has furnished the principal source of information for almost all subsequent writings on Javanese music, I should also point out that at no time does Kunst hint that the sléndro paṭet should be spoken of in the past tense. Mr. Sachs is actually basing his conviction of the "decline of the modes" on the assumption that the modern sléndro scale is tempered. [5]) With the abundant testimony (of the Javanese themselves) to the contrary, how can one reasonably preclude all other considerations? There can be little doubt, it is true, that the logical basis of mode or paṭet must be founded on a scale of non-equidistant intervals, and that if the scale approaches equal temperament, the original *reason* for the establishment of mode is weakened. But since the paṭet concept — whether or not there is a modern tendency toward an equidistant scale (see further pp. 138-42) — *has* maintained itself and by the Javanese is considered fundamental to the whole of their music (and theatre), I should think such a fact would suggest that *in practice* there are residual elements (*e.g.* as shown in this chapter) which in themselves have allowed the preservation of the paṭet idea.

His statement that the main tones of each paṭet "are emphasized by single strokes of the large gong" is rather misleading. The role of the gong ageng in its colotomic function has been adequately explained earlier. [6]) When the first gong tone occurs as the final note of the gongan, it coincides, of course, with the final gong; when it occurs within the gongan, it does not.

His conclusion that Kunst's figures, representing the first gong tone as finalis, mean disintegration is a *non sequitur*. Along this line of reasoning a similar survey of Western music (based on the final note of *every* cadence throughhout a piece of tonal music) would indicate that our concept of "key" was disintegrating.

Mr. Sachs' final remark — that the modes or the melodies ascribed to them

---

1) *Ibid.*, p. 131.
2) *Ibid.*, p. 132.
3) *Loc. cit.*
4) *De Toonkunst van Java*, (Den Haag: Martinus Nijhoff, 1934).
5) Sachs, *op. cit.*, p. 132.
6) Chapter II, pp. 12-14.

matter *only* from the standpoint of time — has been shown earlier in this chapter to be contrary to the available facts.

The question of the origin and evolution of the sléndro scale lies outside the intended scope of this study. A few comments on the existing material, however, are appropriate to the present consideration of the preservation of paṭet. Von Hornbostel's theory of the cycle of blown fifths was considered tenable by a number of musicologists for some years. [1]) Among its proponents was Jaap Kunst, who applied this theory to an explanation of the origin of Javanese scales and tonal systems. [2]) In recent years several writers have questioned the validity of the theory of blown fifths, but none has offered a better explanation of the origin of Javanese scales. Manfred Bukofzer's attempt to show that the structure of the sléndro and the pélog systems is based on the interval of the fourth, [3]) as well as a similar theory in the Harvard Dictionary of Music, [4]) have elsewhere been shown to be untenable. [5]) The results of the present study reinforce this refutation in as much as: first gong tone and dasar represent the interval of the *fifth*, the cadential formula is based on the *fifth*, the melodic material in its development of the cadential formula is founded on the *fifth*, the pitches of the three paṭet are separated by a *fifth*.

In my opinion there has not yet been offered an unequivocably acceptable theory of the origin of Javanese scales, nor is it my intention to propose further speculations. One question which may concern us here, however, arises in connection with the structure of the modern sléndro scale.

In Volume II of *Music in Java* Kunst shows the scale measurements of forty-six gamelan slendro. [6]) On the basis of these statistics he says, "However much this scale may have been, in certain phases of its development, composed of unequal steps . . . in its *modern* form it is practically equidistant. True, in most of the modern gamelans one finds one (sometimes [usually?] two) intervals slightly larger than the others . . ., but these are not always the same two intervals out of the five existing ones, and these deviations from equidistance are therefore *functionally* of no consequence." [7])

Regarding the modern sléndro scale Mr. Bukofzer makes the pronouncement, "This [sléndro] temperament has not yet been accurately realized, but there is no question that it is intended." [8])

In another place Kunst mentions that ". . . according to an oral communi-

---

1) Jaap Kunst, *Around von Hornbostel's Theory* . . . (Amsterdam: Indisch Instituut, 1948), p. 3.

2) *MJ*, I, 24—70.

3) „The Evolution of Javanese Tone-Systems," *Papers* of the International Congress of Musicology (New York: 1944), pp. 241—50.

4) Willi Apel, „Javanese Musik," *Harvard Dictionary of Music* (Cambridge: Harvard University Press, 1950), pp. 373—4.

5) Jaap Kunst, *Around van Hornbostel's Theory* . . ., pp. 27—35.

6) pp. 574—5.

7) *MJ*, I, 64.

8) Manfred Bukofzer, *op. cit.*, 243.

cation from Walter Spies the sléndro scale was not intended to be equidistant; it is supposed to contain two larger intervals, one of which is stable whilst the other is slightly variable — which, of course, can only be expressed vocally." [1])

Colin McPhee stresses the fact that, at least in Bali, the sléndro scale never was nor is in present practice an equidistant scale, but one which contains two larger intervals. [2]) He objects to describing the modern form of sléndro as tending toward equidistance also on the grounds that the instruments of the gamelan are frequently out of tune, "... so that the true scale may only be ascertained with certainty from a pandé krawang, the maker of the metal keys, and also the tuner, or else from a newly tuned instrument." [3])

A close examination of Kunst's statistics based on the measurement of forty-six gamelan supports his conclusion that *functionally* the modern sléndro scale must be considered equidistant — that is, *if*, on the basis of these figures, there is justification in speaking of a *standard* or *true* sléndro tuning. Actually not one of the sléndro scales measured is perfectly equidistant, although six of them (nrs 9, 10, 20, 36, 41, 43) [4]) do not have a difference of more than 30 cents between the largest and the smallest intervals, a modest but significant support of Kunst's contention. The others contain large and small intervals that are more contrasting in size, but — and this is Kunst's strongest argument — there is no apparent consistency in the sequence of those intervals. Choosing at random we find that the intervals of nr 5, for example, run Small Large SSL, and nr 6 LSSSL and nr 33 LSSLS etc. I repeat that *if* there is justification in speaking of a *standard* sléndro tuning, then the tendency is certainly toward equidistance. But perhaps, as I shall try to show presently, this view of the matter is rather too "pure".

It was mentioned earlier that the logical basis of paṭet (or mode) must be founded on a scale of non-equidistant intervals. Now *individually* all of the forty-six measured scales *do* fulfill that requirement; so that if we postulate the preservation of paṭet on the fundamental condition that it be realized on *some* non-equidistant scale, then it must be said that *in practice* each individual gamelan meets that condition.

If McPhee's criticism is valid, there is some doubt whether an average of the collective measurements actually indicates that the modern *true* scale shows a tendency toward equidistance. On the other hand, Kunst's statistics for the scale measurements of thirty-nine gamelan *pélog* [5]) yield an average scale which is uniform in its sequence of small and large intervals. There are two characteristics of the pélog scales, however, which introduce a perceptible advantage in the computation of an acceptable average scale. 1) The difference between the small and large intervals is generally greater in pélog than in sléndro. 2) Each

---

1) *MJ*, I, 90.
2) „The Balinese Wajang Koelit and its Music," *Djawa*, XVI (1936), 10—11.
3) *Ibid.*, 10, footnote 1.
4) *MJ*, II, 574—5.
5) *Ibid.*, 572—3.

of the pélog paṭet selects for its principal tones five of the available seven, and the omission of a tone (in two places in the scale) produces a large interval, between the principal tones lying above and below that tone, which is decidedly larger than the original small intervals of the selected scale. [1]

One further consideration in connection with the difficulty of determining a true sléndro scale may be suggested by Walter Spies' comment that one of the two large intervals is variable. Kunst's observation that such a variation could only be realized vocally is justified in relation to the keys of a *particular* gamelan instrument. But in the process of imitating or reproducing that scale in the tuning of another gamelan there exists the possibility that the variable large interval, by preference, may be copied more in relation to the vocally-raised or -lowered pitch than from the fixed pitch of the bronze key. This whimsy might account for part of the inconsistencies found in the sléndro scale measurements.

The reasons for questioning whether the statistics indicate a tendency toward equidistance in the modern scale can be summarized as follows: 1) a number of the gamelan measured, a number sufficient to obscure the results, may have been out of tune; 2) the difference between the small and large intervals of the true scale in reality may be rather slight; 3) the vocal practice of varying one of the large intervals may have influenced imitations of the scale; 4) even if the given statistics represent "in-tune" gamelan, they still do not indicate that the tendency of the modern "true" scale is toward equidistance but, at the most, rather that in modern practice *there is no true or standard sléndro scale.*

One of the primary concerns of the musicologist is the constant search for the norm, the average, the standard elements of a music, so that these components may be given order and in turn afford understanding. The determination of a true scale is paramount in this endeavor, but I believe there must be a sharp distinction drawn between the *original* form or forms of a scale and the *living, modern, practical* forms of a scale. There seems to be general agreement that the original form of the sléndro scale was made up of unequal intervals. [2] *If* the above-mentioned sléndro statistics represent in-tune gamelan, we can say with certainty that *the original form of the scale has not maintained itself in modern practice.* We can also say that in modern practice a variety of *non-equidistant* sléndro tunings *exist, are living, are being used.* There is not sufficient evidence to support the claim that one aspect of paṭet — the non-equidistant scale — has disintegrated or even shows a tendency toward disintegration (*i.e.* equidistance) so long as the scales in practical usage are non-equidistant. We *cannot* say that the numerical average of these measurements represents an *intended* equidistant scale just because it shows no correlation with the original scale form. In short, statistics should not be made to conform with the standard methods of musicological theory, but rather those standards methods must be evaluated in terms of what they can and cannot show.

1) See further Chapter VIII.

2) *MJ*, I, 64; and Curt Sachs, *Rise of Music* ..., p. 131.

In conclusion: 1) the available statistics do not establish the existence of a true or standard sléndro scale in modern practice; 2) the postulation that the modern scale is intended to be or shows a tendency toward equidistance is based on the assumption that the average of these statistics represents a standard scale, and the postulation, therefore, has been shown to be invalid; 3) the consequent of this postulation, namely, that the paṭet concept is therefore disintegrating, is likewise invalid; 4) the statistics represent either a) in-tune gamelan or b) out-of-tune gamelan: if a) obtains, they indicate that the original form of the scale has not maintained itself in modern practice; if b) obtains, they indicate nothing; 5) there are various non-equidistant sléndro scales — in-tune or otherwise — in current usage; 6) modern practice suggests that intervalic relationship is a lesser consideration in the concept of the sléndro paṭet.

In connection with the last point (nr 6 above) there is an individual exception which by inference suggests another interpretation of Kunst's sléndro statistics. Mr. Kunst tells of an interesting practice followed by the Solonese Prince P. A. Kusumayuda. [1] On occasion P. A. Kusumayuda would hear a particularly fine genḍing played by one of the gamelan sléndro of P. A. A. Paku Alam, Ruling Prince in Jogya, and later would have this same genḍing played by his own gamelan. But he always preferred to transpose a piece that was, for example, originally in *paṭet manyura* to *paṭet sanga*, thereby lowering the pitch of the piece one sléndro step.

The intervalic measurements of the gamelan of both Kusumayuda (nr 4) and Paku Alam (nr 8) are found in the appendix of *Music in Java*. [2] The pitch of the tone barang is almost the same in both gamelan: the vibration number 268.5 in the former and 272.5 in the latter. By lowering the pitch of the genḍing one step Kusumayuda's version would replace the original pitch of barang (272.5) with the pitch 234.5. A sense of absolute pitch would not seem to have motivated the transposition. When we examine the intervalic structure of the two gamelan, we find that nr 4 (Kusumayuda) has the sequence (from low to high) SLSLS and nr 8 the sequence SSLSL. By playing the genḍing one step lower P. A. Kusumayuda shifted the sequence of his own gamelan scale so that in effect it corresponded to that of Paku Alam, as shown below.

				S		L		S		L		S	
nr 4:			barang		gulu		ḍaḍa		lima		nem		barang alit
		S		S		L		S		L			
nr 8:	barang		gulu		ḍaḍa		lima		nem		barang alit		

By sounding the tonic cadential formula in paṭet sanga — gulu-barang-nem-lima or the intervals SSL — Kusumayuda produced a *gapped scale* structure which

[1]) An oral communication from Jaap Kunst.

[2]) *MJ*, II, 574.

corresponds to that of the Paku Alaman gamelan, *e.g.* in the tonic cadential formula in paṭet manyura: ḍaḍa-gulu-barang-nem or the intervals SSL.

If we re-examine Kunst's statistics, looking for *some* (not *one*) arrangement of a gapped scale having the basic structure of two adjacent small intervals and two large intervals separated by a small one, we find that 27 of the 46 gamelan measured have such a structure. While these figures still do *not* yield an *average true scale,* they do suggest rather forcefully that the modern sléndro tuning is *not* tending toward equidistance and further that it has a basic scale sequence of gapped structure.

As stated earlier, a theory of the evolution of Javanese tonal systems is not within the scope of the present study; but one observation seems worthy of mention. The above gapped scale structures and the various "starting points" they represent in the basic sequence SSLSL are strikingly similar to the principal *scale* structures of the three *pélog* paṭet. [1])

The five fundamental aspects of the sléndro paṭet are summarized below:

1) a non-equidistant scale
2) a tonic
3) a dominant
4) the cadential formula
5) the bubuka opaq-opaq

The preservation of the paṭet concept depends on the maintainence of these elements. A *truly* equidistant scale, the loss of a tonic-dominant sense (or a feeling for the principal fifth-interval), a disregard for the cadential formula, *bad* or *standard* bubuka opaq-opaq — any one or any combination of these weaknesses will threaten the preservation of the paṭet. Individual examples of these tendencies, which have been pointed out in the foregoing pages, may be indications of weakness in the concept or simply evidences of artistic license.

There are other circumstances which might be associated with the preservation of paṭet. The several genḍing which are incorrectly labeled may mean that a particular scribe could not associate the *written* music with the *sound* (therefore with the paṭet) which it represented. Or it might mean that its transposition to another paṭet, perhaps through an intermediary gamelan, was not recognized as a change of paṭet but only imitated in the belief that it was the original. The retention of the original bubuka opaq-opaq in transposition might come to be misunderstood. Improvisation among the balungan instruments could destroy the function of the nuclear theme.

The results of the present study, however, establish the fact that the three sléndro paṭet are firmly entrenched and that indications to the contrary are at a minimum.

---

1) See further Chapter VIII.

VIII.

PÉLOG PAṬET LIMA.

IT WAS SHOWN in the foregoing pages that although equidistant sléndro tunings are not to be found, neither is it possible to arrive at a standard or true sléndro tuning which has a gapped structure. The perceptive reader may have noticed in his examination of the sléndro transcriptions that occasionally the melodic line shifts for a short time to a higher or lower tonal center (*e.g.* nr 45 p. 100, nr 58 p. 90). Since a standard gapped scale does not exist, however, it would be meaningless to say that an actual *modulation* has occurred in these passages. In the pélog paṭet, on the other hand, the standard-scale sequence of large and small intervals allows a true modulation [1]). The melodic center may move to an "auxiliary scale" lying a pélog fifth above or below the principal scale, retaining, however the three gong tones (dasar, first gong tone and second gong tone) of the principal scale and thus remaining in the same paṭet [2]).

The Three Pélog Paṭet

The basic scales of the pélog tonal system are constructed from seven available tones as they exist on the keys of the saron. From high to low these tones are: *barang*, *nem*, *lima*, *pélog*, *ḍaḍa*, *gulu* and *bem* (see further pp. 6-7). The gapped structure of this seven-tone sequence gives rise to a rather complicated potential of distinct scale forms. The fundamental scales which can be realized on the saron will be considered according to their paṭet grouping.

In Central Java three pélog paṭet are recognized. Arranged in the order of their occurrence during the wayang night they are: *paṭet lima*, *paṭet nem* and *paṭet barang*. In modern practice these three paṭet are commonly differentiated by a two-part arrangement in which paṭet lima and nem are classified under the one name *pélog paṭet bem* in contradistinction to *pélog paṭet barang*. The justification of this dual classification of "three" and "two" will be most easily understood in

---

1) See *MJ*, I, 91—8.

2) *Ibid.*, 92; the designation „auxiliary scales" was first used by Mr. Bernard IJzerdraat.

the course of the subsequent exposition by referring to the tables given on p. 145 and p. 146 [1]).

Table X is headed with a schematic representation of the seven keys of the saron. The arabic numerals express in cents the sizes of the intervals of the average pélog tuning. The horizontal double lines divide the table according to paṭet, and within the paṭet divisions the five principal tones of each scale are shown by the encirclement of the appropriate intersections formed by the vertical extensions of the schematic keys and the horizontal lines indicating a given scale. For each paṭet the dasar, the first gong tone (lying a pélog fifth below dasar) and the second gong tone (lying two pélog fifths below dasar) are indicated directly above the appropriate tone by the symbols "DASAR", IGT and IIGT, respectively. It should be noted that the term "gong tones" will continue to be used as a convenience in referring to these three tones even though in the pélog paṭet they are not very strictly adhered to as final notes of the gongan [2]). The two tones not included in the scale as principal tones (but which may occur as auxiliary tones) are shown each time beneath the scale name. Below the table is given the substitute or exchange tones (*sorog*) by which a modulation may be accomplished [3]).

Although Table X will serve as a more practical reference in the analysis of the pélog genḍing because the actual distribution of the melodic line will occur within the one-octave limits of the demung (saron) keys, another representation of these scales, given in Table Y, may more easily clarify their relative positions on the basis of a fifth relationship. This table is similar to Table X except that only the principal scale of paṭet nem lies within the range of the saron, all others being extended as they might be realized on a multi-octave instrument.

To return to the discussion of the dual classification system of the pélog paṭet, attention should be called to the scale names appearing in parentheses in the paṭet lima subdivision of Table X. The original principal scale of paṭet lima, indicated in the table by: Low Auxiliary (formerly PRINCIPAL), has gradually fallen into disuse, probably because of the increased sensitivity on the part of the Javanese to one of the five principal tones, namely, the tone *pélog* [4]). The word "pélog" is associated in popular Javanese etymology with *pélo* meaning "deviating" (*miring*) or "prominent", whereas the other six pélog tones are considered *jejeg*, *i.e.* suitable, proper, correct, true, straight [5]). The scale lying a pélog fifth higher, indicated in the table by: PRINCIPAL (formerly High), in which the tone pélog is replaced by the tone ḍaḍa, has become the principal scale in modern practice.

---

1) Adapted from *MJ*, I, 95, and modified to include further details.
2) *MJ*, I, 94 footnote 1.
3) See *ibid.*, 94.
4) *Ibid.*, 75.
5) *Ibid.*, footnote 1.

Table X

PÉLOG

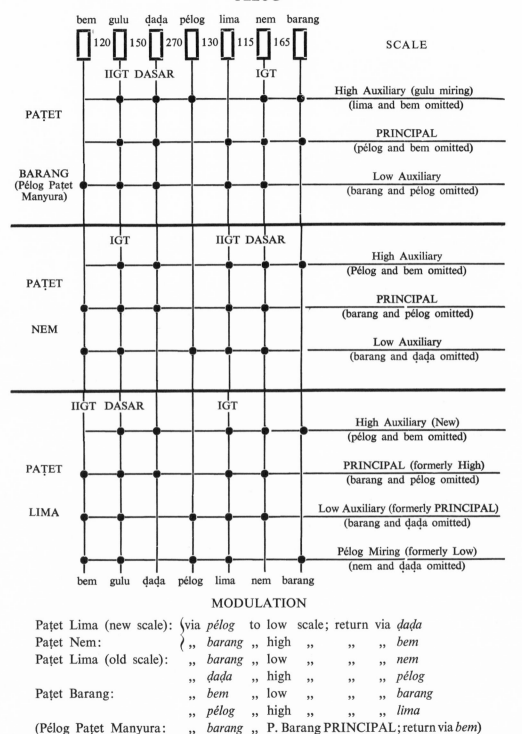

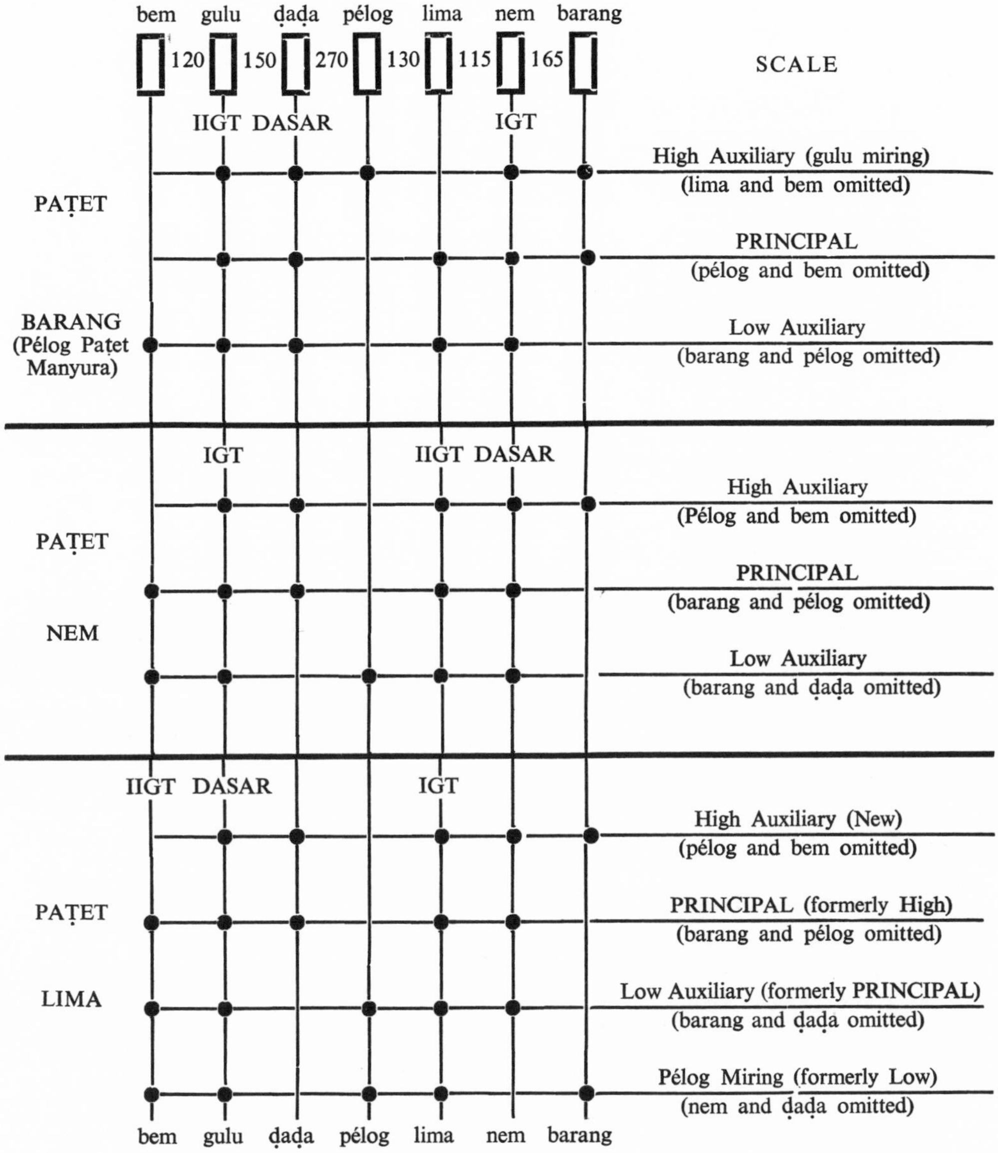

MODULATION

Paṭet Lima (new scale):	via	*pélog*	to	low	scale; return via	*ḍaḍa*
Paṭet Nem:	,,	*barang*	,,	high	,, ,, ,,	*bem*
Paṭet Lima (old scale):	,,	*barang*	,,	low	,, ,, ,,	*nem*
	,,	*ḍaḍa*	,,	high	,, ,, ,,	*pélog*
Paṭet Barang:	,,	*bem*	,,	low	,, ,, ,,	*barang*
	,,	*pélog*	,,	high	,, ,, ,,	*lima*
(Pélog Paṭet Manyura:	,,	*barang*	,,	P. Barang PRINCIPAL; return via *bem*)		

Table Y

PÉLOG

Paṭet	Scale	barang	bem	gulu	ḍaḍa	pélog	lima	nem	barang	bem	gulu	ḍaḍa	pélog	lima	nem	barang	bem	gulu	ḍaḍa	pélog	lima	nem	barang
PAṬET BARANG	High Auxiliary (gulu miring)																	●	●	●		●	●
	PRINCIPAL													●	●	●		●	●				
	Low Auxiliary (Pélog Paṭet Manyura)									●	●	●		●	●								
PAṬET NEM	High Auxiliary													●	●	●		●	●				
	PRINCIPAL									●	●	●		●	●								
	Low Auxiliary					●	●	●		●	●												
PAṬET LIMA	High Auxiliary (New)													●	●	●		●	●				
	PRINCIPAL (formerly High)									●	●	●		●	●								
	Low Auxiliary (formerly PRINCIPAL)					●	●	●	~~●~~	●	●	~~●~~											
	Pélog Miring (formerly Low)	●	●	●		●	●																

As a result of this shift to the scale lying a fifth higher, the principal scales of paṭet lima and paṭet nem now consist of the *same five principal tones;* the chief remaining difference is in their respective designations of dasar, first gong tone and second gong tone. The extent to which other residual differences, *e.g.* final notes, modulation practice, etc., are present will best be ascertained during the course of the analysis.

The common properties of the two paṭet, lima and nem, account for their combined classification of *pélog paṭet bem*, and the word „bem" is a fitting generic designation because this tone is one of the principals of paṭet lima and nem but is replaced by the tone barang in the third pélog paṭet, paṭet barang. In a general sense it might be accurate to regard the three-part classification of pélog paṭet as proper for the inclusion of the old paṭet-lima scale forms and the two-part division as suitable for the new forms (although more will be said in this connection presently). To Western ears the two-part distinction is readily apparent and has even been approximated in familiar tonalities: "... pieces in *pélog bem* strike the ear as being written in *B flat major* or *d minor;* pieces in *pélog barang* sound to it as if they had been written in *F major* or *a minor;* the two tonalities, therefore, differing by a fifth. This is rendered possible by the 'neutral' pitch of the tone *gulu* which, owing to its intermediate position, is 'corrected' in *pélog bem* to *E flat*, and in *pélog barang* to *E natural* ..." [1]). Many Javanese themselves are not able to differentiate between paṭet lima and paṭet nem and merely use the ambiguous designation *pélog paṭet bem* [2]).

I must confess that in the course of this study, as the 100 genḍing of the Jogyanese collection were analyzed and re-analyzed many times over, the two paṭet which remained inscrutable as to their differences — if such differences existed — were paṭet lima and paṭet nem. The problem was rendered particularly difficult by the circumstance that although there are twenty-two paṭet nem genḍing in the collection, only four genḍing are listed in paṭet lima — not a very convincing number on which to base conclusions of any significance. But this handicap proved to be something of a blessing.

In the original search for source material I had passed over a Solonese collection of twenty-eight genḍing in cipher script, for two reasons: first, it was a younger manuscript dating from about 1924—5; second, I thought that in the interests of stylistic uniformity a single collection would be more suitable for comparative purposes. Since, however, these two collections were the only manuscripts of any size available in the original notation [3]), my only recourse was to begin transcribing the fortunately large number (seventeen) of paṭet lima genḍing contained in the Solonese manuscript. The transcriptions revealed that although the collection was written down (or copied) at a relatively recent time, a majority of the paṭet lima genḍing employ the old form of scales, shown above the scale lines within the parenthesis of Table X. This not only indicates that part of the Solonese *repertoire* (not manuscript) is older than the one from Jogya (in which the paṭet lima genḍing use the new scales) but also suggests that the old form of scale may still be in use, at least as late as the mid 20's, to a considerably larger extent than was heretofore suspected [4]). This in turn suggests the possibility that the *pélog paṭet bem* classification, while it has some justification as applied to the modern paṭet lima and paṭet nem scales, may have extended its sphere, at least in some quarters, to include both the old and new scale forms of paṭet lima or that in recent times many of the Javanese have lost contact with the identifying characteristics of this old form. But the subject can be discussed more fully in Chapter XI under the general conclusions reached through the analyses of the pélog genḍing.

---

1) *MJ*, I, 74.

2) According to a verbal communication from Jaap Kunst.

3) The extensive Seelig collection of 200 genḍing (see bibiliography) consists of *transcriptions* including a three-octave range, therefore representing a combination of nuclear theme and panerusan elaboration which obscures the structural line.

4) Cf. *MJ*, I, 92—3; and J. S. Brandts Buys, „Een en Ander over Javaansche Muziek", *Programma van het Congres* (Gehouden van 27 tot en met 29 December 1929 . . . ter gelegenheid van het Tienjarig Bestaan van het Java Instituut), p. 53.

The seventeen genḍing of the Solonese manuscript and the three [1] paṭet lima genḍing of the Jogyanese collection provide a suitable numerical balance for comparison with the twenty-two paṭet nem genḍing.

Returning once again to an examination of Tables X and Y we may, for the time being, suffice with a few more explanatory remarks. The lowest paṭet lima scale shown, designated as: Pélog Miring (formerly Low), is recognized by Poensen [2] and also by Groneman [3]; but Kunst points out that such a scale is considered by the Javanese ear as having a tone sequence which differs too much from the original scale and for that reason is generally avoided [4]. The lowest scale form shown in the paṭet barang subdivision of the tables, designated as: Low Auxiliary, is sometimes classed as a *fourth* paṭet in pélog, (Pélog Paṭet Manyura), related to paṭet barang but yet distinct from it because the tone barang is replaced by bem. This scale, according to Kunst, is not frequently used [5].

The extent to which the various scale possibilities of each paṭet actually appear and the manner in which modulation is effected will most easily be shown in the subsequent analyses.

The scale given below is used for the transcription of the pélog genḍing. As in the transcription of the sléndro genḍing the scale shown does not represent actual pitches, but the approximation becomes somewhat closer if on the average the "f" is thought of as being about 20 cents higher and the "b" about 25 cents lower than the European tempered tone indicates. Again I ask the reader's indulgence and shall refer to the tones of the melodic line only by their Javanese names, so that any tendency to associate Western pitches with tonal designations may be at a minimum. See further p. 19 for an explanation of the transcriptions from the cipher script notation.

The terminology used in the analyses will be similar to that employed in the sléndro studies except, of course, as new situations demand. The terms "tonic" and "dominant" will again designate the two tones of the principal fifth-interval, and the reader is informed in advance that often the final notes of pélog genḍing do *not* coincide with either of the two tones so designated. The seven tones

---

1) The fourth genḍing (nr 66) of the Jogyanese MS appears to be incorrectly labeled by the scribe and will be included in Chapter X with the pélog paṭet barang genḍing. The other three pieces, nr 61, 62, 63, use the new scale and, for the sake of convenience, will be considered in Chapter IX, immediately following the analysis of pélog paṭet nem.

2) „De Wajang", *Mededeelingen vanwege het Nederlandsche Zendelinggenootschap*, XVI (1872), 59.

3) *De Gamelan te Jogjakarta*, (1890), p. 11.

4) *MJ*, I, 92.

5) *Ibid.*, 88, 93.

will appear in the structural charts (at gongan and kenongan divisions) in the following abbreviations: ba = barang, n = nem, l = lima, p = pélog, d = ḍaḍa, g = gulu, bm = bem.

Paṭet Lima

The three gong tones of paṭet lima are the dasar *gulu*, the first gong tone *lima* and the second gong tone *bem*. The original or old scale forms given in Tables X and Y have the following composition: the (formerly) principal scale on the keys of the saron consists of nem, lima, pélog, gulu and bem — barang and ḍaḍa may appear as auxiliary tones. The (formerly) high auxiliary scale contains the tones nem, lima, ḍaḍa, gulu and bem — barang and pélog may be used as auxiliary tones. The (formerly) low auxiliary scale has the sequence lima, pélog, gulu, bem and barang — nem and ḍaḍa may serve as auxiliary tones. Modulation from the principal scale to the high auxiliary scale is accomplished by the substitution of ḍaḍa for the tone pélog, and the return to the principal scale is realized conversely by the substitution of pélog for ḍaḍa. Modulation to the low scale is achieved by substituting barang for nem, and the substitution is reversed for the return to the principal scale.

Analysis of the Genḍing

In order to cover the widest possible sampling of paṭet lima genḍing the representative examples chosen from the Solonese collection have not been restricted to ladrang and ketawang (the only two forms appearing in the preceding chapters) but also include the larger genḍing consisting of bubuka opaq-opaq, mérong and munggah [1]). These last two sections will be discussed presently.

Four of the old scale genḍing and two of the new scale pieces will be presented in detail. The principal features of each of the seventeen genḍing will be summarized in the final part of the chapter (also see footnote 1, p. 148).

"Chondro Sari"

Genḍing nr 26, Solonese MS pélog paṭet lima

bubuka opaq-opaq B. Op. intro$_{bm}$

4 6 5 . 4 2 1 . 2 1 . 1 GN I A_g B_n C_n D_{bm}

2 4 5 4 6 4 $\overset{o}{5}$. 4 2 $\overset{g}{1}$

transcribed (see appendix pp. 287—8)

1) See p. 14.

Although "Chondro Sari" lacks a bubuka genḍing and consists, therefore, of only the bubuka opaq-opaq and one long gongan (in the complete transcription each kenongan is eight measures in length), it is a concise representative of old-scale paṭet lima genḍing. References made to the *principal* and *high* scales will indicate those scale forms designated parenthetically in Tables X and Y (p. 145 and p. 146) as *formerly* principal and *formerly* high.

Bubuka opaq-opaq

The introduction begins in the principal scale (nem, lima, pélog, gulu and bem) with the two neighbor notes of lima. The half note lima is the first tone of a descending scale passage ending with the half note bem of measure three. This is a T1 cadential formula which includes all three gong tones: lima as dasar, gulu as first gong tone, and bem as second gong tone. After a short extension the retrograde formula T2 begins in measure four and is extended by the neighbors of lima in bar five. Measures 6—7 are a repetition of the T1 cadence.

The two tones which carry the principal emphasis, created both by their position and their half-note values, are lima and bem. If the T1 formulas of the sléndro paṭet are called to mind, it may be remembered that the inclusion of the second gong tone as the ultimate note is rather the exception which confirms the rule, *viz.*, that unless the second gong tone lies *within* the formula — *e.g.* the typical formula of sléndro paṭet nem: the sequence nem-*lima*-ḍaḍa-gulu (nem as dasar, *lima* as second gong tone, gulu as first gong tone) — a *three-tone* formula beginning on the dasar and ending on the first gong tone is normally used. It was shown further that a three-note formula, resulting from the omission of the second gong tone, is never the typical cadence of a given paṭet [1]), and that the inclusion of the second gong tone (as in the T3 cadences of sléndro paṭet sanga [2]) or manyura [3]) or the T1 cadence of sléndro paṭet nem), therefore, seems to be an *essential part* of the typical formula.

On the assumption that the pélog genḍing may also follow this tendency we might describe the principal fifth-interval as *lima-gulu* (tonic and dominant, respectively) and consider the T1 formula shown above as extended to include the second gong tone bem. This tentative hypothesis will serve to some advantage during the subsequent analyses and in Chapter XI will be re-examined for its validity.

Gongan I

The first half of kenongan one (four measures long in the transcription) is a literal quotation of the bubuka opaq-opaq beginning with gulu of bar three and continuing to the final bem in measure seven. The second half of kenongan one introduces the tone ḍaḍa (in substitution for pélog) and an abrupt modula-

---

1) See pp. 55—6 and p. 111.
2) See p. 85.
3) See pp. 111—12.

tion to the high scale. The last two measures consist of a descending scale from nem to ḍaḍa, followed by a T1 formula which is extended to gulu as the kenong beat falls.

The melodic high points of this kenongan merit some attention. The first half, as a reiteration of part of the bubuka opaq-opaq, consists of a T2 and a T1 formula. The manner in which ḍaḍa is introduced in the second half of the kenongan is very sudden. To anticipate one of the hallmarks of pélog paṭet nem it should be stated that the exchange tones ḍaḍa-pélog are characteristically introduced and quitted in a step-wise motion in contrast to the appearance of ḍaḍa, in this instance, after a leap up from bem. The reiteration of ḍaḍa for two successive measures may, in fact, be prompted by this abrupt substitution as a means of confirming or, better, insisting on the modulation to the high scale. The next passage nem-lima-ḍaḍa might be viewed as a secondary dominant (nem) proceeding scalewise, through a T1 formula, to land finally on the dominant (gulu) as the last note of the kenongan. It is perhaps worthy of note, since it is not uncommon in paṭet lima, that the secondary dominant nem is also preceded by its dominant ḍaḍa.

The second kenongan continues in the high scale with the principal melodic emphasis on the ḍaḍa-nem-gulu relationships mentioned directly above. The ḍaḍa-nem relationship is clearly evident in the descending scale ḍaḍa-gulu-bem-nem (measures 18—19 of the transcription). The last half of the kenongan is similar to the close of kenongan one except that now the nem-gulu-nem goal is stressed by the omission of the tone bem in the final T1—T2 formulas (resulting in a three-note formula between tonic and dominant) and the extension to the final nem.

Kenongan three after a rest repeats twice the same pattern which appears in the last half of kenongan two. The last half of kenongan one and all of kenongan two and three are related to the bubuka opaq-opaq with, of course, the substitution of ḍaḍa for pélog. Throughout this section nem serves as a bridge or transition tone.

The fourth kenongan begins abruptly on pélog (approached by a leap down from the final nem of the preceding kenongan), and interestingly enough is repeated six times while the introduction of ḍaḍa merited four repetitions. This is followed by the neigbor note nem and an exact quotation of the entire bubuka opaq-opaq, confirming, at the same time, the return to the principal scale.

General Summary

The bubuka opaq-opaq provides the basis of melodic development for the one gongan. The literal quotation of the introduction at the end of the gongan produces a short three-part form which is further emphasized by the high-scale middle section in contrast to the principal-scale beginning and ending.

Although the duration of the high-scale passage is short, its length is proportionate to the whole of the genḍing, and the repetition of the exchange tones in their respective scales leaves little doubt that an actual modulation occurs. The introduction of both exchange tones is abrupt, each of them being approached and quitted by a leap.

The melodic importance of each tone:

Lima has a major importance as tonic of the principal fifth-interval.
Gulu, although it is only prominent in the middle section, shares a principal importance with lima as its dominant.
Bem is important as the final note of the bubuka opaq-opaq and the single gongan.
Pélog is melodically sensitive as an exchangeable tone.
Nem functions as a transition tone in a secondary dominant capacity.
Ḍaḍa is sensitive as a modulation tone and has a minor importance in relation to nem.
Barang does not appear.

"Retnaningsi"

Ladrang nr 2, Solonese MS — pélog paṭet lima

bubuka opaq-opaq	B. Op.	intro$_1$	
6 1 2 1 6 1 5 3 2 1 $\overset{o}{2}$.	B. Gd.	A_1 A_1 B_g C_1	A
1 6 $\overset{g}{5}$	GN I	D_1 D_1 E_{bm} C_1^*	B
	GN II	D_1 D_1 E_{bm} C_1^*	

C* first two notes changed

transcribed (see appendix p. 288)

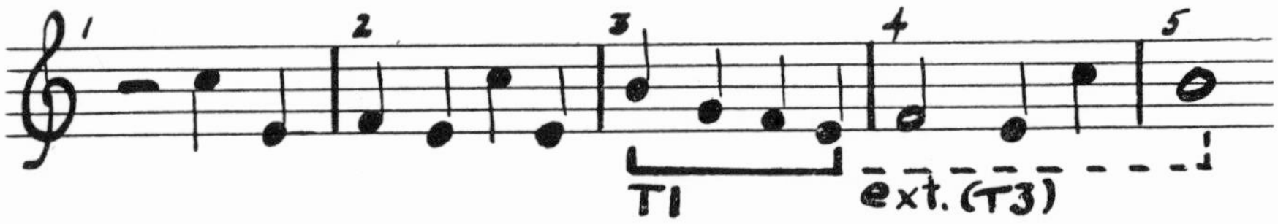

The binary form of "Retnaningsi", in which *A* consists of the bubuka genḍing and *B* of gongan I and II, is further emphasized in the modulation scheme. The first part is in the high scale of the old paṭet lima types (scale designations, therefore, will be the same as in the preceding analysis), and the second part is in the principal scale.

Bubuka opaq-opaq

The introduction opens with the secondary dominant in an ascending scale to the dominant gulu (first note of measure two). The scale passage is then reversed and is followed by a repetition of the opening passage which is not completed (being interrupted by the T1 cadence) until the first note of measure four. The T1 cadence of measure three includes the second gong tone bem and is extended to gulu in bar four, followed in turn by a continuation of that extension in the form of a T3 formula (bars 4—5).

Our tentative assumption that lima-gulu comprise the principal fifth-interval (see p. 150) is supported by the occurrence of those two tones alternately as the first note of each measure and by the weight of their half-note value in measures four and five. It should be noted, however, that the second gong tone bem is included in the T1 cadence of measure three.

Bubuka genḍing

The first two kenongan are identical and consist of an augmentation (precise except for the extra *bem* connecting the two kenongan) of the bubuka opaq-opaq beginning with measure one and continuing to the lima of bar three. Kenongan three begins with a repetition of bem (the second note being a whole note) followed by a half-measure rest and the T4 formula given here:

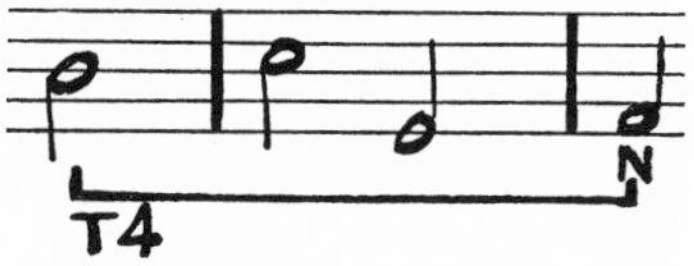

This formula is extended in kenongan four, and the gongan closes with a T3 cadence.

The secondary-dominant function of nem again appears to be delayed at the end (but not in the first half) of kenongan one and two by the tone lima until the end of kenongan three, where the ascending T4 formula leads to the dominant gulu. The tone bem is used at the beginning of the second kenongan and more especially the third kenongan in cadential support of tonic-dominant (and even of the secondary dominant).

Gongan I, II

Gongan I and II are identical and are in the principal scale. Kenongan one consists of lima in reiteration and its neighbors. The tone pélog is introduced abruptly in a leap down from nem and quitted by a return leap up to nem. Kenongan two is the same as the first kenongan. Kenongan three consists of a T1 formula with a delayed extension on gulu-bem (an augmentation of bars 3—4 of the bubuka opaq-opaq but with bem prolonged instead of gulu), which confirms the principal scale. The fourth kenongan contains a T4 formula extended to lima. The importance of gulu and lima as the principal fifth-interval may be seen from the manner in which the extension is accomplished, given in a transcription of this kenongan below.

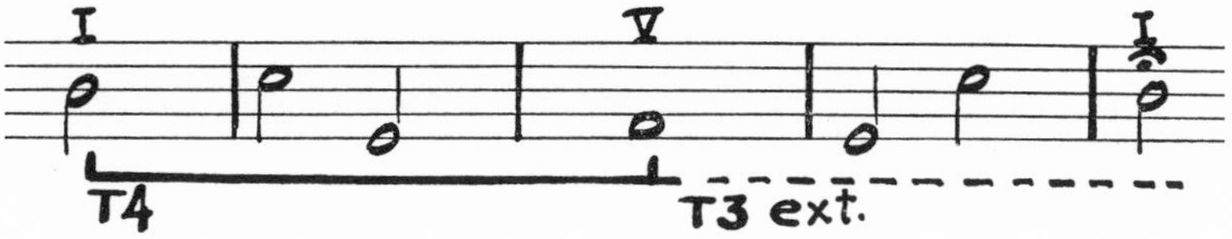

Since the T1 formula of kenongan three confirms the principal scale, however, it is possible that this T1 cadence should be considered as primary and the formulas of kenongan four as comprising a long extension.

After the repetitions of lima (tonic), the introduction of pélog in the first two kenongan, and the usage of three of the four theoretical cadential formulas in the last half of the gongan, there is no doubt that the ladrang ends in the principal scale.

General Summary

The bubuka opaq-opaq provides the basis of melodic development for the genḍing, the tone ḍaḍa of the introduction being replaced by pélog in gongan I and II. The three critical sections are related melodically and cadentially. The ladrang begins in the high scale and modulates abruptly at the beginning of the *B* section to the principal scale.

The melodic importance of each tone:

Lima as the final note of the bubuka opaq-opaq, all three gongan, and most of the kenongan subdivisions and as the tonic of the principal fifth-interval is one of the most important tones.
Gulu is melodically prominent in the bubuka opaq-opaq and as the dominant of lima shares its importance.
Bem is used in cadential support of the principal fifth-interval.
Pélog is melodically sensitive as an exchangeable tone.
Nem as a secondary dominant to gulu appears as a bridge or transition tone.
Ḍaḍa is sensitive as a modulation tone.
Barang is not used.

"Larajola"

Genḍing nr 7, Solonese MS — pélog paṭet lima

bubuka opaq-opaq						
	B. Op.				intro$_{bm}$	
5 5 6 5 4 2 4 . 2 4 . 4	Mérong	A_{bm}	A_{bm}	B_{l}	C_{bm}	A
5 6 5 2 1 . 5(o) 6 1 2 1(g)	Trans.	———			D_{bm}	
	GN I	E_{bm}	E^{*}_{bm}	F_{bm}	G_{bm}	B

E* first 2 notes omitted

transcribed (see appendix p. 289)

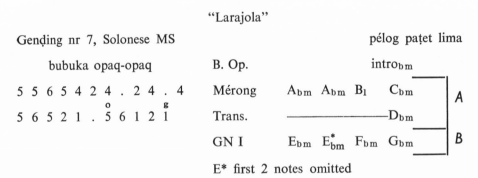

"Larajola" is a genḍing in the large form, consisting of three parts: the bubuka opaq-opaq, the mérong and the munggah. The third section, the munggah (GN I in this example) is considered the genḍing proper. The mérong is usually repeated several times, and the last time a *transitional* kenongan (indicated by the letter "D" in the structural chart given above) leads to the munggah. This transition, therefore, will replace the bubuka genḍing of the ladrangan form as the second "critical section" in our analyses, so that the three critical sections in the larger genḍing are: the bubuka opaq-opaq, the transitional kenongan and the final gongan. Each kenongan in the transcription is eight measures long, and, as another common feature of the large genḍing, the basic note value of the munggah is twice as great as that of the mérong (see the complete transcription p. 289).

The modulation scheme of "Larajola" is the following: the bubuka opaq-opaq is in the (old) principal scale; the mérong modulates to the high scale and returns to the principal scale in the last kenongan; the transitional kenongan and the munggah (the genḍing proper) are in the principal scale.

Bubuka opaq-opaq

The first five measures of the bubuka opaq-opaq contain the principal cadences: a slightly elaborated combination of a T1 and T2 formula (without the inclusion of the second gong tone bem). This is extended by the I—V interval of measure five, continuing in a three-note descending scale to lima of bar six and the T4 formula of measure six — the last formula itself being extended by the note bem. Lima and gulu are melodically prominent as the principal notes of the cadences. In measure three the return to the half-note pélog, the tie over the bar line of measures 3—4, and the reiteration in measure four also give pélog a melodic importance. Bem, too, has some prominence in the weight of the half note of measure five and the final note ending the introduction.

Although it might be argued that the final T4 formula is the principal cadence of the bubuka opaq-opaq, I believe that the stress through prolongation of the T1 and T2 cadences has the primary emphasis and that the notes following are actually an extension. In the interests of avoiding a subjective interpretation, however, (and because the I—V interval of measure five could be considered as a break in the continuity of the preceding cadences) I have entered the T4 formula in the statistical summary (p. 165) as the primary cadence.

Mérong

The first two (eight-measure) kenongan are identical. They begin with a continuation of gulu-bem which closed the bubuka opaq-opaq, followed by a T3 formula with lima appearing as a whole note. An elaboration of the T4 formula, which within its extension features bem in repetition (as a cadential support) and introduces ḍaḍa in a stepwise motion, ends the kenongan. This formula with its extension is given below.

It should be noted that ḍaḍa (marked by +) is introduced in bar thirteen by an ascending scale and quitted in bar fourteen by a descending scale. Both kenongan are based on the T4 formula (the T3 being its retrograde form) of the sixth measure of the bubuka opaq-opaq.

The first half of kenongan three is the same as that of the two preceding kenongan. In the second half the scalewise extension is simplified and proceeds to the conjunct formulas T3—T1—T2 in which pélog effects the return to the principal scale. The passage is given below for comparison with the above example, and it should be pointed out that pélog (+) is introduced by a stepwise motion.

The T1—T2 formulas are derived from the bubuka opaq-opaq.

The final kenongan, after a slight extension in the beginning, is an exact quotation of the bubuka opaq-opaq, and confirms the principal scale.

Transition

The transitional kenongan is also a confirmation of the principal scale and is based on the T1 and T2 formulas of the bubuka opaq-opaq. It opens with three alternations between pélog and lima, followed by the neighbor note nem and a T1 formula descending to bem and continuing to a reiteration of nem. Nem serves as a bridge or transition tone leading to the closing combination cadence: T1—T2—T1. The final T1 cadence is slightly elaborated by a return to pélog (foreshadowed in bars 2—3 of the bubuka opaq-opaq?) and an extension to bem.

Gongan I (Munggah)

The genḍing proper begins with an augmentation of the last three notes of the transitional kenongan. The remainder of the first kenongan is an augmentated elaboration of the T1—T2 formulas and ends with the same extension which closed the transitional kenongan. The second kenongan is the same as kenongan one except that the first two notes are omitted.

The first half of kenongan three consists of a reiteration of gulu (dominant), and the last half continues in an ascending scale passage to the tone barang and then descends to bem as the kenong beat falls. This brief (and only) appearance of barang followed almost immediately by the tone bem does not, of course, establish a modulation. It would be extremely surprising if such a modulation (in which barang is substituted for bem) did occur in the old scale form of paṭet lima since, theoretically, such a modulation exists only in the new paṭet lima form (*i.e.*, the high auxiliary scale lacking the tones bem and pélog, shown in Tables X and Y, p. 145 and p. 146).

The final kenongan begins with a reiteration of nem as a tone of transition leading to the final cadences, the whole eight measures, actually, being an augmentation of the last half of the transitional kenongan.

General Summary

The bubuka opaq-opaq provides the basis of melodic development throughout the piece. The three critical sections — the bubuka opaq-opaq, the transition and the final gongan (munggah) — are related melodically and cadentially. In the mérong a modulation to the high scale is effected by the substitution of ḍaḍa for pélog, and a return to the principal scale via pélog occurs in the latter part of the gongan. Both ḍaḍa and pélog are introduced and quitted in a stepwise motion.

The melodic importance of each tone:

Lima has a primary importance as the tonic of the principal fifth-interval.
Gulu as the dominant of lima shares its importance.
Bem, with one exception, marks the close of all gongan, kenongan, and the bubuka opaq-opaq. It has a principal role, therefore, as the final note of all sections and has a minor role as the cadential support of tonic and dominant.
Pélog is melodically sensitive as an exchangeable tone.
Nem appears in a transitional or bridge-tone function.
Ḍaḍa is melodically sensitive as a modulation tone.
Barang appears only once.

"Laras Bronto"

Genḍing nr 9, Solonese MS — pélog paṭet lima

bubuka opaq-opaq						
	B. Op.				$intro_{bm}$	
4 6 4 . 4 2 1 . 1 . 1 2	Mérong a)	A_{bm}	B_{l}	C_{bm}	A_{bm}	A
4 5 4 6 4 $\overset{o}{5}$. 4 2 $\overset{g}{1}$	Mérong b)	D_{l}	B^{*}_{l}	C_{bm}	A_{bm}	A
	Trans.	———	———	———	E_{bm}	A
	GN I	F_{bm}	F_{bm}	G_{bm}	D^{*}_{bm}	B

B* first measure omitted
D* rhythmic change in first 2 notes

transcribed (see appendix p. 290)

"Laras Bronto" is another example of the large genḍing. It affords some interest in comparison with the foregoing example (nr 7), and the pertinent points will be mentioned in the course of the analysis. The mérong (the *A* section) consists of two regular gongan, each containing four four-measure kenongan, and the transitional kenongan is eight measures in length. The *B* section consists of one long gongan having eight-measure kenongan. The entire genḍing is in the old form of principal scale.

Bubuka opaq-opaq

The introduction begins with an incomplete T1 formula (including bem) in which the tonic lima is omitted and the tone pélog is emphasized in bars 1—2 (cf. nr 7, bars 3—4). After a short extension on bem (bars 3—4) a T2 cadence finally resolves to the delayed lima on the first beat of measure five. Lima is extended by its neighbors and in measure 6—7 descends in a T1 cadence to bem. The emphasis on pélog, the principal T2—T1 cadences and the stress of the tone bem in bars 3—4 and again as the final note are features in common with the bubuka opaq-opaq of nr 7 (cf. the weight of bem in bars five and seven). The tone lima is particularly emphasized in the introduction of "Laras Bronto" by its delay until measure five and by its extension to bar six, where it occurs as a half note.

Mérong a)

The first kenongan, except for the omission of one "bem", is the same as the bubuka opaq-opaq beginning with the third measure. The second kenongan features a long reiteration of the tone lima and concludes with lima and its neighbors. The third kenongan continues with lima and its neighbors and ends in a T1 formula. Kenongan four is the same as the first kenongan, *i.e.* a combination T2—T1 cadence.

Mérong b)

Kenongan one begins with a repetition of the tone bem and then abruptly introduces ḍaḍa in an upward leap. Ḍaḍa descends stepwise to bem, and the kenongan closes with a T3 formula. Kenongan two is the same as that of Mérong a) except that the two lima are omitted in the first bar. Kenongan three and four are identical to those of Mérong a).

The one appearance of ḍaḍa followed by lima and its neighbor pélog (approached by a leap down from nem) does not effect a modulation.

Transition

The transitional kenongan begins with a repetition of nem as a bridge tone and secondary dominant. This is followed by pélog and nem, as neighbors of lima, and a Tl formula descending to gulu; a T2 formula returns to lima, and a final Tl cadence extended to pélog and bem closes the kenongan (cf. nr 7, the last half of the transitional kenongan).

Gongan I

The first two kenongan of the munggah are identical. They open with an emphasis on nem and its neighbors and then proceed to a slightly elaborated T2—Tl combination which ends with the same extension as that of the transitional kenongan (cf. nr 7, first two kenongan of the munggah). The third kenongan consists of a long reiteration of lima followed by its neighbor notes and a Tl formula extended to bem. The fourth kenongan, except that the first two notes appear a half measure earlier, is the same as the transitional kenongan.

General Summary

The entire genḍing is based on the bubuka opaq-opaq. The three critical sections are related melodically and cadentially. The principal scale is used throughout, the one abrupt substitution of ḍaḍa and the disjunct return of pélog occurring too swiftly to establish a modulation.

The melodic importance of each tone:

Lima as it is featured throughout the genḍing in reiterated passages and as the tonic of the principal fifth-interval has a primary importance.
Gulu as the dominant of lima shares its importance.
Bem is prominent as the final note of all but two kenongan, of all gongan and the bubuka opaq-opaq.
Pélog achieves some importance in the bubuka opaq-opaq and is melodically sensitive as an exchangeable tone.
Nem is used as a tone of transition.
Ḍaḍa is melodically sensitive as an exchange note for pélog.
Barang does not appear.

"Horang Haring"

Ladrang nr 3, Solonese MS — pélog paṭet lima

bubuka opaq-opaq	B. Op.				intro_{bm}	
1 1 1 2 3 5 3 . 3 5 6 5 6	B. Gd.	A_{bm}	A^*_d	B_d	C_{bm}	A
5 3 . 3 2 $\overset{o}{3}$ 2 1 2 $\overset{g}{1}$	GN I	A_{bm}	A^*_d	B_d	D_g	A
	GN II	E_l	E_l	F_l	G_{bm}	B

A* last 2 notes changed

transcribed (see appendix p. 291)

The ladrang "Horang Haring" is an example of the paṭet lima *new-scale* forms. The designations *principal* scale and *low* scale indicate those scale forms so designated outside the parenthesis in Tables X and Y, p. 145 and p. 146. The genḍing has a binary form with the *A* section consisting of the bubuka genḍing and gongan I and the *B* section of gongan II. A short modulation from the new principal scale (using *ḍaḍa* as one of its principal tones) to the low scale (using *pélog* in substitution for ḍaḍa as a principal tone) occurs in the first half of gongan II. The latter half of the gongan returns to the principal scale.

"Horang Haring" is particularly interesting in as much as it has retained the predominant features of those compositions written in the old-scale forms (as will be revealed in the statistical summaries).

Bubuka opaq-opaq

The bubuka opaq-opaq is comprised of a T2 cadence and an elaborated T1 cadence extended to bem. These two cadences are linked by the neighbor note ḍaḍa in measure three. The rhythmic distribution of the T1 cadence creates some emphasis on the interval nem-ḍaḍa or, including measure three, ḍaḍa-nem-ḍaḍa. This is suggested by the occurrence of nem on beats one and three of the fourth measure, by the melodic weight of ḍaḍa in bars three and five, and by the return to ḍaḍa in measure six. The initial T2 cadence and the prominence of lima and bem in the T1 cadence, however, establish the primary importance of these two tones.

Bubuka genḍing

The first kenongan is an augmentation of the opening five notes of the bubuka opaq-opaq plus a stepwise return to bem. The second kenongan is an augmentation of the same figure continued to include the first beat of bar three of the introduction. Kenongan three continues the quotation to the first beat of bar five, using the upper neighbor barang, however, instead of the lima on beat two of measure four. The fourth kenongan completes the quotation of the bubuka opaq-opaq (a T1 cadence with a long extension to the final bem) with one change: lima replaces the first ḍaḍa of measure five.

Ḍaḍa occurs as a *neighbor note* in kenongan one, as the *last note* of kenongan two and *begins* kenongan three in a scale passage to nem (plus the neighbor barang), and returns as the *final note* of the kenongan. The slight modification of the bubuka opaq-opaq in the bubuka genḍing even further highlights the ḍaḍa-nem interval; but the principal fifth-interval lima-gulu is the major goal as the gongan closes in an extended T1 cadence.

Gongan I

The first three kenongan are identical to those of the bubuka genḍing. Kenongan four begins with the nem-ḍaḍa interval (bars 4—5 of the bubuka opaq-opaq) and ends with a T1 cadence (including bem) extended to gulu.

In both the bubuka genḍing and gongan one, nem appears in a transitional or bridge-tone function as a secondary dominant of gulu (N.B. the final goal of gongan I). In the extended T2—T1 cadential structure which forms the framework of these gongan the tone bem serves in cadential support of tonic and dominant (kenongan one and two).

Gongan II

The second gongan begins with a repetition of the tone pélog in an abrupt modulation to the low scale. The passage proceeds stepwise to nem and then again descends to pélog. The first and second kenongan are identical, and the melodic material has a simplified relationship (pélog being substituted for ḍaḍa) to bars 3—4—5 of the bubuka opaq-opaq.

The third kenongan quits the preceding pélog with a leap up to nem which leads to lima and subsequently a T3 formula extended to ḍaḍa and back to lima. The fourth kenongan, an abbreviation of the entire bubuka opaq-opaq, closes the ladrang with a T2—T1 cadence extended to bem.

General Summary

The bubuka opaq-opaq provides the basis of melodic development throughout the genḍing. The three critical sections are related melodically and cadentially. Although the modulation in gongan II lasts for only two kenongan, the insistence of the tone pélog firmly establishes the low scale.

It is worthy of note that "Horang Haring" as a ladrang in the new-scale forms has in common with the compositions in the old scale the following general features: a) the T1 and T2 cadences in the critical sections and in the body of the genḍing; b) the tone bem used as a final note and prominent throughout the piece; c) the abrupt introduction of the exchange tone (pélog, in this instance); d) the single appearance of barang as a neighbor note; e) the prominence of ḍaḍa (a replacement for pélog in the new scale) in the bubuka opaq-opaq (cf. the similar importance of pélog in the introduction of nr 7, nr 5, nr 9).

The melodic importance of each tone:

> *Lima* as the tonic of the cadential formulas of the principal fifth-interval has a primary importance.
>
> *Gulu* is the final note of gongan I and shares the importance of lima as the dominant of the principal fifth-interval.

Bem has a particular importance as the final note of the bubuka opaq-opaq, bubuka genḍing and the final gongan, and a secondary importance in cadential support of tonic and dominant.
Nem has a minor importance as a tone of transition.
Ḍaḍa is conspicuous in the bubuka opaq-opaq, has a minor role in relation to nem, and is melodically sensitive as an exchangeable tone.
Pélog is melodically sensitive as a modulation tone.
Barang appears once as a neighbor note.

"Pacharchina"

Ladrang nr 13, Solonese MS — pélog paṭet lima

bubuka opaq-opaq	B. Op.				intro$_g$	
2 5 3 . 2 5 3 5 5 6 $\overset{o}{1}$ 2	B. Gd.	A_g	A^*_d	B_d	C_g	A
3 1 $\overset{g}{2}$	GN I	A_g	A^*_d	B_d	D_l	A
	GN II	E_l	F_{ba}	G_d	H_l	B
	GN III	E_l	I_n	G_d	J_{bm}	B
	GN IV	K_{bm}	K_{bm}	L_l	M_g	B

A* last 2 notes reversed

transcribed (see appendix p. 291)

"Pacharchina" is a ladrang using the new-scale forms. It has a binary structure with the *A* section consisting of the bubuka genḍing and gongan I and the *B* section of gongan II, III and IV. In the *B* section a modulation occurs to the new high-auxiliary scale in which barang replaces bem as a principal tone (see Tables X and Y, p. 145 and p. 146).

Bubuka opaq-opaq

The introduction opens with a repetition of the dominant-tonic interval separated by the half-note ḍaḍa. This forms a spun-out T2 cadence (without bem) which is completed in bar three and followed by a somewhat extended T4 formula. Lima and gulu are featured, and a minor prominence is given to ḍaḍa by the use of a half note in bar two and the neighbor note in bar four.

Bubuka genḍing

The first kenongan features the ḍaḍa-nem interval in a secondary dominant capacity resolving to the dominant gulu as the final note. Kenongan two is the same except that the position of the last two notes is reversed, resulting in an augmentation of the same figure appearing in bars 3—4 of the bubuka opaq-opaq: nem-bem-gulu-ḍaḍa. The first half of these two kenongan, then, can be seen as the retrograde form of this figure: ḍaḍa-gulu-bem-nem. As in the bubuka opaq-opaq, the passage resolves to gulu — in this case at the beginning of the third kenongan. Kenongan three and four are an exact augmentation of the entire bubuka opaq-opaq; and the transitional function of nem is now recognizable in the first two kenongan.

Gongan I

The first three kenongan are identical to those of the bubuka genḍing. The first note of the fourth kenongan completes the T2 cadence of the preceding kenongan and proceeds to the dominant gulu and a reiteration of the tonic lima (with one appearance of the neighbor note nem).

Gongan II

The first kenongan consists of a retrograde form of the figure from bars 2—3 of the bubuka opaq-opaq: lima-ḍaḍa-lima-lima. Kenongan two modulates to the high auxiliary scale by means of a scale passage from lima to a repetition of barang. The third kenongan contains a descending scale from barang to gulu and then begins a T2 formula which is completed in kenongan four. The last kenongan restates the T2 formula with a slight extension closing the gongan.

Gongan III

The first kenongan is the same as that of gongan II. The second kenongan is similar to that of gongan II but finishes on gulu instead of barang. Kenongan three is identical to that of gongan II; the T2 formula, however, is not completed in the fourth kenongan but returns to gulu-ḍaḍa-gulu followed by a T1 cadence which is extended to bem as a modulation back to the principal scale.

Gongan IV

Kenongan one and two are identical and emphasize chiefly the tone bem in confirmation of the principal scale. The third kenongan consists of a prolonged T3 formula, and kenongan four closes the piece with a slightly extended T4 cadence similar to that which terminates the introduction.

General Summary

The bubuka opaq-opaq provides the basis for melodic development throughout the genḍing. The three critical sections are related melodically and cadentially.

The modulation to the high scale is accomplished by the substitution of the tone barang for bem as one of the five principal tones in gongan II and III.

Barang is introduced and quitted in a scale passage. A modulation back to the principal scale occurs at the end of gongan III when bem returns as the ultimate note of a T1 cadence.

The modulation to the high auxiliary scale, the avoidance of the tone pélog, and the closing T3 and T4 cadences of the final gongan suggest that "Pacharchina" departs somewhat from the old-scale practices. On the other hand, the return to the principal scale via a T1 formula extended to bem, the use throughout the genḍing of this formula, and the reiteration of bem in gongan IV as a confirmation of the principal scale are evidence of a close tie to the principal features of the old-scale paṭet lima genḍing.

The melodic importance of each tone:

Lima as the final note of gongan I and II and as the tonic of the principal fifth-interval has a major importance.
Gulu shares this importance as the dominant of lima and as the final note of the bubuka opaq-opaq, the bubuka genḍing, and the final gongan.
Bem is melodically sensitive as an exchangeable tone and appears as the final note of gongan III.
Nem functions as a tone of transition.
Ḍaḍa has a minor importance in the introduction and in relation to nem.
Barang is melodically sensitive as a modulation tone.
Pélog does not appear.

Summary and Conclusions

Even though examples of both the old and the new forms of paṭet lima scales are represented in the Solonese collection, these genḍing appear to have certain features in common — aside from the chief difference in one of their principal tones (pélog and ḍaḍa). The regularity of these features can best be seen in a summary of the seventeen genḍing.

The usual summary of architectonic forms and the correspondence of two of the critical sections on the basis of identical kenongan (Table I of the sléndro chapters) will not be included. A summary of compositional forms, in this instance, would have little value because both ladrang and the large genḍing are represented. A correspondence between the bubuka genḍing (or transitional kenongan) and the final gongan on a melodic basis has been adequately established in the detailed analyses. A cadential relationship can be seen in Table I below.

A summary of the patterns of kenongan repetition in the gongan (Table II of the sléndro chapters) will also be omitted since the genḍing in the large form contain both four- and eight-measure kenongan.

Table I gives a summary of the cadences closing the three critical sections of the genḍing, the scale classification (old or new), and the modulation scheme (P = principal, H = high auxiliary, L = low auxiliary). The designation "P" in the modulation column must be referred to the scale classification for an indication of whether pélog or ḍaḍa is being used as one of the principal tones (also see Tables X and Y, p. 145 and p. 146). The cadential symbols have the same general meaning as in the corresponding tables of the previous chapters. The T1 or T2 formulas include the second gong tone bem unless shown with an asterisk, *e.g.* T1*, indicating that the cadence omits bem and consists, therefore, of lima-pélog-(or ḍaḍa-) gulu.

Table I

Genḍing	B. Op.	Trans. (B. Bd.)	Final GN	Scales	Mod.
nr 1 Sembawa	T1	T1	T1	new	P
„ 2 Retnaningsi	T1 + T3	T4 + T3	(T1)T4+T3	old	H-P
„ 3 Horang Haring	T1	T1	T1	new	P-L-P
„ 4 Welas Tangis	T4 + gulu	T4 + gulu	T4 + gulu	new	P-H-P
„ 6 Kombangmara	T1 + lima	T1	T1	old	H-P-H-P-H-P
„ 7 Larajola	(T1/T2)T4 + bem	T1	T1	old	P-H-P
„ 8 Tlutur	I/V	T1 + T2	T1 + T2	old	H-P-H-P
„ 9 Laras Bronto	T1	T1	T1	old	P
„ 12 Blabak	T1 + nem	T1 + nem	T1 + nem	new	P-H-P
„ 13 Pacharchina	T2 + T4	T2 + T4	T4	new	P-H-P
„ 20 Taliwongsa	T1 + T4	T1 + T3	T1	old	P-H-P
„ 21 Peksi Kudasi	T2	T1 + gulu	T1* + T2	old	H-P-H-P
„ 22 Kembangmara	(T1)T4 + bem	T1* + T2	T1* + T2	old	H-P-H-P
„ 23 Logondang	T1 + T3	T1 + T3	T1 + T2	new	P
„ 24 Jalaga	T1 + T2	T2 + ḍaḍa	T1 + nem	new	P-H-P
„ 26 Chondro Sari	T1	———	T1	old	P-H-P
„ 28 Muntap	T2 + gulu	T1	T1	old	P-H-P-H-P

Summary:	T1	T2	T3	T4	I/V	
B. Op.	10	3	0	3	1	= 76.5% T1 or T2
Trans. (B. Gd.)	12	2	0	2	0	= 87.5% T1 or T2
Final GN	14	0	0	3	0	= 82.4% T1 or T2

10 genḍing use the old scale
7 „ „ „ new „

Table II shows the melodic importance of each tone. Certain columns used in similar tables in preceding chapters have been omitted since the analyses indicate no need for their inclusion, *e.g.* true or quasi-pancher, tone of melodic variety (the variety afforded by the exchange tones themselves, for example, needs no further mention). The new or old form of scale is again indicated for each genḍing as a convenience for comparison with the other principal features. The column headed "Omitted" refers to a tone that does not appear in a given genḍing. The heading "Subs." designates tones which are used as exchange tones for one of the five principals, *e.g. ḍaḍa* indicates that this tone is substituted (in the old form of scales) within the course of the genḍing for pélog (the reverse substitution being understood).

Table II

Gd.	Scales	Final	Pr. 5th	Trans.	Cad. Sup.	Omitted	Subs.
nr 1	new	bem	lima-gulu		bem	pélog	
,, 2	old	lima	,, ,,	nem	,,	barang	ḍaḍa
,, 3	new	bem	,, ,,	,,	,,		pélog
,, 4	new	gulu	,, ,,		(,,)	pélog	barang
,, 6	old	bem	,, ,,	nem	,,		ḍaḍa
,, 7	old	,,	,, ,,	,,	,,		,,
,, 8	old	lima	,, ,,	,,	,,	barang	,,
,, 9	old	bem	,, ,,	,,	(,,)	,,	
,, 12	new	nem	,, ,,	,,	(,,)		barang
,, 13	new	gulu	,, ,,	,,	(,,)	pélog	,,
,, 20	old	bem	,, ,,	,,	,,		ḍaḍa
,, 21	old	gulu	,, ,,	,,	,,		,,
,, 22	old	lima	,, ,,	,,	(,,)		,,
,, 23	new	,,	,, ,,	,,	,,	barang	
,, 24	new	nem	,, ,,	,,	(,,)		ḍaḍa
,, 26	old	bem	,, ,,	,,	(,,)	barang	,,
,, 28	old	,,	,, ,,	,,	,,		,,
Summary:		bem 8 lima 4 gulu 3 nem 2	lima-gulu	nem	bem	barang pélog	ḍaḍa barang pélog

The summary given below Table I indicates that the typical cadence for the paṭet lima genḍing of the Solonese collection is the T1 formula (or occasionally its retrograde form the T2) *with the inclusion of the second gong tone bem.* The four theoretical formulas, any of which may occur within the body of the genḍing or at inner gongan, are given below for both the old and new scales.

Although the tone *pélog* in the old scale and the tone *ḍaḍa* in the new form

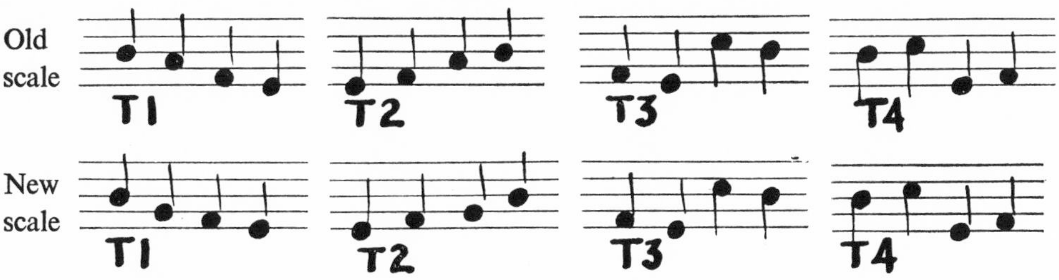

identify their respective scale genders by the manner and frequency of their appearance throughout the genḍing as a whole, the possibility that these are regarded as peculiarly essential tones may be a partial explanation for the preference given to the T1 and T2 formulas, in which they are included, rather than the T3 or T4, in which they are not. The same line of reasoning also leads us back to our earlier supposition that the second gong tone may be an essential part of the typical cadential formula. The addition of bem after the descending or before the ascending scale passage between tonic (lima) and dominant (gulu) seems to support this supposition.

Table I indicates the following modulation practice: *the genḍing using the old scale* never modulate to the low auxiliary scale [1]), in which the tone barang is substituted for nem; they frequently modulate to the high auxiliary by the substitution of ḍaḍa for pélog; they may begin in either the principal or high scale but always end in the principal. *The genḍing using the new scale* rarely modulate to the low auxiliary scale (one example), in which pélog is substituted for ḍaḍa; they frequently modulate to the high auxiliary by the substitution of barang for bem; they begin and end in the principal scale.

In the detailed analyses it was seen that the modulation tone is characteristically introduced abruptly in both the old- and new-scale genḍing. A modulation to an auxiliary scale or the return to the principal scale is often established by the reiteration of the exchange tone which, in the latter instance, is followed by a T1 cadence in confirmation of the principal scale.

The summary below Table II indicates that bem is the final note of paṭet lima genḍing more than half the time, and that lima (tonic) and gulu (dominant) also appear in that capacity in about an equal number of genḍing. It may or may not be significant that the two examples (nr 12 and nr 24) which end on nem are both new-scale genḍing. The extent to which new-scale pieces have been influenced by the regular features of pélog paṭet nem will be discussed at the appropriate time; meanwhile, such speculations in connection with the Solonese collection are probably without value since the new-scale genḍing for the most part exhibit the typical features of the old-scale pieces. The general conclusion may be formulated that although any of the four tones — bem, lima, gulu and nem — may be used as the final note of both the old- and new-scale

[1]) Cf. p. 148.

genḍing, bem is preferred in that capacity. The avoidance of pélog, one of the five principal tones of the old scale, as a final note is probably due to the particular regard in which pélog is held by the Javanese, namely, that it is *miring* or deviating [1]). In the new-scale genḍing the avoidance of ḍaḍa as a final note suggests that these examples have retained this old-scale practice even though ḍaḍa — which, like the other principal tones, is regarded as *jejeg* [2]) — has been substituted for pélog as a principal tone.

The interval lima-gulu is the most prominent fifth-interval in paṭet lima genḍing. The appropriateness of Western terms "tonic-dominant" in connection with these two tones would appear to be questionable since bem is preferred as a final note. It will be convenient, however, if this discussion is deferred until Chapter XI.

Nem frequently appears as a tone of transition and/or secondary dominant. Bem is used in cadential support of tonic and dominant, as well as the functions mentioned above. In the old-scale genḍing the tone barang appears as a passing note or is omitted entirely. In the new-scale genḍing this tone is substituted for bem in the modulation from the principal to the high scale, but even then it is not conspicuous (cf. nr 13, appendix pp. 291—2). Any of the modulation tones except ḍaḍa may be omitted.

A comparison of the columns of Table I headed "Scales" and "Mod." with the two columns of Table II headed "Omitted" and "Subs." reveals that although an exchange tone might not be omitted neither is it really used as a substitute tone. This indicates that the appearance of the exchange tone is too fleeting to effect an actual modulation [3]).

A brief summary of the principal points:

1. The bubuka opaq-opaq is a particular elaboration, combination or variation of cadential formulas, the principal cadence being the T1 formula extended to include the second gong tone bem. The bubuka opaq-opaq provides the basis of thematic development for the entire genḍing.
2. Through the thematic development of the bubuka opaq-opaq the T1 cadential formula becomes the melodic framework of the genḍing. The particular variation of that formula in the bubuka opaq-opaq accounts for the distinctiveness of the introduction and the genḍing itself.
3. The three critical sections of the genḍing are related melodically and cadentially.
4. The "inner gongan" may be related to the bubuka genḍing (or transitional kenongan of the larger genḍing), may be a distinct development of the melodic material or a modulatory section, may be a combination

1) See p. 144.
2) See p. 144.
3) Cf. nr 9, p. 158.

of these conditions or may be chiefly of a transitional nature. Any of the theoretical cadences may be found at these inner gongan.

5. In either the old- or new-scale genḍing modulations to their respective high auxiliary scales are common but modulations to the low auxiliary scales are rare. Genḍing of both scale genders always end in their respective principal scales. The modulation tone is characteristically introduced abruptly, often in reiteration, and a return to the principal scale is confirmed by the repetition of the (principal) exchange tone leading to a T1 cadence. An exchange tone may appear so briefly that a true modulation does not occur.
6. The typical cadence of paṭet lima genḍing is the T1 formula which is extended to include the second gong tone bem. Any of the four theoretical cadences may be used within the body of the genḍing.
7. The dasar gulu, the first gong tone lima, and the second gong tone bem share the principal melodic and structural importance. Lima and gulu form the principal fifth-interval, and bem is the preferred final note and has a minor role in cadential support of lima and gulu. Nem functions as a tone of transition. Pélog and ḍaḍa are principal tones in their respective scale genders and serve as exchange tones in modulations. Barang is omitted or used as a passing note in the old-scale genḍing and in the new-scale pieces is substituted for bem in modulations to the high auxiliary scale.
8. Of the five tones of both the old and the new principal scales only pélog in the former and ḍaḍa in the latter never appear as the final note.
9. The old- and new-scale genḍing of the Solonese collection have the same general features.

IX.

PÉLOG PAṬET NEM.

THE THREE GONG TONES of pélog paṭet nem are the dasar *nem*, the first gong tone *gulu* and the second gong tone *lima*. Tables X and Y, p. 145 and p. 146, indicate that the principal scale consists of the tones nem, lima, ḍaḍa, gulu and bem — the tones barang and pélog may be used as auxiliary notes. The high auxiliary scale contains the tones barang, nem, lima, ḍaḍa and gulu — pélog and bem are auxiliary tones. The low auxiliary scale has the sequence nem, lima, pélog, gulu and bem — barang and ḍaḍa serving as auxiliaries. Modulation from the principal to the high auxiliary scale is accomplished by substituting the tone barang for bem, and the return to the principal scale is realized by substituting bem for barang. Modulation to the low scale is achieved when the tone pélog is substituted for ḍaḍa, and the substitution is reversed in returning to the principal scale. The particular manner in which these substitutions occur will be seen in the course of the analyses.

Analysis of the Genḍing

The genḍing nr 67 through nr 88 of the Jogyanese collection are listed by the scribe in pélog paṭet nem. [1]) Of these twenty-two pieces seven are presented as representative examples, and all twenty-two are included in the statistical summaries. After the summary and conclusions of the paṭet nem analyses the Jogyanese pélog paṭet lima genḍing will be discussed and briefly compared with the paṭet nem genḍing.

Ladrang nr 76 "Pangluntursih" pélog paṭet nem

bubuka opaq-opaq

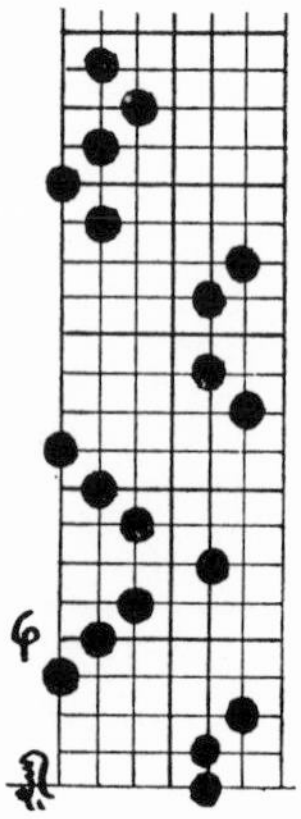

B.Op.			intro$_l$		
B.Gd.	A_l	B_l	C_{bm}	D_l	A
GN I	A_l	B_l	C^*_{bm}	D_l	A
GN II	A_l	B_l	C_{bm}	E_l	A
GN III	F_{bm}	G_l	H_l	I_l	B
GN IV	A_l	B_l	C^*_{bm}	D_l	A′

C* one note added

kenḍang 2

[1]) nr 64 is a gangsaran and has been omitted from the analyses (see p. 15).

transcribed (see appendix p. 292)

"Pangluntursih" has a ternary structure in which *A* consists of the bubuka genḍing, gongan I and II; *B* consists of gongan III; and *A′* of gongan IV. The entire genḍing is in the principal scale.

Bubuka opaq-opaq

The introduction is composed of an elaborated T3 cadence extended by a T4 formula, a short bridge passage, and a final T3 cadence in simple form. This final descending scale begins on gulu (tonic), continues through nem (dominant) and ends on lima, the second gong tone. (An extension of the cadential formula to include the second gong tone was also encountered in the typical cadence of paṭet lima genḍing.[1]) Gulu and lima, in this instance, carry the principal melodic emphasis. The extended formulas of bars 1—4 are linked to the final cadence by a bridge passage in which lima may be described as a tone of transition used in cadential support of tonic and dominant.

Bubuka genḍing

Kenongan one is an augmentation of the simple T3 cadence (measure five of the bubuka opaq-opaq), and kenongan two adds to this same formula a short quasi-pancher on bem and diminishes the note value of the preceding kenongan by half. The third kenongan begins with an ascending scale passage from the tonic gulu to the dominant nem (a T2 formula). This is followed by ḍaḍa-lima-nem— which might be interpreted as secondary-dominant-to-dominant — and the transition tone lima. The last four notes of the kenongan are the beginning of a quotation of the whole bubuka opaq-opaq, which is completed in kenongan four.

Gongan I

The first two kenongan and the fourth kenongan are identical to those of the bubuka genḍing. The third kenongan is the same as that of the bubuka genḍing except for the addition of the tone bem in the second full measure.

Gongan II

The first three kenongan are identical to those of the bubuka genḍing, and the fourth kenongan is similar, the only change being that the final cadence becomes a T4 formula extended to bem (cf. bars 3—4 of the bubuka opaq-opaq).

---

[1] Cf. pp. 166—7.

Gongan III

Kenongan one consists of an alternation of T3 and T4 formulas (the last one being completed on the first note of kenongan two); the first two and the last two are linked by the secondary dominant ḍaḍa. This kenongan is an elaboration of the first four measures of the bubuka opaq-opaq. The second kenongan continues a more exact quotation from that point and adds a T2 formula extended to lima. Kenongan three begins with nem-barang and then, following the tone lima, introduces pélog in a stepwise motion proceeding to gulu. This substitution for ḍaḍa is immediately followed by an ascending scale in which ḍaḍa replaces pélog. A combination T4—T3 formula extended to ḍaḍa and lima ends the kenongan. In kenongan four pélog is again substituted for ḍaḍa in a scale passage which is similar to the cadential bridge of measure four in the bubuka opaq-opaq. The kenongan closes with an elaborated T3 cadence extended to ḍaḍa (once more replacing pélog in a stepwise motion) and lima.

The rapid substitutions of pélog and ḍaḍa are too swift to establish an actual modulation. The tone pélog, on the other hand, is rather too prominent to be dismissed as a passing tone. For the sake of future reference we shall call this and similar examples a "neutral" passage. It is worthy of mention that ḍaḍa appears in the beginning (as the neighbor of gulu) and in the extension (as a neighbor of lima) of the T3 cadence which confirms the principal scale after the neutral passage.

Gongan IV

Gongan IV is the same as gongan I.

General Summary

The bubuka opaq-opaq provides the basis of thematic development throughout the genḍing. The three critical sections are related melodically and cadentially. Only the principal scale is used, although a short neutral passage occurs in gongan III. The substitutions between pélog and ḍaḍa, which establish this neutral section, are introduced in a stepwise motion.

The melodic importance of each tone:

Gulu is prominent in the bubuka opaq-opaq and throughout the genḍing as the tonic of the principal fifth-interval.

Nem shares the importance of gulu as its dominant.

Lima is important as the final note of the bubuka opaq-opaq, all gongan and most of the kenongan; it also serves as a tone of transition.

Ḍaḍa is melodically sensitive as an exchangeable tone and has a conspicuous role in relation to the dominant nem.

Bem is used chiefly as a passing note.

Pélog is melodically sensitive as an exchange tone for ḍaḍa.

Barang does not appear.

"Langen Asmoro"

Ladrang nr 73 pélog paṭet nem

bubuka opaq-opaq

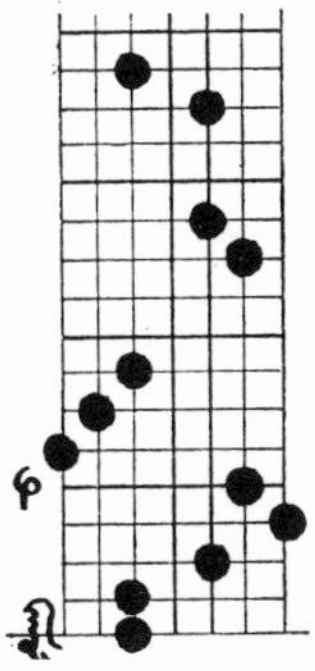

B.Op.			intro$_d$		
B.Gd.	A_d	B_{bm}	C_{bm}	D_d	A
GN I	A_d	B_{bm}	C_{bm}	D_d	A
GN II	E_{ba}	F_l	G_n	H_g	B
GN III	I_n	J_l	K_l	L_d	B
GN IV	M_g	B^*_{bm}	C_{bm}	D_d	A′
GN V	A_d	B_{bm}	C_{bm}	D_d	A′

B* first 2 notes changed

kenḍang 2

transcribed (see appendix p. 293)

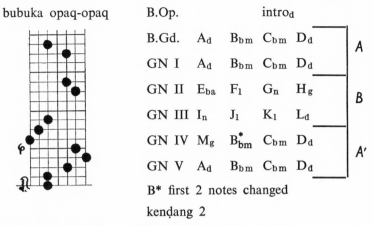

"Langen Asmoro" has a ternary structure which is further emphasized by a modulation to the high auxiliary scale in the *B* section. *A* consists of the bubuka genḍing and gongan I, *B* of gongan II and III, and *A′* of gongan IV and V. In this ladrang the tone ḍaḍa occupies an unusual prominence.

Bubuka opaq-opaq

The first two measures of the introduction establish the importance of the ḍaḍa-nem interval, and lima is given some weight by its repetition and by the dotted half note. The T3 cadence beginning in measure three is preceded by ḍaḍa. This anacrusis on ḍaḍa might be interpreted as being related to the nem beginning bar four and the final ḍaḍa closing the introduction. The T3 cadence includes the upper neighbor of nem (barang) before descending to lima and the extension to ḍaḍa.

Bubuka genḍing, gongan I

The first kenongan features the nem-ḍaḍa interval and the second gong tone lima — a passage based on the opening two measures of the bubuka opaq-opaq. The second kenongan introduces the tone pélog in a stepwise movement between gulu and lima which finally descends to barang. Ḍaḍa reappears in kenongan three (approached by a skip up from bem) and leads to lima. The line descends to gulu and then leaps up to the bridge tone lima followed by the dominant nem. The last two notes are the beginning of an extended T3 cadence which in kenongan four becomes an almost precise augmentation of the bubuka opaq-opaq commencing with measure three.

The melodic highpoints of the gongan can be summarized. Kenongan one features the dominant (and its dominant) leading to: the tonic (and the tone of cadential support) in kenongan two; kenongan three continues, in principal, the melodic aims of the preceding kenongan and leads to an extended T3 cadence in kenongan four, which closes on ḍaḍa.

Gongan I is identical to the bubuka genḍing.

Gongan II

Kenongan one begins with the transition tone lima leading stepwise to barang and the high auxiliary scale. The pattern is repeated and extended. Kenongan two, three and four continue to use barang in substitution for bem and feature the ḍaḍa-nem interval (secondary dominant and dominant) which finally resolves to gulu (tonic), the final note of the gongan. The material is based primarily on bars 1—2 of the bubuka opaq-opaq with barang, as a neighbor note, managing a melodic importance by the frequency of its occurrence.

Gongan III

The first three kenongan feature material similar to that of the preceding gongan; the principal change occurs in kenongan four. The fourth kenongan consists of an extended T3 cadence ending on ḍaḍa (from the bubuka opaq-opaq) in which the tone barang continues in substitution for bem.

Gongan IV

The first kenongan begins with the dominant nem (following the preceding secondary dominant ḍaḍa), the bridge tone lima and a (three-note) T3 cadence in which bem reappears. This confirms a return to the principal scale. The cadence is extended by a T4 formula including ḍaḍa as the penultimate note. Kenongan two begins with the bridge tone lima leading to a T1 formula extended to bem and introducing pélog as a passing note. This kenongan is the same as kenongan two of the bubuka genḍing except for the first two notes.

Kenongan three and four are identical to those of the bubuka genḍing.

Gongan V

The entire gongan is the same as the bubuka genḍing.

General Summary

The bubuka opaq-opaq provides the melodic material for the entire genḍing. The three critical sections are related melodically and cadentially. The modulation in the *B* section to the high auxiliary scale is accomplished by a stepwise substitution of barang for bem. The return to the principal scale (kenongan one, gongan IV) introduces bem in a stepwise motion and confirms the original scale by a T3 cadence. The importance of the ḍaḍa-nem interval and barang is anticipated in the introduction.

The melodic importance of each tone:

Gulu has a primary importance as the tonic of the principal fifth-interval and is the final note of gongan II.
Nem, as the dominant of gulu, shares this importance and is prominent in the high auxiliary scale section.
Lima is used as a tone of transition and in cadential support of tonic and dominant.
Ḍaḍa has a primary importance in its relation to nem and as the final note of the bubuka opaq-opaq and all gongan except gongan II. It is also melodically sensitive as an exchangeable tone.
Bem is sensitive as an exchangeable tone and is used chiefly in passing.
Barang is sensitive as a tone of modulation and achieves some melodic importance by the frequency of its occurrence.
Pélog is melodically sensitive as an exchange tone used as a passing note.

"Langen Bronto"

Ladrang nr 72 pélog paṭet nem

bubuka opaq-opaq

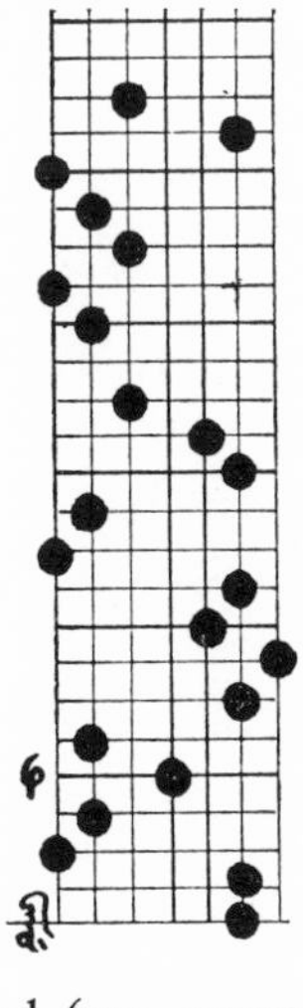

B.Op.				intro$_n$	
B.Gd.	A_g	A_g	B_l	C_n	A
GN I	A_g	A_g	B_l	C_n	A
GN II	A_g	A_g	B_l	D_{bm}	A
GN III	E_n	F_g	G_g	H_d	B
GN IV	I_d	I_d	J_n	K_n	B
GN V	A_g	A_g	B_l	C_n	A′

kenḍang 2

transcribed (see appendix p. 294)

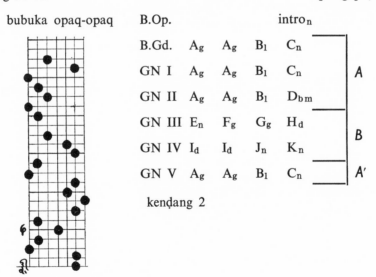

"Langen Bronto" has a ternary structure in which the *A* section consists of the bubuka genḍing, gongan I and II; the *B* section of gongan III and IV; and the *A′* section of gongan V. The entire ladrang is in the principal scale.

Bubuka opaq-opaq

The introduction is comprised of a series of cadential formulas featuring the dominant and tonic (nem and gulu) as the primary tones. The T4 cadence and both T3 cadences are essentially *three-note* formulas which do *not* include the second gong tone lima; the tones lima and barang in measure five are used only as lower and upper neighbors returning to nem, the three notes together, therefore, being a short extension of the T3 cadence. The position of the neighbor note barang, occurring as it does between bem of bar four and six, does not constitute a modulation to the high scale nor does its single appearance create a "neutral" passage. In measure six the tone pélog is used as the neighbor of gulu in substitution for ḍaḍa, suggesting, but not establishing the low auxiliary scale. The initial T4 formula is preceded by ḍaḍa as a secondary dominant leading to nem, and the nem-ḍaḍa interval is again suggested by the neighbor note ḍaḍa in measure two.

Bubuka genḍing, gongan I

Kenongan one and two are identical and consist of an augmentation of measure one to the first note of measure three of the bubuka opaq-opaq. Kenongan three and four complete the augmented quotation with the addition of gulu as the penultimate note. This slight elaboration results in a tonic-dominant interval within the final T3 cadence. After the appearance of pélog in bar six of the introduction the immediate recurrence of ḍaḍa at the beginning of this gongan assures the continuation of the principal scale.

Gongan I is an exact repetition of the bubuka genḍing.

Gongan II

The first three kenongan are the same as those of the bubuka genḍing. Kenongan four begins with bem, instead of barang as in the preceding gongan, and continues to nem and a closing T3 cadence extended to bem.

Gongan III

The first kenongan begins with the transition tone lima, followed by a T4—T3 formula slightly extended. The second kenongan continues the extension to include a nem-to-ḍaḍa scale passage which returns to nem and a T1 formula. Kenongan three contains a T2—T1 formula ending on gulu. This continues to nem (a T3 formula) in kenongan four and then ascends to lima and returns to ḍaḍa. The gongan is based on the cadential formulas of the bubuka opaq-opaq and ends with ḍaḍa as a secondary dominant leading to the first note, nem, of gongan IV.

Gongan IV

The first two kenongan are identical and consist of an initial nem (as the dominant following ḍaḍa of the preceding gongan) followed by the tone of cadential support, lima, and a T3 formula which ascends to ḍaḍa. The material is based on measures 1—2 of the bubuka opaq-opaq. Kenongan three begins with a reiteration of lima as a bridge tone leading to nem and subsequently the ascending figure ḍaḍa-lima-nem. The fourth kenongan introduces pélog in an ascending and descending passage between gulu and lima, followed by a T3 cadence slightly elaborated by the addition of gulu as the penultimate note (also see the bubuka genḍing, gongan I and IV). Lima, in this instance, is used in cadential support of tonic and dominant; pélog is a passing note. Kenongan four is based on bars 5—6 of the bubuka opaq-opaq.

Gongan V

Gongan V is the same as the bubuka genḍing.

General Summary

The bubuka opaq-opaq is used as the basis of thematic development throughout the genḍing. The three critical sections are related melodically and cadentially. Both barang and pélog appear as passing tones and establish neither a modulation nor a neutral passage. From beginning to end the ladrang remains in the principal scale. Pélog is always introduced in a stepwise motion.

The melodic importance of each tone:

Gulu as the tonic of the principal fifth-interval has a primary importance.
Nem as the final note of the bubuka opaq-opaq, bubuka genḍing, gongan I, IV and V and as the dominant of the principal fifth-interval shares the importance of gulu.
Lima functions as a bridge tone and is used in cadential support of tonic and dominant.
Ḍaḍa has a considerable importance in relation to nem and is melodically sensitive as an exchangeable tone.
Bem is used chiefly as a passing note.
Pélog is melodically sensitive as an exchange tone and is used as a passing note.
Barang is used as an upper neighbor of nem.

"Megarsi"

Ladrang nr 70 pélog paṭet nem

bubuka opaq-opaq

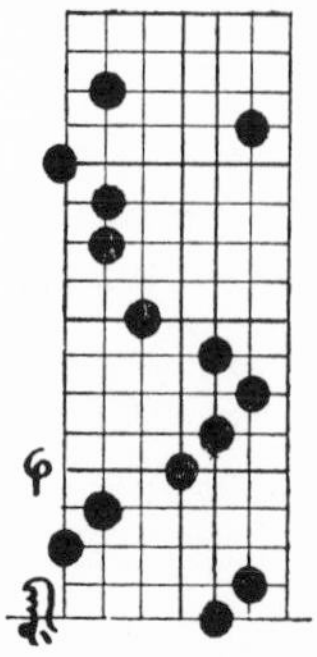

B.Op.				intro$_l$	
B.Gd.	A_d	B_l	C_g	D_g	*A*
GN I	E_n	F_n	G_d	H_d	*B*
GN II	H_d	I_{bm}	J_l	K_l	
GN III	A^{*}_{d}	B_l	C_g	D_g	*A′*

A* rhythmic subdivision

kenḍang 2

transcribed (see appendix p. 296)

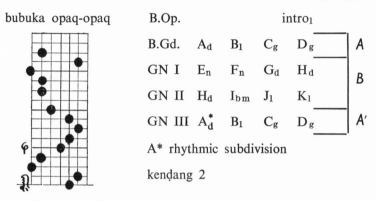

The ternary form of "Megarsi" has the following construction: *A* consists of the bubuka genḍing, *B* of gongan I and II, and *A′* of gongan III. The ladrang uses the principal scale, and a neutral passage occurs during the course of the genḍing.

Bubuka opaq-opaq

The introduction opens with the tonic-dominant interval and a T4 formula and closes with a T3 cadence extended to include the second gong tone lima. These two cadences are connected by a T2—T1 formula. The opening I—V interval, the half-note gulu in bar two, the half-note lima as a final note, and the four combined formulas result in a major emphasis on the three gong tones.

Bubuka genḍing

The first two kenongan feature the dominant nem, its dominant ḍaḍa and the bridge tone lima; bem occurs in the second kenongan as a passing note. The material is based on measure three of the bubuka opaq-opaq. Kenongan three continues the same pattern, followed by a T1 cadence; and the fourth kenongan appears to be a long extension of this cadence. The last two kenongan are derived from the material of bars 3—4 of the bubuka opaq-opaq with the substitution of ḍaḍa for pélog in the T1 formula.

Gongan I

Kenongan one begins on the transition tone lima and proceeds to a slightly extended T2 cadence which descends in kenongan two in a T1 cadence introducing the tone pélog in substitution for ḍaḍa. After another reference to the bridge tone lima the kenongan ends with a T2 formula in which ḍaḍa again replaces lima. Kenongan three continues similar patterns. The material of the three kenongan is based on bars 2—3—4 of the bubuka opaq-opaq. Kenongan four features the dominant and tonic and ends on ḍaḍa. The one exchange of ḍaḍa and pélog in the first part of the gongan is too brief to establish either a modulation or a neutral passage.

Gongan II

Kenongan one is identical to kenongan four of the preceding gongan. The start of an ascending scale at the end of this kenongan continues in kenongan two as a T2 formula which, after the upper neighbor barang, descends in a T1 formula extended to bem. The pattern continues in kenongan three and ends with the first three notes of a T1 cadence with pélog appearing as a substitute for ḍaḍa. The fourth kenongan, after a repetition of pélog, finishes the T1 formula on gulu. This is followed by lima in cadential support of the final T3 cadence. The second kenongan is based on bars 2—3—4 of the introduction, and the last two kenongan are a close quotation of the entire bubuka opaq-opaq beginning with nem of measure one.

Gongan III

Aside from a rhythmic subdivision of nem in the first kenongan, gongan III is the same as the bubuka genḍing.

General Summary

The bubuka opaq-opaq serves as the basis of melodic development throughout the genḍing. The three critical sections are related melodically; but the primary cadences of the bubuka genḍing and the final gongan are the secondary cadences of the bubuka opaq-opaq.

The melodic importance of each tone:

Gulu has a primary importance as the tonic of the principal fifth-interval and as the final note of the bubuka genḍing and gongan III.
Nem shares this importance as the dominant of gulu.
Lima is important as the final note of the bubuka opaq-opaq and gongan II and functions as a tone of transition and in support of tonic and dominant.
Ḍaḍa is melodically sensitive as an exchangeable tone and is important in relation to nem.
Bem is used chiefly as a passing note.
Pélog is melodically sensitive as an exchange note.
Barang appears once as a passing note.

"Madu Kentar"

Ladrang nr 85 pélog paṭet nem

bubuka opaq-opaq

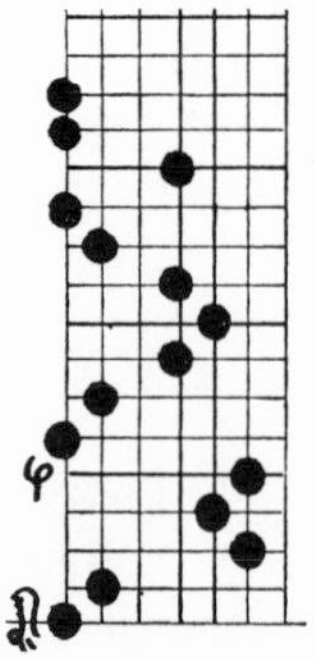

B.Op.			intro$_{bm}$		
B.Gd.	A_{bm}	B_l	C_l	D_l	A
GN I	E_l	F_{bm}	G_g	H_l	B
GN II	I_{bm}	J_{bm}	K_l	L_{bm}	
GN III	A^*_{bm}	M_l	C_l	D_l	A′

A* quasi-pancher added on ḍaḍa kenḍang 1

transcribed (see appendix p. 296)

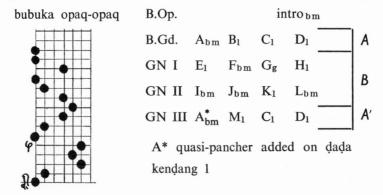

"Madu Kentar" is the only example among the twenty-two pélog paṭet nem genḍing which manages a true modulation tɔ the low auxiliary scale, *i.e.* the replacement of ḍaḍa by pélog as one of the principal tones (see Tables X and Y, p. 145 and p. 146). The ladrang has a ternary structure with *A* consisting of the bubuka genḍing, *B* of gongan I and II, and *A′* of gongan III.

Bubuka opaq-opaq

The introduction does not contain the tone ḍaḍa. This may indicate either of two possibilities: the bubuka opaq-opaq is announcing a piece which uses the old paṭet *lima* principal scale; the ladrang is really in paṭet nem but begins in the low auxiliary scale. The analysis indicated by the brackets in dotted lines (above the transcription) applies to an old-scale paṭet lima interpretation. From this viewpoint the principal cadence is a combination T2—T1 formula extended by a T3 which is in turn extended by nem-gulu-bem. The T2 and T1 formulas are typical for paṭet lima, *i.e.* are extended to include the (paṭet-lima) second gong tone bem. The T3 extension, particularly the way in which *it is extended*, is *not* characteristic of paṭet lima. The last tone bem, on the other hand, is quite eligible as a final note.

Let us consider the introduction from the standpoint of qualifying as the low auxiliary scale of paṭet nem. The principal cadence (indicated by the solid bracket below the transcription) is a T3 formula extended by dominant-tonic and the final half-note bem. If we bear in mind that this is the *low* scale and implies modulation, it is not unreasonable that bem should end the introduction. Now, the first part of the bubuka opaq-opaq must be accounted for.

The introduction begins with lower and upper neighbors of the tonic gulu. Perhaps this means is used to announce pélog as early as possible. From gulu of measure two the line ascends to lima — the tone used in cadential support of dominant and tonic — and once again descends, this time to the T3 cadence with its extension. Tentatively, the paṭet-nem analysis seems at least as plausible as the former and has the advantage of being in agreement with the scribe's listing. But judgement can be withheld until the final summary.

Bubuka genḍing

The first kenongan is a continuation of the last two notes of the bubuka opaq-opaq in augmentation (whole notes in the transcription). Kenongan two begins with the tonic-dominant interval followed (in half notes) by a T3 cadence extended to include the second gong tone lima. Thus far, no reference to ḍaḍa. The third kenongan begins with a repetition of pélog and proceeds in quarter notes with an elaboration of the tonic-dominant interval, leading to the transition tone lima. The passage includes pélog as an upper neighbor of gulu and a lower neighbor of lima. Kenongan four begins with an ascending-descending scale gulu-to-lima-to-gulu, continues with a reference to the tonic-dominant interval, and closes with a slightly extended T3 cadence in which ḍaḍa replaces pélog. The last two kenongan are rather freely based on the bubuka opaq-opaq, *e.g.* bars 2—3 and 3—4.

The first three kenongan continue the low auxiliary scale announced in the introduction; and kenongan four returns via ḍaḍa to the principal scale, which is confirmed by a T3 cadence (ḍaḍa being repeated in the extension).

Gongan I

In kenongan one the tone pélog is introduced stepwise (from lima of the preceding gongan) and after some reiteration ascends to nem. The kenongan continues with the dominant-tonic interval and a T3 cadence extended to lima retaining, the whole time, the tone pélog instead of ḍaḍa. Kenongan two begins with a combined T2—T1 formula which also uses pélog. After its lower neighbor (bem) gulu leaps to the transition tone lima and a scale passage descending to bem containing the stepwise return of ḍaḍa.

Kenongan three and four feature ḍaḍa in reiteration and the ḍaḍa-nem interval; and the gongan closes with a T3 cadence extended to lima in confirmation of the principal scale.

Gongan II

The first kenongan begins with a T4 formula starting on lima and continues through kenongan two with a principal emphasis on gulu and nem, ḍaḍa having a secondary importance to the dominant. Kenongan three opens with a reiteration of bem and begins an augmentation of the entire bubuka opaq-opaq, which is completed at the end of kenongan four.

The first half of the gongan is in the principal scale and the last half modulates to the low auxiliary.

Gongan III

The first kenongan is the same as that of the bubuka genḍing except for the addition of a quasi-pancher on ḍaḍa which establishes a return to the principal scale. Kenongan two is an elaboration of kenongan two of the bubuka opaq-opaq, including a rhythmic subdivision of gulu, a T1 formula and a slightly extended T3 cadence confirming the principal scale. Kenongan three and four are identical to those of the bubuka genḍing.

The first half of the gongan is in the principal scale, the third kenongan in the low auxiliary, and the final cadence confirms a return to the principal scale.

General Summary

The material of the genḍing is rather freely based on the bubuka opaq-opaq. The three critical sections are related melodically and cadentially. The introduction is in the paṭet-nem low auxiliary scale, and the body of the ladrang alternates between the principal and low scales, finally ending with a confirmation of the principal scale. In each instance, the return to the principal scale is confirmed by a T3 cadence.

The melodic importance of each tone:

Gulu has a primary importance as tonic of the principal fifth-interval.
Nem shares its importance as the dominant.
Lima is prominent as the final note of the bubuka genḍing and gongan I and II; it is used as a transition tone and in cadential support of tonic and dominant.
Bem has some importance as the final note of the bubuka opaq-opaq and gongan II.
Ḍaḍa is melodically sensitive as an exchangeable tone and has a minor importance in relation to nem.
Pélog is sensitive as a modulation tone.
Barang does not appear.

"Gondo Mastuti"

Ketawang nr 88 — pélog paṭet nem

bubuka opaq-opaq

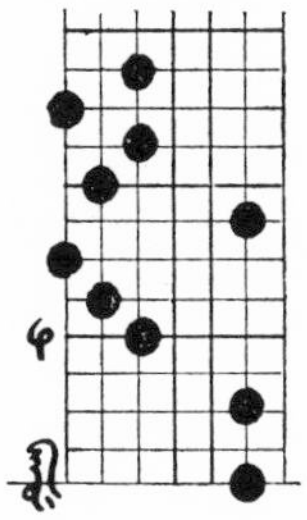

B.Op.		$intro_n$		
B.Gd.	A_{bm}	B_n	A	
GN I	A^*_{bm}	B'_n		theme
GN II	C_g	D_n		and
GN III	C_g	D_n	B	variations
GN IV	E_{bm}	F_n		
GN V	A^*_{bm}	B''_n	A'	

A* and B′ quasi-pancher on lima added

B″ penultimate lima becomes gulu

kenḍang 2

transcribed (see appendix p. 297)

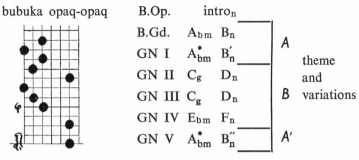

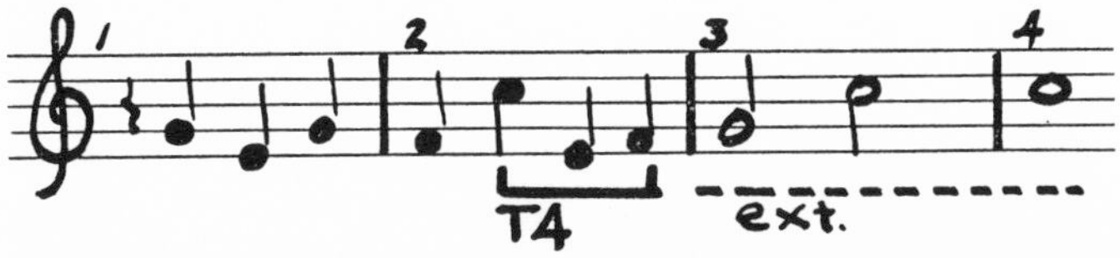

"Gondo Mastuti" is the only ketawang among the pélog paṭet nem genḍing. It employs a kind of variations technique in its melodic development, and the structure can be described in the larger sense as ternary in form (see the structural chart above). The piece uses the principal scale throughout.

Bubuka opaq-opaq

The introduction is very short — the neighbors of gulu in measure one lead to the tonic-dominant interval of bar two and the T4 cadence extended by ḍaḍa (as a secondary dominant) and nem (the dominant).

Bubuka genḍing

The eight-measure gongan of the bubuka genḍing appears to establish more exactly the "theme" which is to form the basis of the subsequent variations. The first kenongan contains four notes, and these are the intervals from the beginning of the bubuka opaq-opaq — ḍaḍa-barang and ḍaḍa-gulu — but used in the reverse order. The second kenongan also uses the reverse order, this time of the sequence from bars 2—3 of the introduction, namely, nem-bem-gulu-ḍaḍa.

If the gongan is considered as a whole, it will be seen that it represents in essence a T3 cadence (ending on nem) in which the upper neighbor of gulu (ḍaḍa) has a secondary importance. This may be seen more easily with another word of explanation. The gulu and bem of kenongan one fall on the kempul and kenong beats, respectively, and are therefore felt as being slightly more important than the two keṭuk beats on which ḍaḍa occurs. [1]) In the second kenongan the cadence is more compact (actually continued). It begins with an anacrusis on ḍaḍa (weak stress by the keṭuk), proceeds to gulu on the kempul beat (secondary emphasis), bem on the keṭuk beat (weak stress), and nem on the final kenongan-gong (principal emphasis).

The variations technique used in the following gongan will be most easily seen in the transcription on pp. 297—8. A few comments, however, may be in order.

Gongan I

This is identical to the bubuka genḍing except for the addition of a quasi-pancher on lima.

Gongan II, III

Gongan II and III are identical. The first kenongan begins with a reiteration of nem followed by a T3 formula extended by a T1 formula to gulu. This is further extended by gulu and its neighbors in the second kenongan, and the gongan close with a T3 cadence (diminution of kenongan two of the bubuka genḍing).

Gongan IV

Gongan IV begins with a reiteration of nem followed by its upper and lower neighbors and a T2 cadence (in which pélog is substituted for ḍaḍa) extended to bem. The second kenongan begins with the return of ḍaḍa and the bridge tone lima and ends with a slight variation of the T3 cadence (resulting in the final tonic-dominant interval).

Gongan V

The final gongan is the same as gongan I except for the penultimate note. In this last gongan lima is replaced by gulu to form a T3 cadence varied by a tonic-dominant ending.

General Summary

The bubuka opaq-opaq forms a melodic nucleus which provides the basis for a set of short variations. The three critical sections are related melodically and cadentially. The single substitution of pélog and the two appearances of barang as a neighbor note accomplish neither a modulation nor a neutral section.

The melodic importance of each tone:

Gulu as the tonic of the principal fifth-interval has a primary importance. *Nem* shares this importance as the dominant of gulu and as the final note of the bubuka opaq-opaq and all gongan.

---

[1]) See the explanation of colotomic structure, pp. 12—14.

Lima serves as a quasi-pancher.
Dada has a minor relation to nem and is melodically sensitive as an exchangeable note.
Bem is used chiefly as a passing note.
Pélog appears once as a passing note.
Barang is used as a neighbor note.

"Udan Mas"

Ladrang nr 83 — pélog paṭet nem

bubuka opaq-opaq

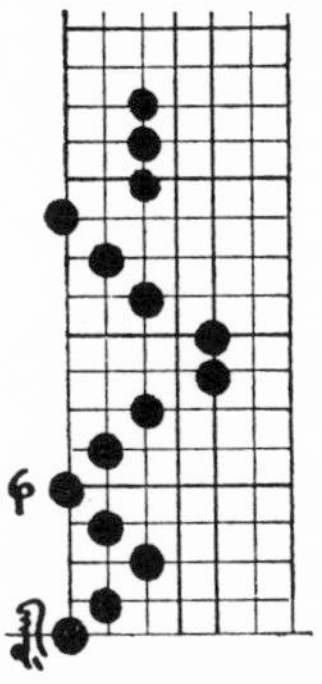

B.Op.			intro$_{bm}$		
B.Gd.	A_l	A_l	B_n	A_l	A
GN I	A_l	A_l	B_n	A_l	
GN II	C_d	D_l	E_{bm}	F_{bm}	B
GN III	C_d	D_l	E_{bm}	F_{bm}	
GN VI	A_l	A_l	B_n	A_l	A
GN V	A_l	A_l	B_n	A_l	
GN VI	C_d	D_l	E_{bm}	F_{bm}	B
GN VII	C_d	D_l	E_{bm}	F_{bm}	
GN VIII	A_l	A_l	B_n	A_l	A′

kenḍang bibaran

transcribed (see appendix p. 298)

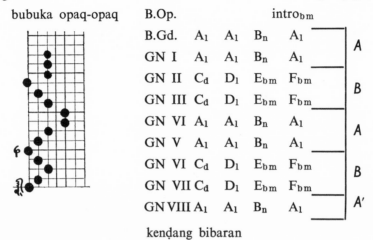

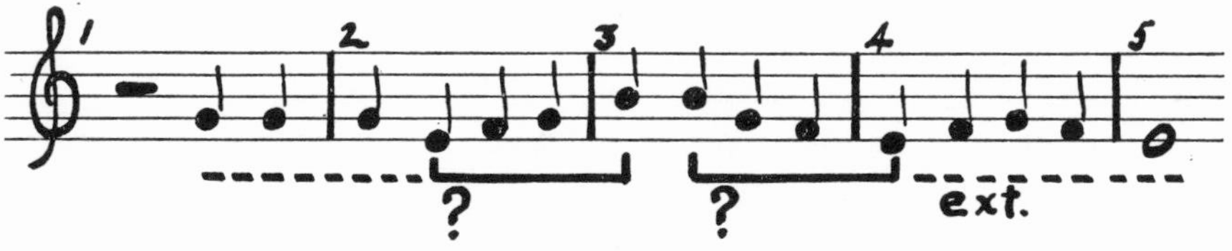

The rondo form, the interesting bubuka opaq-opaq, and the kenḍang bibaran [1]) make "Udan Mas" (Golden Rain) an interesting example for consideration. [2]) The tones barang and pélog are not used.

The first four gongan are repeated eight times and then proceed to the last four gongan which are also repeated eight times but at a faster tempo (see the appendix p. 299). It should be noted that the *ngenchot* (rhythmic subdivisions) are omitted in the faster section.

---

1) „Kenḍang bibaran is heard only during the winding-up of a wayang performance or festival meeting (*bibar*, Low Javanese *bubar* = finish, all over) or when the chief personnage departs from a ceremony". *MJ*, I, 208; also cf. p. 338.

2) nr 82 „Tropongan" has a similar bubuka opaq-opaq and also calls for kenḍang bibaran. The principal features of nr 82 will be found in the statistical summaries.

Bubuka opaq-opaq

The brackets in the above transcription indicate the primary cadences with their elaboration or extension but have not been labeled according to formula type. The ascending formula has the general form of a T2 cadence and the descending formula that of a T1 cadence — but not in paṭet nem! These are typical cadences of the *new-scale paṭet lima genḍing.* [1]) The absence of nem and the stress on lima and bem — especially the position of bem at the end of the T1 cadence (first note of bar four) and as the final note of the introduction — leave little doubt that this interpretation is correct. The following gongan will indicate whether: 1) the piece is actually incorrectly labeled and is really in paṭet lima; 2) artistic license has prompted this "wrong-paṭet" introduction; 3) or the bubuka opaq-opaq has been retained in transposition.

Bubuka genḍing, gongan I, IV, V, VIII

These gongan are all identical.

The first two kenongan are alike and consist simply of a *paṭet nem* T3 cadence including the second gong tone lima. The third kenongan reverses this pattern in a T4 formula, and the fourth kenongan, like the first two, is a simple T3 cadence.

Gongan II, III, VI, VII

These gongan are identical and consist of an augmented quotation of the bubuka opaq-opaq, indicating, therefore, *paṭet lima.*

Conclusions

The usual summary can be dispensed with in this example.

The "paṭet-lima" character of the introduction is completely denied in the strong confirmation of paṭet nem (via the T3 cadences) in the bubuka genḍing and gongan I. Gongan II and III, by quoting the bubuka opaq-opaq, return to paṭet lima. The return of the *A* section in gongan IV and V again confirms paṭet nem. One more such exchange closes the genḍing in the principal scale of paṭet nem.

Each pair of gongan, as it were, are alternately in a different paṭet, the melos of each, therefore, lying a fifth apart. The introduction and the final single gongan are also in different paṭet. The symmetry of the double-gongan construction is preserved in repetitions of the genḍing proper (beginning with gongan I) because gongan IV and I in the slow section and gongan VIII and V in the fast section each form a complete pair, *i.e.* another *A* section.

The particular arrangement of the gongan suggests that artistic choice has

[1]) Cf. pp. 166—7.

produced a musical mixture — a kind of melodic argument between paṭet lima and paṭet nem in which the latter finally triumphs. [1]) Modulation to the low auxiliary scale of paṭet nem has not occurred because the tone *pélog*, the replacement for ḍaḍa necessary to effect such a modulation, does not appear. Only five tones are used: nem-lima-ḍaḍa-gulu-bem, and these form the principal scales of both paṭet nem and (the new-scale) paṭet lima.

"Udan Mas" is a very simple but effective illustration of the fundamental difference between two paṭet which share the same five tones for their principal scales but can be distinguished by their three gong tones and respective typical cadential formulas.

Summary and Conclusions

A summary of the principal features of the twenty-two pélog paṭet nem genḍing will be presented in four tables similar to those used for the sléndro genḍing.

Table I indicates the architectonic form of the genḍing, the modulation scheme, and the correspondence between the bubuka genḍing and the final gongan on the basis of identical kenongan (the one ketawang is not included). In the column headed "Mod." the letters "P & N" indicate that the genḍing is in the principal scale and that the occasional brief substitution of pélog for ḍaḍa produces a neutral section but not a true modulation. The letters "P-H-P" indicate that the piece begins in the principal scale, modulates to the high auxiliary via barang and returns to the principal scale via bem. The meaning of an asterisk after the letters will be explained later. "L & P alt." indicates the one example in which an actual modulation to the low auxiliary scale occurs in alternation with the principal scale. "P & P5 alt." is an abbreviation for the principal scale of paṭet nem and the principal scale of paṭet lima used in alternation (see nr 83, above).

---

1) A similar basis of contrast seems to be the intention of the *sléndro paṭet sanga* ladrang „Udan Sejati" (Real Rain), pp. 66—70. The bubuka genḍing, gongan II and IV employ the typical cadence (T3) of paṭet sanga; gongan I and III use the less-obvious, non-typical cadences (T4—T3 *strong*) of paṭet nem with the tone lima appearing in its usual transitional role at the kenongan subdivisions. Gongan V and VI return to paṭet sanga via the final extented T3 cadences. Further comparison between the two „Udan" is left to the reader.

Table I

Title	Form	Mod.	B.Gd./ final GN
nr 67 Pasang Bandar	Intro — ternary	P-H-P-H-P*	4
„ 68 Durmo	„ — „	P & N	4
„ 69 Larasati	„ — „	P-H-P*	4
„ 70 Megarsi	„ — „	P & N	4
„ 71 Rangsang Tuban	„ — „	P & N	4
„ 72 Langen Bronto	„ — „	P	4
„ 73 Langen Asmoro	„ — „	P-H-P*	4
„ 74 Megarsari	„ — „	P-H-P*	4
„ 75 Pisang Megar	„ — „	P-H-P*	3
„ 76 Pangluntursih	„ — „	P	4
„ 77 Pamikatsih	„ — „	P	4
„ 78 Lagu	„ — „	P-H-P*	4
„ 79 Tejo Bronto	„ — „	P	4
„ 80 Lung Gaḍung Madura	„ — „	P-H-P*	4
„ 81 Bekso Wiromo	„ — „	P-H-P*	4
„ 82 Tropongan	„ — „	P & N	3
„ 83 Udan Mas	„ — Rondo	P & P5 alt.	4
„ 84 Honang-ngonang Manis	„ — ternary	P-H-P*	2
„ 85 Madu Kentar	„ — „	L & P alt.	2
„ 86 Puspo Kanṭi	„ — „	P-H-P	2
„ 87 Moro Semu	„ — „	P-H-P*	1
„ 88 Gondo Mastuti	„ — „ (variations)	P	ketawang

Summary: 21 genḍing are ternary (1 of which is a form of variations)
1 „ is a rondo

11 genḍing modulate to the high auxiliary scale
1 „ modulates „ „ low „ „
1 „ is a mixture of paṭet nem and paṭet lima
4 „ contain neutral passages.

On the basis of identical kenongan appearing in the bubuka genḍing and the final gongan: of the 21 ladrang 21 have at least 1 kenongan identical in both sections, and of these 21:

15 ladrang have 4 kenongan identical in both sections
2 „ „ 3 „ „ „ „ „
3 „ „ 2 „ „ „ „ „
1 „ has 1 „ „ „ „ „

In these ladrang the last kenongan of the bubuka genḍing and the final kenongan of the piece are the same.

Table II indicates the patterns of kenongan repetition in the gongan and is arranged according to type. It shows the number of each type used in every ladrang (the ketawang is omitted).

Table II

Gendịng	ABCD	AABC	AABB	AAAB	AAAA
nr 67	9				
„ 68	4				
„ 69	6				
„ 70	4				
„ 71	4			1	
„ 72	1	5			
„ 73	6				
„ 74	3	3			
„ 75	6				
„ 76	5				
„ 77	5				
„ 78	1	4			
„ 79	1	4			
„ 80	1	1		5	
„ 81	1	4			
„ 82	2	1		2	
„ 83	2			4	
„ 84	5				
„ 85	4				
„ 86	5				
„ 87	3	1	1		
„ 88	6				
Total:	84	23	1	12	0

Summarized on the basis of a total of 120 gongan:

70.0% repeat no kenongan — ABCD
19.2% „ 1 „ — AABC
0.8% „ 2 „ — AABB
10.0% „ 1 „ 3 times — AAAB

Table III gives a summary of the cadences closing the three critical sections of the genḍing. The symbols are similar to those employed in the previous chapters. An asterisk appearing after the T3 symbol, *e.g.* T3*, indicates that the formula ends on nem and is *essentially* a three-note cadence (an extension to lima as a neighbor note again returning to nem is considered in this category). T3 without the asterisk indicates that lima terminates the formula. For an explanation of the question marks appearing under the bubuka opaq-opaq of nr 82 and nr 83, see pp. 185—6.

Table III

Genḍing	B.Op.	B.Gd.	Final GN
nr 67	T3* + V/I	T3* + V/I	T3* + V/I
„ 68	T3 + T4/bem	T1 + lima	T1 + lima
„ 69	I/V	T2	T2
„ 70	T3	T1	T1
„ 71	T3* + I/V	T3	T3
„ 72	T3*	T3*	T3*
„ 73	T3 + ḍaḍa	T3 + ḍaḍa	T3 + ḍaḍa
„ 74	T3*	I/V	I/V
„ 75	T3 + I/V	T2	T2
„ 76	T3	T3	T3
„ 77	T3	T3	T3
„ 78	T3* + ḍaḍa	T3 + ḍaḍa	T3 + ḍaḍa
„ 79	T3*	T3	T3
„ 80	T3	T3	T3
„ 81	T3 + I/V	T3 + I/V	T3 + I/V
„ 82	?	T3	T3
„ 83	?	T3	T3
„ 84	T3	T3	T3
„ 85	T3 + V/I/bem	T3	T3
„ 86	T3*	T3*	T3*
„ 87	T3*	T3 + T1	T3 + T1
„ 88	T4 + ḍaḍa/nem	T3*	T3*

In summary:	T3	T4	T1	T2	I/V	?	
B.Op.	18	1	0	0	1	2	= 86.4% T3 (or T4)
B.Gd.	17	0	2	2	1	0	= 81.8% T3
Final GN	17	0	2	2	1	0	= 81.8% T3

Table IV indicates the melodic importance of each tone. Lima appears both as a tone of transition and in support of tonic and dominant; these functions are combined under the heading "Trans". The column headed "Omitted" indicates the omission of a tone, and the heading "Subs". indicates the tone used in substitution to establish a true modulation. The only example of a quasi-pancher (continuing for at least eight measures) has been given in the detailed analysis. A true pancher is not indicated for any of the genḍing.

Table IV

Genḍing	Final	Pr.5th	Trans.	Omitted	Subs.
nr 67	gulu	gulu-nem	lima		barang
„ 68	lima	„ „	„	barang	
„ 69	nem	„ „	„		barang
„ 70	gulu	„ „	„		
„ 71	lima	„ „	„		
„ 72	nem	„ „	„		
„ 73	ḍaḍa	„ „	„		barang
„ 74	nem	„ „	„		„
„ 75	„	„ „	„		„
„ 76	lima	„ „	„	barang	
„ 77	„	„ „	„	„	
„ 78	ḍaḍa	„ „	„		barang
„ 79	lima	„ „	„	barang	
„ 80	„	„ „	„		barang
„ 81	nem	„ „	„		„
„ 82	lima	„ „	(„)		
„ 83	„	„ „	(„)	pélog/barang	
„ 84	„	„ „	(„)	pélog	barang
„ 85	„	„ „	„	barang	pélog
„ 86	nem	„ „	„		barang
„ 87	gulu	„ „	„		„
„ 88	nem	„ „	(„)		
Summary:	lima 10	gulu-nem	lima	barang	barang
	nem 7			pélog	pélog
	gulu 3				
	ḍaḍa 2				

From the foregoing tables certain general conclusions can be formulated which in Chapter XI can serve as a basis for comparison with the other two pélog paṭet.

Table I indicates that these paṭet nem genḍing have a ternary construction. Even the ketawang (nr 88) which uses a variations form may, in the larger sense, be described as a three-part structure.

Modulations to the high auxiliary scale via the tone barang and a return to the principal scale via the tone bem are rather frequent. Only one genḍing manages a modulation to the low auxiliary scale (using pélog in substitution for ḍaḍa as a principal tone), although several ladrang contain "neutral" passages in which the pélog-ḍaḍa substitution is too tentative to establish an actual modulation. The detailed analyses show that in both types of modulation and in the neutral passages the exchange tones are characteristically introduced in a stepwise motion.

The high percentage of kenongan identical in both the bubuka genḍing and the final gongan establish a close melodic and cadential relationship between these two sections. The detailed analyses show that the bubuka opaq-opaq provides the basis of thematic development for the entire genḍing. These two considerations together indicate a strong melodic relationship among the three critical sections of the genḍing, and Table III indicates an equally strong cadential bond.

The summary given in Table III shows that among the four theoretical cadences the T3 formula, usually extended to include the second gong tone lima, is the typical cadence for genḍing in pélog paṭet nem. The analyses reveal that ḍaḍa sometimes appears as the upper neighbor of gulu at the beginning of the cadence or as the lower neighbor of lima as the penultimate tone of the cadence. Pélog, of course, may be substituted for ḍaḍa in any of the formulas. These several variations of the T3 cadence and all four basic formulas are given below, the second gong tone being indicated by "+".

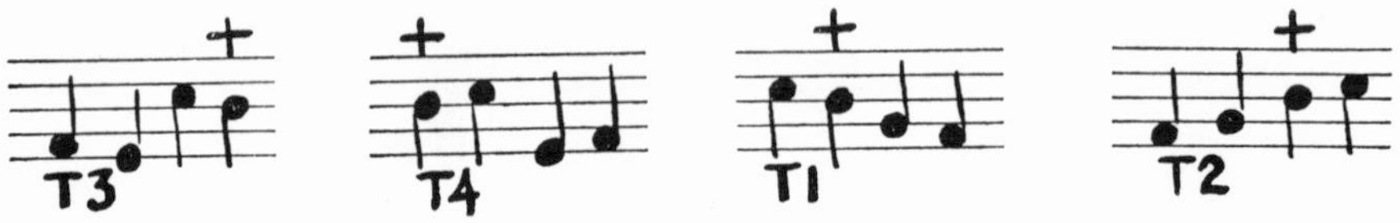

(typical)

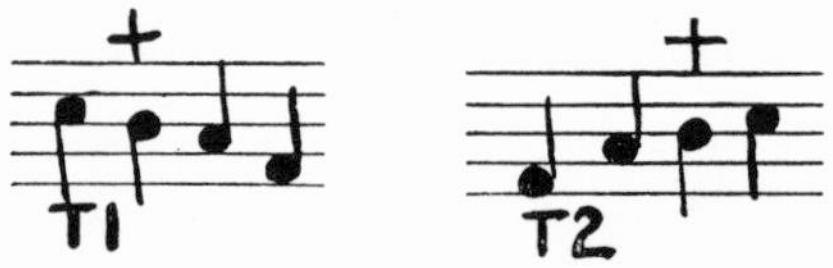

T3 variations (pélog subs.) (pélog subs.)

(3-tone) (with ḍaḍa) (pélog subs.)

Any of the theoretical formulas may be found within the body of the genḍing or at the close of the inner gongan (see the transcriptions in the appendix p. 292ff.).

The tone appearing most often as the final note is lima; nem functions almost as frequently in this capacity; gulu and ḍaḍa are occasionally used; and bem, pélog, and barang are avoided entirely as the final note of the genḍing.

The principal fifth-interval is gulu-nem, first gong tone and dasar, respectively. In addition to its role as the preferred final note, the second gong tone lima functions as a tone of transition and in cadential support of gulu and nem. Thus, the three gong tones occupy the principal melodic importance in pélog paṭet nem.

Ḍaḍa and pélog are melodically sensitive as exchange tones in neutral passages and in the one example of modulation to the low auxiliary scale. Ḍaḍa also has a secondary dominant relationship to nem. Bem and barang are melodically sensitive as exchange tones in modulations to and from the high auxiliary scale and are otherwise used chiefly as passing tones. The asterisks appearing in the "Mod." column of Table I indicate that in ten of the eleven genḍing employing the high auxiliary scale the tone barang achieves a melodic prominence through reiteration or the frequency of its occurrence. The two modulation tones barang and pélog are sometimes omitted entirely.

A brief summary of the principal points:

1. The bubuka opaq-opaq is a particular elaboration, combination or variation of cadential formulas, the typical cadence being the T3 formula. The bubuka opaq-opaq provides the basis of thematic development for the entire genḍing.
2. Through the thematic development of the bubuka opaq-opaq the T3 cadential formula becomes the melodic framework of the genḍing. The particular variation of that formula in the bubuka opaq-opaq accounts for the distinctiveness of the introduction and the genḍing itself.
3. The three critical sections of the genḍing — the bubuka opaq-opaq, the bubuka genḍing and the final gongan — are closely related melodically and cadentially.
4. The "inner gongan" may be related to the bubuka genḍing, may be a distinct development of the melodic material or a modulatory or neutral section, may be a combination of these conditions or may be chiefly of a transitional nature. Any of the theoretical cadences may be found at these inner gongan.
5. Modulations to the high auxiliary scale, via the tone barang, are of short duration but occur in about half the paṭet nem genḍing. Modulations to the low auxiliary scale, via the tone pélog, are rare. Occasionally neutral sections or tentative fluctuations between the principal and low scales result from an exchange of pélog and ḍaḍa which is too rapid or, through the subsequent avoidance of either of these sensitive tones, too indefinite to establish a new scale center.
6. The characteristic manner in which exchange tones are introduced in modulatory or neutral passages is by a stepwise motion.

7. The typical cadence of paṭet nem is the T3 formula extended to include the second gong tone lima. Variations of this formula include a three-tone cadence ending on the dasar nem. Any of the theoretical cadences may be used within the body of the genḍing.
8. The first gong tone gulu and the dasar nem form the principal fifth-interval; and nem frequently appears as a final note. The second gong tone lima is usually included in the typical formula, is the preferred final note, and is used as tone of transition and in support of gulu and nem. These three gong tones occupy the chief melodic and structural positions. Ḍaḍa and pélog are melodically sensitive as exchange tones, and ḍaḍa has a secondary-fifth relationship to nem. Bem and barang are melodically sensitive as exchange tones and are used chiefly as passing note; barang is melodically prominent in sections of the genḍing which use the high auxiliary scale. Both pélog and barang are sometimes omitted altogether.
9. Of the five tones of the principal scale lima and nem are preferred as final notes; gulu and ḍaḍa are occasionally used; bem never appears in this capacity.

Pélog Paṭet Lima Compared
(Jogyanese Collection)

The paṭet lima genḍing of the Jogyanese manuscript show a partial or complete adoption of paṭet-nem characteristics. The scribe has listed four ladrang as belonging to paṭet lima. One of these, nr 66, appears to be incorrectly labeled and will be considered in Chapter X, after the summary of paṭet barang genḍing.

"Rijem-Rijem", nr 61, is entered in the appendix (p. 300) for the reader's convenience in comparing its general features to those of the paṭet nem genḍing immediately preceding. According to the transposition table in the appendix (p. 261) this ladrang is listed in two sources in paṭet lima. For the most part, however, "Rijem-Rijem" seems to be indistinguishable from the genḍing of paṭet nem. Gongan III (the penultimate gongan) closes with a slightly extended paṭet-lima T1 cadence;[1] the midpoint (end of kenongan two) of the bubuka genḍing, gongan I, II and IV also use the T1 cadence — but none of these structural points is particularly prominent, and similar examples can be found in paṭet nem. The bubuka opaq-opaq features the paṭet-nem T3 cadence; the bubuka genḍing and final gongan (IV) close with such a cadence, although a weak case might be made that the T1 cadence preceding it suggest paṭet lima. The exchange tones in the neutral sections and in the high auxiliary modulation of gongan III are introduced according to the paṭet-nem characteristic manner, *i.e.* stepwise motion.

The two remaining examples, nr 62 "Kemong-Kemong" and nr 63 "Juru Demung", are more suggestive of paṭet lima. The ladrang "Kemong-Kemong" is representative of these two and is briefly analyzed below.

1) But cf. the bubuka opaq-opaq of nr 62, p. 195.

"Kemong-Kemong"

Ladrang nr 62 pélog paṭet lima

bubuka opaq-opaq

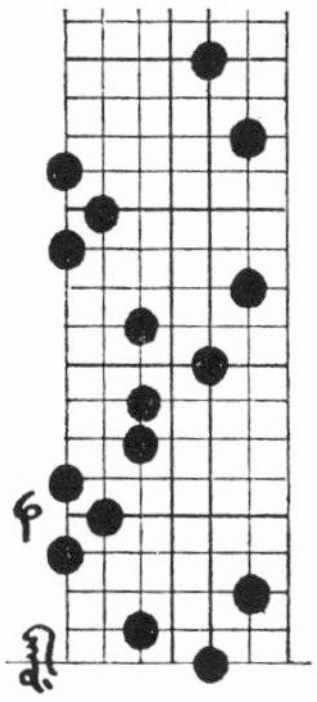

B.Op.			intro$_l$		
B.Gd.	A_l	B_n	C_g	D_l	A
GN I	E_l	F_n	C_g	D_l	A
GN II	G_l	H_n	I_n	J_l	B
GN III	K_{bm}	F_n	C_g	D_l	A′
GN IV	E_l	F_n	C_g	D_l^*	A′

D* penultimate note ḍaḍa not pélog

kenḍang 2

transcribed (see appendix p. 301)

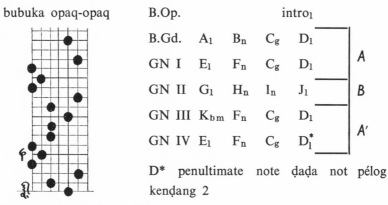

The development of the melodic material of the bubuka opaq-opaq in the body of the genḍing is reasonably apparent and for the sake of the present purpose need not concern us in detail. The discussion will be limited to paṭet-lima and paṭet-nem characteristics. All designations of formula type will refer to paṭet lima unless otherwise indicated. The individual gongan will be examined particularly at the midpoint and the end.

Bubuka opaq-opaq [1)]

The beginning and end of the bracketed cadences clearly outline the paṭet lima tonic-dominant interval lima-gulu. Except for the cadence starting in measure three, however, the formulas used are non-typical; they are in fact typical of paṭet nem. Even the descending T1 cadence of bar three is slightly weakened by the juxtaposition of bem and gulu as the final note of the formula. In conclusion it might be said that the introduction contains a vestige of paṭet lima (new-scale) practice but is otherwise indistinguishable from a paṭet-nem bubuka opaq-opaq.

Bubuka genḍing

The quotation of the bubuka opaq-opaq is altered slightly in kenongan two by the omission of the anticipatory bem. The result, however, still does not yield a T1 formula because the extension continues to nem. The final cadence of the

1) The same as nr 61 except for the initial lima; cf. p. 300.

gongan could be interpreted as a slightly extended (three-note) T1—T2 cadence in which pélog is substituted for ḍaḍa. Although the conjunct position of the preceding formulas makes it difficult to determine where exactly the principal cadence begins, such an extension — especially with pélog in substitution for ḍaḍa — is not characteristic of paṭet nem. [1]) Even though the final three-note cadence is not *typical*, it seems to suggest paṭet lima.

Gongan I

The second kenongan begins with the ḍaḍa-nem interval (common in both paṭet lima and paṭet nem), is followed by a typical T1 formula including bem, and is then extended by a (paṭet-nem?) T3 cadence. The final kenongan is the same as that of the bubuka genḍing.

Gongan II

Kenongan two consists of two ascending scales, gulu-to-nem and ḍaḍa-to-nem, which lead to a paṭet-nem T1—T2 formula in kenongan three and a short modulation to the high auxiliary scale via barang. The fourth kenongan closes with a three-note paṭet-lima T2 cadence slightly extended.

Gongan III

The first kenongan returns to the principal scale. The midpoint and final cadence of gongan III are the same as those of gongan I.

Gongan IV

The midpoint of gongan IV is the same as that of gongan II. The fourth kenongan is the same as that of the bubuka genḍing, gongan I and III except for one small change. The penultimate note substitutes ḍaḍa for pélog introduced by a leap down from nem. Although all pélog substitutions throughout the piece create neutral passages rather than modulations, this return to ḍaḍa in the final T1—T2 cadence appears to be a confirmation of the principal scale.

In every instance except the last the exchange tones are introduced in the genḍing by a stepwise motion characteristic of paṭet nem practice.

Conclusions

Although the introduction is acceptable as a paṭet nem bubuka opaq-opaq, the cadences of the subsequent gongan suggest that this might actually be a weak paṭet lima introduction. The final cadences of all gongan seem to be non-typical, three-note T1—T2 cadences in paṭet lima. The manner of introducing the exchange tones is characteristic of paṭet nem; the single exception occurs, perhaps significantly, at the end of the piece. In conclusion, "Kemong-Kemong" could be called a very weak example of a new-scale paṭet lima genḍing or one which has taken on many of the paṭet nem characteristics.

---

[1]) The substitution of pélog for ḍaḍa in the *T3* cadence of paṭet nem is not unusual; but such a substitution in the T2—T1 formulas is unlikely, especially at a critical point.

X.

PÉLOG PAṬET BARANG.

THE THREE GONG TONES of paṭet barang are the dasar *ḍaḍa*, the first gong tone *nem* and the second gong tone *gulu*. The Tables X and Y on p. 145 and p. 146 show that the principal scale consists of the tones barang, nem, lima, ḍaḍa, gulu — pélog and bem may be used as auxiliary tones. The high auxiliary scale (gulu miring) contains the tones barang, nem, pélog, ḍaḍa, gulu — lima and bem are auxiliary tones. The low auxiliary scale (sometimes called pélog paṭet manyura [1])) has the sequence nem, lima, ḍaḍa, gulu, bem — barang and pélog may be used as auxiliary tones. Modulation from the principal scale to the high auxiliary form is accomplished by substituting the tone pélog for lima, and, conversely, the return to the principal scale is realized by substituting lima for pélog. Modulation to the low scale is achieved when the tone bem is substituted for barang, and the substitution is reversed in returning to the principal scale. We shall discover the methods or rules of these substitutions in the course of the analysis.

Analysis of the Genḍing

The genḍing nr 89 through nr 100 of the Jogyanese collection are listed in paṭet barang. [2]) Nr 91 "Pengsih" and nr 93 "Megarsih" [3]) bear different titles but are otherwise identical ladrang and will be designated by the double number nr 91—93 or by this number together with the two titles. The analysis, therefore, is based on eleven different genḍing in pélog paṭet barang. Five of these are presented as representative examples, and the complete group is included in the statistical summaries.

The ladrang nr 66 "Wirogo" is listed by the scribe in pélog paṭet lima. In the probability that this genḍing is actually an example of the rather rare pélog paṭet manyura or the low auxiliary scale form of pélog paṭet barang, [1]) it is also presented

---

1) See Tables X and Y, p. 145 and p. 146, and also see p. 148.

2) nr 65 is a gangsaran omitted from the analysis; see p. 15.

3) This is not a transposition of the genḍing (nr 70) of pélog paṭet nem, which has the same title, but is a completely different piece.

in a detailed analysis. Because there is some question whether this scale form should be considered as a *fourth* pélog paṭet, the genḍing will not be included in the statistical summaries but will follow the paṭet barang conclusions.

"Rangu-Rangu"

Ladrang nr 97 pélog paṭet barang

bubuka opaq-opaq

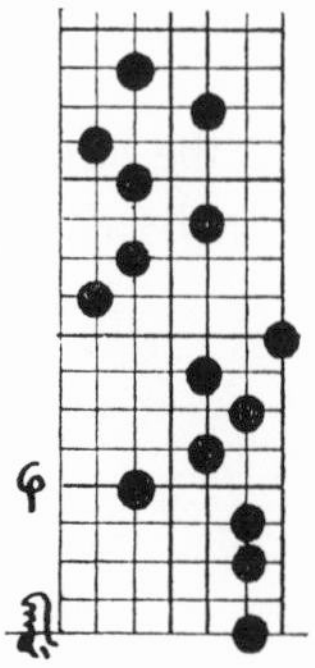

B.Op.			intro$_n$		
B.Gd.	A_n	A_n	B_{ba}	C_{ba}	A
GN I	A^*_n	A^*_n	B^*_{ba}	C_n	
GN II	D_{ba}	E_l	F_d	G_{ba}	B
GN III	H_{ba}	H_{ba}	B_{ba}	C_n	
GN IV	A^*_n	A^*_n	B_{ba}	C_n	A′

A* is an elaboration of A

B* substitutes pélog for ḍaḍa at the beginning of the third measure

kenḍang 1

transcribed (see appendix p. 302)

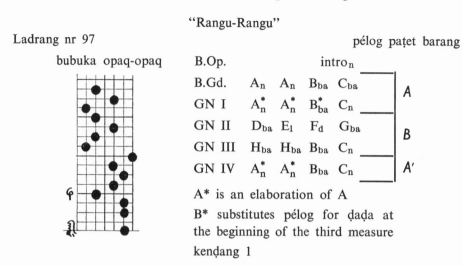

The ternary form of "Rangu-Rangu" has the following structure: *A* consists of the bubuka genḍing and gongan I; *B* consists of gongan II and III, with a transition in the last half of the gongan which leads to the *A′* section, gongan IV.

Bubuka opaq-opaq

The first two measures consist of ḍaḍa and its neighbors used as a spun-out beginning of the T3 cadence (indicated by the first bracket) which is extended by a T1 formula (shown by the second bracket) and finally closes on the tonic nem. The first lima of measure three is used as the lower neighbor of nem and, as will be seen in later examples, is not a part of the essential cadence but characteristically functions as a bridge tone. The entire bubuka opaq-opaq is an elaborated and extended T3 cadence.

Bubuka genḍing

The first two kenongan are identical and consist of a variation or re-arrangement of the four notes of the T3 cadence. The combinations produce two pairs of tones at the interval of a fifth: ḍaḍa-barang (the dominant and its dominant) and gulu-nem (the tone of cadential support and tonic); but the most important interval is probably formed by the first and last notes of the kenongan, *i.e.* ḍaḍa-nem or dominant-tonic. Kenongan three is an exact augmentation of the first two bars of the bubuka opaq-opaq, the T3 cadence being concluded in the first part of kenongan four. As in the bubuka opaq-opaq, the tone lima functions as a bridge tone and gulu serves in cadential support of ḍaḍa in the prolonged beginning of the cadence.

Kenongan four continues the augmented quotation of the introduction but alters the last measure by amplifying the dominant-tonic to an incomplete T3 cadence. In Chapter III we promised the reader not to attempt to justify minor deviations in the music by attributing the responsibility to the custom of *intentionally* recording one or two errors in the original checkered-script notation. [1]) A comparison of this kenongan with the final kenongan of gongan I and gongan IV, however, suggests one of two possible explanations for the use of barang as a final note instead of nem: 1) the close of the T3 cadence on nem is intentionally delayed (as an artistic device) until the end of kenongan one of gongan I; 2) the final tone barang is an intentional (in accordance with the tradition referred to above) or accidental error on the part of the scribe.

Gongan I

The first two kenongan are an elaboration of those of the bubuka genḍing and represent a variation of the T3 cadence. The change in the first note of the third (full) measure, from gulu in the bubuka genḍing to ḍaḍa in gongan I, reinforces the interpretation given in the bubuka genḍing, namely, that the important interval is ḍaḍa-nem or dominant-tonic. The prolonged cadence contains a dominant and secondary dominant approach to nem as shown below:

The employment of barang as a dominant of the dominant will be rather frequently seen.

The third kenongan is identical to that of the bubuka genḍing except for the use of the tone pélog instead of ḍaḍa at the beginning of the second (full) measure. Pélog appears only in passing and is replaced by ḍaḍa in the next measure. This is the only occurrence of pélog in the entire genḍing.

The fourth kenongan is identical to that of the bubuka genḍing except that the last note of the final T3 cadence is — as it should be — *nem.*

---

1) See pp. 19—20.

Gongan II

Kenongan one and two feature barang as a tone of melodic variety (by repetition) and lima as a tone of transition. The three-note figure barang-nem-lima comes from bar three of the bubuka opaq-opaq. In the second kenongan this figure ascends to include gulu before the final return to lima.

The first two and a half measures of kenongan three are like those of kenongan three in the bubuka genḍing; and the last measure and a half closes on a T1 cadence (bars 3—4 of the bubuka opaq-opaq). The fourth kenongan is based on bars 3—4 of the bubuka opaq-opaq with the addition of the tone gulu.

Gongan III

The first two kenongan are identical except that for the initial note of kenongan two a choice of either dominant or tonic is indicated. [1]) The material of these two kenongan is based on a condensation of bars 2—3—4 of the bubuka opaq-opaq (*i.e.* the interval formed by the two neighbors of nem — barang-lima — is omitted).

Kenongan three is the same as that of the bubuka genḍing. Kenongan four is identical to that of gongan I.

Gongan IV

Kenongan one, two and four are identical to those of gongan I. The third kenongan is the same as that of the bubuka genḍing.

General Summary

The bubuka opaq-opaq furnishes the melodic material for the entire genḍing. The three critical sections are related melodically and cadentially. The genḍing employs only the principal scale; the single appearance of the tone pélog in gongan I, followed immediately by lima and ḍaḍa, does not indicate an actual substitution but only a passing-note function.

The melodic importance of each tone:

Nem alternates with barang as the final note of the gongan. As the tonic of the principal fifth-interval nem is one of the most important tones.
Ḍaḍa as the dominant of nem shares its importance.
Gulu achieves some importance in cadential support of dominant and tonic.
Lima occurs as a bridge tone.
Barang is featured as a tone of melodic variety (so designated because it is melodically prominent and is not one of the three gong tones) and alternates with nem as the final note of the gongan. It also has a minor importance as a secondary dominant.
Pélog appears only once as a passing note.
Bem is not used.

1) See the transcription on p. 302.

"Megar Semu"

Ladrang nr 90 — pélog paṭet barang

bubuka opaq-opaq

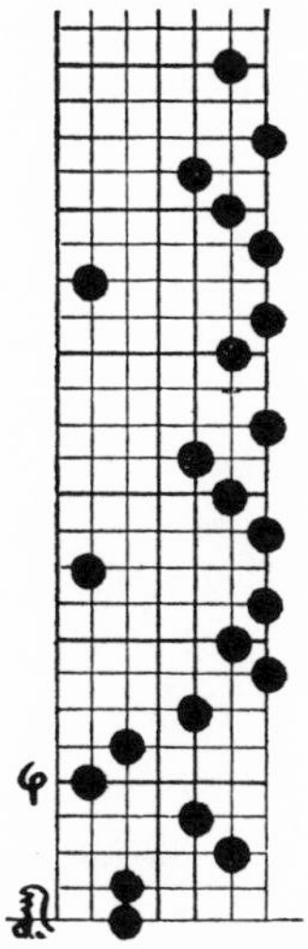

B.Op.			intro$_d$		
B.Gd.	A_d	A_{ba}	B_{ba}	C_d	A
GN I	A_d	A_{ba}	B_{ba}	C_d	A
GN II	A_d	A_{ba}	B^*_g	D_{ba}	A
GN III	E_{ba}	F_d	G_d	H_l	B
GN IV	I_l	J_g	K_g	H^*_l	B
GN V	L_n	L_n	L_n	M_d	B
GN VI	A_d	A_{ba}	B_{ba}	C_d	A′

B* last note omitted

H* first 2 notes changed

kenḍang 2

transcribed (see appendix p. 303)

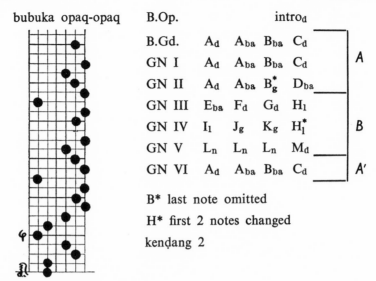

"Megar Semu" has a ternary construction. The *A* section consists of the bubuka genḍing, gongan I and II; the *B* section contains gongan III, IV and V; and the brief return of the first material in gongan VI comprises the *A′* section.

Bubuka opaq-opaq

The long introduction features the two tones of the principal fifth-interval, nem and ḍaḍa. In the first measure nem is stressed in the beginning half note, followed by the two neighbors barang and lima, with a return to nem in measure two. The second measure continues with an ascending scale passage to gulu, which returns to nem at the beginning of bar three. The pattern of measures 1—2 are repeated in measures 3—4. The T1 cadence of bar five introduces ḍaḍa in a weak position, proceeds to gulu-lima-nem in measure six and finally closes on ḍaḍa in anticipation of the stressed ḍaḍa of measure seven.

The tones of the principal scale are employed here in characteristic functions: nem and ḍaḍa have the primary importance through the constant return to nem and the final close on ḍaḍa; gulu is used in cadential support of tonic (in measures two and four) and dominant (-tonic-dominant in measure six); lima and barang appear as neighbors of nem, the former as a bridge tone in measure six and the latter as a tone of melodic variety which appears seven times (once more than nem) but never challenges the primary importance of tonic and dominant because of its passing- and neighbor-note usage.

In the cadential summaries of paṭet barang genḍing (p. 215) the bubuka opaq-opaq of "Megar Semu" is shown as "I/V", only the very close of the introduction being regarded as a definite cadence (or, actually, cadential outline). The T1 cadence might be considered eligible as the primary cadence, but the extension ending on I—V seems to break the normal downward descent of the T1 cadence which should continue (in bar six) to *barang*-nem instead of lima-nem in a T3 formula. But there is yet another possible interpretation of the bubuka opaq-opaq.

The melodic weight of the seven measures might be summarized in the following order, based on the importance of each tone: *nem* (as the first beat of the first five measures), *barang* (as the most frequently used tone), *gulu* (prominent in bars two and four because of its low position on the keys of the demung), *ḍaḍa* (as the final note of the introduction). This sequence — nem, barang, gulu, ḍaḍa — is a T4 cadential formula in paṭet barang and is shown in the example. Although this formula is never stated in its simple, basic form, the T4 cadence is, in my opinion, the primary cadence implicit in the melodic outline of the bubuka opaq-opaq.

Bubuka genḍing, gongan I, VI

The bubuka genḍing, gongan I and the final gongan VI are identical. The first two kenongan of these gongan are identical except for the final note which is ḍaḍa in the first kenongan and barang in the second. The eight measures are constructed on a repetition of the three-note figure lima-nem-ḍaḍa (from measure six of the bubuka opaq-opaq) preceded each time by nem, with the result that nem serves as a kind of quasi-pancher. The final barang of kenongan two together with the nem preceding it form the first half of a T4 formula which is completed at the beginning of kenongan three.

The third kenongan is the beginning of a prolonged T3 cadential formula (*N.B.* the secondary-dominant function of barang) which is not fully revealed until kenongan four, where it is followed by an extension continuing the downward scale to ḍaḍa. The figure of kenongan three is based on the gulu-barang interval of bars two and four in the bubuka opaq-opaq with the addition of the (implied) ḍaḍa. Kenongan four begins with ḍaḍa and then follows quite closely an augmentation of the bubuka opaq-opaq beginning with the gulu-nem interval of measure four and continuing through lima of bar five. The rest of the quotation is shortened to the first and last notes of measure six.

Gongan II

The first two kenongan are identical to those of the bubuka genḍing. The third kenongan is the same as that of the bubuka genḍing except for the omission of the last note. The fourth kenongan is similar to that of the bubuka genḍing in as much as it consists of a T3 cadence with an extension. The formula begins, however, one note later (the gulu-ḍaḍa-gulu of the preceding kenongan being repeated), and the extension is limited to the neighbors of nem and ends on barang.

Gongan III

Kenongan one features the tone barang in reiteration followed by the retrograde and normal sequence of the three-note figure from bars 1—2 of the bubuka opaq-opaq: lima-nem-barang. Kenongan two and three are built on the scale passage of measures 5—6 of the bubuka opaq-opaq and consist of a combined T2—T1 cadence. Barang begins kenongan three as a secondary-dominant-to-dominant followed by a T2—T1 cadence — or, in outline, V—I—V. The position of barang between the T2 and T1 cadences give it a neighbor-note function. Kenongan four begins with the transition tone lima and a T3 cadence which is extended to ḍaḍa and finally ends on lima.

Gongan IV

Kenongan one and two are based on bars 5—6 of the bubuka opaq-opaq. Kenongan one begins with the interval nem-ḍaḍa (tonic-dominant) followed by the bridge tone lima (bar six of the bubuka opaq-opaq) and a T1 formula which is extended by the neighbors of nem in the first half of kenongan two. The latter half of kenongan two repeats the opening nem-ḍaḍa-lima and closes on ḍaḍa-gulu. The eight measures feature the nem-ḍaḍa interval with lima appearing in a transitional role between cadential formulas or the I—V outline.

In kenongan three the tone lima continues in its transitional or bridge function, and the kenongan ends with the beginning of an extended T3 cadential formula concluded in kenongan four. The fourth kenongan, except for the first two notes, is the same as that of gongan III. That small change, however, results in the much more prolonged T3 cadence beginning in kenongan three and ending with the extension to the final bridge tone lima. The whole pattern (beginning with the last two notes of kenongan three) is based on the bars 4—5—6 of the bubuka opaq-opaq.

Gongan V

The first three kenongan are identical and are an exact augmentation of the bubuka opaq-opaq beginning with barang of the first measure. The two-measure pattern of the bubuka opaq-opaq is repeated three times (instead of two, as in the introduction), and the fourth kenongan completes the augmented quotation (bars 5—6 of the bubuka opaq-opaq), adding one extra note, lima, before the final ḍaḍa.

General Summary

The bubuka opaq-opaq provides the material for thematic development in the entire genḍing. The three critical sections are melodically and cadentially related. Only the principal scale is used, the tones pélog and bem being omitted altogether.

The importance of each tone:

Nem as the tonic of the principal fifth-interval and its prominence in the cadential formulas is one of the most important tones.
Daḍa as the final note of the bubuka opaq-opaq, bubuka genḍing, gongan I, V and VI and as the dominant of nem shares the importance of tonic.
Gulu has a lesser importance as the tone of cadential support.
Lima functions as a neighbor note and, as a bridge tone, is the final note of gongan III and IV.
Barang is prominent as the neighbor of nem and (especially conspicuous by the wide leap) as the "neighbor" of gulu. It is used as the final note of gongan II and has a ninor role as a secondary dominant. This secondary function will not be especially pointed out in the following analyses but can be recognized in every example.
Pélog does not appear.
Bem is not used.

"Grompol"

Ladrang nr 95 — pélog paṭet barang

bubuka opaq-opaq

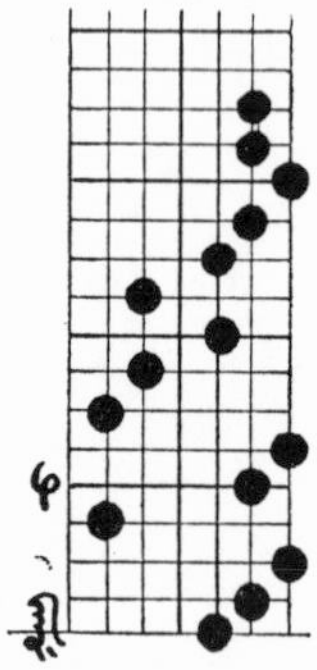

B.Op.	intro_l				
B.Gd.	A_{ba}	A_{ba}	A_{ba}	B_l	A
GN I	C^*_{ba}	A_{ba}	A_{ba}	B_l	A
GN II	D_g	E_g	F_l	G_l	B
GN III	C^*_{ba}	A_{ba}	A_{ba}	B_l	A′

C* is an elaboration of A

kenḍang 2

transcribed (see appendix p. 304)

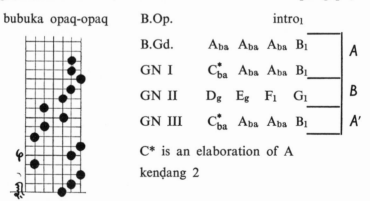

The ladrang "Grompol" has a ternary structure with *A* consisting of the bubuka genḍing and gongan I, *B* of gongan II, and *A′* of gongan III.

In the two previous examples of paṭet barang genḍing the tone pélog appears once as a passing note in one genḍing and is omitted altogether from the other. In "Grompol", however, pélog is used as a substitute for lima.

Bubuka opaq-opaq

The bubuka opaq-opaq consists of two cadential formulas, a T1 and a T3, separated by the bridge tone lima. The T3 cadence is extended by a repetition of the last three notes of the regular formula, gulu-barang-nem, and the addition of a final lima.

Bubuka genḍing

The first three kenongan are identical and are based on the last three notes of measure three of the bubuka opaq-opaq. This reiterated phrase forms the first three notes of a T3 cadence which is completed in the beginning of kenongan four and subsequently extended by a T1 formula, the tonic (nem), and a final lima. The fourth kenongan seems to be a condensation of the whole bubuka opaq-opaq.

Gongan I

The first kenongan begins with a reiteration of gulu followed by an ascending-descending scale passage gulu-pélog-gulu. We shall see in later examples that this manner of substituting pélog for lima is rigidly observed. The pélog "rule-of-substitution" will be shown in a detailed example after an examination of the next three kenongan. The material of kenongan one appears to be an elaboration of kenongan one of the bubuka genḍing, being based on measure three of the bubuka opaq-opaq with pélog used in substitution for lima.

The second, third, and fourth kenongan are identical to those of the bubuka genḍing. The return of lima in kenongan four, after the substitution of pélog in kenongan one, is accomplished in a *descending* scale passage following an extended T3 cadence which begins in kenongan two on the tone ḍaḍa.

Gongan I is given below in its entirely, and the two requirements of the pélog rule-of-substitution are indicated by the appropriate brackets.

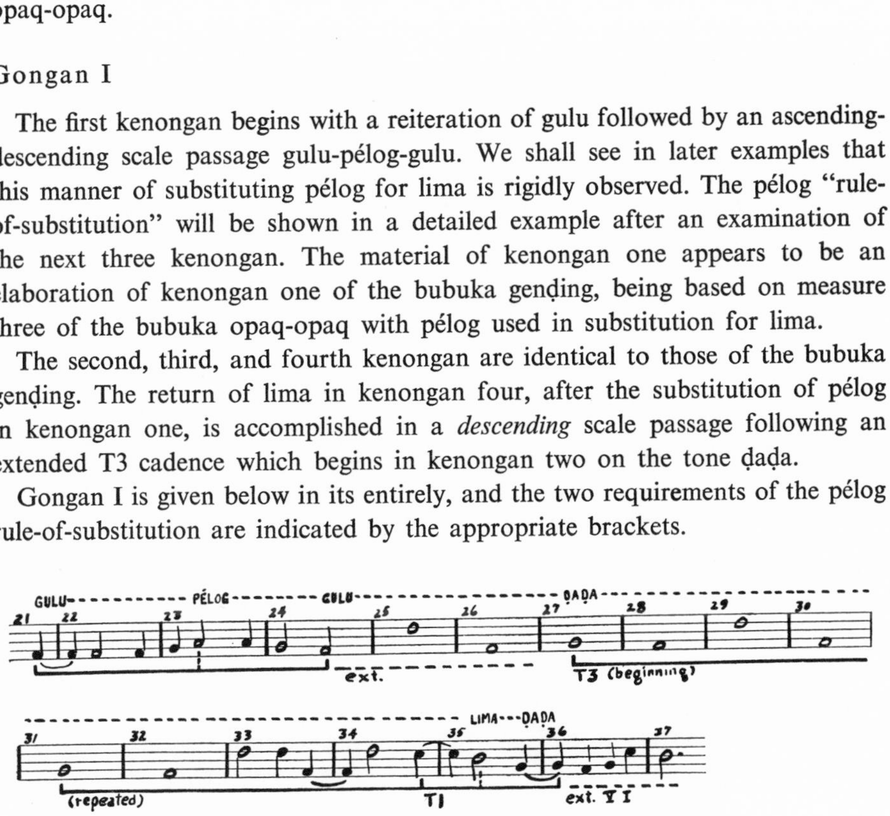

The first bracket indicates the initial substitution gulu-*pélog*-gulu, and the dotted line shows a barang-gulu extension. The long T3 cadence beginning in measure 27 is a descending scale which reaches nem (tonic) in bars 34—35 and *lima* in replacement of pélog in measure 35. The T3 cadence is further extended by the completion of a T1 formula, the neighbor gulu, V—I, and a final lima. The fundamental requirements of the pélog rule-of-substitution appear to be: 1) in substitution for lima the tone pélog must be approached by an ascending scale passage, probably starting on gulu, and quitted by a descending scale passage, probably ending on gulu; 2) lima must replace pélog in a descending scale passage, probably beginning on ḍaḍa in a T3 formula and perhaps ending on ḍaḍa in a T1 extension.

Gongan II

Kenongan one is based on bars 2—3 of the bubuka opaq-opaq, using both a retrograde and normal sequence of the pattern. After the beginning ḍaḍa-lima a long scale passage begins on ḍaḍa. So that this kenongan may be more easily understood as a series of conjunct figures, the kenongan is given below with the appropriate "T" numbers and brackets.

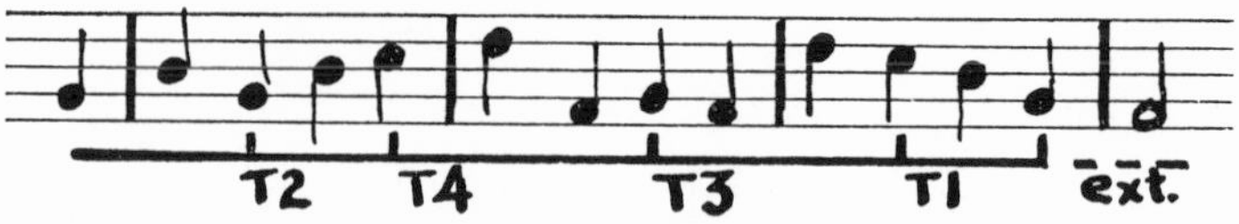

Kenongan two continues the extension with the upper neighbor of ḍaḍa (lima), returns to ḍaḍa and proceeds with practically the same material as kenongan one. The third kenongan, after a reiteration on the tone barang, continues in much the same manner as kenongan one. In kenongan four the quarter- and sixteenth-note figures slow down to half notes in the form of an extended T3 cadence ending on lima.

Gongan III

The final gongan is the same as gongan I.

General Summary

The bubuka opaq-opaq provides a general basis for the melodic development of the genḍing. The three critical sections are closely related melodically and cadentially.

The substitution of the tone pélog for lima is accomplished in an ascending-descending scale. In both gongan I and III the tone pélog appears only in the first kenongan, and the second and third kenongan are "neutral", *i.e.* neither pélog nor lima are used. Lima replaces pélog in a descending scale passage in the fourth kenongan. Thus, although the "modulation" tone pélog is substituted for lima, an actual modulation is not effected. Gongan I and III can be designated as having a neutral character.

The importance of each tone:

Nem, although it does not appear at kenongan or gongan divisions, is important as the tonic of the principal fifth-interval.
Ḍaḍa shares the importance of nem as its dominant and is more prominently used than the tonic.
Gulu is used in cadential support and introduces pélog in accordance with the "rule-of-substitution".
Lima is melodically sensitive as an exchangeable tone and is important as the final note of the bubuka opaq-opaq and all gongan.
Barang is prominent as a tone of melodic variety.
Pélog is sensitive as an exchange tone.
Bem does not appear.

"Ronggo Lasem"

Ladrang nr 98 pélog paṭet barang

bubuka opaq-opaq

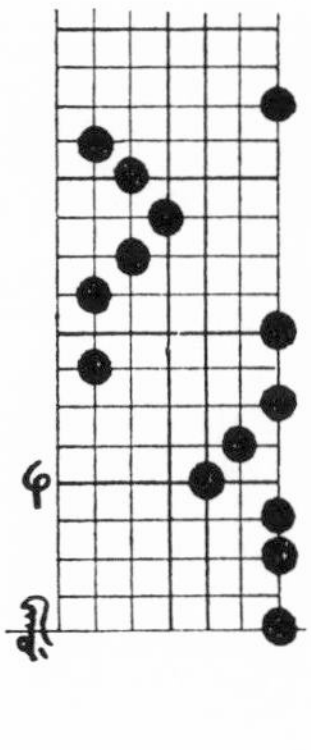

B.Op.				intro$_{ba}$	
B.Gd.	A_{ba}	B_n	C_n	D_g	*A*
GN I	E_n	F_n	F'_n	G_l	
GN II	H_n	F''_l	F'''_n	G_l	*B*
GN III	I_g	J_{ba}	J^*_{ba}	K_{ba}	
GN IV	L^*_{ba}	M^*_n	C_n	D_g	*A'*

F′ extra ḍaḍa added at beginning
F″ last 2 notes changed; gulu added at beginning of last bar
F‴ gulu added at beginning of last bar
J* rhythmic change; one ḍaḍa replaced by ngenchot on pélog
L* and M* elaboration of A and B
kenḍang 1

transcribed (see appendix p. 305)

"Ronggo Lasem" is an example of modulation from the principal to the high auxiliary scale. This ladrang has a ternary construction in which the *A* section (the bubuka genḍing) returns slightly elaborated in gongan IV (the *A′* section). The *B* section is binary, gongan I and II comprising the first part and gongan III the second part. The same bubuka opaq-opaq is used for nr 96 "Teḍak Saking" and nr 99 "Barang Asmoro". These three ladrang are related to one another melodically to about the same extent as those sléndro paṭet sanga genḍing (nr 27, 28, 32) which have a common bubuka opaq-opaq and were compared in Chapter V. Nr 96 and nr 98 contain a modulation to the high auxiliary scale, and nr 99 has a neutral passage.

Bubuka opaq-opaq

The scale passage in the first two measures of the introduction, gulu-pélog-gulu, fulfills the first requirement of the pélog rule-of-substitution; and in bars 3—4 lima, as the extension of a T3 cadence, meets the second requirement by replacing pélog in a scale passage descending from ḍaḍa (cf. nr 95). The T3 cadence is extended in bars 4—5 by the two neighbors of nem. The initial barang appears to be used as a neighbor note which is not essential to the gulu-pélog requirement of the substitution rule (cf. the beginning of gongan III) but which may be added before gulu (cf. the end of kenongan two, gongan III) or after gulu (bar three of the bubuka opaq-opaq, and cf. nr 95).

Bubuka genḍing

The first kenongan is based on the last two measures of the bubuka opaq-opaq and features barang-lima. The second kenongan begins with lima as a bridge tone leading to an extended T2 formula. The third kenongan continues the importance of nem by reiteration of the tone, followed by a T2 formula and a further reiteration of nem with its neighbors. The fourth kenongan begins with a repetition of the tone barang followed by a T1 formula and concludes with a T4 cadence extended by the tone gulu. The material is freely derived from the bubuka opaq-opaq.

Gongan I

The first kenongan stresses the tone nem and the tonic-dominant interval by the employment of the T1 and T2 formulas. This material is also used at the beginning of kenongan two and is followed by an extended T3 cadence. Kenongan three is the same as kenongan two except for the addition of an extra ḍaḍa at the beginning. The fourth kenongan is the same as that of the bubuka genḍing except for the last measure, which ends on an extended T1 cadence instead of a T4 formula. The whole gongan is rather freely derived from the bubuka opaq-opaq.

Gongan II

The first kenongan features the tonic-dominant interval (with the neighbors of nem) and a reiteration of the tone lima. The last half of the kenongan consists of a T4 and a T3 formula. The second kenongan is like that of gongan I except for the following minor changes: the last two notes are altered to end on lima instead of nem; gulu is added at the beginning of the last measure; the initial lima is omitted, a simple I—V being used instead of the T1 formula which links the first two kenongan of gongan I. The third kenongan is like that of gongan I except for the addition of the tone gulu at the beginning of the last measure. The fourth kenongan is the same as that of gongan I. The material is freely based on the bubuka opaq-opaq.

Gongan III

Gongan III begins with an elaboration of the first two measures of the bubuka opaq-opaq (minus the initial tone barang) and firmly establishes a modulation to the high auxiliary scale by the insistent repetition of the gulu-pélog scale passage. This continues until the T3 cadence (from bars 2—3 of the bubuka opaq-opaq) at the end of kenongan two. The third kenongan is essentially the same as the second. It contains the following minor changes: gulu becomes the first note and the tones ḍaḍa and pélog are moved forward one beat; the initial beat of the first full measure becomes two sixteenth notes instead of a quarter note; and the second beat becomes pélog instead of ḍaḍa. Kenongan four begins with lima as an extension of the preceding T3 formula. This indicates a modulation back to the principal scale which continues the extension with a T1 formula including lima and ends on ḍaḍa in the second full measure. The kenongan closes on an extended T1 cadence. The material of gongan III is very closely related to the bubuka opaq-opaq.

Gongan IV

The first two kenongan are elaborations of the first two kenongan of the bubuka genḍing. The last two kenongan are identical to those of the bubuka genḍing.

General Summary

The bubuka opaq-opaq provides a general basis for melodic development in the body of the genḍing. The three critical sections are related melodically and cadentially; the bubuka opaq-opaq closes with an extended T3 cadence, and the bubuka genḍing and the final gongan (IV) end with the retrograde form of that cadence, a T4, slightly extended.

Modulation to the high auxiliary scale is achieved in gongan III in accordance with the two requirements of the pélog rule-of-substitution.

The melodic importance of each tone:

Nem as tonic of the principal fifth-interval is one of the most important tones; it is rather prominent at the kenongan divisions.

Ḍaḍa is prominent as the dominant of nem in the cadential formulas and

introduces the descending scale (*i.e.* a T3 cadence) which continues to lima as a confirmation of the return to the principal scale.
Gulu is used in cadential support of dominant and tonic and begins and ends the ascending-descending scale in the pélog substitution. It is the final note of the bubuka genḍing and the final gongan.
Lima has a minor role as a tone of transition and is melodically sensitive as an exchangeable tone. It is used as the final note of gongan I and II.
Barang is a tone of melodic variety and serves as the final note of the bubuka opaq-opaq and gongan III.
Pélog is melodically sensitive as a modulation tone.
Bem does not appear.

"Srimalélo"

Ketawang nr 100 — pélog paṭet barang

bubuka opaq-opaq

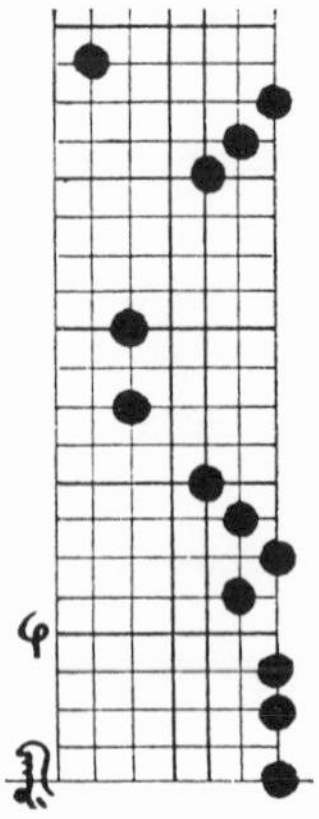

B.Op.		$intro_{ba}$	
B.Gd.	A_l	B_{ba}	A
B.Gd.	C'_l	D'_{ba}	A
GN I	C''_l	E^*_{ba}	A
GN II	F_n	G_l	B
GN III	H_n	I_g	B
GN IV	J_g	K_l	B
GN V	L^*_l	D''_{ba}	A′
GN VI	C''_l	D''_{ba}	A′
GN VII	C''_l	D''_{ba}	A′

Theme and Variations

C′ elaboration of A
C″ slight variation of C′
D′ elaboration of B
D″ rhythmic alteration
E* elaboration of B
L* related to C′
kenḍang 2

transcribed (see appendix p. 306)

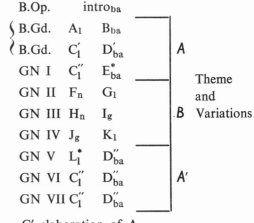

The ketawang "Srimalélo" is the second of the only two examples in the entire Jogyanese collection which use a variations form of melodic development. [1]

[1] See nr 88, p. 183 ff.

Each eight-measure gongan can be thought of as a different variation, although similarities exist among certain of these gongan, which allow the three-part division indicated in the structural table.

Bubuka opaq-opaq

The beginning of the bubuka opaq-opaq might be considered an incomplete T3 formula extended to lima, which, after a prolongation of lima, sounds twice the tone ḍaḍa that was missing at the start. In this interpretation lima functions as a bridge tone between the introductory passage of bar one and the T2 cadence beginning in bar three (rather than the middle tone of a rhythmically questionable T1 formula). The same passage might also be thought of as a descending scale from gulu (second gong tone) to the fifth below, lima — an interval of a fifth beginning with the tone often used in cadential support of dominant and tonic and ending with the tone characteristically used as a bridge- or transition-note. Either view of the matter amounts to the same evaluation of its purpose: an introductory phrase for the principal T2 cadence beginning with ḍaḍa in measure three and extended to the final barang.

Bubuka genḍing, gongan I

The two eight-measure gongan comprising the two halves of the bubuka genḍing and the eight measures of gongan I can be considered together since there is a close melodic relationship among them.

The first eight-measure gongan of the bubuka genḍing is in whole notes and follows, in augmentation, the bubuka opaq-opaq quite exactly. It begins with the first note of bar one, omits the second ḍaḍa of bar three, proceeds to the first note (lima) of bar four, and ends with a repetition of the first two notes. The second gongan of the bubuka genḍing is an elaboration of the first. The transition tone lima occurs at the midpoint, and the latter half of the gongan finishes the quotation of the bubuka opaq-opaq with a slight elaboration occurring in the final measure. This variation closes with a T2—T1 cadence extended to barang. Gongan I is a slightly more-elaborated variation of the same material, closing with a T2 cadence extended to barang.

Gongan II, III, IV

The three gongan of the *B* section again are melodic variations of the bubuka opaq-opaq, but each is developed in an individual manner.

Gongan II begins with a strong reiteration of the tone barang and continues with a variation based on the bubuka opaq-opaq starting on barang of measure one and proceeding to the end. Lima receives some emphasis in the second half of the gongan, and the final cadence, an ascending scale from gulu to lima, appears to be (perhaps not accidentally) related to the *descending* scale which establishes the opening gulu-lima interval of the bubuka opaq-opaq.

Gongan III begins with the gulu-to-lima scale and a reiteration of the tone lima. The rest of the gongan is rather closely related to the corresponding section of gongan II and is a rather free development of bars 3—4 of the bubuka opaq-opaq. The gongan closes on a T4 cadence extended to gulu.

Gongan IV begins with a pélog substitution. With the inclusion of the three notes of the preceding gongan, the introduction of this tone is accomplished in accordance with the rule-of-substitution. After a T3 cadence lima replaces pélog by the rule-of-substitution with a slight variation of the formula-and-extension, caused by the anticipation of lima (before nem), immediately justified by the continuation to ḍaḍa. This brief exchange of "sensitive" tones creates neither a modulation nor a neutral passage. The line continues with a T2—T1 cadence extended to gulu at the kenongan division. The second half of the gongan is based on the first three measures (plus the first beat of measure four, lima) of the bubuka opaq-opaq; the gongan closes on a descending gulu-to-lima scale slightly extended.

It is worth noting that the final notes of these three gongan are: *lima* of gongan II, *gulu* of gongan III, *lima* of gongan IV — the interval which provides the core of melodic development in the *B* section.

Gongan V, VI, VII

The last three gongan are very closely related to the second and third gongan (and therefore to the first also) of the *A′* section. Other than the first half of kenongan one, gongan V, the deviations are so slight that they may most easily be seen by referring to the notes directly below the structural table on p. 210.

General Summary

The material of the bubuka opaq-opaq provides a "theme" for a set of short melodic variations in the body of the genḍing. The three critical sections have a strong melodic relationship and a general cadential relationship. The genḍing is in the principal scale throughout, the brief occurrence of pélog being replaced almost immediately by lima.

The importance of each tone:

Nem as the tonic of the principal fifth-interval is one of the most important tones.

Ḍaḍa as the dominant of the principal fifth-interval shares the importance of nem.

Gulu occurs as a final note in gongan III and serves in cadential support of dominant and tonic.

Lima has some importance as a tone of transition, as the fifth of gulu, and as the final note of gongan II and IV. It is melodically sensitive as an exchangeable tone.

Barang assumes considerable importance as the final note of the bubuka opaq-opaq and all gongan except those three just mentioned in connection with gulu and lima. It also appears as a tone of melodic variety. Although the functions of barang are quite different from those of the tonic and dominant, its prominence gives it an importance equal to that of nem and ḍaḍa. *Pélog* replaces lima in accordance with the rule-of substitution.

Bem is not used.

Summary and Conclusions

The preceding analyses show that the genḍing of paṭet barang are marked by their variation in structural details. By way of example, each genḍing employs a rather distinct cadential form in the three critical sections, although these cadential elements are constructed on the same principal fifth-interval. The reader may have observed as another indication of individuality that among the five representative genḍing no two have the same final note. As regular features, however, only the five notes of the principal scale are used for final tones; the tone pélog is used sparingly and when substituted for lima always appears in a prescribed manner; the tone bem is avoided entirely.

The basis of compositional practice in paṭet barang will be most easily seen by a summary of the principal features of each of the eleven genḍing. Tables similar to those used in the previous chapters will suffice.

Table I indicates the architectonic form of the genḍing, the modulation scheme, and the correspondence of the bubuka genḍing and the final gongan on the basis of identical kenongan (the one ketawang is not included). In the column headed "Mod." the letters "P & N" indicate that a genḍing employs the principal scale and that the substitution of pélog for lima produces a neutral section but not a true modulation. The latters "P-H-P" indicate that the piece begins in the principal scale, modulates to the high auxiliary, and returns to the principal.

Table I

Title	Form	Mod.	B.Gd./ Final GN
nr 89 — Jong Keli	Intro — verse-refrain	P	2
„ 90 — Megar Semu	„ — ternary	P	4
„ 91—93 — Pengsih-Megarsih	„ — „	P & N	4
„ 92 — Jongjongan	„ — „	P	4
„ 94 — Sobrang Betawan	„ — „	P	4
„ 95 — Grompol	„ — „	P & N	3
„ 96 — Teḍak Saking	„ — rounded binary	P-H	4
„ 97 — Rangu-Rangu	„ — ternary	P	4
„ 98 — Ronggo Lasem	„ — „	P-H-P	2
„ 99 — Barang Asmoro	„ — „	P & N	2
„100 — Srimalélo	„ — „ (variations)	P	ketawang

Summary: 9 genḍing are ternary (1 of which is a form of variations)
1 ,, is a rounded binary form
1 ,, ,, ,, verse-refrain ,,

2 genḍing modulate to the high auxiliary scale
3 ,, contain neutral passages

On the basis of identical kenongan appearing in the bubuka genḍing and the final gongan: of the 10 ladrang 10 have at least 2 kenongan identical in both sections, and of these 10:

6 ladrang have 4 kenongan identical in both sections
1 ,, has 3 ,, ,, ,, ,, ,,
3 ,, have 2 ,, ,, ,, ,, ,,

The last kenongan of the bubuka genḍing and the final kenongan of the piece are the same (except for a negligible rhythmic subdivision in nr 100).

Table II indicates the patterns of kenongan repetition in the gongan and is arranged according to type. It shows the number of each type used in every ladrang (the ketawang is omitted).

Table II

Genḍing	ABCD	AABC	AABB	AAAB	AAAA
nr 89		3			
,, 90	2	4		1	
nr 91—93	5				
nr 92	2			3	
,, 94	1			3	
,, 95	1	2		1	
,, 96	2			2	
,, 97	1	4			
,, 98	2	3			
,, 99	2	3			
,, 100	ketawang				
Total:	18	19	0	10	0

Summarized on the basis of 47 gongan:

38.3% repeat no kenongan — ABCD
40.4 ,, 1 ,, — AABC
21.3 ,, ,, ,, 3 times — AAAB

Table III gives a summary of the cadences closing the three critical sections of the genḍing. The symbols used are similar to those employed in the previous chapters. A cadence enclosed in parenthesis and preceding another cadence, *e.g.* (T4) I/V, indicates that the parenthetical cadence may or may not be considered the principal cadence. The symbols "T3 — nem + gulu" indicate a T3 cadence lacking the final nem (which, however, is included in the subsequent gongan) and extended to gulu.

Table III

Genḍing	B.Op.	B.Gd.	Final GN
nr 89	T3 + gulu	T3 + T1	T3 + T1
„ 90	(T4) I/V	T3 + T1	T3 + T1
nr 91—93	T3 — nem + gulu	(T3-ḍaḍa) T1 + lima	(T3-ḍaḍa) T1 + lima
nr 92	T1 + T2	T1 + T2	T1 + T2
„ 94	T3 + barang	T3 + barang	T3 + barang
„ 95	T3 + lima	T3 + lima	T3 + lima
„ 96	T3 + barang	T3 + barang	T3 + barang
„ 97	T3 + V/I	T3 + T3 — nem	T3 + T3
„ 98	T3 + barang	T4 + gulu	T4 + gulu
„ 99	T3 + barang	T3 + barang	T3 + barang
„ 100	T2 + barang	T1 + barang	T1 + barang

In summary:	T3	T4	T1	T2	I/V	=	
B.Op.	8	0	1	1	1	=	72.7% T3
B.Gd.	7	1	3	0	0	=	72.7% T3 (or T4)
Final GN	7	1	3	0	0	=	72.7% (or T4)

Table IV indicates the melodic importance of each tone. The column headings are similar to those used in the preceding chapters. In the column headed "Subs." the letter "R" following the tone name "pélog" indicates that the substitution is made in accordance with the rule-of-substitution and that lima subsequently returns also in accordance with the rule (see pp. 205-6).

Although a comparison of the principal practices of paṭet barang with those of the other two pélog paṭet will be reserved for Chapter XI, the following conclusions can be formulated from these four tables.

Table I indicates that the genḍing in paṭet barang are predominantly ternary in form. One of these genḍing, a ketawang (nr 100), is a set of short variations of the bubuka opaq-opaq. Each variation is eight measures long, and the large form of the composition can be described as a ternary structure.

Two genḍing manage a modulation to the high auxiliary scale through the substitution of the tone pélog for lima. There are no examples of a modulation to the low auxiliary scale, which is theoretically possible through the substitution

Table IV

Gḍ.	Final	Pr.5th	Trans.	Cad. Spt.	Mel.Var.	Omitted	Q-pancher	Subs.
nr 89	ḍaḍa	nem-ḍaḍa	lima	gulu		pélog/bem		
,, 90	,,	,, ,,	,,	,,	barang	,, ,,	nem	
nr91—93	lima	,, ,,	,,	,,	,,	bem		pélog-R
nr 92	nem	,, ,,	,,	,,	,,	pélog/bem		
,, 94	barang	,, ,,	,,	,,	,,	bem		pélog-R
,, 95	lima	,, ,,	,,	,,	,,	,,		,, ,,
,, 96	barang	,, ,,		,,	barang/pélog	,,	gulu	,, ,,
,, 97	nem	,, ,,	lima	,,	barang	,,		
,, 98	gulu	,, ,,	,,	,,	,,	,,		pélog-R
,, 99	barang	,, ,,	,,	,,	,,	,,		,, ,,
,, 100	,,	,, ,,	,,	,,	,,	,,		,, ,,
Sum- mary:	barang 4 nem 2 ḍaḍa 2 lima 2 gulu 1	nem-ḍaḍa	lima	gulu	barang (pélog)	pélog/bem	vari- able	pélog

of bem for barang. 1) Three genḍing employ neutral passages in which the pélog-lima exchange is too tentative to establish an actual modulation.

Table IV indicates that in each instance in which pélog is substituted for lima, the following rules are observed:

1) pélog is approached by an ascending and quitted by a descending scale beginning and ending on gulu:

2) lima returns preceded by a descending scale in the form of a T3 formula extended to lima and usually ḍaḍa:

These two rules indicate that *neutral* passages or modulations are approached by the less-typical *ascending* form of scale 2) as a preparation of the exchange tone pélog and that a return to the principal scale is confirmed by the typical *descending* T3 cadential formula (see below) extended to include lima in replacement of pélog. The one example (nr 97) in which pélog does not appear according to these rules is not an example of substitution but one in which pélog is used merely as a passing tone. 3)

---

1) Cf. p. 145 and p. 148.

2) The *typical* cadential formulas of all paṭet are a *descending* scale passage between dominant and tonic; the retrograde form is infrequently used.

3) See further p. 200.

The high percentage of kenongan identical in both the bubuka genḍing and the final gongan (Table I) establishes a close melodic and cadential relationship between these two sections. The detailed analyses indicated that the bubuka opaq-opaq provides the basis of thematic material for melodic development in the body of the genḍing. These two considerations together show a strong melodic relationship among the three critical sections of the genḍing; and Table III indicates an equally strong cadential bond.

The summary of Table III shows that among the four theoretical cadences given below, the T3 formula is the typical cadence for genḍing in paṭet barang. (The second gong tone is indicated by "+".)

Any of the theoretical formulas may be found within the body of the genḍing or at the close of the inner gongan. The T3 formula appears at the close of the critical sections *always* with an extension. The variety produced by these extensions is one of the distinguishing characteristics of paṭet barang.

Another aspect of this variety may be seen in the first column of Table IV. The tone used most frequently as the final note of the genḍing, barang, serves in that capacity only 36.4% of the time. The remaining final notes are about evenly distributed among the other four tones of the principal scale. The sanction of variety in this selection is somewhat strengthened by the fact that barang — the tone which has priority — is *not* one of the three principal or gong tones, *i.e.* dasar, first or second gong tone. Since barang is, however, a hallmark of paṭet barang — bem, its counterpart in the two pélog paṭet bem, being studiously avoided — it is not illogical that this tone should be given some preference as a final note.

The principal fifth-interval is nem-ḍaḍa. These two tones share the primary melodic importance, notwithstanding frequent cadential extensions to one of the other tones of the principal scale. Lima is melodically sensitive as an exchangeable tone and also has a minor role as a tone of transition. The second gong tone gulu is used in cadential support of dominant and tonic and also achieves some importance in its relation to pélog in the rule-of-substitution passages. The tone barang has already been discussed as a final note; its importance is further increased by its frequent appearance as a tone of melodic variety and as the ultimate note of cadential extensions. Pélog is melodically sensitive as a modulation tone or as an exchange tone in neutral passages; it appears once (nr 96) as a tone of melodic variety! (established by the frequency of its occurrence and by reiteration within the high-scale section). The tone bem is avoided altogether. The pedal note or quasi-pancher is variable.

A brief summary of the principal points.

1. The bubuka opaq-opaq is a particular elaboration, combination or variation of cadential formulas, the typical cadence being the T3 formula. The bubuka opaq-opaq provides the basis of thematic development for the entire genḍing.
2. Through the thematic development of the bubuka opaq-opaq the T3 cadential formula becomes the melodic framework of the genḍing. The particular variation of that formula in the bubuka opaq-opaq accounts for the distinctiveness of the introduction and the genḍing itself.
3. The three critical sections of the genḍing — the bubuka opaq-opaq, the bubuka genḍing and the final gongan — are closely related melodically and cadentially.
4. The "inner gongan" may be related to the bubuka genḍing, may be a distinct development of the melodic material or a modulatory or neutral section, may be a combination of these conditions or may be chiefly of a transitional nature. Any of the theoretical cadences may be found at these inner gongan.
5. Modulations to the high auxiliary scale, via the tone pélog, are not frequent. Occasional neutral sections or fluctuations between the principal and high auxiliary scales result from an exchange of pélog and lima which is too rapid or, through the subsequent avoidance of either of these sensitive tones, too indefinite to establish a new scale center. Modulation to the low auxiliary scale, via the tone bem, does not occur.
6. In modulatory or neutral passages the tone pélog is introduced by an ascending scale beginning with gulu and is quitted by a descending scale ending with gulu. A return to the tone lima and the principal scale is preceded by a descending T3 cadence extended to lima and usually to ḍaḍa.
7. The typical cadence in paṭet barang is the T3 formula, which always includes some kind of extension. The variety produced by these extensions is one of several examples of artistic license characteristic of genḍing in paṭet barang. Any of the theoretical cadences may be used within the body of the genḍing.
8. The first gong tone nem and the dasar ḍaḍa form the principal fifth-interval and occupy the chief melodic and structural positions. Barang is used to the complete exclusion of its exchange tone bem. Probably because the tone barang does not occur in either pélog paṭet lima or pélog paṭet nem as a principal tone, it is considered especially qualified as a preferred final note. It is also prominent as a tone of melodic variety. Gulu, the second gong tone, is used in cadential support of nem and ḍaḍa and has some importance in the scale passages introducing the tone pélog. Lima has a minor role as a bridge or transition tone, and both

lima and pélog are melodically sensitive as exchange tones. Bem is completely avoided.

9. The final note of the genḍing is variable. Although any tone of the principal scale may serve in that capacity, some preference is given to barang

Pélog Paṭet Manyura

The ladrang "Wirogo", listed by the scribe as belonging to pélog paṭet lima, appears to use only the paṭet barang low auxiliary scale. If this interpretation is correct, the term *pélog paṭet manyura* has some justification as a fourth pélog paṭet. [1])

It was shown in the foregoing summary that the typical cadence of paṭet barang genḍing is the T3 formula. Although no modulations to the low auxiliary scale, in which bem is substituted for barang, were found, there exists in this connection the possibility of still another theoretical cadential formula. The typical paṭet barang cadence and the theoretical formula with bem in substitution for barang are given below.

T3

(typical)

T3

(bem replacing barang)

The T3 cadence in which bem replaces barang will be found in the following brief analysis of "Wirogo". Any designations of a T3 formula will indicate this type.

"Wirogo"

Ladrang nr 66 — pélog paṭet manyura(?)

bubuka opaq-opaq

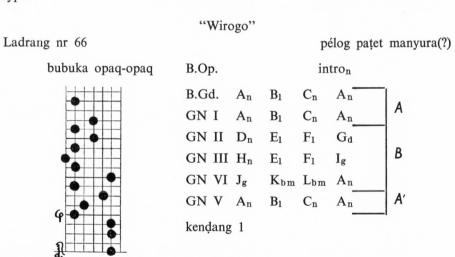

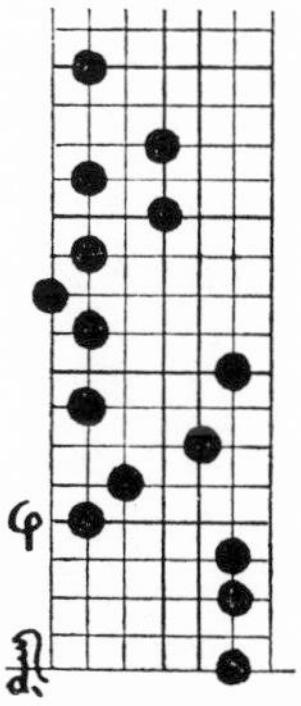

B.Op.			intro$_n$		
B.Gd.	A_n	B_l	C_n	A_n	A
GN I	A_n	B_l	C_n	A_n	A
GN II	D_n	E_l	F_l	G_d	B
GN III	H_n	E_l	F_l	I_g	B
GN VI	J_g	K_{bm}	L_{bm}	A_n	B
GN V	A_n	B_l	C_n	A_n	A'
kenḍang 1					

[1]) See further pp. 145-6 and p. 148.

transcribed (see appendix p. 307)

Bubuka opaq-opaq

The introduction gives little indication of paṭet. The x's below the transcription mark the probable melodic highpoints but do not contribute very much to the solution of our problem. These tones suggest the tonic-dominant of pélog paṭet nem, although the lack of a recognizable cadential formula (unless the passage delimited by the second and third x is accepted as a non-typical formula) and the material which appears later in the genḍing do not support such an interpretation. The tonic and dominant of paṭet lima (the tones lima and gulu) are not established nor are any of the theoretical formulas. The case for paṭet barang is equally weak.

Bubuka genḍing, gongan I

These two gongan are identical. The first kenongan consists of the T3 formula (in whole-note values), ḍaḍa-gulu-bem-nem. The second kenongan contains the interval ḍaḍa-nem returning to ḍaḍa and the transition tone lima. Kenongan three contains the four tones gulu-pélog-bem-nem, which may be intended as a variation of the T3 formula. The fourth kenongan is like the first, a T3 cadence. The interval ḍaḍa-nem of kenongan two is the dominant-tonic of paṭet barang (low auxiliary scale) or pélog paṭet manyura, used, together with the bridge tone lima, to form a link between the T3 formulas preceding and following it. The use of pélog as an auxiliary note in kenongan three is foreshadowed in the bubuka opaq-opaq.

Gongan II

The first kenongan alternates between bem and nem, and in kenongan two the pattern includes gulu and is extended to the bridge tone lima. The third kenongan consists of tonic-dominant-tonic followed by the transition tone lima (and is therefore similar to kenongan two of the preceding gongan). Kenongan four begins on bem and ends the gongan in a three-note T1 cadence from tonic to dominant.

Gongan III

The first two kenongan appear to be a spun-out T3 formula extended to lima. The last half of the gongan begins with tonic-dominant followed by a three-note T1 formula extended to the second gong tone gulu. Kenongan two and three are identical to those of the preceding gongan.

Gongan V

The final gongan is the same as the bubuka genḍing.

Conclusions

One example of pélog paṭet manyura does not allow more than passing speculation on some of its features. The prominence of the T3 cadence (in which bem replaces barang) as a basis of the whole genḍing seems to be its one distinguishing hallmark. In other respects it resembles the general features of paṭet barang. This T3 formula does not exist among the theoretical cadences of paṭet lima and paṭet nem; so that the designation of a fourth pélog paṭet seems justified. Purely in the realm of speculation one cannot help but wonder if the key to the bubuka opaq-opaq might not be (the second time I violate my promise) an error on the part of the scribe, *e.g.* if the second note of measure four were bem instead of nem, the final cadence of the introduction would be a T3 formula.

XI.

PÉLOG: SUMMARY AND CONCLUSIONS.

THE STRUCTURAL CHARACTERISTICS of the pélog paṭet are presented in summary and comparison in an effort to determine both their common and individual features. An occasional reference to Chapter VII will avoid repetition in the substantiation of general principals previously established by example and documentation in the summary of the sléndro paṭet. Certain structural details may be more easily defined by drawing on similar or contrasting practices found in the sléndro genḍing. Otherwise, in the interests of simplicity, the exposition is restricted to pélog material, the principal comparison of sléndro and pélog being reserved for the final chapter. Unless stated to the contrary, references to pélog paṭet lima pertain to the genḍing found in the Solonese manuscript. Until further defined the terms "tonic" and "dominant" will continue to be used to designate the principal fifth-interval of a given paṭet.

The Seven Pélog Tones

The melodic importance of each of the seven pélog tones varies from one paṭet to another. The principal functions are summarized below:

BARANG — in paṭet lima (old-scale) is omitted or used as a passing note; in new-scale paṭet lima is the *modulation tone* to the high auxiliary scale.
— in paṭet nem is the *modulation tone* to the high auxiliary scale where it may achieve some melodic importance; otherwise it is used chiefly as a passing note
— in paṭet barang is the preferred *final note* and the *tone of melodic variety.*

NEM — in paṭet lima is the *tone of transition* and secondary dominant
— as dasar in paṭet nem is the *dominant* and frequently the final note
— as first gong tone in paṭet barang is the *tonic.*

LIMA — as first gong tone in paṭet lima is the *tonic*
— as second gong tone in paṭet nem is the preferred *final note*,

the tone of transition and is used in cadential support of tonic and dominant

— in paṭet barang is melodically sensitive as an *exchangeable tone*.

PÉLOG — in paṭet lima (old-scale) is melodically sensitive as an *exchangeable tone*; in new-scale paṭet lima is a *modulation tone* to the low auxiliary scale.

— in paṭet nem is a *modulation tone* to the low auxiliary scale

— in paṭet barang is a *modulation tone* to the high auxiliary scale.

ḌAḌA — in paṭet lima (old-scale) is a *modulation tone* to the high auxiliary scale; in new-scale paṭet lima is melodically sensitive as an *exchangeable tone*

— in paṭet nem is melodically sensitive as an *exchangeable tone* and serves as a secondary dominant

— as dasar in paṭet barang is the *dominant*.

GULU — as dasar in paṭet lima is the *dominant*

— as first gong tone in paṭet nem is the *tonic*

— as second gong tone in paṭet barang is used in cadential support of tonic and dominant.

BEM — as second gong tone in paṭet lima is the preferred final note and appears in support of tonic and dominant; in new-scale paṭet lima is melodically sensitive as an *exchangeable tone*

— in paṭet nem is melodically sensitive as an *exchangeable tone* and is used chiefly as a passing note

— in paṭet barang never occurs [1])

— in pélog paṭet manyura replaces the tone barang.

The principal particulars can also be arranged according to the characteristic function of the three gong tones:

In all paṭet the *first gong tone* functions as *tonic*.
" " " " *dasar* " " *dominant*.
" " " " *second gong tone* " in support of tonic and dominant; in *paṭet lima* and *paṭet nem* is the preferred *final note*.

And to add the principal exception:

In paṭet barang the *tone barang* is the preferred *final note*.

With the inclusion of the last particular we have accounted for the tonic, the dominant, and the preferred final note for each paṭet. The fact that tonic,

1) Examples of genḍing in pélog paṭet barang which use the tone bem are known outside the collection used for this study; such genḍing are not numerous nor is bem, in those instances, allowed more than a minor role. See further Chapter VIII, p. 148; and see J. S. Brandts Buys, *Djawa*, XVIII (1938), 185.

in this instance, does not coincide with the preferred final note [1]) demands a re-evaluation of our terms "tonic" and "dominant". As designations of the principal fifth-interval in each paṭet these terms were a convenience in the detailed analyses for indicating the two tones which form the melodic core or, better, the principal points of melodic tension throughout the genḍing. The addition of the second gong tone to the typical cadential formulas, however, complicates an interpretation of these two designations in relation to the question of *melodic resolution.*

A consideration of the typical cadential formulas will be necessary before the problem of resolution can be approached. The theoretical formulas, including the second gong tone (marked by +), is given below for each paṭet. The typical cadences are shown in the first two vertical columns.

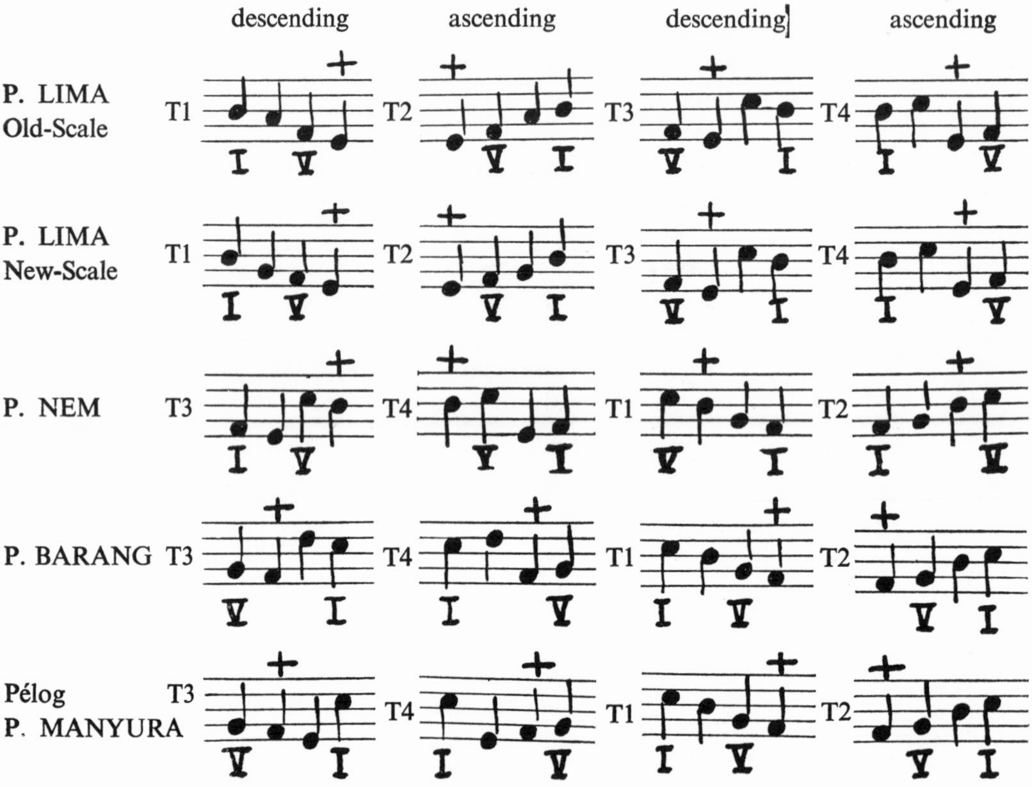

In any of the above formulas the appropriate exchange tones may be substituted for one of the tones of the principal scale [2]). A comparison of these examples reveals that the typical formulas in each paṭet avoid a confusion between "weak" and "strong" cadences [3]), *e.g.* T3—T4 of paṭet lima are avoided

1) Cf. pp. 115—21.

2) See Tables X and Y, p. 145 and p. 146.

3) Cf. pp. 123—4.

because they would be indistinguishable from the typical cadences of paṭet nem [1]). It should be noted that the preferred cadence (column one) is a *descending* scale passage between tonic and dominant [2]) which in paṭet lima and paṭet nem is extended to include the second gong tone.

To return to the discussion of tonic-dominant in relation to melodic resolution, a diagrammatic representation of the typical formulas will somewhat simplify the principal issues of the problem. In the diagrams given below, the principal fifth-interval is indicated by the upper brackets and the interval between the first and second gong tones by the lower brackets.

	PAṬET LIMA			PAṬET NEM			PAṬET BARANG		
PR. 5TH		V	I	I		V		V	I
	bem	gulu	lima	gulu	lima	nem	gulu	ḍaḍa	nem
T. CAD.	a 5th			a 4th			a 5th		

The tones indicated by the lower brackets form the interval of a fifth or a fourth. One might be tempted to speculate on the possibility of assigning *these* tones a tonic-dominant relationship. J. S. Brandts Buys contributes certain information which leads further in that direction, as we shall see in a moment.

The suitability of the terms "tonic" and "dominant" as applied to the sléndro paṭet were confirmed [3]), among other references, by a little publication written by Ki Hadjar Déwantara [4]). In the introduction to that booklet the author states that a similar study, this time devoted to the pélog paṭet, will be forthcoming. The second publication has never appeared. As the next best reference, however, we may consider the few pertinent details which were apparently communicated verbally by Déwantara to Brandts Buys. The references occur in two different places and unfortunately are somewhat contradictory, even though the later passage (by some four years) begins with a reference to the earlier one. With the aid of the diagrams given above we may be able to resolve the contradiction and at the same time make some progress in our consideration of melodic resolution.

The first reference appeared in 1934:

> „De bekende paedagoog speciaal ook op muziekgebied, de Heer Ki Hadjar Déwantara (R. M. Soewardi Soerjaningrat), beschouwt in pélog bem den toon lima als grond- of hoofdtoon, en nummert die dus in zijn cijferschrift

1) See pp. 194—6.

2) Cf. p. 124.

3) See pp. 115—22.

4) *Leidraad behoorende bij den Cursus over De Javaansche Muziek*, (Groningen: J. B. Wolters, 1930).

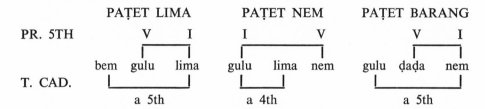

met een 1; maar in barang heeft de toon goeloe, (die een quint hooger, of een quart lager ligt), deze positie en dat nummer" [1]).

(The well-known educator, especially in the field of music, Mr. Ki Hadjar Déwantara (The Honorable Suwardi Surjaningrat), considers the tone lima as the tonic in pélog bem and accordingly numbers this as 1 in his cipher-script [solmization system]; but in [paṭet] barang the tone gulu, (which lies a fifth higher or a fourth lower), has this position and number.)

In a footnote he then arranges the two series according to their tone names and corresponding solmization numbers (N.B. within the one-octave range of the saron):

PÉLOG BEM					PAṬET BARANG				
bem	gulu	ḍaḍa	lima	nem	gulu	ḍaḍa	lima	nem	barang
3	4	5	1	2	1	2	3	4	5

The second reference appeared in 1938:

"... Ki Adjar Déwantara, die vroeger, (zie Dj. XIV, 152, waar we notities hebben verwerkt, gemaakt bij een onderhoud met den Hr. D.), in Pélog de paṭet Barang noteerde met den toon lima [sic] als uitgangstoon, als 1 van zijn cijfertoonschrift, maar voor de beide pélog-bem-paṭet's: Nem and Lima den toon bem [sic] als uitgangspunt had, heeft dit notatiesysteem niet gehandhaafd. In de paṭet Lima schrijft hij thans de reeks bem, goeloe, ḍaḍa,/lima, nem/ met de cijfers 1 tot 5. In paṭet Nem de reeks nem,/bem, goeloe, ḍaḍa,/lima. In paṭet Barang: lima, nem, barang,/goeloe, ḍaḍa/. Hoofdtonen steeds de 1 en de 4. Dus in Lima de quint bem-lima; in Nem de quint nem-ḍaḍa; in Barang de quint lima-gulu.

"Lima en Barang zouden dus gedomineerd worden door wat ons hun leittonenquint lijkt. Nem door de hóógste zijner beide àndere quinten. M.a.w., in het eene, en in het andere geval zijn de reeksen van 1 tot 5 volstrekt niet *functioneel* gelijkwaardig. (Men zie de plaats der groote intervallen, aangeduid door die schuine streepjes.) Een niet zeer gelukkige incongruentie!" [2])

(... Ki Adjar Déwantara has not continued with the system of notation in which he earlier (see Dj. XIV, 152, where we have presented particulars in this connection as a result of an interview with Mr. D.) designated the tone lima [sic] as the beginning tone — as 1 of his cipher-script — in pélog paṭet barang, and in which for the two pélog bem paṭet he designated the tone bem [sic] as a starting point. At present he writes for paṭet lima the series bem, gulu, ḍaḍa,/lima, nem/ with the numbers 1 to 5. In paṭet Nem

1) J. S. Brandts Buys, *Djawa*, XIV (1934), 152.
2) J. S. Brandts Buys, *Djawa*, XVIII (1938), 218.

the sequence nem,/bem, gulu, ḍaḍa,/lima. In paṭet Barang: lima, nem, barang,/gulu, ḍaḍa/. Principal tones are in each instance the 1 and the 4. Consequently in Lima the fifth, bem-lima; in Nem the fifth, nem-ḍaḍa; in Barang the fifth, lima-gulu.
Lima and Barang would therefore be dominated by, what seems to us, a leading-tone fifth. Nem by the highest of its two other fifths. In other words, in one case and in the other the two series from 1 to 5 are clearly not equivalent in a *functional* sense. (See the occurrence of the large intervals indicated by the diagonal bar.) Not a very fortunate incongruity!)

(That last remark might well apply to the whole presentation!) The highpoints of the two articles seem to be these:

In the first account the solmization "tonic" of pélog paṭet barang is given as *gulu*, and (according to the number 4) the dominant is *nem*. No differentiation is made between the two pélog paṭet bem, but the tonic is *lima* and the dominant *gulu*. Thus, the tonic-dominant intervals of the two paṭet divisions are: gulu-nem = pélog paṭet barang; lima-gulu = pélog paṭet bem.

In the second account he misquotes his earlier article by describing the tone *lima* (instead of gulu) as the tonic of pélog paṭet barang, and further, assigns to pélog paṭet bem (*i.e.* paṭet lima and/or paṭet nem) the tonic *bem* (instead of lima). He then brings the whole affair up to date by presenting the following tonic-dominant intervals with their corresponding paṭet: bem-lima = paṭet lima; nem-ḍaḍa = paṭet nem; lima-gulu = paṭet barang.

If the reader is still with me, it might be profitable to compare these sundries with the diagrams given above on p. 225.

From the first article: the tonic-dominant of paṭet barang, gulu-nem, corresponds to the fifth-interval indicated by the lower bracket in our diagram, the two tones delimiting the *non-typical cadential formula*. The tonic-dominant of the unspecified pélog paṭet bem corresponds to the lima-gulu (or, in the limits of one octave, gulu-lima) indicated by the lower bracket of paṭet nem, the two tones delineating the *typical cadential formula*.

From the second article: the tonic-dominant of paṭet lima, bem-lima, corresponds to the outer tones of the *typical cadential formula* of paṭet lima, indicated by the lower bracket. As for Mr. Brandts Buys' remark concerning the two "leading-tone" fifths (finally assigned to paṭet lima and paṭet barang) as compared with the tonic-dominant of paṭet nem — in the *functional* sense the incongruity is not merely unfortunate but quite improbable! In my opinion *it is exactly the FUNCTIONAL properties of the paṭet which are identical.*

It has not been my purpose in marshalling the foregoing references to "select" those items which fit neatly with the pairs of tones indicated by the lower brackets of the given diagrams — to the contrary!

The knotty little maze of contradictions establishes two general facts which are of value in the present discussion: 1) designations, by the Javanese, of tonic-dominant in the pélog paṭet indicate vascillation and uncertainty; 2) the fifth-intervals between the first and second gong tones of the pélog paṭet have been included among those eligible.

An evaluation of these two points leads back to the question of melodic resolution. Throughout the analyses and summaries (also in sléndro) I have used the term "final note" to indicate the last tone of the genḍing in order to avoid the larger connotation suggested by the phrase "tone of resolution". In sléndro the two possibilities generally coincide [1]). In pélog the preferred final note in both paṭet lima and paṭet nem is the *second gong tone*, not the first gong tone as in sléndro. In paṭet barang the preferred final note is not even one of the three principal gong tones but the "characterizing" [2]) tone barang. Although there is in each case a *preferred* final tone, it will be enlightening to compare the frequency of *all* final notes in the pélog paṭet. They are presented in the summary following.

PAṬET LIMA	PAṬET NEM	PAṬET BARANG
Final	Final	Final
bem in 8 genḍing	lima in 10 genḍing	barang in 4 genḍing
lima „ 4 „	nem „ 7 „	nem „ 2 „
gulu „ 3 „	gulu „ 3 „	ḍaḍa „ 2 „
nem „ 2 „	ḍaḍa „ 2 „	lima „ 2 „
		gulu „ 1 „

It may be remembered that in defining the "basis of the laras" (tonic) in the sléndro paṭet Déwantara describes it as the "tone with which a song ends" [3]). A glance at the above summary suggests a possible source of his difficulty in deciding which tone in each pélog paṭet must carry a similar designation. In paṭet nem, for instance, a greater number of examples might easily reverse the percentages of the two leading figures. It is also worthy of note that the two tones of the principal fifth-interval in each paṭet might lend certain complications in this endeavor. If there *should* be justification in referring to these two tones as tonic and dominant, then (as was shown in sléndro) either of them could be expected to appear as a final note. Considered together these respective pairs — lima-gulu in paṭet lima, gulu-nem in paṭet nem, nem-ḍaḍa in paṭet barang — represent a total percentage which is about the same as that of the preferred final note.

The second point which emerges from the contradictory references indicates speculation on the suitability of the first and second gong tones as tonic-dominant. In paṭet lima these are lima and bem; in paṭet nem, gulu and

1) See pp. 53, 84, 109.
2) The appropriateness of this word will be examined presently.
3) See p. 118.

lima; in paṭet barang, nem and gulu. This adds a third complication to the problem of melodic resolution.

There is evidence of some confusion, too, in relation to the function of the tone ḍaḍa in paṭet nem. In the second article referred to above, the fifth-interval nem-ḍaḍa was finally given as the tonic-dominant of paṭet nem. It was pointed out in a number of instances during the course of the detailed analyses that in paṭet nem the tone ḍaḍa had a rather clear relation to the tone nem as a *secondary* dominant. It was also seen, however, that the tone nem (the theoretical dominant) in turn resolves to gulu (the theoretical tonic). It was, in fact, only because of the consistent usage of ḍaḍa-to-nem-to-gulu (sometimes elaborated) that by analogy the term "secondary dominant" was introduced.

The principal issues in the problem of melodic resolution are given in summary: 1) the "preferred" final note represents a rather marginal percentage; 2) the two tones of the theoretical tonic-dominant (*i.e.*, in the analyses, the principal or important fifth-interval in relation to the melodic movement as a whole) together represent as final notes a percentage about equal to 1) above; 3) the extension of the typical cadence in paṭet lima and paṭet nem to include the second gong tone results in a fifth-interval which is suggestive of a tonic-dominant; 4) in at least one instance the function of the secondary dominant in relation to the dominant has not been seen in its larger context.

I believe these involved considerations can be reduced to one essential observation and consequent conclusion. The final note in each of the pélog paṭet is variable and therefore cannot be taken as an indication of "tonic".

The melodic importance of the theoretical tonic-dominant or principal fifth-interval has been established in the detailed analyses. These two tones are constantly the melodic core, the melodic referent of modulatory or neutral sections, the melodic goal of the entire genḍing. It has been shown that in paṭet lima and paṭet nem the second gong tone is usually added to the essential cadential formula. I repeat, *added* to the cadence. In paṭet lima, for example, there are a few instances in which this tone has *not* been added [1]; in paṭet nem there are still more cadences of this kind [2]. In paṭet barang the typical cadence *includes* the second gong tone *within* the T3 formula and ends on the (theoretical) tonic. But it was also shown that one of the hallmarks of paṭet barang is the *extension of the typical cadence to one or more other tones* [3].

It has been stated in numerous places that the second gong tone might be considered an essential part of the typical cadence, and in Chapter VII the typical formulas of the sléndro paṭet were seen to include this tone *within* the cadence [4]. It is significant that in pélog paṭet lima and paṭet nem the typical cadence is *extended to include the second gong tone*. Perhaps it is merely coincidence (but

---

1) See p. 165.
2) See p. 190.
3) See p. 215 and p. 217.
4) Chapter VII *passim*.

striking, nonetheless) that the typical cadence of paṭet barang is also extended to *some* tone — the second gong tone being already included *within* the cadence. Through coincidence or not (and I think not), the pélog paṭet characteristically extend the *essential cadence* (*i.e.* the scale passage between the theoretical tonic and dominant) to some other tone.

Finally, there remains one item of unfinished business in connection with the two references cited above. I refer to Mr. Brandts Buys' exclamation regarding the fact that Déwantara's last pairs of tonic-dominant were *functionally* non-equivalent. The three pairs are given below in ascending form from tonic (I) to dominant (V), and a diagonal bar (/) indicates the occurrence of the large interval.

DÉWANTARA'S TONIC-DOMINANT

Paṭet Lima	Paṭet Nem	Paṭet Barang
I V	I V	I V
bem-gulu-ḍaḍa/lima	nem/bem-gulu-ḍaḍa	lima-nem-barang/gulu

His description of paṭet lima and paṭet barang (in contrast to paṭet nem) as being dominated by "leading-tone" fifths neatly defines the incongruity.

I stated earlier, however, that in my opinion it is exactly the *functional* properties of the paṭet which are identical. The ascending form of the *theoretical* tonic-dominant (the principal fifth-interval) of each paṭet is given below.

THEORETICAL TONIC-DOMINANT

Paṭet Lima	Paṭet Nem	Paṭet Barang
I V	I V	I V
lima-nem/bem-gulu	gulu-ḍaḍa/lima-nem	nem-barang/gulu-ḍaḍa

I believe this graphic illustration of their functional equivalence needs no further elaboration.

If, after the foregoing exposition of melodic resolution in the pélog paṭet, the reader feels that a tonic-dominant designation will facilitate his orientation, then I recommend those pairs of tones given immediately above. For my part, the matter is concisely stated in the following conclusions: *melodic resolution* in pélog genḍing is achieved by a final confirmation of the principal fifth-interval. After this resolution a short extension to either of the two tones of that fifth-interval, to the second gong tone, or to *any of the five tones of the principal scale* is allowable. The modulation or exchange tones (i.e. auxiliary tones) never appear as final notes [1]).

Modulation Practice

The summary of the seven pélog tones given at the beginning of this chapter

[1]) Cf. the summary on p. 228.

indicates that five of them function as exchangeable or modulation tones in one scale or another. The two exceptions are nem and gulu. In theory nem might also be included with the other five [1]), but none of the genḍing in the two collections examined admits the possibility [2]). Perhaps it is the central position of gulu and nem, as the principal fifth-interval of paṭet nem — (the principal fifth of paṭet barang lies a pélog fifth higher; that of paṭet lima a pélog fifth lower) — which secures their permanence in all scales.

It has been shown that in each paṭet the substitution of one of the five tones for its respective exchange tone is fundamental to modulation or neutral passages. The characteristic manner in which the modulation tone (and subsequently the principal tone it has replaced) is introduced is slightly different for each paṭet. In paṭet lima an exchange tone is introduced abruptly; in paṭet nem by a step-wise motion; in paṭet barang by a prescribed scale passage. The extent to which these tones actually succeed in accomplishing modulation, *i.e.* by continuing in substitution for a principal tone long enough to establish an auxiliary scale, also varies in each paṭet. A summary of these details is presented below in the following way: the characteristic manner in which an exchange tone is introduced is designated by a key word, *e.g.* "abrupt"; the total number of genḍing is given; and the number of gending modulating to the low or the high auxiliary scale is indicated below the appropriate heading. The old- and new-scale genḍing of paṭet lima, of course, are shown separately.

P. LIMA				P. NEM		P. BARANG	
(old)		(new)					
abrupt		abrupt		stepwise		scale	
10 genḍing		7 genḍing		22 genḍing		11 genḍing	
Low	High	Low	High	Low	High	Low	High
0	9	1	4	1	8	0	2

In each paṭet a decided preference is shown for modulations to the high rather than the low auxiliary scale. The percentage of modulations are noticeably higher in paṭet lima than in the other two paṭet. The fact that nine of the ten old-scale paṭet lima genḍing contain modulations to the high auxiliary scale might be taken as an early indication of the Javanese feeling that the tone pélog is *miring* [3]). In modulations to the high scale these gending minimize the *miring* effect by replacing, for a short time, the tone pélog with ḍaḍa. The examples of genḍing using the new scale in paṭet lima are consistent in this respect in as much as only one of the seven utilizes the low auxiliary scale (*i.e.* in which

1) Cf. Tables X and Y, p. 145 and p. 146.
2) Cf. p. 148.
3) See p. 144.

pélog, in this instance, replaces *ḍaḍa*). The same characteristic is seen in the modulations of paṭet nem. Although there are a number of examples which contain neutral passages or the introduction of the exchange tone as a passing note, in only one genḍing is there an actual modulation to the low auxiliary scale [1]). Neutral passages also occur in paṭet barang, in this instance pélog being substituted for lima, and two genḍing contain modulations to the high auxiliary scale. The tone bem is never used, and consequently there are no examples of modulation to the low auxiliary scale. The one genḍing which uses the low auxiliary scale employs *only* this scale throughout [2]) and is probably an example of the rather rare *pélog paṭet manyura* [3]).

Pélog Paṭet Bem

The dual classification pélog paṭet bem and pélog paṭet barang was discussed in Chapter VIII [4]). It is possible at this time to reëxamine the appropriateness of the term *pélog paṭet bem.*

The detailed analyses and the statistical summaries of the *paṭet lima* genḍing found in the Solonese manuscript show that the old- and new-scale genḍing in that collection exhibit the same general characteristics [5]): a) the use of the T1 (or T2) typical cadence in the three critical sections and in the body of the piece; b) the use of the tone bem as a final note and its prominence throughout the genḍing; c) the abrupt introduction of the exchanges tones; d) the reiteration of the exchange tones to establish modulation; e) a minimal usage of the tone barang (new-scale genḍing, even in modulations to the high auxiliary scale, do not stress barang [6]); f) the complete avoidance of the principal-scale tone pélog (old scale) or ḍaḍa (new scale) as a final note.

Although there are other minor similarities [7]), these principal features may be compared, point for point, with the following constrasting practices in *paṭet nem* [8]): a) the use of the T3 (or T4) typical cadence; b) the complete avoidance of bem as a final note and its customary role being limited to that of a passing note; c) the stepwise introduction of the exchange tones; d) the establishment of modulation by the scalewise reappearance rather than an immediate reiteration of the sensitive tone; e) the prominence of the tone barang in melodic passages using the high auxiliary scale; f) the occasional employment of ḍaḍa as a final note.

---

1) The ladrang „Udan Mas" (pp. 185—7) does not modulate to the low auxiliary scale (which requires that pélog be substituted for ḍaḍa) but „modulates" abruptly to another paṭet, namely, the new-scale paṭet lima.

2) See pp. 219—21.

3) See p. 148 and Tables X and Y, p. 145 and p. 146.

4) See pp. 143—8.

5) See pp. 164—9.

6) Cf., *e.g.* nr 3 appendix p. 291.

7) See nr 3, p. 161.

8) Cf. Chapter IX, *passim.*

This comparison establishes a clear-cut distinction between paṭet lima and paṭet nem based on the analysis of two collections of genḍing. Are the three paṭet-lima examples from the Jogyanese manuscript [1]) sufficient evidence to suggest that this distinction may be disappearing? Does the term *pélog paṭet bem*, by its common acceptance [2]), substantially reinforce that evidence?

I think not. A much wider sampling of new-scale genḍing than is presently available must be compared before that question can be answered categorically. There are several indications, however, which permit considerable doubt that modern practice represents a merger of these two paṭet.

In the first place, there are indications that the old-scale genḍing of paṭet lima may still be in use to a larger extent than was heretofore suspected [3]).

It has been shown, too, that the new-scale genḍing of the Solonese collection maintain those principal compositional features which characterize the old-scale forms. Genḍing of this nature may be *typical* of modern practice, rather than the three examples from the Jogyanese manuscript. Although it is true that the old-scale majority of the Solonese manuscript establishes the age (of part) of the repertoire as being earlier than that of the Jogyanese collection, the fact remains that the manuscript *was written down ca. 1924—5*. It is therefore possible that the new-scale genḍing in this collection are actually more recent than those of the Jogyanese manuscript (dating from *ca.* 1895). It is also interesting that the Groneman Jogyanese collection contains new-scale genḍing in paṭet lima [4]) which exhibit the same general characteristics as those of the Solonese manuscript.

It may be significant, too, that the dual classification (pélog paṭet bem and pélog paṭet barang), although justified on its fundamental distinction between the paṭet using bem and the paṭet using barang as a principal tone, makes no allowance for those paṭet lima genḍing which are clearly distinguishable from those of paṭet nem. In this instance, the three parts of a trilogy are conveniently compared in terms of a duality. This larger division of the whole does not deny the existence of the trilogy, but it may tend to obscure the distinguishing qualities of the three parts solely through the process of common usage.

As another powerful force in preserving the distinction between paṭet lima and paṭet nem I might mention, in passing, the wayang repertoire with its three successive time periods, each characterized by a corresponding paṭet in the sequence: paṭet lima, paṭet nem, paṭet barang. Another example of continued endorsement (if not understanding) of that distinction is the popularity of the ladrang "Udan Mas" which was shown in the detailed analysis to be a sort of

---

1) See pp. 194—6.
2) See p. 147.
3) See p. 147.
4) *De Gamelan te Jogjakarta,* (Amsterdam: Johannes Müller, 1890), p. 83 ff., nr's 28, 29, 30, 31, 32; p. 99 ff., nr's 7, 8; but refer to the corrections of these transcriptions listed in the bibliography under the pertinent titles in *Djawa* by J. S. Brandts Buys.

"text-book case" in illustrating the fundamental difference between these two paṭet [1]).

The principal argument in favor of "merger" — namely, that the two paṭet use principal scales consisting of the same five notes and differ only in their three gong tones — is actually not so convincing. The three sléndro paṭet, by comparison, have managed to maintain themselves under similar conditions and with the additional limitation of not having available exchange tones and the distinguishing modulation practices which arise in connection with auxiliary scales.

Lastly, the fact that such a leading educator as Déwantara was searching for an adequate solmization system for *three* pélog paṭet as recently as 1938 not only suggests that the paṭet lima genḍing of the Jogyanese collection are *atypical* but also offers a recent confirmation that paṭet lima and paṭet nem have maintained their separate identities — recognized, at least, by the musically educated Javanese [2]).

The following conclusions can be formulated:

On the basis of available sources a clear distinction between pélog paṭet lima and pélog paṭet nem has been established. The common usage of the term pélog paṭet bem, although appropriate in contradistinction to pélog paṭet barang, has contributed to the occasional confusion of the two paṭet in practice and, to some extent, may have obscured a conscious knowledge of their essential differences. There being little evidence to the contrary, however, it is highly probable that the individual characteristics of these two paṭet are maintained in modern practice.

Pélog Paṭet Barang

The principal features of pélog paṭet barang readily distinguish it from the other two pélog paṭet. The use of the tone *barang* as a principal tone, in contrast to the principal note *bem* in the pélog paṭet bem, sets paṭet barang apart from the other two paṭet. This difference is further stressed by the appearance of barang as a preferred final note, while in the other two pélog paṭet it never appears in this capacity. Its prominence in paṭet barang is especially emphasized by its function as a tone of melodic variety; its role in the other two paṭet, on the other hand, is minimal by comparison. These factors taken together might furnish some justification in referring to barang as the "characterizing" tone of pélog paṭet barang. The term, however, is better avoided since it may falsely suggest a counterpart in each of the pélog paṭet bem.

In this connection a slight digression will, I believe, illustrate this point. We have the following remarks from Mr. Manfred Bukofzer: "The three tones [bem, pélog, and ḍaḍa] are not ... basic tones such as the tonic. Their function is

1) See p. 187.

2) According to a verbal communication from Jaap Kunst this distinction is recognized by most *niyaga* (thorough musicians) today; and see the quotation from *MJ* in Chapter III, p. 17.

not even that of a *finales* in the ecclesiastical modes. I should prefer to speak of 'characterizing' tones, because they do not have to occur very often, though they impart a peculiar character to the melodic design, which the native recognizes at once as typical of a particular *paṭet*. The European hearer cannot equal the native's speed in recognizing *paṭet* distinctions; he cannot determine the paṭet as readily as he can distinguish major from minor" [1]).

Mr. Bukofzer's remarks preceding this passage are not entirely clear, so that the reader is not quite sure which paṭet is meant to be correlated with each of the three tones; it is therefore difficult to make detailed comment. The meaning of the term *sorogan* seems to be the source of the difficulty [2]). If he means that the occasional appearance of bem as an exchange tone for barang will identify paṭet barang, then all eleven of our paṭet barang genḍing will go unidentified — because these examples establish another of the distinguishing features of paṭet barang: the omission of the tone bem [3]). If he means that the tone bem "characterizes" paṭet nem (which he incorrectly regards as being synonymous with "paṭet bem"), we should point out that this is rather more appropriate for paṭet lima — in which bem is a preferred final note; its behavior, as a matter of fact, is indeed similar to that "of a *finalis* in the ecclesiastical modes". If he means that pélog, as an exchange tone for ḍaḍa, indicates paṭet nem by its occasional usage, then he must also account for the appearance of the tone pélog in both paṭet lima and paṭet barang. Likewise, any combination or cross-relationship which can be established between the three tones indicated and the three pélog paṭet reveals the misapplication of the term "characterizing" and the imposibility of the claimed functions. His implied method of paṭet identification, I am afraid, would yield rather unpredictable results.

As for the implications in Mr. Bukofzer's last statement — to the best of my knowledge there has been only *one* European who could *usually* distinguish the various paṭet on hearing them: Walter Spies [4]).

To continue with the discussion of paṭet barang: in addition to the distinguishing position of barang and the omission of bem, it is only in paṭet barang that the tone *lima* may be exchanged for the tone pélog in modulations to the high auxiliary scale (not too frequent) or neutral passages. In both the pélog paṭet bem the melodic intervals lima-ḍaḍa and lima-pélog appear as indications of modulatory or neutral passages; it is only in paṭet barang that the intervals nem-pélog and ḍaḍa-pélog have this signification. Paṭet barang is further distinguishable by the prescribed manner in which the exchange tones are introduced [5]).

---

1) „The Evolution of Javanese Tone-Systems", *Papers* read at the International Congress of Musicology. (New York: 1944), p. 242.

2) See further Jaap Kunst, *Around von Hornbostel's Theory* . . ., (Amsterdam: Indisch Instituut, 1948), p. 31.

3) See p. 219.

4) J. S. Brandts Buys, *Djawa*, XVIII (1938), 207.

5) Cf. J. S. Brandts Buys, *Djawa*, XIV (1934), 154.

The function of the tone *ḍaḍa* as a theoretical dominant secures its position as one of the principal tones of paṭet barang. In the pélog paṭet bem, of course, ḍaḍa and pélog are exchangeable.

A general hallmark of paṭet barang is the variety of cadential extensions which appear at the termination of the three critical sections.

General Considerations

The general nature and function of the bubuka opaq-opaq and its singular importance are essentially the same in both pélog and sléndro genḍing. The reader is referred to the discussion in Chapter VII, pp. 129—32. The relationship of the three critical sections and its significance as established in Chapter VII also applies in substance to the pélog paṭet.

The structural forms of the genḍing and the patterns of kenongan repetition in the gongan need not be compared since those statistics were omitted from the paṭet lima summaries of Chapter VIII. The reader is referred to Chapters IX and X for a comparison of these details as found in paṭet nem and paṭet barang.

Summary of the main points:

1. The three gong tones have a primary importance in all paṭet.
2. First gong tone and dasar form the principal fifth-interval and function as the theoretical tonic and dominant, respectively.
3. The second gong tone is used in cadential support of the theoretical tonic and dominant.
4. Melodic resolution is achieved through a final confirmation of the principal fifth-interval in the form of the essential cadential formula which in turn may be extended by one or more notes.
5. The final note is variable.
6. The distinct practices of paṭet lima on the one hand and paṭet nem on the other suggest that the term *pélog paṭet bem* is appropriate only as a general designation in contradistinction to paṭet barang.
7. The dual classification, in some instances, may have contributed to a confusion of paṭet lima and paṭet nem in practice and recognition.
8. Paṭet barang is readily distinguishable from the pélog paṭet bem.
9. The three critical sections, individually and in relation to one another, have the same general importances and features as those previously established in connection with the sléndro paṭet.

XII.

SLÉNDRO AND PÉLOG COMPARED.

"A genuine definition of paṭet, *i.e.* one which would convey to us all essential characteristics of the conception, and thereby, indirectly, the differences existing between the different kinds of paṭets, has not yet, as far as I am aware, been formulated." [1]

WITH THE RESTATEMENT of this objective we have come full-circle. A comparison of the principal features of sléndro and pélog may permit the formulation of a definition which meets these requirements.

The Principal Fifth

The melodic foci of all paṭet are the two tones which form the principal fifth-interval, first gong tone and dasar. They occur in a typical cadential formula which not only closes the three critical sections (bubuka opaq-opaq, bubuka genḍing and final gongan) but also provides a melodic framework for the whole composition.

In the final cadence of a sléndro genḍing one of these two tones is usually the final note of the piece, and consequently the tones of the principal fifth-interval are recognized by the Javanese as a kind of tonic and dominant. In pélog, melodic resolution is achieved by a final confirmation of the *essential* cadence (a scale passage between first gong tone and dasar) which may be followed by a short extension to any tone of the principal scale, except, of course, the tone pélog in the old-scale paṭet lima. The final note, therefore, is variable. The tones of the principal fifth-interval in pélog might be termed a "theoretical" tonic and dominant.

In our effort to discover the essential characteristics of this aspect of the paṭet concept I suggest that we eliminate the terms "recognized tonic-dominant" and "theoretical tonic-dominant". In the final analysis, it would seem, I must agree with the critics of "Western-influenced thinking" and suggest that the term "tonic-dominant" *per se*, while it has been a convenience in presenting this

[1] *MJ*, I, 72.

study, is not *essential* to a consideration of melodic resolution in the Javanese paṭet. The appropriateness of such an approach in regard to the pélog paṭet has been established in Chapter XI and briefly mentioned directly above. Sléndro, actually, is no different in principal.

It was pointed out in the summaries of sléndro paṭet nem [1]), paṭet sanga [2]), and paṭet manyura [3]) and again in Chapter VII [4]) that if some tone other than those of the principal fifth-interval occurs as the final note, it is *always* preceded by the typical cadential formula. In the sléndro paṭet the *typical* cadence and the *essential* cadence (*i.e.* a scale passage between the two tones of the principal fifth) are the same. In practice, therefore, melodic resolution in both sléndro and pélog is achieved by a final confirmation of the principal fifth-interval.

Second Gong Tone

The tone lying a fifth below the principal fifth-interval, second gong tone, is used in both sléndro and pélog in cadential support of the important fifth and is an essential part of the typical cadence. In sléndro the second gong tone occurs *within* the typical cadence; in pélog it occurs *within* the cadence (paṭet barang) or as an *extension* of the cadence (paṭet lima and paṭet nem).

The Typical Cadence

In each of the six paṭet the principal fifth appears at cadential points and elsewhere in the genḍing in a typical formula. The three time periods of the wayang night correlate the sléndro and the pélog paṭet in the following parallel pairs:

WAYANG NIGHT

	1st period	2nd period	3rd period
SLÉNDRO	Paṭet Nem	Paṭet Sanga	Paṭet Manyura
PÉLOG	Paṭet Lima	Paṭet Nem	Paṭet Barang

In Chapter VII it was shown that this arrangement is consistent with the corresponding "shapes" of the typical cadential formulas of the first two pairs of paṭet as they occur within the one-octave limits of the balungan instruments [5]). The typical cadences of the six paṭet are given below [6]).

---

1) See p. 53—4.
2) See p. 85.
3) See p. 108 and p. 124.
4) See p. 124.
5) See p. 128.
6) For an explanation of the Javanese tones represented by the transcriptions see (sléndro) p. 20 and (pélog) p. 148.

WAYANG NIGHT

1st period	2nd period	3rd period
SLÉNDRO P. Nem	SLÉNDRO P. Sanga	SLÉNDRO P. Manyura

PÉLOG P. Lima (old) (new) PÉLOG P. Nem PÉLOG P. Barang PÉLOG P. Manyura

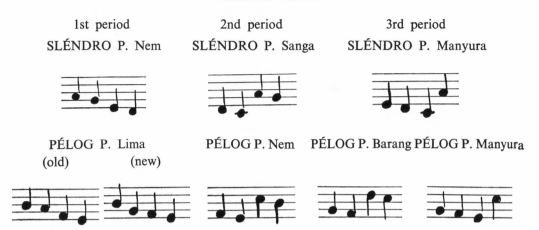

At first glance, sléndro paṭet manyura and pélog paṭet barang seem not to sustain the correlation too perfectly. The pattern of the former is three descending tones followed by a wide leap up to nem, and the pattern of the latter is two descending tones and a leap up to two more descending tones. In other ways, however, they are related as a parallel pair distinct from the other paṭet. It has been shown in the individual summaries of these two paṭet that they are both characterized by the great variety of extensions which follow the typical cadence [1]) (in contradistinction to the other four paṭet). It should also be noted that these paṭet share, in name only, the same principal fifth-interval, *viz.* nem-ḍaḍa, so that perhaps the third pair of paṭet are related on this basis. But there is still something to be said regarding a correlation of typical "shapes".

Pélog paṭet barang cannot achieve a pattern of three-down-and-one-up because the lower tone barang geḍé is not available on the balungan instruments. In the low auxiliary scale, however, barang is replaced by bem; and in our one example of the rare *pélog paṭet manyura* (equivalent to the low auxiliary scale) the typical cadence *does* correspond to that of *sléndro paṭet manyura* (cf. the examples given above). A pertinent question arises in this connection. Why is this fourth pélog paṭet called *manyura*? Since the *names* of the tones of the principal fifth-intervals as well as the other two notes of the typical cadence are identical in sléndro paṭet *manyura* and pélog paṭet *barang*, why is the latter not called pélog paṭet *manyura* and the fourth pélog paṭet (in which *bem* replaces the *tone barang*) by some other name? I can think of one principal reason: the *shape* of the cadential formula of sléndro paṭet manyura and (the fourth) pélog paṭet manyura is the same. Are the Javanese really so conscious of melodic *shape*? There is considerable evidence to support an affirmative answer.

It may seem strange to the Westerner that melodic pattern can assume such

1) See pp. 106—7 and p. 218.

importance. In connection with the music of India Curt Sachs offers the following general analogy:

> "The easiest way to make Westerners understand what melodic patterns are is to compare them with the architectural orders of the Greeks. Hellenic architects obeyed the rules of the Doric, or the Ionic, or the Corinthian style. Each implied certain proportions of the columns, the ground motives of the capitals, the equilibrium of cornices, friezes, gables, and numberless other qualities. The artist's latitude was small and his inventiveness restricted to detail work and general harmony.
>
> "Oriental music has been ruled by the same idea of submitting individual creative power to the binding force of ready-made patterns" [1]).

In addition to the particular arguments advanced in Chapter VII [2]), I call attention to the *preferred* usage of the *one-octave* balungan instruments as strong evidence that the Javanese are conscious of melodic pattern.

One might logically wonder why the Javanese had not extended the range of the saron group to include two octaves or more. There is, in fact, an instrument with fourteen or fifteen metal keys, the *gambang gangsa,* [3]) which would seem to represent approximately a two-octave saron. The gambang gangsa, rarely seen in Java today, appears to be a remnant of early times and recently has been played (at least in the Solonese Kraton) only in the genḍing *Hundur-hundur kajongan* "when the Susuhunan rises himself from his seat to retire to his apartments, or after a dinner, when His Princely Highness gets up to repair to another hall, and, finally, outside the kraton, when he rises to depart" [4]).

Before we too hastily conclude that the multi-octave gambang gangsa is the instrumental forerunner of the saron family and that the three modern versions of this group are a gambang gangsa "fallen apart" [5]), we should know that the earliest representation of the one-octave saron is depicted on one of the reliefs of the great Borobuḍur, dating from the beginning of the 9th century [6]). The co-existence of both forms during very early times is vouched for by the following passage: "Saron-key-ranges have also been recovered from the Hindu-Javanese period, partly completely identical with the existing single-octave forms, and partly of multi-octave range, with keys of the demung-format" [7]). According to the most recent information the age of the keys recovered in these excavations may date from any time between the Middle Hindu-Javanese period (8th—10th century) and the rise of Islam in the 16th century.

These sources indicate that either: 1) the saron and the gambang gangsa

---

1) *The Rise of Music ...*, (New York: W.W. Norton, 1943), pp. 172—3.

2) See pp. 124—9.

3) See illus. p. 317.

4) *MJ*, I, 171—2.

5) Cf. *ibid.*, 171.

6) See further Jaap Kunst, *Hindoe-Javaansche Muziek-Instrumenten* (Weltevreden: Koninklijk Bataviaasch Genootschap, 1927), pp. 94—8.

7) *MJ*, I, 172.

were co-existent in the 9th century; or 2) the saron dates from the 9th century, and the first record of the gambang gangsa appears some time later. We can conclude, then, that the known age of the saron is the same as that of the gambang gangsa or earlier.

By inference it is also possible to tell something of the function of these two instruments through time. The earliest descriptive account of the musical instruments of Java was published in 1817 [1]). Raffles mentions the *gambang kayu* [2]) and the gambang gangsa in a single sentence: "The gámbang káyu has wooden plates, sixteen or seventeen in number; the gámbang gángsa, of which there are several in each band [gamelan], has metal plates" [3]). The saron is included with other instruments in a separate entry [4]). From this brief description it is worthy of note that there is an evident association between the *gambang* kayu and the *gambang* gangsa; and as we know, the gambang kayu plays melodic elaborations of the nuclear theme [5]).

In 1890 Groneman also discusses the two gambang in one entry [6]) and the saron family in another [7]). In the first instance he says, "Elke *gamelan* heeft voorts twee *gambang's*, een houten (g. kajoe) en een metalen (g. gangsa)." (Each gamelan has, besides, two gambang, a wooden one (g. kayu) and a metal one (g. gangsa)). We are also fortunate in „Bijlage C" of the same publication to find a rather complete score with the following note from Land (who transcribed the music examples): „Nadat ik op pag. 13 en 17 slechts de partituur der melodische slaginstrumenten had kunnen beloven, zijn mij nog ter elfder ure de partijen van den *rebab*, den *demoeng*, den *tjelempoeng* en den *kenḍang* toegezonden, met de opmerking, dat de gambang gangsa dezelfde octavo speelt als de houten gambang, doch met dit onderscheid, dat de hoogere noot eerst na de lagere wordt aangeslagen" [8]). (After I had been able to promise, on page 13 and 17, the score of only the melodic instruments, at the eleventh hour the parts for the rebab, the demung, the chelempung and the kenḍang were sent to me — with the notice that the gambang gangsa plays the same octaves as the wooden gambang, but with this difference: the higher note [of the octave] is struck after the lower note [rather than simultaneously]). The two gambang, in other words, are playing almost identical parts, and the score reveals the contrast between the gambang line and that of the saron group [9]). In the score

---

1) Thomas Stamford Raffles, *The History of Java* (London: Black, Parbury, and Allen, 1817), I, 469—72.

2) See p. 12.

3) Raffles, *op. cit.*, I, 469.

4) See *ibid.*, 470.

5) See further pp. 11—12.

6) *De Gamelan te Jogjakarta* (Amsterdam: Johannes Müller, 1890), pp. 36—8.

7) *Ibid.*, pp. 35—6.

8) *Ibid.*, p. 105.

9) *Ibid.*, pp. 106—17.

of „Bijlage D", although the two gambang play different parts, they show the same character in contrast to the balungan melody [1]).

In a more recent reference Brandts Buys states that on rare occasion he has seen the gambang gangsa played, but then only *half* the instrument, either the higher or lower octave, was used to sound the *melody of the nuclear theme.* In short, the multi-octave gambang gangsa was played as a *one-octave* saron and served only to reinforce the sound of the saron group [2]).

In summary the principal points are: 1) the saron is as old or older than the multi-octave gambang gangsa; 2) the traditional function of the latter, in contradistinction to the former, has been to play an *elaboration* of the nuclear theme; 3) the gambang gangsa has fallen into disuse, probably because the softer, wooden gambang was more suited for the role of melodic elaboration; 4) for many centuries, at least, a *multi-octave* instrument of the saron type has been available.

From these facts we can safely conclude that *choice* has restricted the playing of the nuclear theme to the *one-octave* saron. Having established the preferred usuage of the one-octave saron we might ask why it is preferred. It might be suggested that the one-octave instrument is easier to play. In view of the fact that together the principal scales of the three paṭet, in both sléndro and pélog, cover a range of about two and a half octaves (the distance of three conjunct fifths, actually), I am not sure that a one-octave limitation necessarily simplifies the playing of a melody. But on the assumption that it might, *simplicity*, on these grounds, certainly does not extend to the panerusan instruments. The two gambang, the bonang family and the gendèr group (to mention only the idiophones) are far from simple instruments to play. But in spite of their multi-octave ranges they *are* played and *have been* played for many centuries [3]). Simplicity is hardly an explanation of the preference shown for a one-octave saron, especially since the notes of the nuclear theme have comparatively long time values and require, therefore, a minimum of technical facility in execution.

I believe the preference for a one-octave saron as the instrument to be entrusted with the nuclear theme is directly attributable to a desire, conscious or otherwise, to preserve the melodic contour or *shape*, if you will, of the principal melody — the melodic *shape*, I repeat, of the all-important cadential formula which closes the three critical sections, which serves as the framework of the whole genḍing, which, in short, is one of the strongest features in the identification and, consequently, the very preservation of the paṭet concept itself.

Paṭet Transposition

The table on pp. 259—61 indicates that transposition from one paṭet to another

1) *Ibid.*, pp. 118—23.

2) *Djawa*, XVIII (1938), 220.

3) Many ancient bonang kettles which predate the spread of Islam (16th century) have been excavated; see Jaap Kunst, *Hindoe-Javaansche Muziek-Instrumenten*, p. 77; for *gendèr* of 1157 see *ibid.*, pp. 90—4.

occurs much more frequently in sléndro than in pélog. The table also gives some indication that a genḍing is more likely to be transposed from sléndro to pélog than the reverse practice (assuming, for the sake of this comparison, that the larger number appearing in the vertical columns may be taken as indicative of the original tuning system, *e.g.* sléndro). This general practice is confirmed by the following statement from Djajengoetara:

> "Almost all genḍing sléndro are more enjoyable in the pélog system. On the contrary, a pélog piece often should not be played in the sléndro system. Especially not when many wilet show a pélog character. Then it is completely impossible to play it in the sléndro system. The genḍing, therefore, is especially recognized by its wilet. If many wilet are found in a genḍing, then it is certainly pélog. If this is not the case, then it can be loaned to sléndro" [1]).

Wilet in a general sense means "melodic section"; in this instance it probably extends to include "a melodic section having a modulatory (or neutral) character".

Transposition practice from one system to another, *e.g.* from pélog to sléndro, usually follows the general rule which corresponds to the parallel paṭet as they appear in the sequence of the wayang night (see above) [2]). The transposition table in the appendix, for the most part, bears out this correlation. This practice and the principal exception can best be illustrated by using an abbreviated representation of the ladrang "Udan Mas" for comparison.

"Udan Mas", it should be remembered, is in pélog paṭet nem and is constructed of pairs of gongan alternating between pélog paṭet nem and pélog paṭet lima [3]). In the following comparison the time value of each note will be reduced by one quarter, so that the sixteen measure of a gongan will be represented by four measures. The example is further abbreviated by presenting only one of the repeated gongan of the *A* section and one gongan of the *B* section [4]). Thus, the first example is a miniature of the original genḍing. The second example illustrates the transposition of this genḍing from pélog paṭet nem to sléndro paṭet sanga, in accordance with the parallel paṭet of the wayang sequence. The third example (corresponding rhythmically to the faster section, *i.e.* GN V—VIII of the transcription on p. 299 of the appendix) is a transposition from memory: as a beginner on the saron, the first piece I learned to play was "Udan Mas" in sléndro paṭet nem [5]). The fourth example, for the moment, we shall call a "robot transposition" from sléndro paṭet nem (Ex. 3) back to the pélog system (Ex. 4). The Javanese names of the two notes of the

---

1) From a manuscript submitted in competition in 1924: see further J. S. Brandts Buys, *Djawa*, IV (1924), 1—17.

2) See further pp. 126—8.

3) For the complete transcription see pp. 298—9.

4) For the detailed analysis see pp. 185—7.

5) Mr. IJzerdraat, who taught me the basic techniques of the gamelan instruments, never allows his students to *read* music but favors the Javanese method of teaching by immitation or rote.

principal fifth-interval are placed on the corresponding line or space of the transcription; for the key to the sléndro transcriptions see p. 20 and for pélog see p. 148.

"UDAN MAS"

Ex. 1 PÉLOG P. NEM

A section (P. p. nem) *B* section (P. p. lima)

Ex. 2 SLÉNDRO P. SANGA

A section (S. p. sanga) *B* section (S. p. nem)

Ex. 3 SLÉNDRO P. NEM

A section (S. p. nem) *B* section (S. p. sanga)

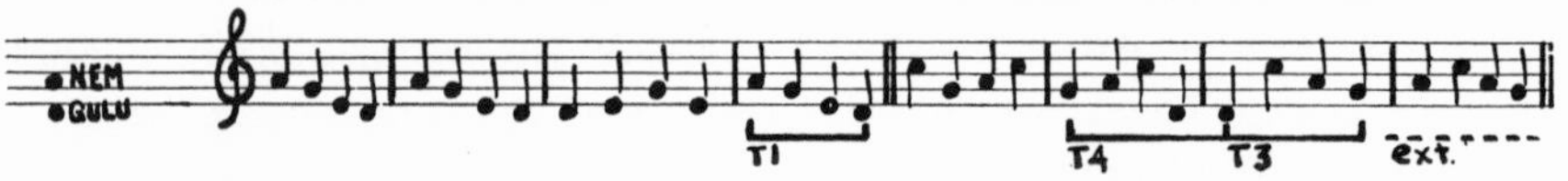

Ex. 4 PÉLOG P. ?

A section (P. p. nem?) *B* section (P. p. ?)

The first two examples present a clear illustration of the correlation between the parallel paṭet of the wayang sequence, *i.e.* the corresponding shapes of the typical cadences between pélog paṭet nem and sléndro paṭet sanga and between pélog paṭet lima and sléndro paṭet nem.

A comparison of examples 1 and 3 reveals that the shapes of the cadential formulas do not correspond; but in the sléndro transcription the cadences are *typical* of their respective paṭet, *e.g.* the T1 formula of sléndro paṭet nem (*A* section). In this less-preferred transposition practice the pélog and sléndro paṭet *do* show a correlation on the basis of their *principal fifth-intervals*, *e.g.* gulu-nem of pélog paṭet nem and gulu-nem of sléndro paṭet nem.

Example 4 is what I have termed a "robot transposition" from sléndro paṭet nem (Ex. 3) to the pélog *system*. This is merely a mechanical transfer on the basis of the tone *names* from sléndro to pélog. Actually, we cannot speak of a "transposition" from a sléndro *paṭet* to a pélog *paṭet* in this example because: 1) the *A* section contains only the non-typical cadences of pélog paṭet nem, and therefore *paṭet nem* is not established; 2) the *B* section resembles no paṭet in the pélog system (the complete absence of ḍaḍa eliminates paṭet barang, for instance). If in the *B* section the mechanical transfer were slightly altered, so that the tone bem is used instead of barang, the "T?'s" of the lower brackets could be labeled T3 in pélog paṭet nem. Even then, however, the character of the piece — which depends on the alternation of *two* paṭet — would be entirely lost since the *A* section (if it can be called anything) is *also* paṭet nem. Example 4, in other words, represents a purely mechanical transfer which has no basis in the paṭet concept. I should point out that I have never heard of this method of transposition being used by the Javanese themselves; it is only presented as an example of *incorrect* transposition.

In summary: the preferred transposition practice from one tonal system to the other follows the parallel paṭet of the wayang sequence, based on the corresponding shapes of the typical cadences. The lesser transposition practice is based on a correlation of corresponding fifth-intervals. In both instances sléndro paṭet manyura and pélog paṭet barang have a correlation based on their principal fifth-intervals and, to a lesser extent, on the shape of their typical cadences.

"*The Enemy Tone*"

In Chapter VII it was pointed out that in each of the sléndro paṭet one tone is generally avoided [1]): in paṭet nem the tone barang, in paṭet sanga the tone ḍaḍa, in paṭet manyura the tones lima and barang. This actually needs some qualification. These tones in their respective paṭet are usually used as passing notes *or*, by contrast, are occasionally "featured". The tone barang is sometimes used for melodic variety in paṭet nem [2]). In paṭet sanga the tone ḍaḍa is normally a passing tone, but in nr 23 it attains a minor prominence [3]). In paṭet manyura the tone barang is frequently a tone of melodic variety but sometimes appears only as a passing note; in this same paṭet the tone lima, as a transition tone, is rarely conspicuous, but in nr 47—48 it is used as a final note and in nr 56 as a tone of melodic variety; in nr 45 both barang and lima appear as tones of melodic variety [4]).

In pélog paṭet lima (old- and new-scale) the tone barang is neglected; in pélog paṭet nem the tone pélog is either avoided or, as a substitute for ḍaḍa, is treated with special care; in pélog paṭet barang the tone bem is avoided (and see p. 223 footnote 1) and pélog, as a substitute for lima, is introduced in a prescribed manner. (The tone pélog in the new-scale paṭet lima receives no special consideration in the abrupt manner in which it is introduced and reiterated.)

The occurrence of these "enemy tones" is consistent with the parallel pairs of paṭet corresponding to the wayang sequence:

---

1) Cf. J. S. Brandts Buys, *Djawa*, XIV (1934), 149; *Djawa*, XVI (1936), 234—5; *Djawa*, XVIII (1938), 208.

2) See p. 56.

3) See p. 66.

4) See nr 47—48, p. 98; nr 56, p. 109; nr 45, p. 101.

WAYANG SEQUENCE

	1st per.	2nd per.	3rd per.
SLÉNDRO	P. Nem barang	P. Sanga ḍaḍa	P. Manyura lima-barang
PÉLOG	P. Lima barang	P. Nem pélog | subs. ↓ ḍaḍa	P. Barang pélog-bem | subs. ↓ lima

The equivalence of the first parallel pair of paṭet is easily seen. The second pair shows a correspondence between ḍaḍa, on the one hand, and pélog as the substitute for ḍaḍa, on the other. The third pair has a correlation between the tone lima and pélog as its substitute in pélog paṭet barang. In this last pair of paṭet the tones barang and bem show an indirect correlation: In sléndro paṭet manyura the tone barang, much of the time, is featured melodically. In pélog paṭet barang the tone barang is also very prominent, but the tone *bem* never appears (see footnote 1 p. 223). In sléndro paṭet manyura the tone *barang*, the nearest equivalent to *bem*, is sometimes inconspicuous as a passing tone.

The Bubuka Opaq-opaq

It has been shown that in all paṭet the three critical sections of a genḍing are related cadentially and melodically. The singular importance of the bubuka opaq-opaq was established in Chapter VII [1]).

Although this short introductory section can be characterized as a source of endless variety, certain general features common to all bubuka opaq-opaq can be shown. If we imagine six prototypes (one for each of the six paṭet), distinguished from one another only by the appropriate scale and cadential formulas, it is possible to describe the collective characteristics and function of this principal element of the Javanese genḍing — the bubuka opaq-opaq.

> Although one of its functions has been loosely compared to the establishment of "mode", it represents something *more* than mode. On the other hand, it is something *less* than a fixed melody (the prototype) but is rather a particular combination of tones or melodic patterns (cadential formulas). One tone, which we may call the *ruling* note or *king* note (first gong tone), functions as a melodic stabilizer, so that although the melody may go anywhere, it is always drawn back again to that tone. This king tone has its *allies* and *followers*, usually the fifth (dasar) and the (too-large) third (or too-small fourth, the second gong tone). There are also *enemy* tones (one,

1) See pp. 129—32.

at least) which are either generally avoided or are "captured" in a particular way, so that their movements are closely controlled. The combination of these tones appears in melodic patterns which have both descending and ascending forms in relation to the stabilizing tonal line maintained by the ruling note. The complex of these several elements establishes a compact structure (the bubuka opaq-opaq) which provides a basis for melodic development or "variations" (if we think of one prototype for sléndro paṭet nem, for example, then in the general sense all the paṭet nem genḍing would be "variations" on this prototype). This basic structure (because it establishes a given paṭet) is associated with certain hours of the day or night.

This description, except for the parenthetical comments, has been freely paraphrased from a lecture given by Prof. D. P. Mukerji of Lucknow, India, during which the above remarks, in substance, were offered as part of a GENERAL DEFINITION OF THE INDIAN RAGA [1]).

I think the reader will agree that the aptness of this figurative definition as applied to the bubuka opaq-opaq or, actually, to *paṭet* is striking. I am not suggesting that the music of India has a *practical* similarity to that of Java. Certainly the division of the octave into twenty-two sruti has no apparent correlation to the five-tone or seven-tone fundamental scales of Java [2]). On the other hand, to the best of my knowledge, there has been no comparative study of the two musics with the interesting objective of determining the relationship which might exist between the raga *concept* and the paṭet *concept*. It is not impossible that the two concepts have much in common, granted that they are *applied* to two different musical expressions. The general definition given above strongly suggests such a possibility.

If future investigation should show that the two cultures are in this way musically related, it would not be surprising. There are countless studies which have established the marked influence of the Hindu culture on Javanese and Balinese art, sculpture, literature, theatre, etc. The Borobuḍur has been one rich source of information and the Hindu epics another. How many stories with a musical theme were included when the Rāmāyaṇa and the Mahābhārata of India became part of the Javanese literature? There are two outstanding publications devoted to a study of the musical instruments of these cultures [3]).

---

1) On September 28, 1953, at the Institute for Social Studies in The Hague.

2) Deviation from these fixed pitches (which is possible on the rebab, suling, chelempung, and the human voice) bring the two practices closer together; see further *MJ*, I, 52—5, 62, 66 ff., 94, 96, 102—3, 354, 388. As many as 17 vocal tones in the sléndro octave have been described by the Sundanese musicologist and teacher R. Machjar Angga Kusumadinata: see *Ringkĕsan Pangawikan Rinĕnggaswara* (Djakarta: Noordhoff-Kolff, (*ca.* 1950), p. 17.

3) Jaap Kunst, *Hindoe-Javaansche Muziek-Instrumenten*; and Claudie Marcel-Dubois, *Les Instruments de musique de l'Indie ancienne* (Paris: Presses Universitaires de France, 1941); in connection with the latter also see Jaap Kunst, „Boekbespreking", *Cultureel Indie*, IV (1942), 226—36.

The Javanese paṭet and the Indian raga as musical concepts might take their place in this chain of cultural ties.

A summary of this chapter and therefore the essence of the entire study will be presented in the form of a definition of Javanese paṭet.

The Paṭet Concept Defined

Javanese *paṭet* is a concept of tonality applied to two non-equidistant and distinct scale systems, the five-tone *sléndro* and the seven-tone *pélog*. In each of these systems the concept distinguishes three principal divisions, the sléndro paṭet: *nem*, *sanga*, *manyura*; the pélog paṭet: *lima*, *nem*, *barang*. These six paṭet are differentiated in the two-part division by their basic scale systems and in the three-part division by the following fundamental structures and practices: their principal scales differ in pitch by the distance of three conjunct fifth-intervals (approximate fifths) which in turn form the core of melodic movement; these fifth-intervals are further identified by the distinctive melodic patterns created through the scale movement of the typical cadences restricted to the one-octave range of the *balungan* instruments (the predominant volume of sound in the gamelan issues from these idiophones which play the nuclear theme or principal melody); the tone lying a fifth below this principal interval supports the cadential points and is characteristically included within a primary cadence or as an extension of such a cadence; melodic resolution is achieved through a final confirmation of the principal fifth-interval sometimes followed by a short extension; the particular function of tones other than those included above, modulation practice and other compositional techniques further distinguish the six paṭet.

The preservation of these principal features is aided by a standard compositional practice: the melodic development of a *genḍing* (orchestral composition) is based on a short introductory theme, the *bubuka opaq-opaq* (*bubuka* or *buka*), uniquely constructed in accordance with the essential paṭet requirements.

Each of the three paṭet of both scale systems is associated with one of the three time periods of *wayang* (theatre) and with certain hours of the day or night in the following parallel pairs: sléndro p. nem — pélog p. lima; sléndro p. sanga — pélog p. nem; sléndro p. manyura — pélog p. barang. The essential relationship of these parallel paṭet is not their principal fifth-intervals but the corresponding "shapes" of their typical cadences as sounded on the balungan instruments. This parallelism is generally, but not always, observed in transpositions from one system to the other. The lesser transposition practice follows an arrangement of the paṭet based on a similarity of the principal fifth-intervals. Transpositions from one paṭet to another occur in sléndro more often than in pélog. Transposition from the five-tone sléndro to the seven-tone pélog are frequent, but the converse practice is limited probably because the modulatory character of pélog cannot be realized in sléndro.

BIBLIOGRAPHY.

Alkema, A. W. and T. J. Bezemer. *Beknopt Handboek der Volkenkunde van Nederlandsch-Indië.* Haarlem: H. D. Tjeenk Willink en Zoon, 1927. 583 pp. 131 illus.

Apel, Willi. *Harvard Dictionary of Music.* Cambridge, Mass.: Harvard Univ. Press, 1950, 833 pp.

Baker, Theodore. *Baker's Biographical Dictionary of Musicians.* 4th ed., rev. and enl. New York: G. Schirmer, 1940. 1240 pp.

Balfoort, Dirk J. "De Indonesische Instrumenten in het Muziekhistorisch Museum Scheurleer te 's-Gravenhage," *Nederlandsch-Indië Oud & Nieuw,* XV (1930—1), 33—43, 153—159, 244—247, 307—319.

"Baliër over Amerikaansche Muziek, Een," *Djawa,* XIX (1939), 185—6.

Belo, Jane. "Balinese Children's Drawing," *Djawa,* XVII (1937) 248—60.

Bernet Kempers, K. Ph. "Het Ontstaan van Toonsystemen," *De Muziek,* VII (1933), 258 ff.

Brandes, J. L. A. "Mededeeling over eenige bijzonderheden der Metriek, het Notenschrift der Javanen," *Notulen* d. Vergaderingen v. het Bataviaasch Genootschap. XXXVII, Vol. II (1899), pp. XLII—LVI.

Brandts Buys, J. S. "Aanteekeningen betreffende enkele Indonesische Muziekinstrumenten," *Djawa,* II (1922), 34—48.

— "Het Gewone Javaansche Toonciferschrift (Het Sålåsche-Kepatihan-Schrift)," *Djawa,* XX (1940), 87—106.

— "Muziek en Dans bij de Huwelijksfeesten," *De Taak,* IV (1920—1), 125—6, 139—40.

— "Over de Ontwikkelingsmogelijkheden van de Muziek op Java," *Djawa,* Prae-adviezen II, Vol. I (1921), 1—90.

— "Over het Onderzoek der Javaansche en daarmee Verwante Muziek," *Koloniale Studiën,* IV (June, 1920), 455—81.

— "Pogingen tot Hervorming van de Gamelan," *De Taak,* IV (1920—1), 6—7.

— "Uitslag van de Prijsvraag Inzake een Javaansche Muziekschrift," *Djawa,* IV (1924), 1—17.

— and A. Brandts Buys-van Zijp. "Een en Ander over Javaansche Muziek," *Programma van het Congres,* gehouden van 27 tot en met 29 December 1929 in de Kapatihan Mangkoenagaran te Soerakarta, ter gelegenheid van het Tienjarig bestaan van het Java Instituut, 1919—29. pp. 39—63.

— and — "Javaansche Genḍing's bij Land en bij Seelig," *Djawa,* XVI (1936), 230—42; XVIII (1938), 182—225.

— and — "Land's Transscripties van Genḍing's," *Djawa,* XV (1935), 174—85.

— and — "Omtrent Notaties en Transscripties en over de Constructie van Gamelanstukken," *Djawa,* XIV (1934), 127—65.

— and — "Over Fluiten," *Nederlandsch-Indië Oud & Nieuw,* XI (1926—7), 57—62, 115—21.

Bukofzer, Manfred F. "The Evolution of Javanese Tone-Systems," *Papers* read at the International Congress of Musicology, held at New York Sept. 11 to 16, 1939 (New York: 1944), pp. 241—50.

— "Kann die 'Blasquintentheorie' zur Erklärung exotischer Tonsysteme beitragen?" *Anthropos,* XXXII (1937), 402—18.

— "Präzisionmessungen an primitiven Musikinstrumenten," *Zeitschrift für Physik,* 99 (1936), 643—65.

Coomaraswamy, Ananda K. *History of Indian and Indonesian Art.* New York: E. Weyhe, 1927. 295 pp. CXXVIII pls.

Covarrubias, Miguel. *Island of Bali.* With an album of photographs by Rose Covarrubias. New York: Alfred A. Knopf, 1942. 417 pp.

— "Theatre in Bali," *Theatre Arts Monthly,* XX (August, 1936), 571—658.

Crawfurd, John. *History of the Indian Archipelago.* Edinburgh: Archibald Constable, 1820. 3 vols.

Cultuurgeschiedenis van Java in Beeld. Samengesteld door W. F. Stutterheim. Weltevreden: Java-Instituut en G. Kolff, 1926. 172 pp.

Déwantara, Ki Hadjar. "Conservatorium voor Indonesische Toonkunst," *Cultureel Nieuws,* No. 5 (1951), 31—2.

— *Een en ander over "Nationaal Onderwijs" en het Instituut "Taman Siswa" te Jogjakarta.* Brochuren-Serie No. NII. Jogjakarta: Wasita, 1935. 16 pp.

— *Leidraad behoorende bij den Cursus over de Javaansche Muziek.* Groningen: J. B. Wolters, 1930. 124 pp.

— *Leidraad behoorende bij den Cursus over de Javaansche Muziek.* Brochuren-Serie No. L. Jogjakarta: Wasita, 1935. 8 pp.

Djajadipoera, R. M. T. "Gegevens met Betrekking tot de Gamelan," *Djawa,* Prae-adviezen II, Vol. I (1921), 91—6.

Djajengoetara, R. Loerah. *Opstel over de Regels in de Javaansche Gending.* MS in the possession of Jaap Kunst at the Koninklijk Instituut voor de Tropen in Amsterdam. 9 numb. leaves; see further J. S. Brandts Buys, *Djawa,* IV (1924), 1—17.

Djakoeb and Wignjaroemeksa. "Lajang anjoeroepake pratikele bab sinaoe naboeh sarto panggawene gamelan," *Volkslectuur,* No. 94 (1913), 135 pp.

Dungga, J. A. "De Huidige Stand van de Indonesische Muziek," *Cultureel Nieuws,* No. 9 (1951), 2—7.

— and L. Manik. *Musik di Indonesia dan beberapa persoalannja.* Djakarta: Balai Pustaka, 1952. 112 pp.

Ellis, Alexander J. "Tonometrical Observations on some existing Non-harmonic Musical Scales," *Proceedings* of the Royal Society, London (Nov., 1884), 374 ff.

Endo, Hirosi. *Bibliography of Oriental and Primitive Music.* Tokyo: Nanki Music Library, 1929. 62 pp.

Faber, G. H. von. "Van Krontjonglied tot 'lagu modern'," *Cultureel Nieuws,* No. 9 (1951), 23—32.

Gironcourt, Georges de. "Recherches de géographie musicale au Cambodge et à Java," *Bulletin,* Société d'Etudes Indochinoises, XIX (1944), 49—81.

Goris, R. *Bali Godsdienst en Ceremoniën.* Foto's door Walter Spies. Batavia: G. Kolff, 1931. 79 pp.

— "Tooneel, Dans en Muziek op Bali," *Djawa,* XIII (1933), 329—33.

Goslings, B. M. *De Wajang op Java en Bali in het verleden en het heden.* Amsterdam: J. M. Meulenhoff, 1939. 103 pp.

Groneman, J. *De Gamelan te Jogjakarta.* Voorrede "Over onze Kennis der Javaansche Muziek" door J. P. Land. Amsterdam: Johannes Müller, 1890. 125 pp.

— *De Garebeg's te Ngajogyakarta.* 's-Gravenhage: Martinus Nijhoff, 1895. 87 pp. XXV pls.

Handschin, J. [Review of Jaap Kunst's *Music in Java* and *Around von Hornbostel's Theory . . .*] *Acta Musicologica,* XXII (1950), 156—71.

Hardouin, E. *Java's Bewoners in hun eigenaardig Karakter en Kleederdracht.* Tekst van W. L. Ritter. Leiden: A. W. Sijthoff, 1872. 164 pp.

Hazeu, Godard Arend Johannes. *Bijdrage tot de Kennis van het Javaansche Tooneel.* Leiden: E. J. Brill, 1897. 203 pp.

Hiss, Philip Hanson. *Bali.* New York: Duell, Sloan & Pearce, 1941. 112 pp.

Holt, Claire. *Théâtre et danses aux Indes néerlandaises, Java, Bali, Célèbes, Sumatra, Nias.* Catalogue et commentaires. Paris: Gustave-Paul Maisonneuve, 1939. 86 pp.

Hooykaas, C. *Proza en Poëzie van Oud-Java.* Groningen: N.V. P. Noordhoff, 1933. 187 pp.

Husmann, Heinrich. "Fünf- und siebenstellige Centstafeln zur Berechnung musikalischer Intervalle," *Ethno-musicologica.* Leiden: E. J. Brill, 1951. 16 pp.

Huyser, J. B. "Indonesische Musikinstrumenten," *Nederlandsch-Indië Oud & Nieuw,* XIII (1928—9), 234—47, 266—74.

Indonesisches Kunstgewerbe. Bilder-Atlas, mit einer Einleitung von T. J. Bezemer. Den Haag: Ten Hagen [no date]. 170 pp.

Izikowitz, Karl Gustav. "Där Primitiva Folk och Högkulturer Mötas," *Primitiv Konst* (Stockholm: 1947), pp. 128—77; 135 figs.

Jacobson, Edw. and J. H. van Hasselt. *De Gong-fabricatie te Semarang*. Leyden: E. J. Brill, 1907. 64 pp. xii pls.

Jogyanese manuscript containing 100 genḍing. In the possession of Jaap Kunst at the Royal Tropical Institute in Amsterdam.

Juynboll, H. H. "Tooneel," *Encyclopaedie van Nederlandsch Oost-Indië*, 2nd ed., IV (1921), 395—404.

Kats, J. *Het Javaansche Tooneel*, I, *Wajang Poerwa*. Weltevreden: Volkslectuur, 1923. 446 pp.

— "Wat kan er gedaan worden, om het Behoud en de Ontwikkeling der Javaansche Toonkunst te Verzekeren?" *Djawa*, Prae-adviezen II, Vol. I (1921), 111—15.

Kennedy, Raymond. *Bibliography of Indonesian Peoples and Cultures*. Yale Anthropological Studies, vol. 4. New Haven, Conn.: Yale Univ. Press, 1945. 212 pp.

Kloss, C. Boden. "Malayan Musical Instruments," *Journal*, Straits Branch, Royal Asiatic Society, XLV (1906), 285—7.

Knosp, Gaston. "Le Gamelan," *Revista Musicale Italiana*, XXXI (1924), 35—58.

— "Le Pantoun javanais," *Vie Musicale*, II (1918), 41—6.

Koechlin, Charles. "Gamelang Salandro (Sultanat de Yogyakarta)," *S.I.M. Revue Musicale Mensuelle*, VI (1910), 548—63.

Kolinski, Mieczyslaw. "Die Musik der Primitivstamme auf Malaka und ihre Beziehungen zur samoanischen Musik," *Anthropos*, XXV (1930), 585—648.

Kool, Jaap. "Over Gongs en Ankloengs," *Nederlandsch-Indië Oud & Nieuw*, VIII (1923—4), 368—78.

Kunst, Jaap. *Around von Hornbostel's Theory of the Cycle of Blown Fifths*. Amsterdam: Indisch Instituut, 1948. 35 pp.

— "Boekbespreking," *Cultureel Indië*, IV (1942), 226—36.

— *The Cultural Background of Indonesian Music*. Amsterdam: Indisch Instituut, 1949. 43 pp.

— *Een en ander over de Javaansche Gamelan*. Amsterdam: Indisch Instituut, 1945. 8 pp.

— *Een en ander over de Javaansche Wajang*. Amsterdam: Indisch Instituut, 1945. 12 pp. 10 pls.

— *Een en ander over de Muziek en den Dans of de Kei-Eilanden*. Amsterdam: Indisch Instituut, 1945. 27 pp. 7 pls.

— "Een en ander over den Vorstenlandschen Gamelan," *Oedaya* (1928), pp. 130—7.

— *A study on Papuan Music*. Weltevreden: G. Kolff, 1931. viii, 97 pp.

— *Hindoe-Javaansche Muziek-Instrumenten, speciaal die van Oost Java*. In collaboration with R. Goris. Studiën over Javaansche en andere Indonesische Muziek, Deel II. Weltevreden: Koninklijk Bataviaasch Genootschap, 1927. 203 pp.

— "Indes néerlandaises," *Musique et chanson populaires*. Paris: Société des nations, Institut internationale de coopération intellectuelle, 1934. pp. 82—6.

— *De Inheemsche Muziek en de Zending*. Voordracht op 1 Mei 1946 gehouden voor de zending-school te Oegstgeest. Amsterdam: H. J. Paris, 1947. 47 pp.

— *De Inheemse Muziek in Westelijk Nieuw-Guinea*. Amsterdam: Indisch Instituut, 1950. 78 pp.

— *Kulturhistorische Beziehungen zwischen dem Balkan und Indonesien*. Amsterdam: Koninklijk Instituut voor de Tropen, 1953. 32 pp. 60 illus.

— "Mededeelingen: 3. Een vergeten musicologische bron: de Instrumentenafbeeldingen in 'Les Hindous' van F. Baltazard Solvyns; 4. Een Novum op Indonesisch Muziekgebied," *Cultureel Indië*, VII (1945), 197—204.

— "Een merkwaardig blaasinstrument: de Maleische Duivenlokfluit," *Cultureel Indië*, II (1940), 47—53.

— *Music in Flores*. Transl. by Emile van Loo. Leyden: E. J. Brill, 1942. 164 pp.

— *Music in Java*. 2nd ed., revised and enlarged, transl. by Emile van Loo. The Hague: Martinus Nijhoff, 1949. 2 vols.

— "Music in Nias," *International Archiv für Ethnographie*, XXXVIII (1939), 1—91.

— *Musicologica*. Amsterdam: Indisch Instituut, 1950. 77 pp.

Kunst, Jaap. "A Musicological Argument for Cultural Relationship between Indonesia — probably the Isle of Java — and Central Africa," *Proceedings of the Musical Association*, LXII (1935—6), 57—76.

— "Musicological Exploration in the Indian Archipelago," *Asiatic Review*, XXXII (1936), 810—20.

— "Musicologische Verzameling," *Jaarboek*, K. Bataviaasch Genootschap van Kunst en Wetenschappen, I (1933), 231—3.

— *Muziek en Dans in de Buitengewesten.* Leyden: Indisch Instituut, 1946. 18 pp. 24 pls.

— "De Muziek in den Mangkoe Negaran," *Djawa*, IV (1924), 24—30.

— "Ein musikologischer Beweis für Kulturzusammenhange zwischen Indonesien — vermutlich Java — und Zentralafrika," *Anthropos*, XXXI (1936), 131—40.

— "Een onbekend Javaansche Muziekinstrument," *Cultureel Indië*, I (1939), 140—3.

— "De l'origine des echelles musicales javano-balinaises," *Journal*, Siam Society, XXIII (1929), 111—22.

— "Over eenige Hindoe-Javaansche Muziek-Instrumenten," *Tijdschrift voor Indische Taal-, Land- en Volkenkunde*, LXVIII (1929), 347—56.

— "Over Soendaneesche Zangmuziek," *Gedenkboek van het Kon. Bataviaasch Genootschap, 1778—1928*, I (Weltevreden: G. Kolff, 1929), 393—407.

— "Een overwalsche Bloedverwant van den Javaanschen Gamelan; Geschiedenis van het Siameesche Orkest," *Nederlandsch-Indië Oud & Nieuw*, XIV (1929—30), 79—96, 354.

— *Over zeldzame Fluiten en veelstemmige Muziek in het Ngada- en Nageh-gebied (West Flores).* Oudheidkundige Dienst in Ned.-Indië: Musicologisch Onderzoek, I. Batavia: K. Bataviaasch Genootschap, 1931. 37 pp.

— *The Peoples of the Indian Archipelago.* Leiden: E. J. Brill, 1946. 9 pp. xvi pls. 31 illus. 2 maps.

— *Songs of North New Guinea.* Oudheidkundige Dienst in Ned.-Indië: Musicologisch Onderzoek, II. Batavia: K. Bataviaasch Genootschap, 1931. 17 pp.

— "Schrijven naar Aanleiding der Gestelde Vragen," *Djawa*, Prae-adviezen II, Vol. I (1921), 123—5.

— *De Toonkunst van Java.* Den Haag: Martinus Nijhoff, 1934. 2 vols.

— *De Waardeering van exotische Muziek in den Loop der Eeuwen.* 's-Gravenhage: Martinus Nijhoff, 1942. 48 pp.

— "Waar komt de Gong vandaan?" *Cultureel Indië*, IV (1942), 241—5.

— and R. Machjar Koesomadinata. "Een en ander over Pélog en Sléndro," *Tijdschrift voor Indische Taal-, Land- en Volkenkunde*, LXIX (1929—30), 320—52.

— and R. Toemenggoeng Wiranatakoesoema. "Een en ander over Soendaneesche Muziek," *Djawa*, Prae-adviezen I, Vol. I (1921), 235—52.

— and C. J. A. Kunst-van Wely. "Over Bali'sche Muziek," *Djawa*, II (1922), 117—46.

— and — "Over Toonschalen en Instrumenten van West Java," *Djawa*, III (1923), 26—40.

— and — *De Toonkunst van Bali, Deel I.* Weltevreden: Koninklijk Bataviaasch Genootschap en G. Kolff, 1925. 248 pp. xix tables; *Deel II.* Weltevreden: K.B.G. en Albrecht, 1925. pp. 249—501.

Kusumadinata, R. Machjar Angga. *Ringkĕsan Pangawikan Rinĕnggaswara.* Djakarta: Noordhoff-Kolff, *ca.* 1950. 48 pp.

Kruyt, Albert Christian. "De Fluit in Indonesië," *Tijdschrift voor Indische Taal-, Land- en Volkenkunde*, LXXVIII (1938), 248—70.

Land, Jan Pieter Nicolaas. "Note sur la musique de l'île de Java," *Actes du Dixième congrès international des orientalistes ...* Genève, 1894. Leyden: E. J. Brill, 1897. Section V, pp. 3—18.

— "Ueber die Tonkunst der Javanen," *Vierteljahrsschrift für Musikwissenschaft*, V (1889), 193—215.

Lange, Daniel de, and John. F. Snelleman. "La Musique et les instruments de musique dans les Indes orientales néerlandaises," *Encyclopedie de la Musique et Dictionnaire du Conservatoire*, ed. Lavignac, V (1922), 3147—69.

Lelyveld, Th. B. van. *De Javaansche Danskunst.* Amsterdam: Van Holkema en Warendorf, 1931. 258 pp.

Lodewijckz, Willem. *D'Eerste Boeck*. De Eerste Schipvaart der Nederlanders naar Oost-Indië onder Cornelis de Houtman, 1595—1597. The Hague: Linschoten-Vereeniging en Martinus Nijhoff, 1915. p. 238, pls. 23 and 25 (pp. 128—9).

M., F. v. d. "Iets over de 'Muziek' en het 'Tandakken' bij de Javanen," *Tijdschrift voor het Binnenlandsch Bestuur*, II (1889), 93—104.

Mangku Nagaran, list of titles in the collection of the. In the possession of Jaap Kunst at the Royal Tropical Institute in Amsterdam.

Marcel-Dubois, Claudie. *Les Instruments de musique de l'Indie ancienne*. Paris: Presses Universitaires de France, 1941. 259 pp.

Mellema, R. L. *De Islam in Indonesië (in het bijzonder op Java)*. Amsterdam: Indisch Instituut, 1947. 52 pp. 34 illus.

— *Wayang Puppets, Carving, Coloring, Symbols*. Transl. by Mantle Hood. Amsterdam: Koninklijk Instituut voor de Tropen, 1954, 80 pp.

Moens-Zorab, M. V. "Arjuna, Prince of Charms," *Sluyter's Monthly* (June, 1922), pp. 442—7.

— "Bima and his Kin," *Sluyter's Monthly* (April, 1922), pp. 270—5.

— "Mintaraga," *Inter-Ocean* (formerly *Sluyter's Monthly*), II (Oct./Nov., 1923), 709—13, 783—8.

— "Salya, the Waverer," *Inter-Ocean*, IX (Oct., 1928), 535—41.

— "Suyudana, the Humiliated," *Inter-Ocean*, I (Nov., 1922), 346—54.

Moojen, P. A. J. *Kunst op Bali. Inleidende studie tot de Bouwkunst*. Den Haag: Adi Poestaka, 1926. 187 pp. ccvi pls.

Music Library Association. "Bibliography of Asiatic Music," *Notes*, 2nd Series, VII (Dec., 1949), 84—98.

McPhee, Colin. "The 'Absolute' Music of Bali," *Modern Music*, XII (1935), 163—9.

— "Angkloeng gamelans in Bali," *Djawa*, XVII (1937), 322—66.

— "The Balinese *Wajang Koelit* and Its Music," *Djawa*, XVI (1936), 1—50.

— "Children and Music in Bali," *Djawa*, XVIII (1938), 309—28.

— *A Club of Small Men*. New York: John Day Co., 1948. 61 pp.

— "Dance in Bali," *Dance Index*, VII, Nos. 7, 8 (1948), 156—207.

— "The Decline of the East," *Modern Music*, XVI (1939), 160—7.

— "Figuration in Balinese Music," *Peabody Bulletin*, XXXVI, No. 2 (May 1940), 23—6.

— "The Five-Tone Gamelan Music of Bali," *Musical Quarterly*, XXXV (1949), 250—81.

— "Gamelan-muziek van Bali, Ondergangschemering van een Kunst," *Djawa*, XIX (1939), 183—5.

— *A House in Bali*. New York: John Day Co., 1946. 234 pp.

— "In This Far Island," *Asia Magazine*, XLIV (1944), 532—7; XLV (1945), 38—43, 157—62, 206, 210, 257—61, 305—9, 350, 354.

— "Musical Exploration in Bali," *Musical America*, LX (Feb. 1940), 120, 263.

— "The Technique of Balinese Music," *Bulletin*, American Musicological Society, No. 6 (August 1942), 2—4.

"Naar een Nationale Indonesische Muziek," *Vrije Pers* (Jan. 1951); reprinted in *Indon. Documentatie* (March 1951), 405 ff.

"Nationale Indonesische Muziek," *Indonesia*, II, No. 5 (1949), 67 ff.

Nieuwenhuis, G. J. "Ueber den Tanz im malaiischen Archipel," *Internat. Archiv für Ethnographie*, XXIII (1916), 183—240.

Overbeck, H. "Javaansche Meisjesspelen en Kinderliedjes; beschrijving der spelen, Javaansche liederteksten, vertaling," *Djawa*, XIX Suppl. (1939), 1—224.

"Pangkur," Konservatori Karawitan Indonesia, 1953, 21 numb. leaves; an orchestral score in cipher notation in the possession of Jaap Kunst at the Koninklijk Instituut voor de Tropen in Amsterdam.

Pigeaud, Th. *Javaans-Nederlands Handwoordenboek*. Groningen: J. B. Wolters, 1938.

— *Javaanse Volksvertoningen*. Batavia: Volkslectuur, 1938. 545 pp.

— "Over den huidigen van de tooneel- en danskunst en de muziekbeoefening op Java," *Djawa*, XII (1932), 155—6.

Poensen, C. "De Wajang," *Mededeelingen vanwege het Nederlandsche Zendelinggenootschap*, XVI (1872), 59—164.

Prawiro, Sastro. "Préludes javanais," *Bulletin Français, So. Internat. de Musique*, V (1909), 839—55.

Prins, Eli. "Het Gamelan-orkest; Indrukken van een terugkeer, 1945," *Vrije Geluiden*, XX, No. 36 (Sept. 1950), 6—7.

Raffles, Thomas Stamford. *The History of Java*. London: Black, Parbury, and Allen, 1817. 2 vols.

Rassers, W. H. "Inleiding tot een Bestudeering van de Javaansche Kris," *Mededeelingen der Koninklijke Nederlandsche Akademie van Wetenschappen*, Nieuwe Reeks, I (1938), 425—83.

— "On the Javanese Kris," *Bijdragen Koninklijk Instituut*, 99 (1940), 501—82.

— "Over den Oorsprong van het Javaansche Tooneel," *Bijdragen tot de Taal-, Land- en Volkenkunde van Ned.-Indië*, 88 (1931), 317—450.

— "Over den Zin van het Javaansche Drama," *Bijdragen tot de Taal-, Land- en Volkenkunde van Ned.-Indië*, 81 (1925), 311 ff.

Sachs, Curt. *The History of Musical Instruments*. New York: W. W. Norton, 1940. 505 pp.

— *Die Musikinstrumente Indiens und Indonesiens*. Zweite Auflage. Berlin: Walter de Gruyter, 1923. 192 pp. 117 illus.

— *Real-lexikon der Musikinstrumente*. Berlin: Julius Bard, 1913. 442 pp.

— *The Rise of Music in the Ancient World East and West*. New York: W. W. Norton, 1943. 324 pp.

— "Sudostasiatische Orchester," *Kultur und Schallplatte*, II (1931), 162—3.

— "Die Tonkunst von Bali," *Bulletin*, Soc. Union Musicologique, V (1925), 1—6.

Sastrasoewignja, Soehardha, in collaboration with R. Wiradat and R. Kodrat. "Ringkesaning kawroeh padalangan ringgit poerwa ing Soerakarta," *Kadjawen*, published by *Volkslectuur*, appearing from No. 70 (Sept. 2, 1931) until No. 54 (July 6, 1932).

Schlager, Ernst. "Bali," *Die Musik in Geschichte und Gegenwart*, I (1949—51), 1110—15.

Seelig, Paul J. *Gending Djawi*. Leipzig: Hug, 1922. 155 pp.

Selleger, L. "L'Orchestre javanais ou 'gamelan'; conference faite à la Société de géographie de Hanoi le 5 décembre 1932," *Cahier, Soc. de Geographie de Hanoi*, XXIV (1933), 5—23.

Serre, Paul. "Note sur la musique aux Indes néerlandaises," *Revue Musicale*, V (1905), 565—6.

Simbriger, Heinrich. "Gong und Gongspiele," *Internat. Archiv für Ethnographie*, XXXVI (1939), 1—180.

Sitompoel, B. "Het Muziekleven in Indonesië," *Cultureel Nieuws*, Nos. 21—22 (1952), 406—13.

— "Naar een Indonesische Muziek," *Cultureel Nieuws*, No. 9 (1951), 8—12.

Snelleman, Joh. F. "Muziek en Muziekinstrumenten," *Encyclopaedie van Nederlandsch Oost-Indië*, 2nd ed., II (1918), 812—24.

Soelardi, R. Bagoes. *Serat pradongga*. Weltevreden: Widyapoestaka, (no date). 65 pp.

Soemitra, R. M. "Een en ander over de Gamelan," *Voordrachten en Mededeelingen der Indische Vereeniging*, II (1913), 69—87.

Soerjowinto, R. "Beschrijving van gamelan-instrumenten," *Nederlandsch-Indië Oud & Nieuw*, V (1920—1), 267—75.

Soeroto, Noto. "Ueber den javanischen Tanz," transl. by Viktor Joss, *Auftakt*, IX (1929), 237—9.

Solonese Kepatihan, list of titles in the collection of the. In the possession of Jaap Kunst at the Royal Tropical Institute in Amsterdam.

Solonese manuscript containing 28 gending. In the possession of Jaap Kunst at the Royal Tropical Institute in Amsterdam.

Soorjopoetro. "Beschouwing over Java's nationale Toonkunst," *Nederlandsch-Indië Oud & Nieuw*, IV (1919—20), 217—24.

— "Javaansche Muziekontwikkeling en Westersche Muziek," *Djawa*, Prae-adviezen II, Vol. I (1921), 117—21.

— "Muziekschrift voor Java's Toonkunst," *Nederlandsch-Indië Oud & Nieuw*, I (1916—7), 375—80.

— "De Sléndro en Pélog Toonladders op de Viool en Violoncel uitgezet, en het daaraan beantwoordende Muziekschrift," *Nederlandsch-Indië Oud & Nieuw*, II (1917—8), 317—23.

— "Van de Javaansche Muziek en hare Verhouding tot andere Aziatische en tot Europeesche Muziek," *Mudato*, I (1919), 37—48.

— "Voorloopige Mededeelingen omtrent het Nieuwste System van Javaansch Notenschrift," *Nederlandsch-Indië Oud & Nieuw*, IV (1919—20), 318—20.
— and Noto Soerto. "Causerieën over Javaansche Muziek," *Nederlandsch-Indië Oud & Nieuw*, I (1916—7), 17—21, 74—8, 115—18, 170—4, 312—14.
Spies, Walter. "Bericht über den Zustand von Tanz und Musik in der Negara Gianjar," *Djawa*, XVI (1936), 51—9.
— "De Gamelan-wedstrijd te Gianjar . . . December 1938," *Djawa*, XIX (1939), 197—207.
— and R. Goris. "Overzicht van Dans en Tooneel in Bali," *Djawa*, XVII (1937), 205—27.
Sturler, J. E. de. "Les Danseuses de cour à Java," *Revue Musicale*, VIII (1908), 442—7.
Stutterheim, Willem F. *Indian Influences in Old-Balinese Art.* London: The India Society, 1935. 41 pp. xxiii pls.
— "Old and New Art of Bali," *Indian Art and Letters*, VI (1932), 1—9.
— *Rāma-Legenden und Rāma-Reliefs in Indonesien.* Ins Deutsche übersetzt von Karl und Hedwig Döhring. München: George Müller, 1925. 2 vols.
Tirtanata, R. *Notenschrift voor Gending Saléndro en Pélog.* MS in the possession of Jaap Kunst at the Koninklijk Instituut voor de Tropen in Amsterdam. 11 numb. leaves; see further J. S. Brandts Buys, *Djawa*, IV (1924), 1—17.
Tjakrahadikoesoema, R. M. Ad. Ar. *De Regelen der Gending.* MS in the possession of Jaap Kunst at the Koninklijk Instituut voor de Tropen in Amsterdam. 7 numb. leaves; see further J. S. Brandts Buys, *Djawa*, IV (1924), 1—17.
IJzerdraat, Bernard. "De Instrumenten van den Javaanschen Gamelan," *Mensch en Melodie*, I (1946), 246, 280, 309; II (1947), 52, 250, 348; III (1948), 181; IV (1949), 18.
— and Suhendro Sosrosuwarno. *Bentara Senisuara Indonesia.* Groningen: J. B. Wolters, 1954, 76 pp.
Zganec, Vinko and Nada Sremec. *Croatian Folk Songs and Dances.* Zagreb: Seljačka Sloga, 1951. 284 pp.
Zoete, Beryl de, and Walter Spies. *Dance and Drama in Bali.* With a Preface by Arthur Waley. New York: Harper and Bros., 1939. xx, 343 pp.

APPENDIX

PAṬET TRANSPOSITION TABLE.

This table indicates the different paṭet in which the genḍing of the Jogyanese collection are known in six other repertoires. The gangsaran, nr's 13, 14, 64, 65, are omitted from the table; the original numbering of the genḍing has been retained, but those pieces which were incorrectly labeled (nr's 4, 12, 35, 38) appear in their proper paṭet; several pairs of genḍing which are identical except for their titles have been listed individually but are paired by an appropriate bracket (*e.g.* nr 47—48) or tie (*e.g.* nr 91—93).

The vertical columns are arranged according to the wayang sequence, so that the corresponding columns of sléndro and pélog indicate parallel paṭet. For example, nr 6 appears in three collections (A-D-E) in sléndro paṭet nem and in collection "B" has been transposed to its parallel paṭet, pélog paṭet lima; within the sléndro system it has also been transposed to paṭet manyura (collection "C") and within the pélog system to paṭet nem (collection "G"). Nr 17 is an example of the lesser transposition practice in which sléndro paṭet nem has been transposed to pélog paṭet nem (or *vice versa*). The bold horizontal lines divide the titles of the Jogyanese collection according to paṭet.

The letter "A" indicates the Jogyanese manuscript of 100 titles; the letter "B" indicates the Solonese manuscript (see Chapter VIII); "C" indicates the list of genḍing given in Vol. II of Kunst's *Music in Java*; "D" represents a list of genḍing in the collection from the Solonese Kepatihan, the palace of the "prime minister" (see further *MJ*, I, 317); "E" indicates the Seelig collection of 200 genḍing (see biblio.); "F" represents the genḍing listed by Groneman in *De Gamelan te Jogjakarta* (see biblio.); "G" represents a list of genḍing from the Mangku Nagara, presented to Jaap Kunst in the 1920's by His Highness P. A. A. Mangku Nagara VII.

It should be noted that these six sources in themselves may contain errors in paṭet designation or two different titles for the same genḍing or a title which corresponds to one of those in the Jogyanese collection but which may actually indicate a different genḍing. The large number of titles represented by these combined collections, however, should minimize the effect of such errors and yield a generally reliable index to paṭet transposition practice.

		SLÉNDRO			PÉLOG		
		Paṭet NEM	Paṭet SANGA	Paṭet MANYURA	Paṭet LIMA	Paṭet NEM	Paṭet BARANG
S. PAṬET NEM	nr 1 Lungkèh	A-B-C-D-E-G					
	nr 2 Dirodo Meto	A-C-G					
	nr 3 Girang-Girang	A-C-F		C			
	nr 5 Peksi Bajah	A-C-D-E-G					
	nr 6 Herang-Herang Kudus	A-D-E		C	B	G	
	nr 7 Gègèr Sakuto	A	G				
	nr 8 Babat Kencheng	A-C-E-G	G	D			G
	nr 9 Pisang Bali	A	C	D		C-D	G
	nr 10 Kandang Walang	A					
	nr 11 Rojo Hanggolo	A					
	nr 15 Gupuh	A		C			
	nr 16 Sekar Gaḍung Puletan	A-C		D			
	nr 17 Rangsang	A-F				G	

		SLÉNDRO			PÉLOG		
		Paṭet NEM	Paṭet SANGA	Paṭet MANYURA	Paṭet LIMA	Paṭet NEM	Paṭet BARANG
S. PAṬET SANGA	nr 12 Wani-Wani		A-G	F *)		G	
	nr 18 Udan Sejati		A				
	nr 19 Uluk-Uluk		A-D-E-F-G			D	
	nr 20 Wirangrong	C	A-C				
	nr 21 Jangkrik Ginggong		A-G				
	nr 22 Dempel		A-C-D-G	G			
	nr 23 Konchang		A				
	nr 24 Gondo Yonni		A				
	nr 25 Sobrang Barang		A				C-E-G
	nr 26 Sulung Ḍayung		A			C **)	
	nr 27 Chlunṭang		A-C-D-G			D	
	nr 28 Madu Bronto		A				
	nr 29 Gondo Suli		A-C-D-G				
	nr 30 Bujang Daleman		A-C				
	nr 31 Bronto Moro		A				
	nr 32 Bronto Asmoro		A				
	nr 33 Bronto Kingkin		A				
	nr 34 Gaḍung Mlati		A-C-G				
	nr 36 Kumandang		A			G	
	nr 37 Laras Dijo		A-C-D-G				
	nr 39 Barang Ganjur		A-C				
	nr 40 Gajah Endro		A-C	D			
S. PAṬET MANYURA	nr 4 Sekar Pépé			A-C-E-G			
	nr 35 Ladrang Kuwung			A-D			D-G
	nr 38 Panji Ketawang			A-C			
	nr 41 Kondo			A-C-D-G			
	nr 42 Liwung	D		A-C			
	nr 43 Richik-Richik			A-C-D-G			
	nr 44 Lèngkèr			A		D-E	
	nr 45 Tlosor			A			
	nr 46 Jagung-Jagung			A			
	{ nr 47 Gajah Bengok			A			
	{ nr 48 Machan Géro			A			
	{ nr 49 Machan Angop			A			
	{ nr 50 Simo Nebak			A			
	nr 51 Chèlèng Mogok			A			
	nr 52 Chèlèng Minggok			A			
	{ nr 53 Panyutro			A			
	{ nr 54 Prawiro Tomo			A			
	nr 55 Semar Mantu			A-D			
	nr 56 Chino Nagi			A			
	nr 57 Gonjang		C-G	A-D-G		D-G	D
	nr 58 Gonjang Sèrèt			A-D-E-G			
	nr 59 Téjo			A			
	nr 60 Sekar Tanjun		E-G	A-C			

		SLÉNDRO			PÉLOG		
		Paṭet NEM	Paṭet SANGA	Paṭet MANYURA	Paṭet LIMA	Paṭet NEM	Paṭet BARANG
P. PAṬET LIMA	nr 61 Rijem-Rijem				A-C		
	nr 62 Kemong-Kemong				A-F		
	nr 63 Juru Demung				A-G		
P. PAṬET NEM	nr 67 Pasang Bandar					A-D	
	nr 68 Durmo					A	
	nr 69 Larasati	D-E-G			D	A-C-F	
	nr 70 Megarsi					A-C	
	nr 71 Rangsang Tuban					A-D-E-G	
	nr 72 Langen Bronto					A	
	nr 73 Langen Asmoro					A-C	
	nr 74 Megarsari					A	
	nr 75 Pisang Megar					A	
	nr 76 Pangluntursih					A	
	nr 77 Pamikatsih					A	
	nr 78 Lagu			D-G		A-C-D-G	
	nr 79 Téjo Bronto					A	
	nr 80 Lung Gadung Madura					A-C	
	nr 81 Bekso Wiromo					A	
	nr 82 Tropongan					A-C-D-G	
	nr 83 Udan Mas					A-C	
	nr 84 Honang-ngonang Manis		D-E-G			A-C-F	
	nr 85 Madu Kentar					A	
	nr 86 Puspo Kanti					A	C
	nr 87 Moro Semu					A	
	nr 88 Gondo Mastuti					A-G	
P. PAṬET BARANG	nr 89 Jong Kèli			D-G			A-C-G
	nr 90 Megar Semu						A
	nr 91 Pengsih						A
	nr 92 Jongjongan						A
	nr 93 Megarsih			C			A
	nr 94 Sobrang Betawen						A
	nr 95 Grompol						A
	nr 96 Teḍak Saking					G	A-D-E-G
	nr 97 Rangu-Rangu						A-C-F-G
	nr 98 Ronggo Lasem						A
	nr 99 Barang Asmoro						A
	nr 100 Srimalèlo						A-C
	nr 66 Wirogo				A in pélog paṭet manyura		

*) But cf. p. 79.

**) Only the pélog system is indicated; "C" is therefore entered in the column which is parallel (in the wayang sequence) to the given sléndro paṭet.

TRANSCRIPTIONS

of

THE GEND̩ING

GENḌING SLÉNDRO.

As a reminder that every genḍing in transcription has been moved forward one beat (see further p. 21) the end of each of the three critical sections — the bubuka opaq-opaq (B. Op.), the bubuka genḍing (B. Gd.), and the final gongan (*e.g.* GN V of ladrang nr 1, below) — is indicated by a dotted double-bar; the divisions of the individual gongan are shown by a single dotted bar-line. It should be noted that in the examples illustrating the text the final note of the bubuka opaq-opaq or any of the subsequent gongan is given its full value as it is actually sounded. In ladrang nr 1, for example, the final note of the bubuka opaq-opaq appears as a half note on page 25; in the complete transcription given below, this is represented by two quarter notes connected by a tie as an indication of the end of the bubuka opaq-opaq and the beginning of the bubuka genḍing.

The translation of the written Javanese musical directions is given in the same order in which it occurs in the original. The directions "HIGH AND LOW REGISTERS" refer to the octave in which the panerusan instruments may play and indicate that some of the specified repetitions are to be high and some low. The directions "STRINGENDO, THEN A RIT." indicate that (usually) the penultimate gongan of the final repetition is accelerated and that the last gongan begins a *ritardando* whichs ends with the final gong. The fermata placed in parenthesis above the last note of the genḍing indicates that this tone is allowed to continue sounding at the close of the final repetition.

The symbols for the colotomic instruments are abbreviations of the following: T = keṭuk, W = wela (a rest), N = kenong, P = kempul, NG = kenong-gong. The Western scale used for the transcriptions of the genḍing sléndro is given below:

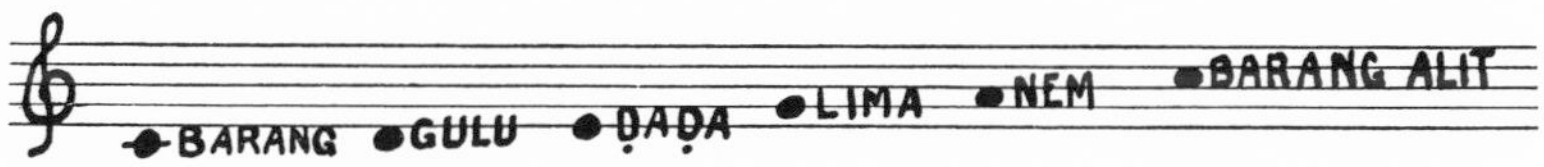

"Lungkèh"

Ladrang nr 1 sléndro paṭet nem

"Dirodo Meto"

Ladrang nr 2 sléndro paṭet nem

"Babat Kencheng"

Ladrang nr 8 sléndro paṭet nem

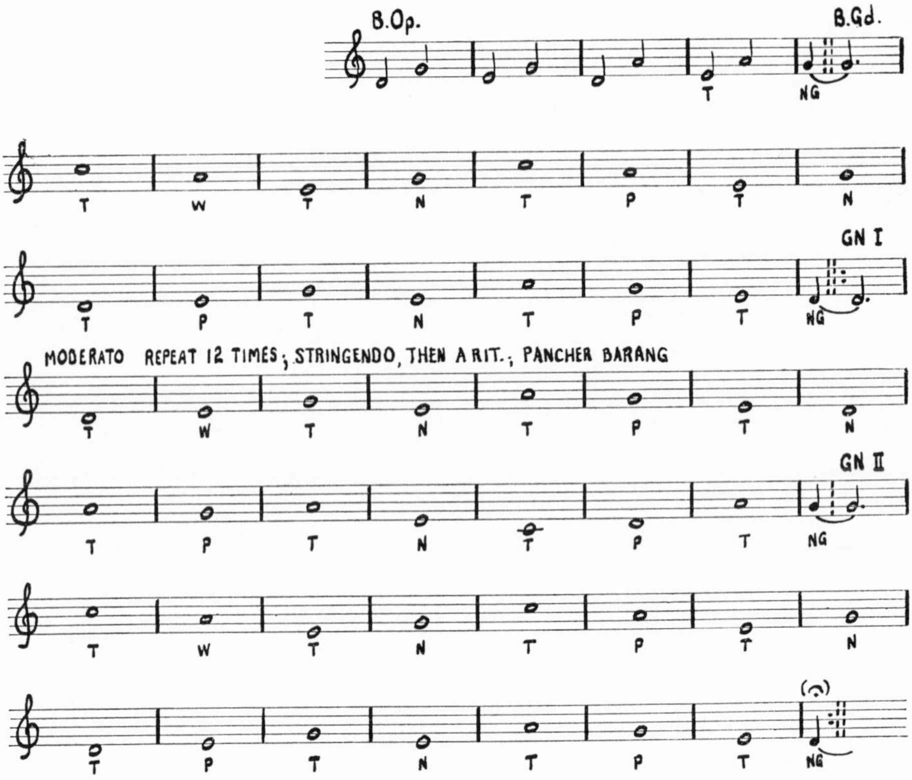

"Kandang Walang"

Ladrang nr 10 sléndro paṭet nem

“Rojo Hanggolo”

Ladrang nr 11 sléndro paṭet nem

‘Gupuh”

Ladrang nr 15 sléndro paṭet nem

"Gègèr Sakuto"

Ladrang nr 7

sléndro paṭet nem

"Uluk-Uluk"

Ladrang nr 19 sléndro paṭet sanga

"Gondo Yonni"

Ladrang nr 24 sléndro paṭet sanga

"Konchang"

Ladrang nr 23 — sléndro paṭet sanga

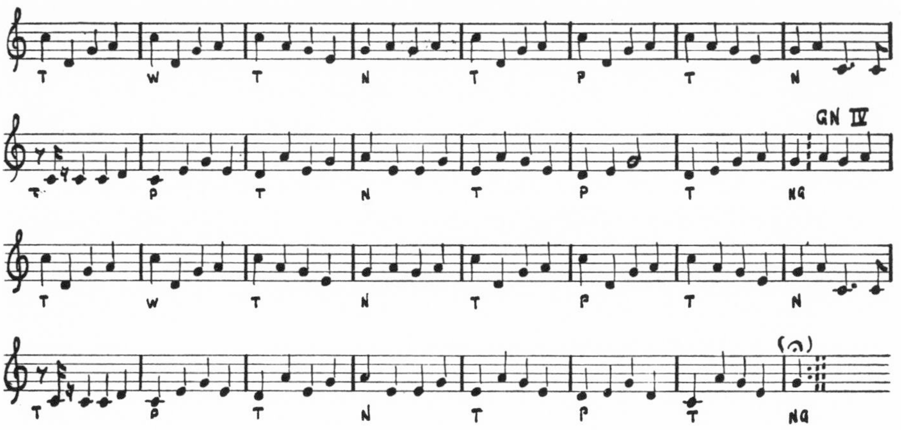

"Udan Sejati"

Ladrang nr 18 slĕndro paṭet sanga

"Madu Bronto"

Ladrang nr 28 slèndro paṭet sanga

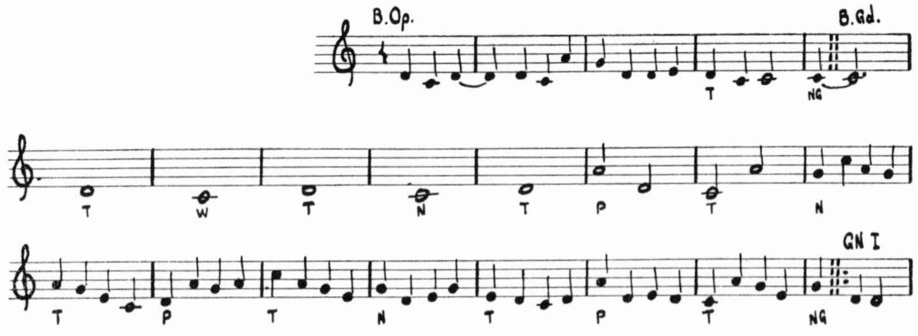

"Bronto Asmoro"

Ladrang nr 32

sléndro pațet sanga

"Chlunṭang"

Ladrang nr 27 sléndro paṭet sanga

"Barang Ganjur"

Ketawang nr 39

sléndro paṭet sanga

"Wani-Wani"

Ladrang nr 12 — sléndro paṭet sanga

"Gonjang"

Ladrang nr 57 — sléndro paṭet manyura

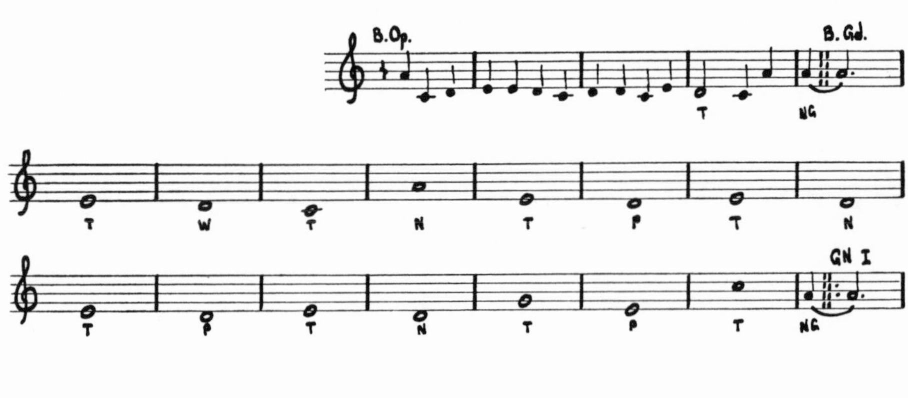

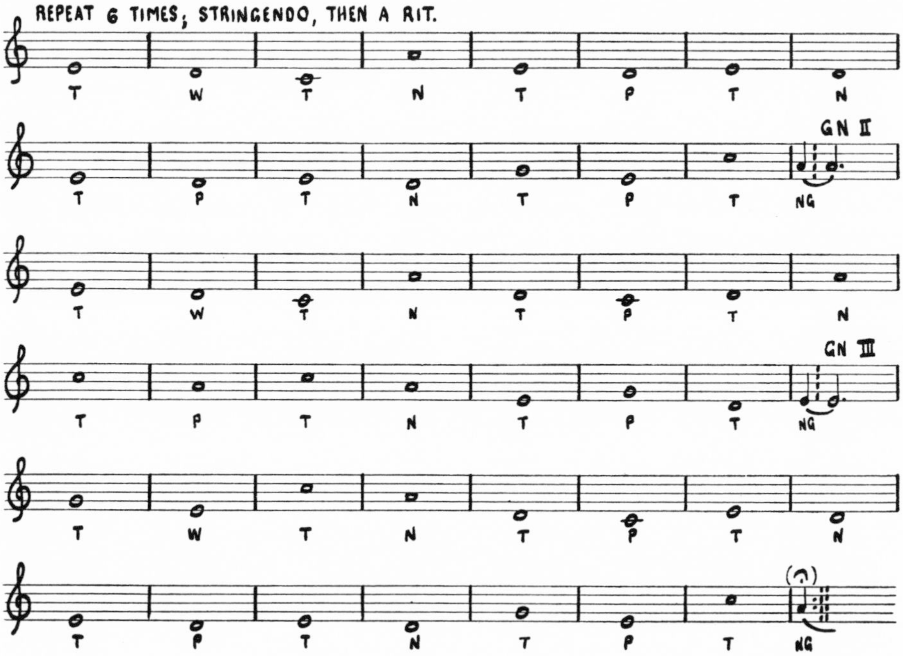

"Gonjang Sèrèt"

Ladrang nr 58 — sléndro paṭet manyura

"Lèngkèr"

Ladrang nr 44 sléndro paṭet manyura

"Chèlèng Mogok"

Ladrang nr 51

sléndro paṭet manyura

"Gaja Bengok" and "Machan Gero"

Ladrang nr 47—48 sléndro paṭet manyura

"Richik-Richik"

Ladrang nr 43 sléndro paṭet manyura

"Tlosor"

Ladrang nr 45 sléndro paṭet manyura

"Liwung"

Ladrang nr 42

sléndro paṭet manyura

GENḌING PÉLOG.

The transcriptions beginning on p. 292 ff. are from the Jogyanese manuscript and follow the same general form used in the transcription of the genḍing sléndro (see p. 265). The first six genḍing are from the Solonese manuscript, and the musical directions are given directly below the individual transcriptions. In nr 7 (p. 289) and nr 9 (p. 290) the *TRANS.* kenongan replaces the bubuka genḍing as the second critical section. Other symbols and abbreviations are the same as those used in the transcription of the genḍing sléndro.

The Western scale used for transcribing the genḍing pélog is given below:

"Chondro Sari"

Genḍing nr 26, Solonese MS pélog paṭet lima

No musical directions given.

"Retnaningsi"

Ladrang nr 2, Solonese MS pélog paṭet lima

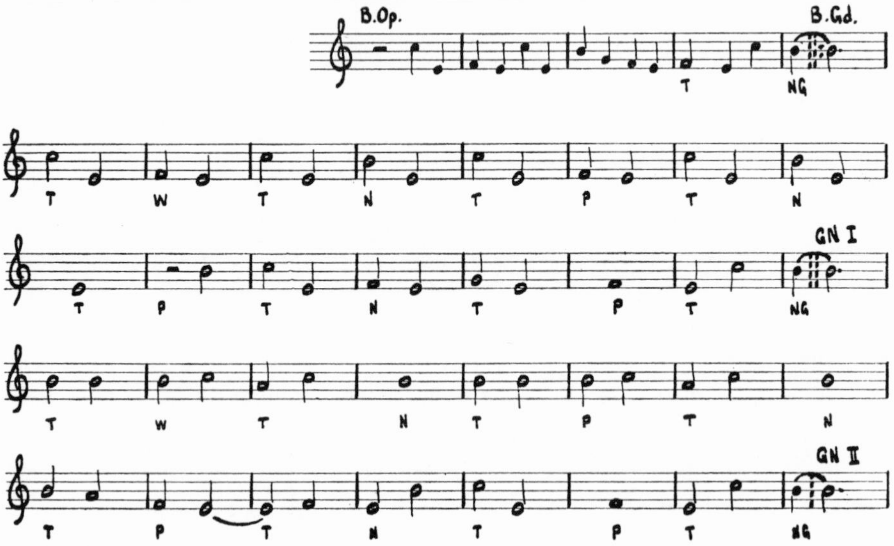

Duration 12 minutes. Fast tempo until the first kenong-gong (NG), then retard to a slow tempo. After this, return to a fast tempo for one gongan playing the first three kenongan in the high register. Conclude with several slow gongan.

Genḍing nr 7, Solonese MS "Larajola" pélog paṭet lima

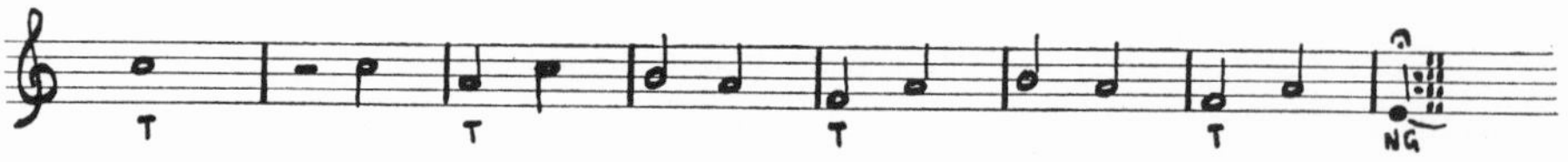

Duration 20 minutes. Fast tempo until the first kenong-gong (NG), then play one kenongan slowly. (In the *mérong*) when playing in the high register, use a fast tempo; (on the final repetition of the *mérong*) after three kenongan (jump from the sign + to the *Trans.* kenongan and) retard until the gong falls (end of *mérong*, beginning of *munggah*). The repetitions of the *munggah* are played in a slow tempo. Two kenongan before the end (of the last repetition) begin *stringendo*, then *ritardando* on the last kenongan until the final gong falls.

Genḍing nr 9, Solonese MS Laras Bronto“ pélog paṭet lima

Duration 20 minutes. (Further directions similar to nr 7 above.)

"Horang Haring"

Ladrang nr 3, Solonese MS pélog paṭet lima

Duration 12 minutes. (Further directions similar to nr 2 above.)

"Pacharchina"

Ladrang nr 13, Solonese MS pélog paṭet lima

No musical directions given.

"Pangluntursih"

Ladrang nr 76 pélog paṭet nem

"Langen Asmoro"

Ladrang nr 73 — pélog paṭet nem

"Langen Bronto"

Ladrang nr 72 pélog paṭet nem

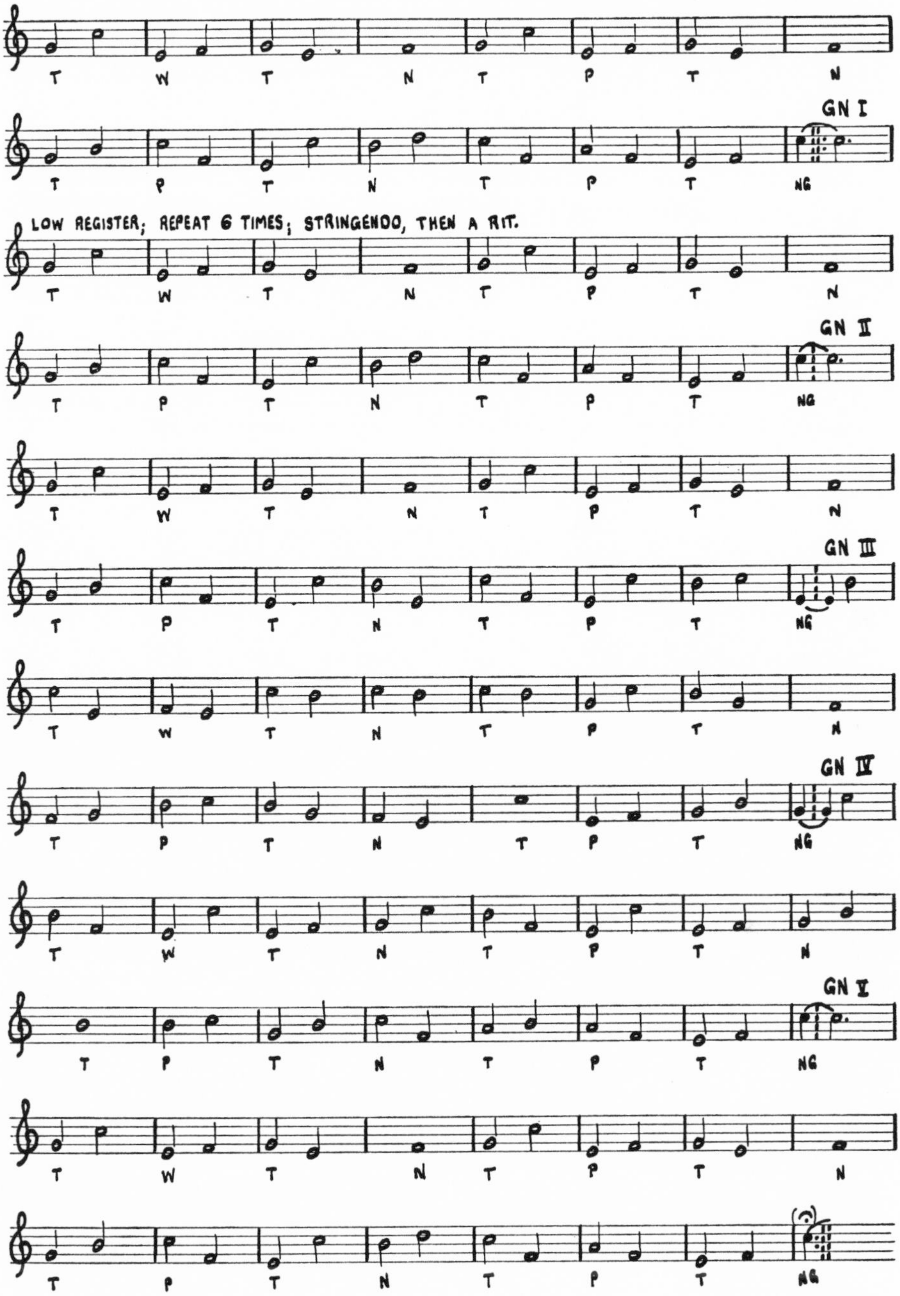
T W T N T P T N
GN I
T P T N T P T NG
LOW REGISTER; REPEAT 6 TIMES; STRINGENDO, THEN A RIT.
T W T N T P T N
GN II
T P T N T P T NG
T W T N T P T N
GN III
T P T N T P T NG
T W T N T P T N
GN IV
T P T N T P T NG
T W T N T P T N
GN V
T P T N T P T NG
T W T N T P T N
T P T N T P T NG

“Megarsi”

Ladrang nr 70 pélog paṭet nem

“Madu Kentar”

Ladrang nr 85 pélog paṭet nem

"Gondo Mastuti"

Ketawang nr 88

pélog paṭet nem

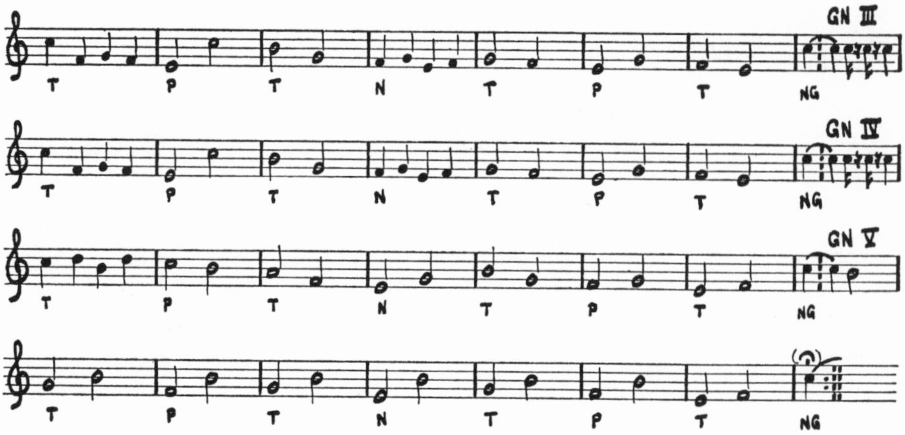

"Udan Mas"

Ladrang nr 83

pélog pațet nem

T W T N T P T N
T P T N T P T NG
GN IV
T W T N T P T N
T P T N T P T NG
GN V
LOW AND HIGH REGISTERS; STRINGENDO; REPEAT 8 TIMES, THEN A RIT.
T W T N T P T N
T P T N T P T NG
GN VI
T W T N T P T N
T P T N T P T NG
GN VII
T W T N T P T N
T P T N T P T NG
GN VIII
T W T N T P T N
T P T N T P T NG

"Rijem-Rijem"

Ladrang nr 61 pélog paṭet lima

“Kemong-Kemong”

Ladrang nr 62 pélog paṭet lima

“Rangu-Rangu”

Ladrang nr 97 pélog paṭet barang

"Megar Semu"

Ladrang nr 90 pélog paṭet barang

"Grompol"

Ladrang nr 95 pélog paṭet barang

"Ronggo Lasem"

Ladrang nr 98 pélog paṭet barang

"Srimalélo"

Ketawang nr 100 pélog paṭet barang

"Wirogo"

Ladrang nr 66 pélog paṭet manyura

GN V
T P T N T P T NG
T W T N T P T N
T P T N T P T NG

ILLUSTRATIONS

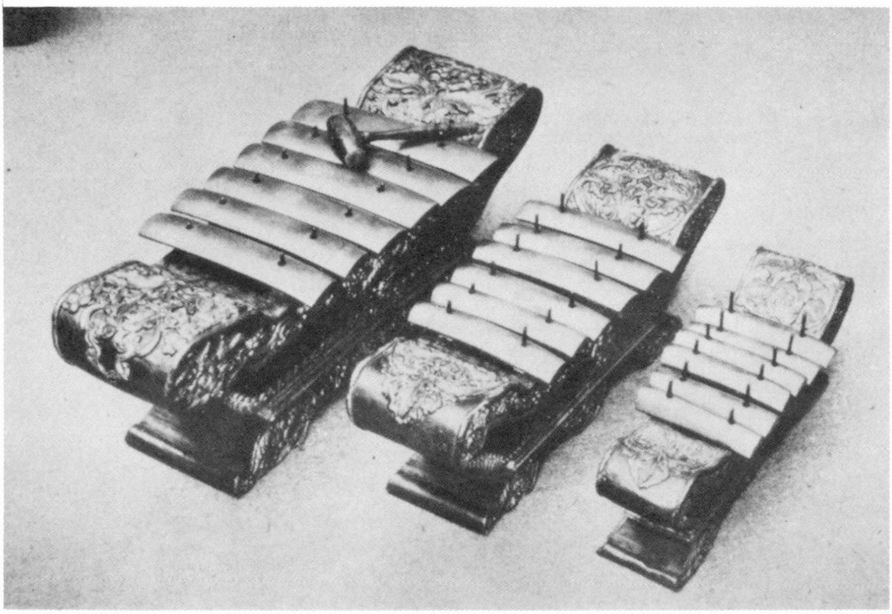

From left to right: the sléndro *saron demung*, *saron barung* and *saron panerus*.

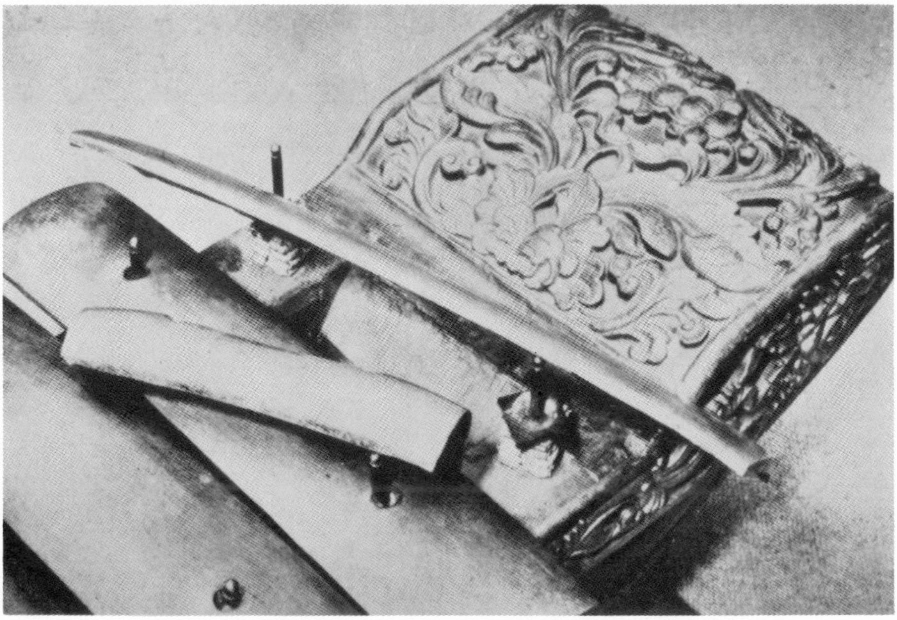

Detail showing the relative size of the largest key of the *saron demung* and the smallest key of the *saron panerus*. Note the ratan *sumpilan* and the felt square above it.

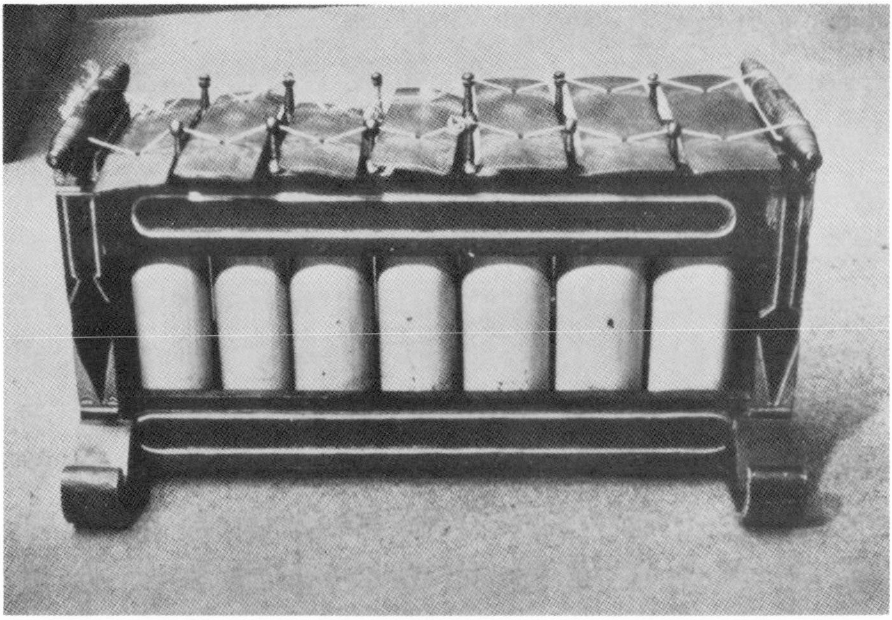

The *gendèr slenṭem.*

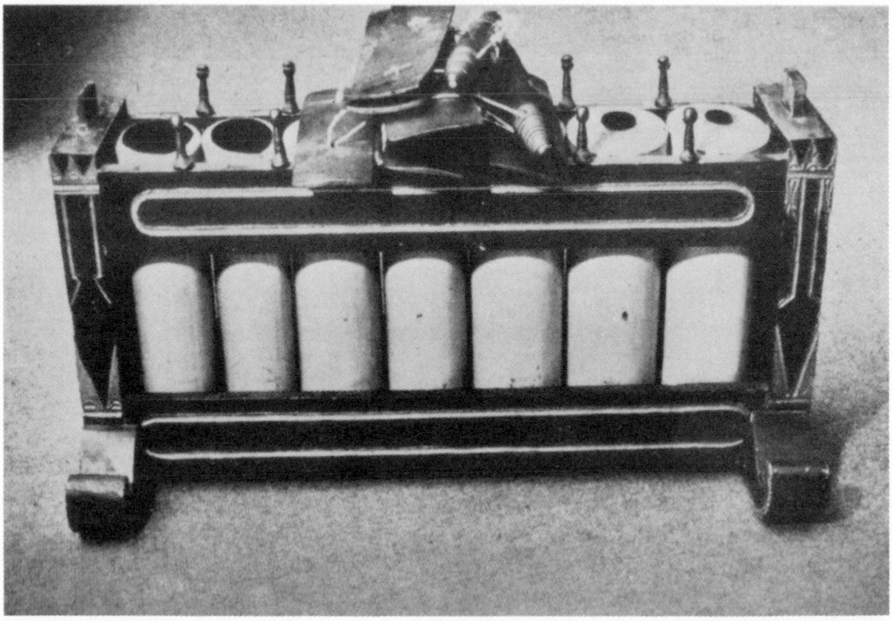

Detail showing the resonators of the *gendèr slenṭem.* Tubes of metal instead of bamboo (found in the smaller gendèr) have been used for this slenṭem; the partially closed ends allow a deep tone in a resonator of minimum length.

From front to rear: the sléndro *bonang panerus*, *bonang barung* and *bonang panembung* (several *kenong* are in the background).

Detail showing the relative size of the largest *bonang panembung* and smallest *bonang panerus* sound kettles (center and right of center); note the frame construction and supporting cords.

After Kunst

The *saron slenṭem.*

The *gong ageng* and the *kempul.*

The *kenong* (left) and the *keṭuk*.

Detail showing the crossed cords and frames which support the *kenong* and *keṭuk*.

The *gambang kayu.*

Detail showing the low, middle, and high keys and the manner in which the keys are held in place by pins.

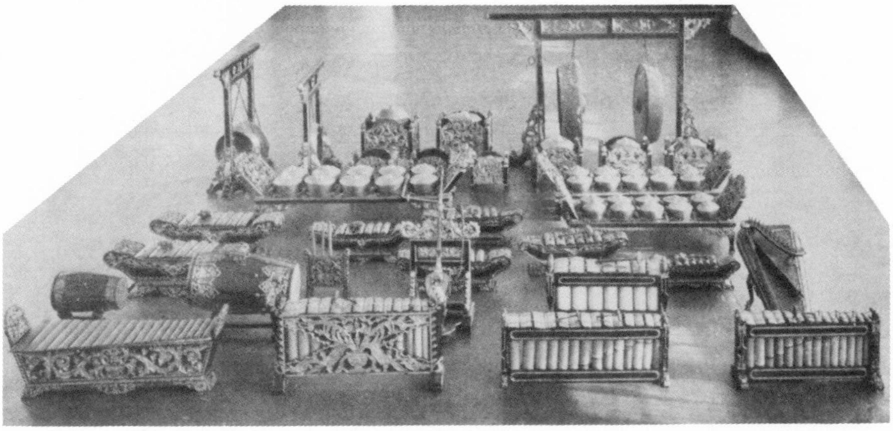

Foto archief Kon. Inst. v/d Tropen

Gamelan sléndro: note the small and large *kenḍang* (left foreground), the case of three *suling* and the *rebab* (center foreground). The *chelempung* (right foreground) is a kind of zither.

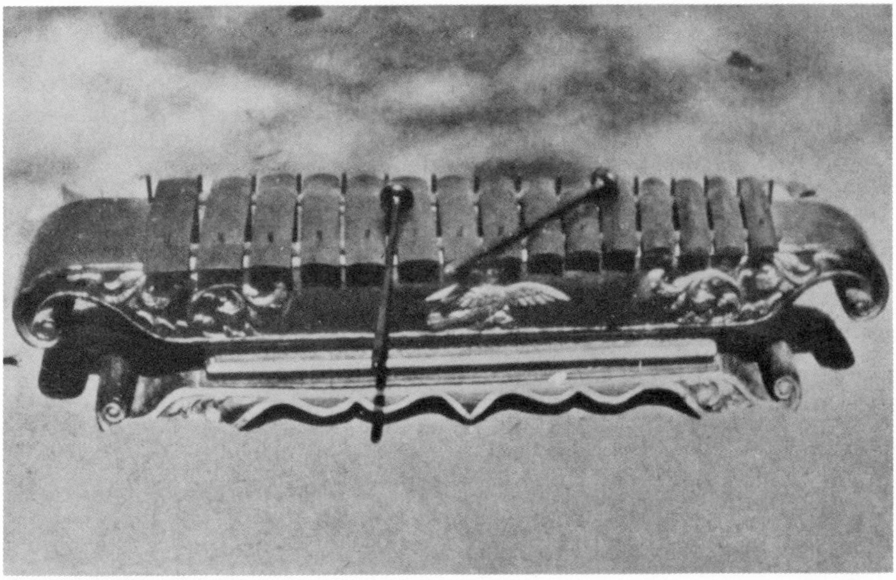

After Kunst

The *gambang gangsa*.

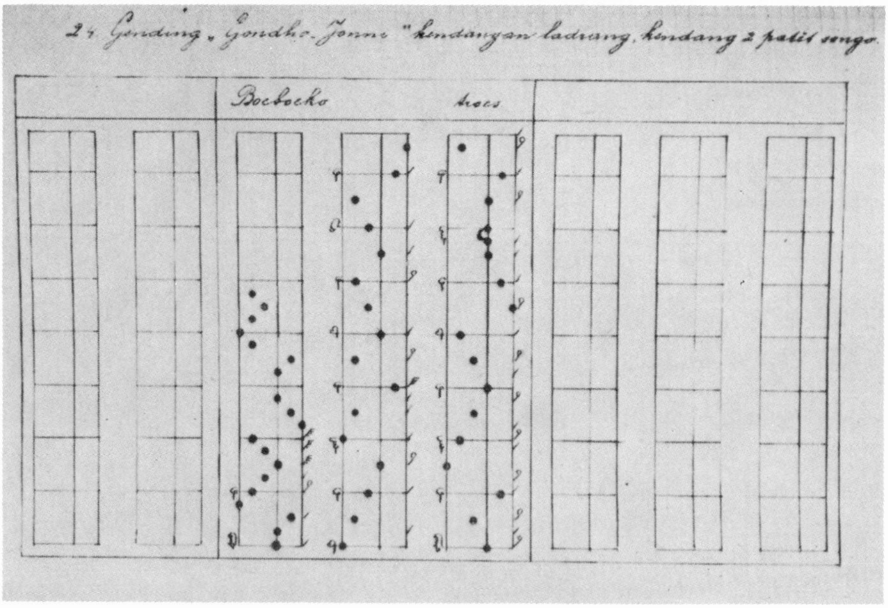

The ladrang "Gondo Yonni," sléndro paṭet sanga, from the Jogyanese manuscript: the bubuka (opaq-opaq) and the bubuka genḍing.

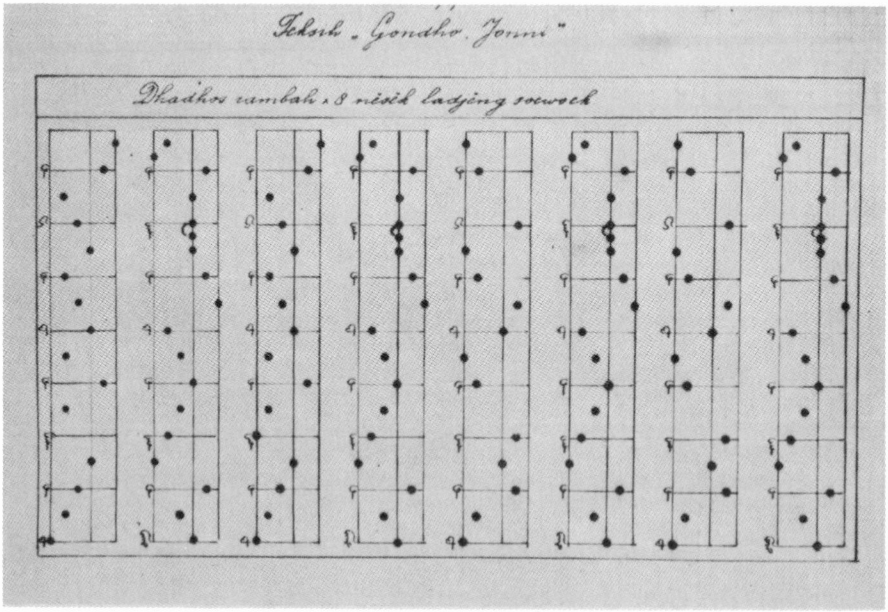

"Gondo Yonni:" the genḍing proper.

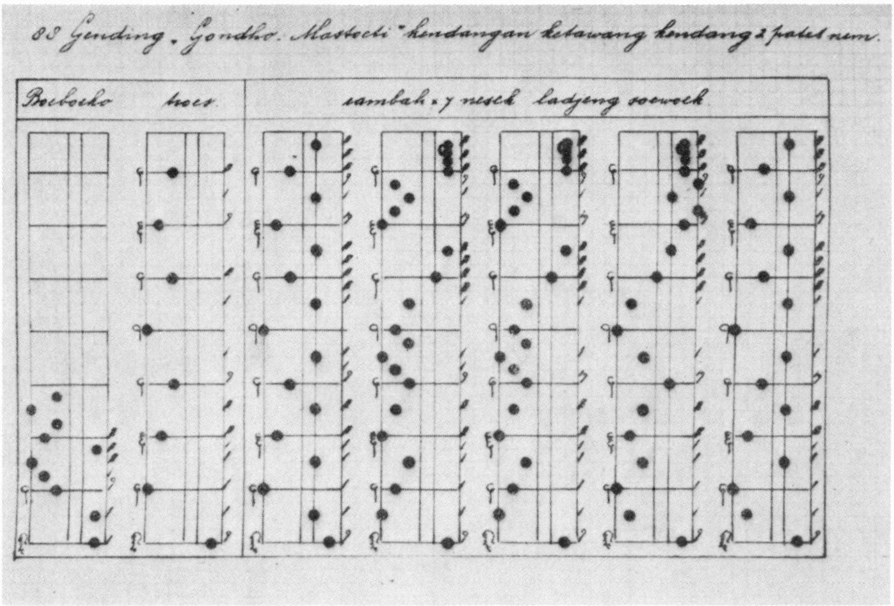

The ketawang "Gondo Mastuti," pélog paṭet nem, from the Jogyanese manuscript.

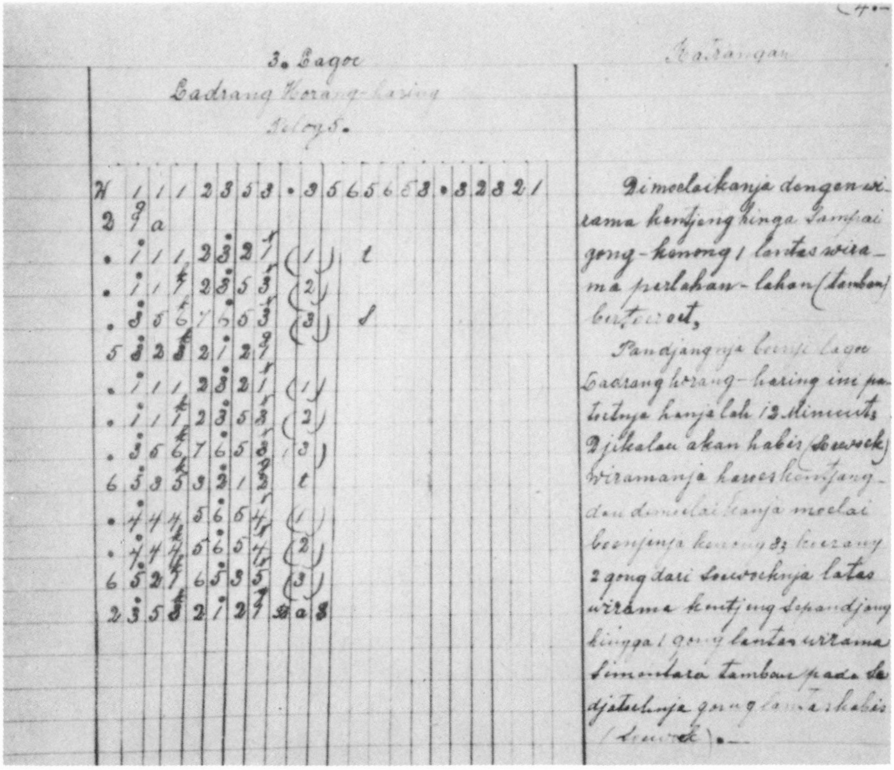

The ladrang "Horang Haring," pélog paṭet lima, from the Solonese manuscript.

INDEX

Various terms used throughout the analyses are paginated in the index only to indicate general or illustrative applications. Specific applications of these terms or other terms not appearing in the index can be located by consulting the appropriate sections listed in the table of CONTENTS.

alus, 12
auxiliary scale, 9, 143—8
"Babat Kencheng", 33, 268
babon ing laras, 118
Bali, 5, 117, 139, 247
balungan, 9, 10, 124, 142, 238—40, 248
balunganing gending, (*vide* nuclear theme), 9
barang, 6—8, 20, 114—15, 119, 143, 145—6, 148, 219, 222
"Barang Asmoro", 208
"Barang Ganjur", 75, 279
batik, 5
bem, 6, 143, 145—6, 148, 219, 223
Bharata, 117
bonang, 10—12, 242; barung, 10—12, 313; panembung, 10, 18, 313; panerus, 11, 12, 313
Borobuḍur, 240, 247
Brandts Buys, 2, 18, 79, 130—1, 225—30, 242
"Bronto Asmoro", 72, 277
bubuka, (buka), 14, 15, 130, 248
bubuka genḍing, 15, 23—4, 122—3, 133—4, 155, 265, 287, 318
bubuka opaq-opaq, 15, 23—4, 74, 122—3, 129—34, 142, 155, 236, 246—8, 265, 318; transposed, 41—3, 45, 48—9, 56, 132, 142
Bukofzer, 138, 234—5
cadence, 22, 30, 40, 122—9, 132—3, 138, 141—2, 224—5, 236, 238—9, 242, 244—6, 248; strong-weak, 55—6, 123—4
cantus firmus, (*vide* nuclear theme), 18
"characterizing" tone, 228, 234—5
Central Java, 116, 143
chelempung, 241, 247, 317
"Chèlèng Mogok", 95, 283
chengkok, 16, 132
"Chlunṭang", 73, 278
China, 1, 2, 117
"Chondo Sari", 149, 288
copyist errors, 19, 20, 61, 68, 199, 221
critical sections, (*vide* bubuka opaq-opaq; bubuka genḍing; kenongan, transitional; gongan, final), 23—4, 125, 133—4, 155, 236—7, 242, 246, 265
ḍaḍa, 6—8, 20, 114, 119, 143, 145—6, 148, 223
dasar, (*vide* dominant), 7, 8, 114—22, 127, 138, 144—6
demung, *vide* saron demung
Déwantara, 115—17, 120—2, 125, 225—30, 234
"Dirodo Meto", 30, 267
Djajengoetara, 127, 243
dji, (sidji), 118—20
dominant, 22, 26, 54—5, 115—22, 142, 148, 168, 222—30, 236—7
ḍongḍing, 125
"enemy" tone, 245—7
exchange tone, (*vide* sorogan), 7, 8, 144—6, 224, 230—2, 235
final note, 121, 124, 223—4, 228—9, 234—7
"Gaja Bengok", 87, 96, 284
"Gajah Endro", 75
gambang gangsa, 240—2, 317
gambang kayu, 12, 130, 133, 241—2, 316
gamelan conductor, 4
gamelan sléndro, 317
gangsaran, 15, 23, 170, 259
gayor, 10
"Gègèr Sakuto", 45, 271
gendèr, 11, 130, 133, 242; barung, 11; panembung, 10, 11; panerus, 11; slenṭem gantung, 10, 11, 312
genḍing, types, 14, 15; large form, 149, 155
"Gondo Mastuti", 183, 297, 319
"Gondo Yonni", 61, 273, 318
gong, ageng, geḍé, 3, 10—13, 18, 19, 137, 265, 314; suwukan, 11
gongan, 10, 12, 24, 137, 150, 265; final, 24, 122—3, 133—4, 265; "inner", 57, 122
gong tones, 7, 8, 23, 54—5, 114—24, 137—8, 143—6, 150, 222—30, 236—8, 246
"Gonjang", 87, 90, 280
"Gonjang Sèrèt", 89, 281